Through a Glass Darkly

RELIGION AND AMERICAN CULTURE

Series Editors

David Edwin Harrell Jr.
Wayne Flynt
Edith L. Blumhofer

Through a Glass Darkly

Contested Notions of Baptist Identity

Edited by Keith Harper

THE UNIVERSITY OF ALABAMA PRESS

Tuscaloosa

Cover illustration: *Church Window*, copyright © Mathiasphotography | Dreamstime.com
Cover designer: Erin Kirk New

Typeface: Caslon

∞

The paper on which this book is printed meets the minimum requirements of American National Standard for Information Sciences—Permanence of Paper for Printed Library Materials, ANSI Z39.48-1984.

Library of Congress Cataloging-in-Publication Data

Through a glass darkly : contested notions of Baptist identity / edited by Keith Harper.
    p. cm. — (Religion and American culture)
    Includes index.
    ISBN 978-0-8173-5712-2 (pbk. : alk. paper) — ISBN 978-0-8173-8614-6 (electronic) 1.
Baptists. 2. Identification (Religion) I. Harper, Keith, 1957–
    BX6332.T47 2012
    286—dc23

                                                                            2012005531

For Samuel S. Hill and Wayne Flynt

Contents

Acknowledgments

It is always a pleasure to acknowledge those whose hard work led to the production of a work such as this. First, I want to thank the contributors. Each author provided an excellent essay, and it was my honor to work with each one. Two essays appeared previously in scholarly journals. Curtis W. Freeman's "E. Y. Mullins and the Siren Songs of Modernity" first appeared in *Review and Expositor* 96 (1999). We offer it here in a slightly modified form that reflects trends in Mullins's scholarship since 1999. Elizabeth H. Flowers's "The Contested Legacy of Lottie Moon" first appeared in *Fides et Historia* 43, no. 1 (Winter/Spring 2011). Both are used in this volume by the kind permission of their respective journals, and it is my privilege to thank these journals for their consideration in this matter. Finally, Michael McEwen and Michael Brake, friends and associates at Southeastern Baptist Theological Seminary, offered a number of helpful suggestions that expedited the project's completion.

Along different lines, I owe Daniel J. J. Ross, former director of The University of Alabama Press, a special note of thanks. I could not believe it when I heard Dan was set to retire in the fall of 2010, but he assured me that he met all the necessary criteria. I am grateful that Dan gave the final approval for this project, but more than that, Dan has been a good friend through the years. He has always been most encouraging, and his advice never failed to be wise. Enjoy retirement, my friend.

Finally, I wish to recognize Samuel S. Hill and Wayne Flynt. Sam challenged an entire generation to rethink their assumptions about race and religion with *Southern Churches in Crisis*. As probing as he is prolific, Sam has a way of challenging pat assumptions about the past with a disarming grace that makes me envious. And, anyone who knows Wayne Flynt thinks of Auburn University, Alabama politics, and Baptists but not necessarily in that order. Wayne set a new standard for studying Baptists at the state level with *Alabama Baptists: Southern Baptists in the Heart of Dixie.* Wayne consistently reminds everyone that poor people matter and that one's social consciousness transcends both region and denomination. When we were all three a good bit younger, Sam and Wayne took an interest in me and my career. I have enjoyed their friendship and counsel through the years, and I dedicate this volume to them as a small token of my enduring gratitude.

Keith Harper
Wake Forest, North Carolina

Introduction

If bibliographies, book lists, and the like are any indicator, North American Baptists ended the twentieth century in the throes of an identity crisis. Little wonder. The world had witnessed a communications revolution that spawned the Internet. The Soviet Union had collapsed. There had been national and international economic upheaval, and by century's end, some contend that a global missionary culture had emerged.[1] If that were not enough, North American Baptists had endured a century of intra- and inter-denominational squabbling. Given the rapidly changing state of things, many began asking, what does it mean to be a Baptist these days?

In 1997, a group of fifty-five scholars affirmed a document titled "Re-Envisioning Baptist Identity: A Manifesto for Baptist Communities in North America." As the title suggests, the manifesto issued a bold call for interested parties to "re-envision" Baptist identity. A postscript to the manifesto noted, "Those of us who originally drafted this statement are but a few among a growing number of Baptists in North America who would like to see our churches take a new theological direction, one that is not 'conservative' nor 'liberal' nor something in between."[2] Between 1999 and 2001, no fewer than four works appeared that explored what it means to be a Baptist.[3] These works were not follow-up volumes to the manifesto's call to "re-envision" Baptist identity. In fact, these reflections on Baptist identity did not even acknowledge the manifesto. Clearly, something was going on.

In searching for identity in the present, is there any value in sifting through the past? Judging by the hundreds of books written by Baptists for Baptists, others have trod this path before. In fact, turning to the past to help define Baptist identity in the present is a regular feature of Baptist writing, and for good reason. Margaret MacMillan notes that among other things, history helps make sense of confusing situations and lends clarity to values when people lose confidence in authority figures.[4] Making sense of the past is important in understanding one's personal and collective identity.

Yet, mining the past for clues to a usable identity in the present can be tricky. Toward the latter part of the twentieth century, denominational history came under fire for being biased, self-serving, self-congratulatory, and parochial. There are a number of possible reasons for this, ranging from partisan historians telling a biased story to historians selectively using elements of the Baptist story to advance a particular viewpoint. Robert Bruce Mullin has detailed the difficulties in writing denominational history; difficulties that will not be rehashed here.[5] Suffice it to say that a skewed view of bygone Baptists may yet wield considerable polemical power but does little to explain who they really were. That is, referencing a distorted image of who Baptists were in the past sends scholars and other interested parties down the wrong trail as they try to figure out who Baptists really are.

Notwithstanding the difficulties, history remains an important component to one's identity. As early twenty-first-century Baptists of all stripes grapple with what it means to be a Baptist, now may be an opportune time to revisit important aspects of Baptist life for new insight on an important question. Historians may be able to help by offering timely correctives to staple themes in Baptist lore. The following essays are about issues, people, and elements of the Baptist story that may help frame Baptist identity from a historical perspective. These essays are not likely to answer every question bearing on Baptist identity over time. Neither will they provide a singular Baptist perspective on the past. Such is not possible. On the other hand, taken together, they demonstrate that "being Baptist" can mean different things to different people at different times. As Bill J. Leonard's aptly titled text *Baptist Ways: A History* implies, there is more than one way to be a Baptist.[6] Moreover, these essays also suggest that Baptist identity is not static; thus, tomorrow's Baptists may resemble yesterday's Baptists, but they will probably not look exactly like them. Nonetheless, if Baptists are at an identity crossroads, historians have a great opportunity to reexamine all aspects of a familiar story. We hope these essays offer fresh insights to those who are interested in the topic.

The essays in this volume are divided under three headings. Part I, Key Themes, explores religious liberty and persecution, two prominent issues in Baptist history. The formal disestablishment of religion opened the door to widespread, if grudging, acceptance for Baptists and other dissenters. It also raised certain important legitimacy issues, namely, in America's emerging religious free market, who represented "authentic" Christianity?[7] Eighteenth-century writers such as Isaac Backus had styled Baptists as good citizens who were hounded by established churches and thereby deprived of their rights. In a word, Baptists were "outsiders" who deserved to be "insiders" on America's religious scene.[8] Early nineteenth-century historian David Benedict carried Backus's work forward in his massive *History of the Baptist Denomination in America*. In his version of Baptist history, Benedict recounted the familiar persecution narrative but with a slight twist. Whereas Backus's history had pitted Baptists as "outsiders" against the standing order "insiders," Benedict's Baptists had gained a measure of acceptance, and their history assumed a slightly different cast. With Benedict, Baptists began using their history as an apologia to their non-Baptist neighbors. Benedict maintained that Baptists were a beleaguered people who had been treated poorly. Their history demonstrated that they deserved better, as Benedict used the past as a vindication for the present.

Soon, other historians began using history for apologetic ends. For some, history became a formal means of defending the "Baptist way." As they moved toward center stage in America's unfolding story, Baptist writers frequently used history to authenticate their doctrine and practice, thereby solidifying their newfound status. From these writings, a number of themes emerged that continue to shape Baptist identity. For instance, Baptists are generally regarded as outspoken advocates of religious freedom. Yet, when it comes to the separation of church and state, Bill J. Leonard's essay, "Baptists, Church, and State: Rejecting Establishments, Relishing Privilege," observes that while Baptists advocated the separation of church and state, they were never united in one understanding of what such a separation might look like.

In a similar vein, there remains a lingering temptation to paint late colonial-era Baptists as persecuted victims. Many Baptist historians are quick to argue that as easterners began pushing westward in the 1780s, these pioneering souls yearned for the religious freedom they could only find on the American frontier. Few, however, have ever explored the implications of how Baptists fit into general westward migration patterns or how they fit in the nation's emerging economic order. In "Democratic Religion Revisited: Early Baptists in the American South," Jewel L. Spangler notes that whatever else may have motivated Baptists to move west, the majority were as interested in making better lives for themselves as everyone else, even to the point of owning slaves whom they claimed as brothers and sisters in Christ.

Part II, Biography, contains five biographical essays that address key figures at pivotal times in Baptist history. Every denomination has its heroes and villains, and biography may be the easiest place to distort the denominational story. Historians face the temptation to turn heroes into superheroes and villains into archvillains. Therefore, it is appropriate to begin this section with an essay on Roger Williams. For some, Williams represents the quintessential Baptist champion of dissent and religious freedom. Others scarcely see him as a Baptist at all, given that he professed to be a Baptist for a mere matter of months. James P. Byrd's essay, "Persecution and Polemics: Baptists and the Shaping of the Roger Williams Tradition in the Nineteenth Century," explains how Williams's legacy grew and changed throughout the nineteenth century.

Arguably, every denomination in America faced great change in the early twentieth century. Much like everyone else, Baptists contended with modernism. Seminary administrators and faculty faced a choice of following a "new way" or sticking with "the old paths." Which way to turn? Edgar Young "E. Y." Mullins served as president of Southern Baptist Theological Seminary, Louisville, Kentucky, from 1899 to 1928. Both a gifted teacher and administrator, Mullins proved to be a genuine Baptist statesman. In "E. Y. Mullins and the Siren Songs of Modernity," Curtis W. Freeman maintains that Mullins tried to steer a middle course that neither espoused modernism nor hewed too closely to "the old paths."[9] It was a course that influenced Southern Baptist thinking for the remainder of the twentieth century.

Similarly, few Southern Baptists influenced the denomination like Charlotte Diggs "Lottie" Moon, missionary to China from 1873 to 1912. Moon was not the first single female Southern Baptist missionary, but she was by far the most articulate. Her impassioned pleas for missions, both public and private, helped shape attitudes toward the missionary enterprise at a time when the denomination was growing and becoming increasingly professionalized. Elizabeth H. Flowers's "The Contested Legacy of Lottie Moon" reflects how Moon's image in Baptist writings changed over time, especially as the South's social, political, and economic conditions changed. By pairing Freeman and Flowers, one sees the essence of one denomination's struggle with shifting theological trends and changing perceptions of gender roles, two of the twentieth century's more hotly contested issues.

Beyond theological controversy, many Baptists struggled to reconcile American prosperity and Christian ethics with widespread poverty and discrimination. Consequently, social justice became as contentious an issue as modernism or women's rights. Christopher H. Evans's "Walter Rauschenbusch and the Second Coming: The Social Gospel as Baptist History" offers a thoughtful reconsideration of Walter Rauschenbusch. Despite his status as the "Prophet of the Social Gospel," Rauschenbusch is also regarded in some quarters as a theological liberal who elevated social work above the Christian gospel. Evans maintains that Rauschenbusch is more evangelical than his critics allow and that he may have carried out his theological convictions better than any other theologian of his day. Edward R. Crowther's "'I Am Fundamentally a Clergyman, a Baptist Preacher': Martin Luther King Jr., Social Christianity, and the Baptist Faith in an Era of Civil Rights" argues that King was more than a political activist. Crowther demonstrates that King advocated a social gospel for African Americans. Ironically, both Rauschenbusch and King are remembered as activists of a sort, but few have noticed what Evans and Crowther argue so convincingly: Rauschenbusch and King acted primarily on theological principle.

Although biography may lend itself to a certain amount of exaggeration, it is not the only area where denominationally oriented history is susceptible to distortion. Part III, Historiography, highlights several of the ways Baptists have used their past to define their present. Perhaps no group of Baptists relies on its history more than the Primitive Baptists. In the early nineteenth century, many Baptists began engaging in organized missionary work to convert the world to Christ. Others became increasingly uncomfortable with Sunday schools and the steadily increasing number of missionary societies. They objected to such measures as unnecessary and innovative. By the mid-1830s, they began to style themselves as "primitive," claiming their polity conformed to the New Testament. Further, they maintained that real primitives stood in a long, distinguished line of dissenters including the Waldenses, Paulicans, and Donatists. Thus, Primitive Baptists began using history as an apologia for their nonparticipation in missionary activity. The first-century churches had not established the precedent, so why should they?[10] John G. Crowley's aptly titled, "'Written that Ye May Believe': Primitive Baptist Historiography," explores some of the early efforts to bridge that past with the primitive present.[11]

The Primitives were not the only nineteenth-century Baptists looking for roots in centuries past. In fact, before the twentieth century, most Baptist historians claimed some connection to the first century. None are more noteworthy than the so-called Landmarkers, who were led by James Robinson Graves, a Baptist preacher, editor of *The Tennessee Baptist*, and master polemicist. Graves and many of his followers espoused a view of Baptist history that claimed modern Baptists could trace their lineage back to the New Testament era through an unbroken line of dissenters.[12] Graves relied on a single text, G. H. Orchard's *History of the Baptists*, which was rejected as a bad history by some of his own contemporaries.[13]

Graves's questionable research did not stop him from using history as an apologetic against rival denominations, especially Methodists and Presbyterians. Because they had "human founders," and Baptists (Graves) claimed Jesus as their founder, these other groups were suspect, and their sacraments unacceptable as genuine reflections of Christian devotion.[14] At any rate, Graves became one of the most outspoken and controversial Baptists of the nineteenth century, and subsequent generations of Baptist historians found him particularly distasteful. Graves and Landmarkism became synonymous with anything that ran contrary to denominational development. Some even accused Graves of espousing high churchism and holding a doctrine that amounted to a Baptist variant of Roman Catholicism.[15] Over time, anti-Landmarkists devised an anti-Landmark history and used it as their own apologetic against Graves and all forms of antidenominational dissent. James A. Patterson's "Reframing the Past: The Impact of Institutional and Ideological Agendas on Modern Interpretations of Landmarkism" suggests that in their efforts to discredit Landmarkism, some historians have outstripped J.R. himself.

By the early twentieth century, Baptist historiography reflected a seemingly boundless confidence. Their histories were basically consensus-driven and celebrated Baptist advancement on all fronts. Toward the end of the twentieth century, however, things began to change. American denominationalism faced a number of changes and most denominations declined precipitously. Moreover, changes in the history profession, most notably the emergence of new social history and, later, the new cultural history, raised new questions and offered new methodologies. By century's end, Baptists saw fewer large-scale works but a growing number of important, focused works that began to challenge a number of cherished assumptions and open the door to new lines of inquiry.

Beyond question, one area needing further exploration is African American Baptist life. It is tempting to think that black Baptists in America have traditionally rallied around one another for mutual aid and support. Paul Harvey's *Redeeming the South: Religious Cultures and Religious Identities among Southern Baptists, 1865–1925* and *Freedom's Coming: Religious Cultures and the Shaping of the South from the Civil War to the Civil Rights Era* have clarified the complex ways that black and white southerners have interacted since the Civil War. Yet, Harvey's "Is There a River?: Black Baptists, the Uses of History, and the Long History of the Freedom Movement" questions the notion that a unified, holistic black Baptist experience ever existed in America.[16]

The rise of the Christian Right in the 1970s and '80s also raised important questions about religion and politics. As Catholics, Mormons, and assorted evangelicals joined forces against abortion rights issues and the Equal Rights Amendment, some began to wonder how closely aligned religion and politics should be. Some even claimed that America was quickly losing its long-standing status as a "Christian nation." How Christian is America? In "Symbolic History in the Cold War Era," Alan Scot Willis argues that "Christian America" became a dominant theme after World War II as Baptists, especially Southern Baptists, became ultranationalistic and fabricated a new understanding for themselves by selectively using early American history.

Finally, in the late twentieth century, Southern Baptists became embroiled in a controversy that has been labeled the Fundamentalist Takeover or the Conservative Resurgence, depending on one's perspective. Rival camps dubbed "moderate" and "fundamentalist" vied for control of America's largest Protestant denomination.[17] It was a situation prime for using history to support rival truth claims, and each camp proved equal to the task. As "moderates" and "fundamentalists" fought for control of the denomination, many wondered which side represented *real* Baptists. Few have observed the controversy with a keener eye than Barry Hankins. His essay, "Southern Baptists and the F-Word: A Historiography of the SBC Controversy and What It Might Mean," explains that historically speaking, Southern Baptist Convention conservatives/fundamentalists fit in the Baptist camp, heated rhetoric notwithstanding.

The contributors to this volume know the pitfalls of writing about

people, places, and things that smack of denominational history. With
that in mind, these essays offer correctives to certain stereotypical interpretations of the Baptist past. They are written for scholars and students
who are interested in Baptist history and identity. They are also for a general readership who occasionally muses, "Who are these people called
Baptists?" Careful readers will notice that while these essays are not exclusively about Southern Baptists, many address Baptists in the southern
United States. As editor of this volume, it was never my intention to slight
any person or any aspect of Baptist history. But for better or worse, Baptists in the South command considerable attention as these essays attest.
As for the title, *Through a Glass Darkly* is a reference to 1 Corinthians 13:12
(King James version) in which the Apostle Paul reminded the church of
Corinth that of all they knew of Christ, their knowledge was incomplete
and imperfect. Hopefully, these essays will offer fresh perspectives on who
Baptists were in the past so that we may more clearly see who they are in
the present.

Notes

1. See Mark A. Noll, *The New Shape of Global Christianity: How American
Experience Reflects Global Faith* (Downers Grove, IL: IVP Academic, 2009).

2. Curtis W. Freeman, et al., "Re-Envisioning Baptist Identity: A Manifesto for Baptist Communities in North America," *Baptists Today*, June 26,
1997, 8–10. In a similar vein see Freeman, "Can Baptist Theology Be Revi-
sioned?" *Perspectives in Religious Studies* 24 (Fall 1997): 273–310. The text of
the manifesto is on 303–10. For a different perspective on Baptist identity see
Walter B. Shurden, *Perspectives in Religious Studies*, 25, no. 4 (Winter 1998):
321–40.

3. See R. Stanton Norman, *More than Just a Name: Preserving Our Baptist
Identity* (Nashville: Broadman & Holman Publishers, 2001) and *The Baptist
Way: Distinctives of a Baptist Church* (Nashville: Broadman & Holman Pub-
lishers, 2005); Tom Nettles and Russell D. Moore, eds., *Why I am a Baptist*
(Nashville: Broadman & Holman Publishers, 2001); Cecil Staton Jr., ed., *Why
I am a Baptist: Reflections on Being a Baptist in the 21st Century* (Macon, GA:
Smyth & Helwys Publishing, Inc., 1999).

4. Margaret MacMillan, *The Uses and Abuses of History* (London: Profile
Books, Ltd., 2009), 8–22.

5. Robert Bruce Mullin and Russell E. Ritchey, eds., introduction to *Reimagining Denominational History: Interpretive Essays* (New York: Oxford University Press, 1994), 3–16.

6. Bill J. Leonard, *Baptist Ways: A History*, foreword by Edwin S. Gaustad (Valley Forge, PA: Judson Press, 2003).

7. See Nathan Hatch, *The Democratization of American Christianity* (New Haven, CT: Yale University Press, 1989) and Jon Butler, *Awash in a Sea of Faith: Christianizing the American People* (Cambridge, MA: Harvard University Press, 1990).

8. Isaac Backus, *A History of New England Baptists with Particular Reference to the Denomination of Christians Called Baptists*, 2nd ed., 2 vols., with notes by David Weston (Newton, MA: The Backus Historical Society, 1871).

9. For Baptists and early twentieth-century modernism, see Grant Wacker, *Augustus H. Strong and the Dilemma of Historical Consciousness* (Macon, GA: Mercer University Press, 1985) and William Vance Trollinger, *God's Empire: William Bell Riley and Midwestern Fundamentalism* (Madison: University of Wisconsin Press, 1990).

10. Some like John Leland raised this issue long before the Primitive Baptists. See Leland's "Missionary Societies," in *The Writings of the Late Elder John Leland*, ed. Miss L. F. Greene (New York: G. W. Wood, 1845), 471–72.

11. See also John G. Crowley, *Primitive Baptists of the Wiregrass South: 1815 to the Present* (Gainesville: University Press of Florida, 1998).

12. Baptist origins is a difficult issue, often charged by inter- and intra-denominational politics. See Morgan W. Patterson, *Baptist Successionism: A Critical View* (Philadelphia: The Judson Press, 1969) and James Edward McGoldrick, *Baptist Successionism: A Critical Question in Baptist History* (Metuchen, NJ: Scarecrow Press, 1994).

13. Compare G. H. Orchard, *A Concise History of the Baptists* (London: George Wightman, 1838) and J. M. Cramp, *Baptist History: From the Foundation of the Christian Church to the Present*, with an introduction by Rev. J. Angus (London: Elliot Stock, 1871). Cramp takes Orchard to task in a lengthy footnote, wherein he documents Orchard's mishandling of evidence; see note on pp. 52–54.

14. See Marty G. Bell, "James Robinson Graves and the Rhetoric of Demagogy: Primitivism and Democracy in Old Landmarkism" (Ph.D. dissertation, Vanderbilt University, 1990).

15. James Tull, *High Church Baptists in the South: The Origin, Nature, and Influence of Landmarkism*, edited and with a preface by Morris Ashcraft (Macon, GA: Mercer University Press, 2000). For the comparison of Landmarkism with nineteenth-century Roman Catholicism, see H. Leon McBeth, *The Baptist Heritage: Four Centuries of Baptist Witness* (Nashville: Broadman Press, 1987), p. 459.

16. See also Paul Harvey, *Redeeming the South: Religious Cultures and Racial Identities among Southern Baptists, 1865–1925* (Chapel Hill: University of North Carolina Press, 1997) and *Freedom's Coming: Religious Culture and the Shaping of the South from the Civil War to the Civil Rights Era* (Chapel Hill: University of North Carolina Press, 2005).

17. There are a number of books available on "the Controversy." See especially David Morgan, *The New Crusades, the New Holy Land: Conflict in the Southern Baptist Convention* (Tuscaloosa: The University of Alabama Press, 1996) and Jerry Sutton, *The Baptist Reformation: The Conservative Resurgence in the Southern Baptist Convention* (Nashville: Broadman & Holman, 2000).

I
Key Themes

I
Baptists, Church, and State
Rejecting Establishments, Relishing Privilege
Bill J. Leonard

> We still pray our lord the king that we may be free from suspect, of
> having any thoughts of provoking evil against them of the Romish
> religion, in regard of their profession, if they are the true and faithful
> subjects to the king. For we do freely profess that our lord the king has
> no more power over their consciences than over ours, and that is none
> at all. For our lord the king is but an earthly king, and he has no au-
> thority as a king but in earthly causes. And if the king's people be obe-
> dient and true subjects, obeying all human laws made by the king, our
> lord the king can require no more. For men's religion to God is be-
> tween God and themselves. The king shall not answer for it. Neither
> may the king be judge between God and man. Let them be heretics,
> Turks, Jews, or whatsoever, it appertains not to the earthly power to
> punish them in the least measure. This is made evident to our lord the
> king by the scriptures.
>
> —Thomas Helwys, *A Short Declaration of the*
> *Mystery of Iniquity (1611/1612)*

Writing around 1612, Baptist founder Thomas Helwys set forth one of the
earliest statements on religious freedom, anticipating liberty of conscience
and religious pluralism.[1] In fact, the paragraph contains in itself some of
the essentials of Baptist approaches to church and state. It (1) attacks establishmentarian religion; (2) emphasizes the centrality of individual conscience; (3) affirms loyalty to the state; and (4) opens the door to state-
supporting religious diversity. It sets forth the idea that God alone is judge
of conscience and thus neither state nor established church can assess the
conscience of the heretic (the people thought to believe the wrong thing)
or the atheist (the people who do not believe at all).

Writing in 1847, British historian Edward Bean Underhill asserted: "It
has been already seen, that the claim, for the church and for the conscience,
of freedom from all human control, was a distinguishing and character-

istic trait of the Baptists in former reigns. The divine saying, 'FAITH IS THE GIFT OF GOD,' moved, animated, strengthened them. Its practical assertion brought them into collision with every form of human invention in the worship of God."[2] Baptist emphasis on religious liberty was there from the beginning, building on the assertions of certain Anabaptist groups and antedating those of the Quakers and various Enlightenment-influenced philosophers.

Why was such freedom so important to early Baptists? The concern for freedom of religion was grounded in a commitment to the reality of a Believers' Church, the conviction that those who would claim church membership should first profess faith in Christ, followed by believer's baptism. A Believers' Church was built on the premise that faith and conscience must remain free, uncoerced by an established church or an arbitrary state.

Edward Underhill understood this to mean that "Faith, God's gift, must not be subjected to man's device, nor enchained by the legislative enactments of parliaments or kings." He concluded that for the earliest Baptists, "To worship God aright, the highest function of humanity, the spirit must be free; true worship can come only from a willing heart. For this [belief] the Baptists bore cheerfully, *cruel mockings, and scourgings; yea, moreover bonds and imprisonments,* and death."[3] Thus, Baptist obsession with religious liberty developed, not out of a flirtation with "secularism," but from their commitment to personal faith in Christ. Perhaps the most distinguishing characteristic of Baptist identity rests in their concern for a Believers' Church grounded in the power of conscience and the inevitability of dissent.[4]

Early Baptist identity was characterized by emphasis on biblical authority, regenerated church membership, and believer's baptism by immersion, congregational church polity, religious liberty, and the priesthood of all believers. Amid those essentially sectarian characteristics, one of their most enduring legacies involves the importance of a regenerate church membership based on faith in Christ. Such a faith required the autonomy of the human conscience and because religious and political establishments inevitably inhibit conscience, dissent was inescapable.

Those who founded the first Baptist church in Amsterdam in 1608–1609 began as an unashamed Christian sect, born of the idea that the church should be composed only of believers, those who could testify to a work of grace through faith in Jesus Christ. Their earliest confession of faith, known as *A Declaration of Faith of English People Remaining at Am-*

sterdam in Holland (1611) sums up this idea in a concise statement: "That the church of CHRIST is a company of faithful people . . . separated from the world by the word & Spirit of GOD . . . being knit unto the LORD & one unto another, by Baptism . . . upon their own confession of the faith . . . and sins."[5] Baptists understood conscience and dissent in light of the need for sinners to be "regenerated," made new through conversion to Christ. Yet in their assertion that conscience could not be compelled by either state-based or faith-based establishments, they flung the door wide for religious liberty and pluralism in ways that even they may not have fully understood. By regeneration, they meant, in the words of the *Orthodox Creed* of 1679: "those who are united unto Christ by effectual faith, are regenerated, and have a new heart and spirit created in them through the virtue of Christ his death, resurrection, and intercession, and by the efficacy of the holy spirit, received by faith."[6]

Conscience and religious liberty were not based on secular theories (although they would influence them), but on the necessity of uncoerced faith mediated through a congregation of Christian believers. A commitment to freedom of conscience led Baptists to oppose religious establishments and develop principles of religious liberty that anticipated modern pluralism.

Baptists began as a community of dissenters. They challenged political and religious establishments in various ways. First, they were nonconformists who often refused to abide by the rules of religious uniformity demanded by the state-based churches of their day. Second, they rejected any laws of church or state that compelled financial or devotional support for a religious communion in which they had no voice. Third, they defied any church that attempted to mandate belief by virtue of birth, economic status, or culture privilege; and they sought to separate from it.

Anglican priest Daniel Featley's description of seventeenth-century Baptists illustrates the basis of their radical nonconformity. His list of Baptist teachings is clearly an establishmentarian nightmare. It also provides insight into how seventeenth-century dissenters were perceived by their religio-political enemies. Featley described Baptists' beliefs as follows:

First, that none are rightly baptized but those who are dipt. [They rejected the culturally mandated mode of baptism.]
Secondly, that no children ought to be baptized. [They cast aside the link between baptism and citizenship—i.e., to be born into a "Christian" state required immediate baptism into the Christian Church.]

Thirdly, that there ought to be no set form of Liturgy or prayer by the Book, but onely [*sic*] by the Spirit. [They demanded the freedom to determine their own spirituality apart from government enforced prayer.]

Fourthly, that there ought to be no distinction by the Word of God between the Clergy and the Laity but that all who are gifted may preach the Word, and administer the Sacraments. [They challenged the status of a privileged religious class that controlled theology and admission to the sacraments.]

Fifthly, that it is not lawful to take an oath at all, no, not though it be demanded by the magistrate. [The oath reflected the loyalty of citizenship. Baptists would swear only to God, not governments.]

Sixthly, that no Christian may with good conscience execute the office of civil magistrate.[7] [Some early Baptists followed their Anabaptist spiritual cousins in rejecting the idea that Christians could serve in public office. Others rejected that idea, but it was a sign of their struggle with church/state relations from the beginning.]

Every article in this list reflects elements of political and religious nonconformity evident among seventeenth-century Baptists, as interpreted by one of their sharpest critics.

Suffice it to suggest that these Baptists were an unruly lot. They challenged the status quo in areas related to theology, church polity, class, economics, and politics. At the same time, their confessions make clear that they wished to be good citizens and honor the government as long as its policies did not interfere with faith and conscience. The *Declaration* of 1611 asserted, "That Magistracie [*sic*] is a Holy ordinance of GOD, that every soul ought to be subject to it not for fear only, but for conscience sake. Magistrates are the ministers of GOD for our wealth, they bear not the sword for naught. They are the ministers of GOD to take vengeance on them that do evil."[8]

The document also distinguishes the group of English Separatists gathering around Baptist ideals in Amsterdam from their Anabaptist neighbors. Unlike the so-called Radical Reformers, the Baptists asserted that believers could indeed serve in political office. The confession suggested that "members of the Church of Christ" could retain "their Magistracie, for no Holy Ordinance of GOD debarreth any from being a member of CHRIST'S Church." They were free to swear oaths of allegiance as might be required in seventeenth-century political culture. The confession noted that it was "Lawful in a just cause for the deciding of strife to take an oath by the Name of the Lord."[9]

The *Standard Confession* written by General Baptists in 1660 suggested that "civil Magistrates" are called of God for "the punishment of evil doers" but warned that if they should "impose things about matters of Religion, which we through conscience to God cannot actually obey, then we with *Peter* also do say, that we ought (in such cases) to obey God rather than men; Acts 5:29."[10] Thus, Baptists accepted the jurisdiction of governments in keeping order and punishing wrongdoers, but they were willing to challenge government when it invaded matters of faith and conscience. It was a similar experience for Baptists in America.

Although he only remained a Baptist for a short time, Roger Williams was instrumental in the founding of the First Baptist Church in America at Providence in what became the colony of Rhode Island, probably around the year 1639. His challenge to the Puritan establishment opened the door for other Baptist responses in colonial America. He claimed that "a Civil Magistrate's power extends only to Bodies and Goods, and outward state of men," and he insisted that the Native Americans, not the English monarch, were the owners of the American land and should be compensated accordingly.[11]

Exiled in 1636 by the Massachusetts church-state establishment, Williams bought land from the Indians to found Providence Plantation. Years later, reflecting on that action, he recalled: "I desired it might be for a shelter for persons distressed for conscience. I then considering the condition of divers of my distressed countrymen, I communicated my said purchase unto my loving friends, who then desired to take shelter here with me."[12]

Dr. John Clarke, Baptist physician and preacher, joined Williams in Rhode Island, founding the town of Newport and the First Baptist Church there by 1640. He insisted that "No such believer, or Servant of Christ Jesus hath any liberty, much less Authority, from his Lord, to smite his fellow servant, nor yet with outward force, or are of flesh, to constrain, or restrain his Conscience, no nor yet his outward man for Conscience sake."[13] Clarke, who never left the Baptist fold, wrote the charter of Rhode Island, the first colony to extend complete religious liberty to all its citizens. The charter states, "No person within said colony at any time hereafter shall be in any wise molested, punished, disquieted or called into question for any differences of opinion in matters of religion . . . but that all and any persons may, from time to time, and at all times hereafter, freely and fully have

and enjoy his and their own judgments and consciences in matters of religious concernments throughout the tract of land hereafter mentioned."[14]
That statement set the tone for much of the Baptist emphasis on religious
liberty during the colonial period.

Over a century later, Isaac Backus took up the cause as an advocate
for the Warren Association of New England Baptists beginning in 1772.
Backus lobbied the Continental Congress at their first gathering in 1774,
urging them to take action on religious liberty. The Congress passed a
resolution dated December 9, 1774, that expressed its hope for providing
"civil and religious liberty" for every group but essentially sending the matter back to the "states." The resolution condescendingly advised the Baptists to take their grievances directly to the "general assembly" of Massachusetts "when and where their petition will most certainly meet with all
that attention due to the memorial of a denomination of Christians, so
well disposed to the public weal of their country."[15]

Although the Massachusetts religious establishment remained intact
until 1833, Baptists gave a continuing witness toward its demise. In 1778,
Backus provided this statement for religious liberty and against the Standing Order:

> Nothing can be true religion but a voluntary obedience unto God's
> revealed will, of which each rational soul has an actual right to judge
> for itself; every person has an inalienable right to act in all religious
> affairs according to the full persuasion of his own mind, where oth-
> ers are not injured thereby. And civil rulers are so far removed from
> having any right to empower any person or persons to judge for oth-
> ers in such affairs, and to enforce their judgments with the sword
> and that their power ought to be exerted to protect all persons and
> societies within their jurisdiction, from being injured or interrupted
> in the full enjoyment of this right, under any pretense whatsoever.[16]

In his study *Soul Liberty*, William McLoughlin suggested that Backus,
unlike Roger Williams, John Clarke, and John Leland, viewed America
as a distinctly Protestant nation. He even looked toward a day when the
Baptist position on adult believers ("antipedobaptism") would prevail in
other Protestant communions. He agreed with the Massachusetts state
constitution that required a religious oath of all magistrates and supported
Sunday regulations on gambling, dancing, theater performances, and card-
playing.[17] McLoughlin wrote: "Backus and the Baptists of eighteenth-

century New England thought primarily of religious liberty in terms of ending compulsory religious taxation, not in terms of a high wall of separation."[18] Generally speaking, however, Baptists were among the strongest advocates for the abolition of state establishments and the legalizing of religious freedom for all or none.

Backus's views are often contrasted with his contemporary, Virginian John Leland, who denied the idea of "Christian" nations and gave renewed emphasis to the breadth of religious pluralism in a free state. He wrote, "No National church, can, in its organization, be a Gospel Church," which alone "takes in no nation, but [only] those who fear God, and work righteousness in every nation."[19] Leland rejected the idea of religious *toleration,* the willingness of an established religion to grant second-class status to minority communions. He declared, "The very idea of toleration, is despicable; it supposes that some have a pre-eminence above the rest, to grant indulgence; whereas, all should be equally free, Jews, Turks, Pagans and Christians."[20]

In Leland's opinion, religious privilege, whatever the sect, was not simply politically incorrect, it was destructive to true faith. He wrote: "The fondness of magistrates to foster Christianity, has done it more harm than all the persecutions ever did. Persecution, like a lion, tears the saints to death, but leaves Christianity pure; state establishment of religion, like a bear, hugs the saints, but corrupts Christianity."[21] He warned that "Bible Christians, and Deists, have an equal plea against self-named Christians, who . . . tyrannize over the consciences of others, under the specious garb of religion and good order."[22] These radical statements have long represented the separationist approach to church-state issues. Later Baptists would divide between the church-state approaches of Isaac Backus and John Leland.

William McLoughlin's work gives attention to a transition in Baptist response to issues of religious liberty and the "culture wars" of pre-Revolutionary America. He insists that following the Revolution, "Baptists became victims of their own success." Their dramatic numerical gains made them, by the 1830s, one of the two largest denominations in the country. They thus entered "the mainstream of American life," no longer "a small sect of outcast and downtrodden martyrs."[23] McLoughlin commented, "It is not too much to say that the Baptists (especially in the South and West) embodied the basic outlook of the American people for most of the nineteenth century."[24] Indeed, his assessment shapes much of the continuing debate among Baptists themselves as to the application of religious freedom and the meaning of "separation of church and state." He wrote:

> By entering the mainstream the Baptists ceased to be critics of American society; their piety relaxed, and they became the captives of the culture against which they had fought for so long. . . . That is, they came to believe that because the American social order had accepted their evangelical views, then America must be the equivalent of a Christian society. . . . To be a good Baptist one should be a good American, and to be a good American one should be a good Baptist. Which meant, in effect, that the Baptists began to act as though they were the establishment. In short, between 1630 and 1833 the Baptists went through the classical evolution from a dissenting sect to an established church.[25]

It is this paradox that is one of the Baptists' most insightful and divisive emphases. On one hand, they are thoroughgoing sectarians, demanding a personal profession of faith (followed by believer's baptism) of everyone who would seek membership in the church. This concern for regeneration required them to insist on the uniqueness and centrality of the Christian revelation and the need for all persons to come to faith in Christ.[26] Their de facto establishmentarian presence in at least certain segments of American society united them with the Protestant privilege that was part of the culture almost from the beginning. At the same time, their emphasis of religious liberty and their strong concern for uncoerced faith for heretic and atheist alike made them the ultimate advocates for religious pluralism, opposing religious establishmentarianism wherever it appeared. Yet as religious liberty and religious pluralism became the norm, specifically in America, and as diversity of religious communions coincided with the rise of secularism and "nontraditional" spiritualities, Baptists found themselves at odds over the nature of the freedom they had so long advocated.

As the twenty-first century gets underway, controversies surrounding the relationship of church and state may be the most divisive issues faced by Baptists in America since the 1845 schism over slavery. In fact, those divisions mirror larger debates over the nature of religion in the American culture and the impact of religious pluralism on Christian Protestant groups that previously represented a religious "norm" in the American public square.

Baylor University professor Barry Hankins offers a helpful analysis of these divisions with particular attention to the Southern Baptist Convention. He suggests that the differences are evident in "Separatist" and "Accommodationist" positions. Separatist Baptists are those who continue to use *separation of church and state* to refer to the need for the state to be neutral in matters of religion, minimizing religious specificity or sectarianism in the public square. He writes:

> If the Baptist Joint Committee [BJC] is representative, moderates argue that any level of government support for religion will likely result in discrimination against minority faiths. Conservatives and moderates share the Baptist goal of full religious liberty, but they differ substantially over how the Baptist tradition should be applied to the Establishment Clause issues. Moderates focus on the state and attempt to head off any aid that might accrue to religion. Conservatives focus on the effects of government policies and ask only whether anyone is being coerced. Theirs is a less rigorous test for the establishment of religion. If no one is coerced, nothing is being established.
>
> Moderates, however, are more vigilant against the possibility that the state might further the cause of religion even when few if any would be directly affected by such action.[27]

In one of its earliest position statements, the BJC clarified its understanding of the nature of church-state separation. It states:

1. Separation of church and state means separation on an official, organizational, legally contractual level. . . . In a free society religion is expected to apply to all of life, to public officials, though partisanship for their particular churches in political action is forbidden.
2. Separation of church and state means that all churches exist on a purely voluntary basis, that they are all equal before the law, and the Government of the State shall not practice discrimination by singling out one or more churches for special recognition or favor, as would be true if it appointed an Ambassador to the Vatican.
3. Church-state separation means there shall be no general assessment of taxes for support of any kind of religious institution. . . .
4. Church-state separation, as construed in the Unites States, means that no religious instruction shall be given by any church in the public schools,

and no facilities of tax-supported public schools shall be used by the churches for their religious doctrines . . .
5. Separation of church and state is best for the church and best for the state.[28]

This separationist approach is evident in a case that developed in 2009–2010 between the American Civil Liberties Union and the Forsyth County Board of Commissioners from North Carolina regarding the use of "deity specific" prayers (i.e., "in Jesus's name") by ministers who volunteer to lead the opening prayer at commissioners' meetings. In 2009, the ACLU went to court to stop such prayers, charging that such action was privileging Christianity above other faiths. In 2010, a U.S. district court judge agreed. In July 2010, the BJC filed a "friend of the court" brief supporting the decision of the judge and arguing "that sectarian prayer at government meetings in effect endorses one particular religion, which undermines the Establishment Clause of the First Amendment."[29] Holly Hollman, general counsel for the BJC, was quoted as saying: "The government can't be in the business of promoting religion. In order to protect our religious liberty, we need clear distinctions between government-sponsored expression and private expression." The action of the Joint Committee illustrates something of its separatist approach to church-state religions.

The accommodationist position is defined by Michael McConnell, one of its advocates, as "government laws or policies that have the purpose and effect of removing a burden on, or facilitating the exercise of a person's or an institution's religion." He believes that this "does not include government action that acknowledges or expresses the prevailing religious sentiments of the community, such as the display of religious symbols on public property or the delivery of a prayer at public ceremonial events." Accommodationists, such as McConnell, insist that the state should reject "neutrality" in favor of aid to all religions. It refuses to discriminate against religion in ways that favor secularism as the dominant framework for cultural identity.[30]

A burgeoning secularism is indeed a major concern for advocates of a more accommodationist position. Many believe that secularism is fast becoming the new religious or nonreligious establishment, a danger that may cause the state to undermine religion all together. Thus, they resist traditional Baptist approaches to separation of church and state as a dated approach to issues that now threaten to destroy the religious and moral fiber of the entire nation.

The effect of a secular establishment dictating cultural and political mores is not lost on accommodationists. In July 2010, Reverend Ron Baity of Berean Baptist Church, Winston-Salem, a North Carolina Independent Baptist congregation, demanded an apology from the state legislature after he was invited to serve as chaplain for a week, in the course of which time he was called on to offer an opening prayer at each legislative session. As the pastor reported it, he informed his hosts on the first day that he intended to conclude each prayer "in Jesus's name." The pastor contended that "he was specifically asked [by the Speaker of the House] not to say Jesus in prayer."[31] When Baity implemented his plan to pray "in Jesus's name," he was told that his services as the weekly chaplain were no longer required. Baity then charged, "They're telling me how I need to pray. That is establishment of religion."[32] From his perspective, the encouragement or mandate to drop a Christian-specific prayer was a form of establishmentarianism.

Accommodationists might well insist that this incident illustrates the way in which a dominant secularism and a mistaken pluralism can undermine the rights of religious people to pray in faithfulness to their traditions, even at government gatherings. As long as the state permits all groups to pray in that faith-based way, no harm has been done, and "accommodations" could be made for all types of prayer.

Church-state Separatists, on the other hand, might assert that such a sectarian prayer in a governmental context privileges one religion over another, especially when that religion reflects the religious majority. Prayers in governmental settings should not alienate, exclude, or coerce persons who are outside the tradition of the person doing the praying. Twenty-first-century Baptists align themselves on both sides of that issue, each claiming a certain degree of historical precedent for their position.

Where is all this headed? Debates over the relationship of church and state often seem to be at the center of certain "culture wars" that divide religious communities over issues related to ethics, education and economics, war and peace, family and sexuality, and the overall role of religion in the public square. As the century deepens, religious, political, and cultural transitions confront Baptist groups across the theological and political spectrum with new challenges that move beyond current arguments. Certain examples must suffice.

First, some things remain the same. In spite of the First Amendment and claims of freedom for all religions, certain segments of American society continue to grant religious liberty grudgingly. It has been like that from the beginning. Colonial Puritans exiled Baptists and executed Quakers for their heretical views in the pre-Revolutionary era. Post-Revolutionary Virginia Anglicans jailed Baptists and other dissenters for, among other things, their refusal to secure a preaching license from the state. Protestants were shooting Mormons in Illinois in the 1840s and gunning down Catholics on the streets of Louisville in the 1850s. The Ku Klux Klan not only harassed African Americans, but Jews, Catholics, and other religio-ethnic minorities as well. During the mid-twentieth century, Jehovah's Witnesses faced significant public sanctions over their refusal to say the pledge of allegiance or serve in the military. African American churches, Jewish synagogues, and Islamic mosques continue to be vandalized, burned, or otherwise defaced even into the twenty-first century. Almost a decade after the terrorist attack on the World Trade Center, a growing number of communities are divided over the construction of new mosques, important signs that Muslims are making their way into towns and cities where their presence had been less evident or less extensive than before.[33] Like Jews, Catholics, Mormons, Jehovah's Witnesses, Christian Scientists, Quakers, and Baptists before them, American Muslims are now compelled to explain why their religion can be compatible with the "American Way of Life." Religious liberty is a right but not necessarily a given in all segments of American society, even in the twenty-first century.

Second, increasing references in some quarters to America's "Judeo-Christian" heritage may reflect an effort to minimize the rising influence of other world religions in towns and cities, large and small. The attempt lacks historical veracity nonetheless. Although talk of America as a "Christian Commonwealth" occurs throughout the nation's history, the assertion that America is a "Judeo-Christian nation" is relatively new. In volume three of *Modern American Religion*, Martin Marty suggested that the term Judeo-Christian cannot be found in American usage until 1899, and "it certainly did not enter the argot of America until World War II."[34] As Jewish immigration increased, Judaism was not immediately recognized as an appropriately "American" religion, as evidenced in formal and informal restrictions required of Jews in schools, private clubs, and the workplace.

Third, Roman Catholicism was a long time coming to full recognition as a valid expression of American Christianity. Indeed, the question is not completely settled for some American Protestants. Although the intensity and animosity of earlier Catholic-Protestant conflicts has abated significantly, some conservative Protestants continue to wonder if Catholics are really "born again," whereas some liberal Protestants wonder if the church's Christian and moral witness is compromised by its positions on women and its response to the predatory behavior of some of its clergy. Certain Protestants continue to denounce Catholicism as a false religion altogether.[35] From an historical perspective, therefore, it is probably best to think of early America as a "Protestant nation" rather than a Judeo-Christian one. Protestant hegemony endured in much of the country well into the twentieth century.

Will Herberg's classic study, *Protestant, Catholic, Jew*, published in 1955, was one of the earliest scholarly recognitions that America had become a "melting pot" of religious pluralism as evidenced in the confluence of three great faiths. Nonetheless, sociologist Herberg fretted over the rising secularism he observed in mid-twentieth-century American life. He called on the three great traditions to reassert their own identities even as they learned to work together in a new cooperative pluralism. Herberg concluded: "America was once almost entirely Protestant; the transformation of Protestant America into the tripartite America of the 'triple melting pot' has taken place, in a measure, through its union with two minority communities very different in ethnic and social composition. Present-day America reflects, at almost every point, the basic fact of its history."[36]

If Herberg probably pressed the melting pot idea in American religious life too far, he did anticipate a new pluralism that was extended to non-Protestant groups who shared Judeo-Christian roots. It involved the recognition that Jews and Catholics, often caricatured as engaged in inappropriate, even false (immigrant) religions, had come of age in American life, as is evident in a greater degree of public acceptance. Marty cites Jewish professor Seymour Martin Lipset's observation that "mainstream Protestants, who were yielding their old claims to monopoly or hegemony and learning to share space and power with others, evidently began to use Judeo-Christian language in order to sound American and to abandon claims for superiority."[37] This process continues, now involving communities of Muslims, Hindus, Buddhists, and lesser known "spiritualties," often creating new challenges for certain Protestant traditionalists.

Fourth, Baptists in America clearly demonstrate diverse responses to issues of church and state with different subgroups giving varied emphases to formative ideals. Most early Baptists were clearly antiestablishmentarians in their reaction to the Standing Order of government-sanctioned faith in England and America. Later, Baptists often relished their privileged status as a majority religion in America, thereby limiting their critique of implicit promotion of Protestantism. Indeed, it could be suggested that the twentieth-century revival of Baptist concern for separation of church and state began in part because of concerns over the rapid increase of Roman Catholics and the fear that they would constitute a new establishment through numerical increase, tax exemption, and other state-granted favors. In point of fact, however, in twenty-first-century America, any religious group that claims advocacy of separation of church and state should probably revisit their use of the phrase given the fact that most ministers, whatever their denomination, are permitted significant tax write-offs not permitted to others employed in the nonprofit sector. Such tax exemptions make it impossible to pontificate too elaborately on true separationism.

Thus, divisions over the religious nature of the Republic, long present in Baptist life, are bound to continue. As secularism and religious diversity extend throughout American life, Baptist division over church and state continues. The real question seems to be whether those divisions really matter in the increasingly secular environment of American society.

Fifth, it is clear that Baptist views on conscience and uncoerced faith contributed significantly to the development of American religious pluralism. The early Baptist insistence that God alone is judge of conscience and neither state nor official church can judge the conscience of anyone, including the heretic or the atheist, provided the foundation for a religiously pluralistic culture. Seventeenth-century Baptists generally believed that all persons should be free to exercise their voice in religious matters whether they accepted a religion or not. No group or individual should be silenced by external establishments that claimed divine prerogatives for themselves.

Amid this concern for pluralism, Baptists did not hesitate to assert the uniqueness and truth of their approach to the gospel. They challenged those whose views were different from their own, sometimes in language that was highly sectarian. Hence the dilemma: Liberal Baptists confront the challenge of discerning and declaring their unique approach to faith rather than succumb to a nebulous syncretism without a center of faith. Conservative Baptists must find ways to assert an unashamed orthodoxy without appearing to be bigoted in response to Christian and non-Christian groups who are outside the parameters of their sectarian approach to the gospel.

Finally, as Baptists lose their cultural and numerical hegemony, and as Baptist individuals, churches, and subgroups continue to struggle with church-state issues, they would do well to recall their origins in a Believers' Church in which faith commitments are required of all who would claim membership. Such a vision of the nature of the church demands an environment where the conscience is uncoerced by religious and political establishments formal or informal, legislative or ecclesiastical. Because religious and political cadres inevitably try to privilege one voice over others, dissent is an ever-present probability. Thus, contemporary Baptist ministers might decide not to pray at any government-sponsored event as a witness and in protest—a witness to the fact that government involvement in religious issues always privileges one voice over another and a protest against the coercion of consciences in a "mixed" public gathering. As faithful communities of believers, Baptists thus resist even the implicit efforts of the state to privilege any conscience or religion, even their own.[38]

Notes

1. Thomas Helwys, *A Short Declaration of the Mystery of Iniquity (1611/1612)*, ed. and introduced by Richard Groves (Macon, GA: Mercer University Press, 1998), 53.

2. Edward Bean Underhill, "Historical Introduction," in *The Records of a Church of Christ Meeting in Broadmead, Bristol, 1640–1687* (London: J. Haddon, 1847), xliv.

3. Ibid.

4. A more extensive survey of this issue may be found in Bill J. Leonard, *The Challenge of Being Baptist: Owning a Scandalous Past and an Uncertain Future* (Waco, TX: Baylor University Press, 2010), 95–99.

5. William L. Lumpkin, *Baptist Confessions of Faith* (Valley Forge, PA: Judson Press, 1974), 119.

6. Ibid., 316.

7. Daniel Featley, *The Dippers Dipt, or, the Anabaptists Duck'd and Plung'd over Head and Eares, at a Disputation at Southward* (London: Nicholas Bourne and Richard Royston, 1646), 36; and Leonard, *The Challenge of Being Baptist*, 96–97.

8. Lumpkin, *Baptist Confessions of Faith*, 122.

9. Ibid., 122–23.

10. Ibid., 233.

11. Edwin Scott Gaustad, *Liberty of Conscience: Roger Williams in America* (Grand Rapids, MI: Eerdmans Publishing Company, 1991), 39; and Bill J. Leonard, *Baptist Ways: A History* (Valley Forge, PA: Judson Press, 2003), 73.

12. Edward Bean Underhill, "Biographical Introduction" to *The Bloudy Tenent of Persecution for Cause of Conscience Discussed*, by Roger Williams (London: J. Haddon, 1848), xxv.

13. H. Shelton Smith, Robert T. Handy, and Lefferts Loetscher, *American Christianity*, 2 vols. (New York: Scribner, 1960–1963), 1:168.

14. Leonard, *Baptist Ways*, 76–77.

15. O. K. Armstrong and Marjorie Armstrong, *The Baptists in America* (Garden City, NY: Doubleday, 1979), 99–100.

16. J. M. Dawson, *Baptists and the American Republic* (Nashville: Broadman Press, 1956), 75, citing the *Backus Collection*, Andover-Newton Theological School.

17. William McLoughlin, *Soul Liberty: The Baptists' Struggle in New England, 1630–1833* (Hanover, NH: University Press of New England, 1991), 268.

18. Ibid., 263.

19. John Leland, *The Writings of John Leland*, ed. L. F. Greene (1845; repr., New York: Arno Press, 1969), 107.

20. Ibid., 118.

21. Ibid., 149.

22. Ibid., 294.

23. McLoughlin, *Soul Liberty*, 2.

24. Ibid.

25. Ibid.

26. Baptists themselves disagreed on who could be saved—the "elect" chosen by God before the foundation of the world (Calvinism), or all who would come on the basis of their free will, repentance, and faith (Arminianism).

27. Barry Hankins, *Uneasy in Babylon: Southern Baptist Conservatives and American Culture* (Tuscaloosa: The University of Alabama Press, 2002), 137. Founded in 1939, the Baptist Joint Committee on Religious Liberty, based in Washington, D.C., is a coalition of multiple Baptist groups that offers advocacy in matters of religious liberty and offers resources for churches and individuals church-state issues. Divisions over the nature of such advocacy between conservatives and moderates in the 1980s led the Southern Baptist Convention to withdraw from the BJC and form its own organization, the Ethics and Religious Liberty Commission.

28. Dawson, *Baptists and the American Republic*, 13–14.

29. Sarah Morayati, "Groups back Judge on Prayer," *Winston-Salem Journal*, July 9, 2010.

30. Hankins, *Uneasy in Babylon*, 140–41.

31. Travis Fain, "House Lacks Formal Policy," *Winston-Salem Journal*, July

10, 2010, A1. (The two examples cited here are current controversies in the state in which I live.) The pastor was Reverend Ron Baity of Berean Baptist Church, Winston-Salem, North Carolina.

32. Ibid., A9.

33. Lauren Green, "Controversy Surrounds Construction of Mosques Across U.S.," FoxNews.com, July 02, 2010. The story reflects on opposition to the construction of mosques in Murfreesboro, Tennessee; Staten Island, New York; Sheboygan County, Wisconsin; and Sheepshead Bay, Brooklyn, New York.

34. Martin E. Marty, *Modern American Religion: Under God Indivisible, 1941–1960* (Chicago: University of Chicago Press, 1996), 332.

35. Those who doubt that this is the case should not overlook the continuing publication of anti-Catholic "tracts" by groups and individuals such as Jack Chick.

36. Will Herberg, *Protestant, Catholic, Jew* (Garden City, NJ: Anchor Books, 1955), 211.

37. Marty, *Modern American Religion*, 333.

38. This conclusion reflects my own separatist-leaning sentiments, born, at least in my own mind, of the witness of the seventeenth-century Baptist forebears.

2

Democratic Religion Revisited

Early Baptists in the American South

Jewel L. Spangler

Virginia Baptist minister James Ireland would never forget the winter of 1769–1770. He spent most of it incarcerated in Culpepper County for preaching without a license. There, dreadful living conditions and worries about his impending court appearance turned out to be the least of his troubles. The Culpepper jailor had it in for the preacher and appeared willing to commit murder, if that was what it would take to silence him. He tried to suffocate the minister with smoke, set off a homemade bomb in his cell, and even resorted to poisoning his food. Ireland responded to every act of persecution by recommitting himself to his ministry to the commonfolk of Culpepper. He bravely carried on preaching to crowds (large ones) that gathered around his cell window to hear him, no matter what might come next. Opposition to his work soon spread beyond the walls of the jail itself. Gangs of well-placed local men took to galloping their horses through his congregation to break up these meetings and grabbed the slaves in his audience to be whipped. A few of them even pulled benches over to the windows of the jail, jumped up on them, and urinated on the minister through the bars to shut him up.[1]

Ireland's story of persecution, endurance, and ultimate triumph (after being released in 1770, he went on to establish and lead several congregations in the Shenandoah Valley and become a beloved pillar of the church in the South in the founding generation) is well-known to Baptist historians in the United States. It has been told many times over, as have dozens of other stories about the hardships faced by the first Baptist ministers and converts in the American South. The tale primarily has its basis in Ireland's memoir, *The Life of the Rev. James Ireland*, dictated from the preacher's deathbed in 1806 and posthumously published in 1819. The story also

secured a safe place in the historical record because of early published re-
tellings by other ministers of Ireland's cohort, most notably Robert Baylor Semple and James B. Taylor.[2]

It is interesting to note, however, that stories such as this one have
remained familiar even while other incidents in Ireland's life have been
almost completely passed over and forgotten by Baptist historians over
time, even tales that were just as dramatic and well-documented. A glaring example is an attempted murder in 1792, which is detailed in the final
chapters of the autobiography, but did not make it into Semple and Taylor's writings and has rarely been mentioned since. Ireland's two house
servants—one a free, white girl in her teens, the other a young adult slave
mother—laced the family's evening tea with arsenic after a previous attempt to poison Ireland alone had failed. Ireland's whole household was
desperately sickened in the attack, and his youngest son died after he sneaked
some sips of poisoned tea from his mother's unattended saucer. The incident was reported in the local newspaper, and court records confirm that
the women were barely acquitted of murder in the child's death and that
considerable evidence of their involvement in a poisoning plot had been
compiled.[3]

What can one make of the fact that this narrative of rebellion in the
Ireland household has been largely passed over by those whose business it
is to remember and tell Baptist stories, when other parts of Ireland's life
are so well-known and often repeated? This sort of forgetting can certainly be understood as part of the "normal" process of selectivity in storytelling. In fact, most of the past is forgotten as a matter of course, and a
wide range of influences come into play to help a few stories to get retold
and remembered over time. It can be argued, though, that the poisoning
story, in particular, was ripe for omission because it fits a bit awkwardly
with the narrative framework storytellers have typically imposed on Ireland's life. Descriptions of Ireland as a heroic Baptist founder are stream-
lined and easier to tell without the poisoning episode to contend with, as
the incident has the potential to raise some awkward questions in readers' minds. It hints that all was not quite well in the Ireland household at
some point. Though no motive for the poisoning is explained in either
Ireland's memoir or the court records, the very fact of the attack tempts
readers to wonder why these women may have committed such a serious
crime against him. Even though the memoir mentions that they were encouraged in their crimes by some unidentified neighbors, readers could
speculate on whether the poisoning might be read as an act of personal

retaliation in some sense. Such musings have the potential to clash with long-accepted narratives of Ireland's conversion, imprisonment, and ministry, which all rest on his unimpeachable personal merits and his deep commitment to godly living. The story also raises the specter of Ireland as a slaveholder, and an unpopular, or at least not fully successful, one at that. It is a well-known and noncontroversial fact that some early southern Baptists were slaveholders, but drawing particular attention to Ireland's role as a slave master by retelling the poisoning story has the potential to confuse and dilute narratives about early Baptist struggles and triumphs as religious and social underdogs in the early American South.

This essay focuses on the rise of the Baptists as dissenters in Virginia between the 1750s and 1800. It means to reconsider some of the stories often told about the Baptist past by seeking to square the dominant narrative with some forgotten tangents. It argues that by looking closely at the church minute books that detailed daily life among the Baptists, and by considering carefully the information revealed there, even if it does not fit easily with dominant narratives about the Baptist founding generation, one can develop a more complex, nuanced, and, one would hope, accurate picture of early Baptists on the rise. That picture does not so much replace the dominant view as add new depth to it. Virginia is important in the history of southern Baptists of all stripes, and to Baptists in the United States as a whole, as it was the largest colony and state in terms of population in this period, and by 1800, it had developed a large Baptist population relative to other states. Virginia produced more westward immigrants than any other state in the postwar years, sending Baptist converts to Kentucky, Tennessee, the old Southwest, and the old Northwest in astonishing numbers.[4] To reconsider stories of the rise of the Baptists in Virginia is to get at the root of the Baptist past in America as a whole in a significant way.

What is the dominant narrative about Virginia's Baptist beginnings? To be sure, there is not complete agreement on this point, but a few key features of the story do come to mind. Many writers have correctly pointed out that Baptist dissent emerged in a context of Anglican establishment— that early Baptists struggled against sometimes extreme legal and extra-legal persecution to gain a toehold between 1750 and 1775. Ireland's published life story reconfirms this theme several times over, not only in his imprisonment, but also by describing more informal encounters with Anglican leadership and local officials who sought to suppress Baptist expansion. In most Baptist histories, the Revolutionary War acts as a turning point for Baptist dissent. Not only did Baptists overwhelmingly support the patriot cause and improve their image with their patriot neighbors by their defense of the independence movement, but in the wartime context, Baptists pushed for disestablishment of the Anglican Church and to define a true policy of religious liberty. In these activities, Baptists became revolutionary leaders of a sort, who found common cause with some of the best-known political grandees of the day, most especially James Madison and Thomas Jefferson. The war not only allowed Baptists to assert their loyalty to Virginia and the emerging United States, but also to advance the idea of separation of church and state, a principle that was instrumental in the relatively persecution-free expansion of Baptist churches after the war's end.[5]

That Baptists were in some sense political revolutionaries is not terribly controversial, but such Baptist political activity has also been widely linked to an evangelical social agenda that is less uniformly supported by the historical record. That reputed social agenda is the focus of this essay. Many writers have highlighted "popular" discomfort with early Baptist dissenters because of their beliefs, style, and, most especially, their presumed "social leveling." Baptist work for religious liberty, so the argument goes, went hand-in-hand with a distinctive vision of the social order that was more welcoming of and less oppressive to those who had traditionally been discriminated against in the plantation colony of Virginia. Baptist challenges to the social hierarchy of a slaveholding society began in the demography of the membership. Plain folk of every description, so the standard narrative goes, flocked to the Baptist meetinghouse, and men of modest backgrounds and limited education could even find their way into the pulpit, whereas half-empty Anglican churches were presided over by educated men from families of at least modest wealth, who kowtowed to the slaveholding elite. Further, traditional household dependents in a patriarchal society, such as women and slaves, experienced increased opportunities for public activity and less discriminatory treatment in early Baptist churches. Some have focused on the two decades after the Revolutionary War as a moment when antislavery politics even got a hearing among Virginia Baptists, though in the end, the movement was defeated and proslavery ideology took hold in the nineteenth century. Baptist congregationalism, in sum, has been characterized as producing a "people's religion" that was in some sense an affront to the class, race, and gender hierarchies that ordered secular Virginia, helping to explain both their ability to attract converts among plain folk and the backlash against them by secular and religious authorities alike in the first generation of fellowship.[6]

There is plenty of evidence to suggest that the classic telling of the Baptist story rests on firm ground. Yet recent works on early southern Baptists, including my own *Virginians Reborn: Anglican Monopoly, Evangelical Dissent, and the Rise of the Baptists in the Late Eighteenth Century*, have "problematized" this narrative in various ways to produce a more complex story.[7] Much of this work rests, at least in part, on eighteenth-century church minute books. These records cannot be considered compelling reading, and they do not readily contribute to memorable narratives of the Baptist past, but they collectively provide a detailed portrait of congregational life among early Baptists. In them, the first generation of Baptist converts listed the names of their members, noted when individuals joined the church, and kept an account of the business meetings of the congregation. Congregations typically met on Saturdays to hear the conversion experiences of potential members, to vote on accepting those individuals into the group, to hear reports from the membership about fellow Baptists who had strayed in some way, to decide how to reprove the errant, to hear confessions and contrition from sinners, and to decide whether the contrite could be held in fellowship. At business meetings, congregations discussed what constituted sin and what overarching policies the church would have. They decided who had the gift of preaching, they hired ministers, and they fired those that did not work out. They settled disputes among members and required that the congregation be "in fellowship" with one another. They raised and then spent the funds that supported the church.

From a close look at the surviving church records of both Regular and Separate Virginia Baptists through the 1780s, for example, it is possible to consider anew the standard interpretation of early Baptists as a plain people of modest backgrounds. That idea is so widely held that it is difficult to find anyone who disagrees with it. H. Leon McBeth describes Separate Baptists in the 1750s and 1760s as swarming "over the country, appealing to the common folk." Robert G. Torbet points out the perception "in the popular mind, [that] Separate Baptists occupied a clearly defined social status which often was described by their critics as ignorant, poor, awkward, and even uncouth." Rhys Isaac put it this way: "[o]nly isolated converts were made among the gentry, but many among the slaves."[8]

There is no question that the first Baptist congregations did reach out successfully to the plainer sort. But comparisons of church membership rolls and county tithable and tax records suggest an important modification to that characterization. Though many first-generation converts were simple folk before 1785, a few were significantly wealthier than was average for their county, a number were sturdy yeomen, some were completely dispossessed, and a small percentage were enslaved. What stands out from this sort of quantitative project is not the poverty of Baptists so much as their social range. Plain folk predominated, but the initial rise of the Baptists cannot be explained as a class-based movement, nor can its nature be a reflection merely of small farmers' social and religious vision. There were many kinds of people in early Baptist congregations, all negotiating a way forward together.[9]

Although true planter elites were few among the first Baptist converts, slaveholders were many. Using social history methodologies such as tracing lists of Baptist names in tax and court records, it becomes clear that early southern Baptists were well integrated into the economic and social world of their day in ways that are hardly surprising but that tend to be overlooked in tellings of the Baptist past. For example, significant minorities of Baptist church members lived in or headed up slaveholding households. Baptists and non-Baptists alike were additionally called on by county government to perform various civic duties in which they dealt with and protected the institution of slavery, including assessing estates for division when household heads died intestate (which involved deciding the fate of slave property) and serving on slave patrols. Although some among early Baptists were certainly "an ignorant illiterate set," clearly the whole first generation of Virginia Baptists just cannot be characterized that way.[10] It should hardly be surprising that Baptist converts comprised a cross section of revolutionary Virginia's population, as later generations were certainly so, and conversions over the generations, in all probability, ran through family networks.

Early Baptists were unquestionably a distinctive people with a unique faith and practice. However, framing the rise of the Baptists in oppositional terms—as a democratic or egalitarian counterpoint to the authoritarian and patriarchal order of the dominant culture—distorts the ways in which Baptist distinctiveness came into play to some degree. Without question, opponents of the Baptists sometimes expressed concern that the dissenters threatened the traditional system of order and needed to be suppressed. A classic rendition of this claim was published in the *Virginia Gazette* in February 1772. An anonymous open letter to then-imprisoned Baptist preachers in Caroline County described the Baptists as violators of "common Conduct" who flouted earthly authority. The letter specifically framed Baptist practices as a threat to household government, which the author conceived of as the foundation of social order. Through Baptist teachings, the letter explained, "Wives are drawn from their Husbands, Children from their Parents, and Slaves from the Obedience of their Masters. Thus the very Heartstrings of those little Societies which form the greater are torn in sunder, and all their Peace destroyed."[11]

It is widely understood that in the early American South, patriarchy served as the foundation of white male authority. Women, children, unpropertied men, and slaves were conceived of as dependent members of households and, therefore, were virtually barred from the public life of the community. Propertied white men were able to come together in the public sphere as relative equals at times precisely because of the dependent and unequal status of most household members, whether these were kinfolk, hired laborers, or slaves. The centrality of the patriarchal household to the southern social structure provided the basis for white male political equality, even as it ensured that the overall extent of social equality was importantly circumscribed. Slavery served as an extension of familial patriarchy, and its continuation reinforced those values.[12]

Many Baptist historians have correctly suggested that early evangelical congregations in some ways challenged Virginia's traditional social order by elevating household dependents, such as women and slaves, and reconfiguring household relations in some measure. C. Douglas Weaver has explained especially nicely the connections seen by many writers. He has linked Baptist disestablishment activity to "the high tide of the egalitarianism of the revolutionary era" and has posited that "evangelical conversion was made attractive by unequal social conditions," because in Baptist churches "voluntarism and freedom trumped some of the privileged elements of patriarchal hierarchical society."[13] It is virtually standard to describe Separate Baptists, in particular, as a group in which women could begin to find their voice—sometimes merely by participating in church business meetings, sometimes by acting as deaconesses and eldresses, sometimes through preaching—at least until Baptists began to self-consciously modify their "radical" social ways in the nineteenth century as part of a broader quest for social respectability and a more general move toward the religious mainstream in a slaveholding society.[14] Similarly it has been posited that eighteenth-century Virginia Baptist churches were places where slaves could sometimes speak and be heard and where the master's power met with some moral limits. Some historians have been at least passingly impressed with the antislavery tendencies of the first generation of Virginia Baptists, viewing evangelical proslavery as mostly a nineteenth-century development, born of a necessity to make the faith acceptable in a slaveholding society in order to continue to attract new converts.[15]

By focusing on the subtle relationships between Baptists within households and in congregations, as revealed in the church minutes, a more complex and sometimes contradictory picture of Baptist egalitarianism emerges. To be sure, one can point to moments when early Baptists defied racial and gender norms, but the centrality of the patriarchal household to everyday Baptist life is also apparent. The management of Baptist churches often proceeded from a hierarchical, patriarchal social vision as much as it demonstrated nascent democratic tendencies. What stands out is the lack of a single voice or vision, as well as the multiplicity of stories one might tell about early Baptists that run in different directions.

Without a doubt, women took up roles as public authorities among the early Baptists from time to time. No discussion of southern Baptist women would be complete without mention of the popular exhorting of Daniel Marshall's wife, Martha Stearns Marshall, or the sometimes legally suppressed preaching of Margaret Meuse Clay.[16] However, the daily lives of the vast majority of Baptist women in the first generation of Virginia fellowship was far less disruptive to patriarchal norms, even if women were understood to be the spiritual equals of Baptist men.[17] A handful of early churches may have allowed women a vote at business meetings for a time, but no church records have survived that unambiguously reveal that women enjoyed sustained political rights in Virginia's early Baptist congregations. Those records do reveal that the vast majority of churches likely barred women from voting on church matters from their founding. The membership of Chesterfield Baptist Church addressed the matter most directly when they queried "whether a sister has a right to give their votes in a church." They answered in August 1773, "we think not from our present light in it." In 1776, Antioch Baptist Church signaled women's lack of political power in the church more indirectly, which was a far more common approach, when it ruled that only male members were required to attend discipline conferences.[18] Black Creek Baptist Church more pointedly spoke to the question of women's public voice when it ruled in 1785 that its female members could not preach or exhort and again in 1793 when it ruled that they could not speak in meetings.[19] These decisions reflected a widely held principle in the Old Dominion that women's public voices were to be expressed through their husbands, in which they were legally and socially subsumed.

It was rare and, therefore, noteworthy for women to hold official posts of governance in Baptist churches, even in the revolutionary age. Women did sometimes receive appointments as housekeepers for the meeting-house itself, a post in keeping with the expectation that women would support but not lead. Some Separate Baptist churches on the eve of the Revolution also nominated women to the office of deaconess. This office might sound equivalent to the male office of deacon, but it was not nec-essarily a position of comparable authority in the church. It appears that deaconesses did not carry out the decisions of the congregation so much as act as nurturers to sick church members and facilitators for female mem-bers, tasks that accorded well with women's supporting roles within their households.[20] In terms of church discipline, women occasionally acted as go-betweens who investigated the sins of other women or entreated with them to repent, but they almost never participated in the discipline cases of male church members, which would have upended traditional lines of patriarchal authority.[21]

When Baptist congregations called their members to account for their sins and demanded repentance to avoid expulsion from fellowship, they expected both men and women to conform to the same moral standards. At the same time, special behavioral standards applied to female converts, pertaining to fulfilling their roles as women, wives, and mothers. As one historian, writing about a slightly later period, has put it, "Precisely be-cause the recognition of women as moral individuals had the potential to reconfigure relations of power between husband and wife, precisely be-cause it could disrupt customary lines of authority within the household and undermine deeply engrained assumptions about coverture, evangelical congregations were vigilant in countering the suspicion that such was their intention."[22] Women's relationships to their husbands, for instance, were matters of public discussion within the church, which sought to ad-vance an understanding of marriage as an institution in which women were expected to submit to male authority, even if it meant putting their own desires, happiness, and even safety aside. Hartwood-Potomac Baptist Church expressed this understanding very clearly when it examined the behavior of William and Phyliss Sturdy in May 1776. William had been "getting into great passions and swearing and acting in all his conduct dis-orderly," activities that brought him under church censure. The congrega-tion disapproved of his behavior, but expected his wife to exhibit tolerance and patience. William's behavior was so far beyond the pale that his con-gregation ultimately excommunicated him, but the church first expelled Phyliss from fellowship because she had "of late transgressed and swerved from the line of the gospel by absconding from her husbands house and abstinately persisting in the unlawfull measure contrary to the particular admonishion of her brethren."[23] William may have been in a dangerous rage, but the church felt justified in judging Phyliss an even more egregious sinner for trying to escape him. When Meherrin Baptist Church censured Mary Ellis in 1776 for "unbecoming conduct to her Husband," congregants acted on their expectation that women would not only conduct themselves properly, but also appear to act appropriately toward their mates when caught in the public gaze. Baptist husbands, like their unconverted counterparts, had a right to expect both a proper wife in fact and the public appearance of such a partner. In this sort of discipline, Baptist churches echoed the gendered expectations of the wider society.

Both women and men were subject to church discipline for a wide variety of sins, including alcohol abuse, excessive revelry, and breaking the Sabbath. However, early Baptist congregations in Virginia also held female converts to specific, gendered standards. For example, both men and women were expected to speak the truth, avoid oaths, and demure from expressing anger verbally. In addition, women were chastised for scolding and gossiping, sins that their husbands, sons, and fathers were almost never accused of.[24] Meherrin Baptist Church excommunicated Mary Fullerlove for "the sin of lying, falting, and some other loose behavior," suggesting that women's speech was, in some sense, analogous to women's chastity, something to be carefully and vigorously monitored and controlled. The scolding or gossiping woman gathered the power of language to herself, a power that Virginians widely believed should not belong to women and could be dangerous if handled recklessly. When Black Creek Baptist Church reproved Frances Barnes for "Falsehood, & speaking disrespectful of the proceedings of the brethren," and Meherrin congregation censured Margaret Wood for "continual anger, & unbecoming language to some of the Brethren," these congregations signaled that they expected women to maintain an attitude of submission to male authority in their speech.[25]

Even as parents, women's power was rather circumscribed in early Baptist churches. Even though mothers were certainly expected to guide their children in the faith, the ultimate responsibility for children's religious education resided in the male head of household well into the nineteenth century. So it was that while West Tynes and his wife were both reproved by Black Creek Church in 1776 for "neglecting Family Prayr," Mill Swamp Baptist Church proclaimed it a duty that "Brethren should . . . keep their

Children in subjection in time of Divine Worship." Meherrin Baptist Church, moreover, singled out only men for discipline if they should "suffer any . . . domesticks (children or servants) in open sin uncorrected."[26]

In the end, what is striking is the mixed message that Baptist congregations collectively sent with respect to women. Female empowerment could certainly be found in some Baptist churches. In addition to preaching, exhorting, and public roles in church government, women networked with one another, supported one another in faith and daily life, and had their self-worth confirmed in the church's support for their daily walk in Christ. In fact, Baptist worship probably provided most congregants, both male and female, with a means of publicly expressing themselves in ways more overt than they could have expected to find through civic and Anglican institutions. Nevertheless, these upstart congregations were important sites of patriarchal authority, and Baptist fellowship did not liberate the vast majority of women from the confines of their established social roles. Instead, Baptist churches widely defended these roles, prompting all family members to live up to expectations, to carry the burdens of their responsibilities, and to exercise their rights judiciously.

In no way were the limits of Baptist democracy more apparent than in church dealings with slaves. Slaves were, in theory, spiritual equals among early Baptists, but in practice, they were treated as dependents of the lowest order. Baptist congregations were contested space—slaves and free southerners struggled with one another and churches could never fully and forever define slaves as Baptist "noncitizens," but that struggle also highlights the limits to Baptist antislavery in the Age of Revolution.

The daily workings of Black Creek and Meherrin Baptist churches, on Virginia's Southside, may illustrate the point. Both congregations have been held up as examples of Baptist antislavery from time to time. At Black Creek, the minister, David Barrow, and a number of key congregants freed at least some of their slaves after the Revolutionary War, and the church as a whole ruled that slavery was "unrighteous" in 1786. Even though Black Creek's declaration was not quite an emancipationist policy, it was among the clearest statements of concern about slavery that any Virginia Baptist church would make in the Revolutionary era.[27] At Meherrin, the discipline cases revealed congregational struggles with respect to slavery. In 1772, two slave members complained to the white male membership that Rebeckah Johnson, a church member, had committed "the sin of anger and unchristian language, also offering something like parting of a black bro and sister (man and wife)." The church actively investigated these charges and worked to bring mistress and slaves back into a state of harmony, actions that might be interpreted as intervention to protect slaves' rights. The following year, the church declared it "unlawful" to burn a slave and expelled Charles Cook for that offense, and in 1775, the church considered bringing Sherwood Walton under discipline after he was accused by slaves of fathering a child with one of his slaves.[28]

Yet even in these congregations, slaves were daily defined by the church leadership as the least among equals. In spite of Black Creek's pronouncement against slavery, congregants did not follow through to clear their membership of slaveholders in following years. In point of fact, over 35 percent of the free membership continued to own at least one slave throughout the 1780s and 1790s. And some who could not afford to purchase a slave outright hired bondpeople on annual contracts.[29] A handful of congregants did persist in their commitment to rid the membership of slaveholders by refusing to take communion until the matter had been addressed, but this group was ultimately persuaded to give up their cause and extend the right hand of fellowship to the slaveholders among them.[30] Three members freed all of their slaves by deed of manumission in these years. These members were clearly a committed antislavery contingent within the congregation, who defined slavery as a violation of the "Golden Rule" and freedom as "the Natural and Unalienable right of all Mankind."[31] That any slaves at all found their way out of bondage through the Baptist Church is significant and must have made a deep impression on potential slave converts, who may not only have been encouraged to give the Baptist faith a hearing but also to expect to assert their worth as Christians when they became congregants. Yet it must be remembered that these few manumissions represent one of the greatest collective achievements of Virginia Baptist churches on this subject. The small number of manumitting Baptists at Black Creek, in the end, could not fundamentally challenge the understandings of their fellow Baptist converts about the nature and place of slaves in their society.

At Meherrin Baptist Church, the disappointments were similar. Church intervention on behalf of slave members must have sent a message of hope, and news of these cases undoubtedly helped some unconverted slaves to find their way to Baptist fellowship, at least partly from a desire to participate in a faith that held out even the barest promise of social justice in a society that entirely barred them from it. Slaves may have been further encouraged by the church's May 1772 ruling that it was sinful for church members to whip Baptist servants and children unless verbal persuasion had failed to bring a change in behavior.[32] The actual results of discipline cases related to slaves, on the other hand, were undoubtedly cause for some disappointment. Rebeckah Johnson and her slave Esther may stand as a case in point. Johnson, who was accused of regaling Esther with curses and threats of separation from her spouse, came to an understanding with her slave, with church guidance. However, there is little evidence that Esther's marriage survived this crisis. The vagueness of the church record leaves open the possibility that Esther was forced to accept the sale of her husband as part of a bargain to remain in fellowship. The case of Charles Cook, who burned a slave as a means of correction, is equally ambiguous. Slaves must have been heartened that the church expelled Cook for his cruelty and that they promised expulsion to any who followed Cook's example. One wonders, though, whether slave members were truly ready to extend the hand of fellowship to him the very next month when the congregation voted to restore him, or the very next year when they gave him a license to preach.

The story of these two churches echoes broader trends with respect to the subordination that African Americans experienced in Virginia's biracial Baptist congregations. Occasionally, slaves did find their way to Virginia's eighteenth-century Baptist pulpits and preaching circuits. That even a handful of African American preachers, slave and free, were able to take up such leadership roles is meaningful. Yet the majority of slaves made do on a day-to-day basis in congregations that accorded them a decidedly second-class membership status, much the way that white women did. Most slaves had virtually no official function in the church. Business meetings occurred on Friday or Saturday, when slaves were unlikely to be able to obtain permission from their masters to attend.[33] When slaves missed business meetings, they were excluded from the discussion of questions of practice, from voting for deacons and representatives to be sent to higher levels of Baptist government, from the process of disciplining other members, and from helping to settle disputes among church members. There are few instances of slaves giving testimony in discipline cases involving free members. Many slaves, in sum, were confined to the entirely passive role of attending Sunday services and receiving discipline when their behavior was reported to the church fathers, in spite of isolated examples to the contrary.[34]

Like white women, slaves were sometimes held to a special code of conduct commensurate with their subordinate role in the household in early Baptist churches as well. Slaves could be called before the congregation for the sin of treating free people with disrespect or for disobeying their masters (even if their masters were not Baptists). For example, when a slave named Humphrey was charged by Black Creek congregation in 1793 with the sin of shooting his master's dog, the church not only required public contrition among the brethren, but also ordered Humphrey to go with a white church member to confess his sin to his master and ask forgiveness.[35] Baptist congregations appeared to operate from an understanding that masters had previous claim on the time and movements of slaves. Masters were usually consulted when slaves were requested to attend business meetings. For example, at Meherrin Church, in the process of investigating the charges against Rebeckah Johnson, the congregation discovered that the master and husband of that household, Joseph Johnson, intended to use his authority to prevent both his wife and slave from appearing at a business meeting to settle the matter. The church bowed to the master's authority and sent a committee onto his plantation to adjudicate the case under his watch and care.[36] At Mill Swamp Baptist Church, the minister refused to even baptize slaves without their masters' permission.[37]

The Baptist men who ran early Virginia Baptist churches sometimes chose to allow slaves some uncommon opportunities in the church. They allowed a few men to preach and exhort; they occasionally decided to use the discipline power of the congregation to limit slaves' mistreatment; and they sometimes recognized the contribution of slave members to the work of the church as a whole. At the same time, slaves themselves contested unequal treatment in Baptist space and asserted themselves when they could. They used their voices to inspire one another in informal preaching; they brought complaints about their treatment to the congregation for a hearing; and they sometimes even broke away from biracial churches altogether to create another form of Baptist worship in which they were, decidedly, in charge. All this is true. Yet biracial eighteenth-century Virginia Baptist congregations typically operated in ways that reflected, more than challenged, the patriarchal order.[38] Those men who owned slaves themselves were probably primarily responsible for shaping church policy with regard to slaves, as it was husbands and fathers who were undoubtedly responsible for defining the subordinate place of women and children in the congregation and the complex array of reciprocal duties and rights that bound families together as households in Christ. One important lesson to be gleaned from these churches, then, is that some Baptists came into the church, even in the earliest years, already well versed in proslavery and patriarchy, ideas that undergirded planter power in Virginia.

Why should it matter that early Virginia Baptists are understood both as challengers to the rigidity of the patriarchal, proslavery social order and also as instrumental supporters of it? Why is it important to consider the Reverend James Ireland both as astoundingly persistent under Anglican and government persecution and also as the object of a personal attack from his disgruntled household dependents? Historical writing is, inevitably, a process of selection and narrative crafting. One can never truly get at the "real story" in its entirety, to everyone's complete satisfaction, for the ages. But, by seeking and embracing multiple, and sometimes conflicting, narratives of the past, it is possible to at least get closer to the truth that the past is complex, meanings conflict, and that simple lessons from history are hard to come by.

Notes

1. James Ireland, *The Life of the Rev. James Ireland Who Was, for Many Years, Pastor of the Baptist Church in Buck Marsh, Waterlick and Happy Creek, in Frederick and Shenandoah Counties, Virginia* (Winchester, VA: James Foster, 1819), 158–81.

2. Robert B. Semple, *A History of the Rise and Progress of the Baptists in Virginia* (Richmond, VA: John O'Lynch, 1810), 425–27; James B. Taylor, *Lives of Virginia Baptist Ministers,* 2nd ed. (Richmond, VA: Yale and Wyatt, 1838), 114–25. A selected list of more recent historical work that makes reference to Ireland's imprisonment story would include William Henry Brackney, *The Baptists* (New York: Greenwood Press, 1988), 96; Keith E. Durso, *No Armor for the Back: Baptist Prison Writings, 1600s–1700s* (Atlanta: Mercer University Press, 2007), 239–47; Lewis Peyton Little, *Imprisoned Preachers and Religious Liberty in Virginia* (Lynchburg, VA: J. P. Bell Co., 1938), 159–71; and H. Leon McBeth, *The Baptist Heritage* (Nashville: Broadman Press, 1987), 271. For a quick guide to Baptist persecution in Virginia in the 1760s and 1770s, see particularly Little, *Imprisoned Preachers.*

3. Ireland, *Life of Ireland,* 199–209; Bowen's *Virginia Centinel and Gazette,* or *The Winchester Political Repository,* May 21, 1792; June 4, 1792; September 3, 1792; Frederick County Court Minute Book, 1790–1793, pp, 195–99, Library of Virginia, Richmond, Virginia (hereafter LVA); Frederick County Court Order Book No. 23, 1791–1792, microfilm reel 76, LVA, pp. 467–70; loose papers in Frederick County District Court End Causes, September–

December 1792, box 6, LVA. For a more complete treatment of the poison-ing, see Jewel L. Spangler, "Poison Stories: A Re-Reading of Revolutionary Virginia's Baptist 'Revolt,'" in *Master Narratives: Storytelling, History, and the Postmodern South,* ed. Jason Phillips (Baton Rouge: Louisiana State Univer-sity Press, forthcoming). It should be noted that the poisoning has certainly been mentioned from time to time. Keith E. Durso devotes a full paragraph to the poisoning in his treatment of imprisoned preachers, and the incident is highlighted in the introduction to a new edition of Ireland's memoir. See *No Armor for the Back;* Keith Harper and C. Martin Jacumin, eds., *Esteemed Re-proach: the Lives of Rev. James Ireland and Rev. Joseph Craig* (Macon, GA: Mer-cer University Press, 2005), 3–4.

4. David Hackett Fischer and James Kelly, *Bound Away: Virginia and the Westward Movement* (Charlottesville: University Press of Virginia, 2000), 137–46, 201.

5. These themes are common to most publications about the early Bap-tists in the American South, whether the historian is a Baptist or not. See, for example, Thomas E. Buckley, *Church and State in Revolutionary Virginia* (Charlottesville: University of Virginia Press, 1977); H. J. Eckenrode, *Separa-tion of Church and State in Virginia: A Study of the Development of the Revolution* (1910; repr., New York: De Capo Press, 1971); Charles Irons, "The Spiritual Fruits of Revolution: Disestablishment and the Rise of the Virginia Baptists," *Virginia Magazine of History and Biography* 109 (2001): 159–86; Bill J. Leonard, *Baptists in America* (New York: Columbia University Press, 2005), 158–61; Robert G. Torbet, *A History of the Baptists,* 3rd ed. (Valley Forge, PA: Jud-son Press, 1980), 234–43; C. Douglas Weaver, *In Search of the New Testament Church: The Baptist Story* (Macon, GA: Mercer University Press, 2008), 68–78.

6. Some element of these arguments has been developed in James D. Essig, *Bonds of Wickedness: American Evangelicals Against Slavery, 1770–1808* (Philadelphia: Temple University Press, 1982); Wesley M. Gewehr, *The Great Awakening in Virginia, 1740–1790* (Gloucester, MA: Peter Smith, 1965), 187–218; Christine Leigh Heyrman, *Southern Cross: The Beginnings of the Bible Belt* (New York: Knopf, 1997); Rhys Isaac, *The Transformation of Virginia, 1740–1790* (Chapel Hill: University of North Carolina Press, 1984); Donald Ma-thews, *Religion in the Old South* (Chicago: University of Chicago Press, 1977), 25–28; Gregory A. Wills, *Democratic Religion: Freedom, Authority, and Church Discipline in the Baptist South, 1785–1900* (New York: Oxford University Press, 1996), 50–66, among others.

7. Jewel L. Spangler, *Virginians Reborn: Anglican Monopoly, Evangelical Dissent, and the Rise of the Baptists in the Late Eighteenth Century* (Charlottes-

ville: University of Virginia Press, 2008). See also Charles F. Irons, *The Origins of Proslavery Christianity: White and Black Evangelicals in Colonial and Antebellum Virginia* (Chapel Hill: University of North Carolina Press, 2008); Janet Moore Lindman, *Bodies of Belief: Baptist Community in Early America* (Philadelphia: University of Pennsylvania Press, 2008); Randolph Ferguson Scully, *Religion and the Making of Nat Turner's Virginia: Baptist Community and Conflict, 1740–1840* (Charlottesville: University of Virginia Press, 2008).

8. McBeth, *Baptist Heritage*, 269; Torbet, *History of the Baptists*, 223. See also Rhys Isaac, *The Transformation of Virginia, 1760–1790* (Chapel Hill: University of North Carolina Press, 1984), 166; J. Stephen Kroll-Smith, "Tobacco and Belief: Baptist Ideology and the Yeoman Planter in 18th Century Virginia," *Southern Studies* 21 (1982): 354; Mechal Sobel, *The World They Made Together: Black and White Values in Eighteenth-Century Virginia* (Princeton: Princeton University Press, 1989), 180; Weaver, *In Search of*, 65. An important exception to many of the assertions about the dominant narrative made here is Bill J. Leonard, *Baptists in America* (New York: Columbia University Press, 2005). Leonard takes pains to note the presence of both slaveholders and slaves in early congregations, suggesting a range of social backgrounds.

9. Spangler, "Becoming Baptists: Conversion in Colonial and Early National Virginia," *Journal of Southern History* 69 (2001): 243–86; Spangler, *Virginians Reborn*, 121–27. Richard Beeman, in *The Evolution of the Southern Backcountry A Case Study of Lunenburg County, Virginia, 1746–1832* (Philadelphia: University of Pennsylvania Press, 1989), found less social variation than my study, but nevertheless did identify a range of wealth holdings for converted Baptists on the Virginia Southside. Rodger M. Payne, in "New Light in Hanover County: Evangelical Dissent in Piedmont, Virginia, 1740–1755," *Journal of Southern History* 61 (1995): 666–67, has made a similar argument with respect to early Virginia Presbyterians.

10. Quotation from William Fristoe, *A Concise History of the Ketocton Baptist Association* . . . (Staunton, VA: William Gilman Lyford, 1808), 64. For a fuller explanation of Baptist participation in local government, as illustrated through court records, see Spangler, *Virginians Reborn*, 125, 127–32.

11. The letter is reprinted (and misdated) in Little, *Imprisoned Preachers*, 255–56.

12. For a useful discussion of the household in this period, Carole Shammas, *A History of Household Government in America* (Charlottesville, Va., 2002), 24–52. For a particularly clear discussion of household order, evangelicals, and slavery in the American South, see Stephanie McCurry, *Masters of Small Worlds: Yeoman Households, Gender Relations, and the Political Culture of the*

Antebellum South Carolina Low Country (New York: Oxford University Press, 1995), 171–238.

13. Weaver, *In Search of,* 77, 78.

14. Weaver, *In Search of,* 65, 82–85. Recent literature has modulated this theme, recognizing both the potential for women's public roles and the patriarchal order in Baptist churches. See particularly Leonard, *Baptists in America,* 208–9; Lindman, *Bodies of Belief,* 115–33; Monica Najar, *Evangelizing the South: A Social History of Church and State in Early America* (New York: Oxford University Press, 2008).

15. Probably the most straightforward expression of these various ideas can be found in W. Harrison Daniel, "Virginia Baptists and the Negro in the Early Republic," *Virginia Magazine of History and Biography* 80 (1972): 60–69; James D. Essig, "A Very Wintry Season: Virginia Baptists and Slavery, 1785–1797," *Virginia Magazine of History and Biography* 88 (1980): 170–85; Robert G. Gardner, "Virginia Baptists and Slavery, 1759–1790: Part I," *Virginia Baptist Register* 25 (1985):1212–20; Sobel, *World They Made Together,* 178–213; Mathews, *Religion in the Old South.* Recent work has tended to highlight slaves' agency in biracial Baptist congregations while recognizing long-standing proslavery tendencies in these churches. See especially Scully, *Religion and the Making of Nat Turner's Virginia;* Charles F. Irons, *Origins of Proslavery Christianity.*

16. Leonard, *Baptists in America,* 208–09.

17. In addition to previous citations, for a discussion of women's participation in evangelical churches, see Susan Juster, *Disorderly Women: Sexual Politics and Evangelicalism in Revolutionary New England* (Ithaca, NY: Cornell University Press, 1994) and Blair A. Pogue, "'I Cannot Believe the Gospel That Is So Much Preached': Gender, Belief, and Discipline in Baptist Religious Culture," in *The Buzzel About Kentuck: Settling of the Promised Land,* ed. Craig Thompson Friend (Lexington: University of Kentucky Press, 1999), 217–42.

18. Minute Book of Chesterfield Baptist Church, MS, LVA, August 1773; Minute Book of Antioch Baptist Church, MS, LVA, September 1776. Women were at least partially excluded from decision-making processes in all congregations in Virginia that discussed the matter for which records are extant, with one exception. Waterlick Baptist Church ruled in 1787 that women were at liberty to vote on church affairs (Minute Book of Waterlick Baptist Church, 1787–1817, MS, Virginia Baptist Historical Society, Richmond, Virginia, 1787). Many church records are simply silent on the voting rights of women, but one should be cautious about equating silence with women's empowerment, given prevailing trends in the minutes.

19. Minute Books of Black Creek Baptist Church, MS, LVA, February 1785,

February 1793. In 1798, the Roanoke Baptist Association urged its churches to keep female members silent and exclude them from governing church proceedings, citing the scriptures in support of their position. See Minute Book of Roanoke Association, MS, LVA, October 1798.

20. For the use of deaconesses, see Morgan Edwards, *Materials Toward a History of the Baptists, Volume One* (Danielsville, GA: Heritage Papers, 1984), 46, 50, 51, 54, 56, 59, 60, 61; Lindman, *Bodies of Belief,* 121.

21. Susan Juster has found expanded public roles for women in Baptist churches in New England before the Revolution. She argues that Baptist churches directed themselves to the control of women as part of their struggle for legitimacy and their move toward the religious mainstream. See *Disorderly Women,* 41–45, 78–79, 86–88, 145–79. For southern Baptist women, the records do not demonstrate a transition from a previous period when women enjoyed more authority in churches and sin was less closely associated with feminine qualities. The most thorough study of early southern women's participation in Baptist church life to date is Lindman, *Bodies of Belief,* 112–33. Stephanie McCurry has found that by the 1830s, women were even more circumscribed in their church activities. See *Masters of Small Worlds,* 179–81.

22. McCurry, *Masters of Small Worlds,* 195.

23. Minute Book of Hartwood-Potomac Baptist Church, MS, LVA, May 1776.

24. Susan Juster observed a similar pattern with respect to verbal sins in New England's Baptist churches. See *Disorderly Women,* 151, 158–60.

25. Minute Book of Antioch Baptist Church, MS, LVA, May 1776; Minute Book of Black Creek Baptist Church, MS, LVA, May 1776; Minute Book of Meherrin Baptist Church, MS, LVA, December 1771, January 1772.

26. Minute Book of Mill Swamp Baptist Church, MS, LVA, March 1785.

27. Minute Book of Black Creek Baptist Church, MS, LVA, November 1786.

28. Minute Book of Meherrin Baptist Church, MS, LVA, February 1772, September 1775. For interpretations of these episodes, see Beeman, *Evolution of the Southern Backcountry,* 108–9; Sobel, *World They Made Together,* 194, 195–96.

29. Minute Book of Black Creek Baptist Church, MS, LVA, February 1787, July 1787. When five members refused to continue in fellowship until slaveholders had been expelled from the church, they included those who hired slaves as well (Minute Book of Black Creek Baptist Church, MS, LVA, June 1791).

30. Minute Book of Black Creek Baptist Church, MS, LVA, November

1786, February 1787, July 1787, June 1791, August 1791, February 1794, March 1802.

31. Black Creek members Toomer Joyner, Henry Jones, and Giles Johnson submitted deeds of manumission to the county court in the winter of 1787–1788, freeing five slaves between them (Southampton Court Minute Book, MS, LVA, 1786–1790, December 1787, February 1788). For their stated reasons for manumission, see Southampton County Deed Book 6, 1782–1787, microfilm reel 3, LVA, p. 208; Southampton County Deed Book 7, 1787–1793, microfilm reel 3, LVA, pp. 41, 65.

32. Minute Book of Meherrin Baptist Church, MS, LVA, May 1772. For a discussion of slaves' motives for joining dissenting churches in the South in this period, see Frey and Wood, *Come Shouting to Zion,* 80–117. Frey and Wood point out that in addition to the hope of finding justice or even freedom through worship, the nature of evangelical belief and style of worship were also particularly appealing to slaves.

33. Meherrin Baptist Church held business meetings on both Saturdays and Sundays, so slaves could conceivably at least have been present for some official church activities. Not surprisingly, the majority of churches from the pre-Revolutionary period with surviving records held business/discipline meetings on days other than Sunday. Linville's Creek Baptist Church explained in their founding covenant why this would be so: "no Matter of Debate, [should] be handled in the Church on the Lords Day, least a Contention should arise, to the polution of the Day, the Dishonour of God, and the disturbance of the Churches Peace &c." See Minute Book of Linville's Creek Baptist Church, MS, LVA, p. 5.

34. In no churches is there positive evidence that slaves were empowered with the vote. A few, such as Hartwood Baptist Church, required slaves to attend all meetings, but it would be reckless to assume, in the absence of direct evidence about voting, that slaves had the vote even in these congregations. In a few instances, however, slaves were expressly denied the vote. Antioch Baptist Church accorded voting rights only to men in their September 1776 meeting and made it clear four years later that slaves were not numbered among the "men" of the congregation. South Quay Baptist Church ruled in 1778 that slave members were to attend business meetings when convenient "for instruction." Their role as students suggests that they probably did not have voting power. See Minute Book of Antioch Baptist Church, MS, LVA, September 1776, May 1780; Minute Book of South Quay Baptist Church, MS, LVA, October 1778.

35. At Black Creek, Lawrence's Will was charged with "rude Behavior

among Women" (Minute Book of Black Creek Baptist Church, MS, LVA, May 1791), and at Meherrin, Mr. Wood's Sharper was censured for "unchristian behaviour to some of the Brethren" (Minute Book of Meherrin Baptist Church, MS, LVA, January 1772). For the case of Humphrey, see Minute Book of Black Creek Baptist Church, MS, LVA, June 1793, August 1793. See also the case of William Barnes's Moses, May 1790.

36. Minute Book of Meherrin Baptist Church, MS, LVA, May 1772. See also Minute Book of Black Creek Baptist Church, MS, LVA, August 1793, December 1792.

37. Minute Book of Mill Swamp Baptist Church, MS, LVA, June 1777.

38. This point is also made from different evidence by Andrew Lee Feight. See "The Good and the Just: Slavery and the Development of Evangelical Protestantism in the American South, 1700–1830," (Ph.D. dissertation, University of Kentucky, 2001), 85–86, 174–78.

II
Biography

3
Persecution and Polemics
Baptists and the Shaping of the Roger Williams Tradition in the Nineteenth Century
James P. Byrd

Controversy has always surrounded Roger Williams. Soon after arriving in New England, he engaged Puritan leaders on several issues. He denied the validity of their church because it was still aligned with the corrupt Church of England. He denied the validity of their colony, arguing that King Charles I had no right to authorize colonization of lands that rightfully belonged to Native Americans. Finally, he denied Massachusetts Bay's civil and religious government, arguing that civil authorities had no jurisdiction over religious life—a direct offense to Puritan efforts to establish a colony of "visible saints." For these reasons and more, Puritan leaders banished Williams from Massachusetts Bay in 1635. But the controversy did not stop there; it had only begun. Over the next several decades, Williams published several works—mostly polemical attacks on the religious persecution of New England and mostly published in London for an English audience that included Parliament.[1] Given the polemical life that he lived, it is perhaps appropriate that after his death, Williams's controversies continued, though the difference was that he became the center of the debate. Williams the polemicist became a polemic. His reputation became entangled within a variety of controversies, especially over religious liberty, the separation of church and state, and Native American rights. More than these debates, however, scholars became intrigued with Williams himself—the nature of the man, his character, and the origins of his innovative ideas that seemed so ahead of his time. The controversies over Williams rose to such a level that historians became entangled not only with uncovering Williams's history, but also in assessing his historiography. There have been so many examinations of his historiography that one could write a substantial essay on the historiography of Williams's historiography.[2] Even today, Williams claims the attention of scholars in various fields. To cite one prominent example, Williams was a central figure in Martha C. Nussbaum's 2008 book *Liberty of Conscience*. Nussbaum, a professor of law and philosophy at the University of Chicago, calls Williams "a hero" who "can help us greatly as we grapple with problems that are not unlike those he confronted in the seventeenth century."[3] Nussbaum is one of the latest of many recent scholars who have found Williams relevant to contemporary issues. Although interpretations of Williams have never lagged, a major turning point for modern views of Williams came half a century ago in the work of Perry Miller. As was often true of Miller's work, his interpretations tended to establish new benchmarks for scholarship. Such was the case with Miller's interpretation of the Puritans, Jonathan Edwards, and Roger Williams. After Miller's treatment of Williams, historians had to take seriously what Edmund Morgan called "Miller's Williams," a radical thinker acknowledged as much for the theological context of his thought as for his innovative concept of religious liberty.[4]

Much has been gained from the work of scholars since Miller, who have delved into Williams's thought and lifted out his relevance on a variety of topics. Yet with the advancement of so much scholarship on Williams, one aspect of his life and thought has received less notice: his Baptist identity. This neglect is not altogether inappropriate. Even though Williams played a central role in founding the first Baptist church in America, he was not a Baptist for very long—just how long is debatable, but possibly only for a few months. At some point, Williams came to doubt the validity of the Baptist church, and all churches for that matter, believing that Christianity needed to be restored to its primitive purity, and that restoration could not come from human efforts alone. Only Christ, or perhaps his apostles, could reset Christianity on new foundations, Williams believed. Until then, founding new churches, even Baptist churches, would do no good. So one could argue that Williams's brief sojourn among the Baptists discredited much of his relevance for the movement's long history. Moreover, the issues Williams engaged spanned far beyond one particular denomination or tradition. Still, without assessing Williams's reputation among the Baptists, historians miss a crucial part of Williams's status in American history. In the eighteenth and nineteenth centuries, Baptists wrote the majority of works on Roger Williams. And when Baptists wrote on Williams, they did so in ways that not only informed further perspectives on Williams, but they also revealed much about Baptist agendas during a crucial period of Baptist growth. As Baptists flourished in America, they contemplated Williams, often heralding him as essential to their historical legacy and to their contemporary relevance in America. Though Baptists knew that Williams had not been a Baptist for long, they continued to tell his story because he formed a critical perspective on their identity and the issues that mattered to them. Most of all, they wrote about Williams in ways that reflected the struggles that consumed them—controversies about their own contested position in the denominational marketplace and their own identity as Americans. At a time in which the new nation was teeming with new denominations, all competing for members and many claiming to be the truest form of Christianity, Baptists had a stake in the game that closely involved Roger Williams.

This essay assesses key Baptist interpretations of Roger Williams in the eighteenth and nineteenth centuries, revealing how Williams's reputation evolved throughout Baptists' struggles to establish themselves in the new nation. As Baptists worked to establish their American credentials, a process that required historical grounding, Roger Williams became crucial. And as Baptists identified themselves in relation to Williams, they shaped a narrative of Williams as a courageous witness for convictions that they shared. Baptists were keen to identify themselves not only with Williams's ideas, but with his experience as a persecuted outsider. As such, Baptist interpretations of Williams resonate with R. Laurence Moore's analysis of outsider rhetoric in American religious history.[5] Specifically, Moore argued that, beginning with the Revolution, outsiders became insiders—that is, the best way for one to be recognized as a true American was to secure an outsider identity. In a culture enthused with liberty and revolution against tyranny, the persecuted became patriots, and those who suffered unjustly achieved distinction and respect in the new nation. This outsider-to-insider dynamic was especially true for American religion, Moore argued, and he analyzed a variety of groups that achieved insider status by playing up their predicament as outsiders. Whereas Moore focused on recognized outsiders such as Latter-Day Saints, Jews, and Christian Scientists, we can recognize a similar process at work with Baptists. Even though Baptists became numerical insiders in the nineteenth century, they were vocal outsiders in the seventeenth and eighteenth centuries. Beginning with Roger Williams, Baptists were the most assertive advocates for religious liberty, especially in opposition to New England church establishments. Baptists never lost their persecuted status. Even when their numbers increased substantially, to the point that they rivaled the Methodists for Protestant dominance in the nineteenth century, Baptists continued to position themselves as persecuted outsiders. This outsider status shaped Baptist rhetoric in debates with other denominations, and it became the basis for Baptists' claims that they were both authentically biblical in their faith and authentically American in their polity. As Baptists positioned themselves as patriotic outsiders through relating their history and debating their adversaries—and often these agendas overlapped—Roger Williams was an invaluable asset. When it came to establishing their reputation as advocates of liberty—both civil and religious—and as a persecuted people, Williams served Baptists well, so well that his contributions to Baptist identity far overshadowed the minor problem that, technically, he was only a Baptist for a short time.

This essay illustrates how Baptists shaped a Roger Williams tradition in the eighteenth and nineteenth centuries. Even though my selection of sources could not be exhaustive, hopefully it is illustrative of how Baptists interpreted their tradition in light of Williams's legacy. Through biographies, sermons, and denominational squabbles that involved Congregationalists, Methodists, and even a president of the United States, Baptists shaped a useful interpretation of Roger Williams that both raised his visibility and served their own purposes in shaping Baptist identity in the denominational marketplace.

An Originating Vision: Isaac Backus, John Leland, and Williams's Legacy as a Baptist Outsider

One of the major shapers of Williams's reputation was Isaac Backus, perhaps the most influential Baptist in colonial America. In his lifetime, Backus witnessed the explosive growth of Baptist churches, from less than twenty-five churches at his birth in 1724 to over three hundred churches and nearly 25,000 members when he died in 1806.[6] Moreover, many of these new Baptists came to the movement just as Backus did, beginning as converts of New England revivals who separated from Congregationalist churches and eventually decided that believer's baptism was an essential practice of revivalistic, evangelistic Christianity. Baptists, Backus believed, were the true heirs of revivalism, even of the Puritan tradition as a whole. For fifty years, he labored for the Baptist cause, as a minister in Middleboro, Massachusetts, as a leader in Warren Association of Baptists congregations, as an activist for religious liberty, and as a church historian with a particular focus on the Baptists.

In his appeals for religious liberty, especially in defense of the Baptists who were forced to pay taxes to support established churches, Backus adapted the republican political terminology of Revolutionary America. Just as colonial patriots asserted republican principles of freedom in rejection of British tyranny, Backus used these republican images to oppose the tyrannical oppression of Baptists in New England. Colonial leaders rejected British tyranny in the state, Backus realized, but they endorsed tyranny in the church by forcing dissenters to support established churches.[7] By pointing out the hypocrisy of colonial leaders' inconsistent republicanism, Backus made the case for religious liberty and for the Baptists. Just as he believed that the Baptist churches were the rightful heirs of heartfelt Puritan piety, he also believed that the Baptists were the legitimate pioneers of the American zeal for liberty. In securing Baptist credentials on both counts, Backus wrote history, and in his history, he held a special place for Roger Williams. Accordingly, in his depiction of Williams, Backus stressed Williams's witness for religious liberty no less than his credentials as an orthodox Puritan and founder of the first Baptist church in America.

In making the case for Williams, however, Backus knew he had taken on a difficult task, for Williams's reputation in New England at the time was that of an unstable religious radical. In contesting these charges, Backus asserted that Williams was neither destructive nor erratic; Williams was a noble witness for religious liberty who engaged religious persecution firsthand when Massachusetts authorities banished him from their colony. Williams's experience of persecution was important to Backus, most likely because in Williams's struggles he found the same pattern of persecution that later Baptists would encounter in New England. Most importantly for Backus, Williams's true character shone after his banishment when he escaped Massachusetts authorities, negotiated for land among the Narragansett, befriended them, and even became an invaluable diplomatic asset to the colonial leaders in Massachusetts—his very persecutors—by negotiating with the Narragansett to prevent them from joining with the Pequot in attacking the colonists. Yet Massachusetts leaders did not repay Williams by lifting his banishment, even though he was, in Backus's view, "the greatest instrument of saving New England of any one man that lived in that day." In the end, however, history redeemed Williams. From the perspective of Revolutionary America, Backus found in Williams a political visionary, one who founded in Rhode Island the first civil government based on full liberty of conscience, thereby erecting "the best form of civil government that the world had seen in sixteen hundred years."[8] As such, Backus lifted Williams up as the pioneer of a future American political ideal, a vision that reigned supreme in the Revolutionary era.

Williams's status as a political visionary was essential for Backus. But equally important were his Baptist credentials. Although Williams was only briefly Baptist, Backus emphasized Williams's Baptist identity and defended him against charges from those who "imposed the name of Seeker upon him" and branded him a heretic. Although Backus admitted that Williams came to doubt the purity of any existing church, his debates against the Quakers late in life demonstrated that he remained firmly Christian in his theological convictions. At his death, Backus praised Williams as "the first Baptist minister in New England, and the first founder and supporter of any truly free civil government upon earth, since the rise of antichrist."[9] In Backus's view, therefore, the brevity of Williams's Baptist career did not diminish the power of his prophetic vision for liberty in church and state. By making the case for Williams's Baptist identity, Backus strengthened the republican credentials of Baptist convictions. Most important among Williams's credentials were his qualifications as a martyr for religious liberty, one who suffered for his convictions. In Puritan New England, Williams was the ultimate outsider. It was this outsider status that sealed Williams's credibility as a suffering witness who felt the pain of Baptists in Backus's era. In Williams, therefore, Backus found the perfect American origins of the Baptist tradition for a Revolutionary age.

After Backus, the most influential Baptist champion for religious liberty in the Revolutionary era was John Leland. Like Backus, Leland was born in New England and battled the established churches there. But whereas Backus was a lifelong New Englander, Leland was a traveling evangelist who spent fourteen years advocating religious liberty in Virginia before returning to New England. Leland, who was thirty years younger than Backus, lived long enough to see the full explosion of republican influence in the new nation. No minister was more enraptured by the democratization of American life in the early republic than Leland was. A thoroughgoing populist, Leland battled established churches as fiercely as Backus did, but Leland moved beyond Backus in advocating the liberty of individuals against various authorities, including the authority of the clergy. The contrast between the two is clear. Even after Backus joined the Baptist movement, he remained staunchly Calvinist, an enthusiastic admirer of Jonathan Edwards, and he never questioned the authority of the clergy as a professional class in society. In contrast, Leland had little use for formal theology. Instead of choosing sides in debates over the freedom of the will, for instance, Leland opted for a position that accepted "the doctrine of sovereign grace in the salvation of souls, mixed with a little of what is called Arminianism." Moreover, Leland had an anticlerical streak and was especially suspicious of self-serving "modern" clergy who transformed "preaching" into "a science and a trade" by which "many grand estates are made."[10]

Leland's advocacy of religious liberty led him to lobby for support from likeminded politicians, and sometimes his notoriety led politicians to lobby Leland. It is very likely that James Madison negotiated with Leland to secure his support for the Constitution in Virginia, where the support of Baptists and other dissenters was critical to ratification. Leland especially admired Thomas Jefferson, whom he praised as a defender of the spirit of the Revolution against Federalist challenges, the leader who called "back the government, and the people, from their wanderings, into the path of Republicanism." Theologically, Jefferson the deist had little in common with Leland the Baptist, but the two agreed that church establishments were evil machinations of corrupt power and that an educated, refined clergy was nothing more than tyranny hidden under the veil of piety. Leland admired Jefferson for his leadership and his intelligence—"genius and research are not always connected with firmness and perseverance," Leland observed, but "when they are, they produce a Jefferson." Often Leland described Jefferson in biblical terms, as a virtual saint; though the title was often used for others, for Leland, Jefferson was the true "Apostle of Liberty."[11]

In 1802, Leland made headlines by presenting President Jefferson with a 1,235-pound cheese inscribed "Rebellion to tyrants is obedience to God."[12] The cheese was a gift from the Republicans of Cheshire, and the inscription aptly indicated the nature of Leland's defense of liberty in church and state. Leland was almost equally exuberant with praise for Andrew Jackson. As he did with Jefferson, Leland spoke of Jackson in religious terms as an American savior of the republican tradition. When "the government degenerated from its virgin purity" and became overtaken by ambition, Leland asserted, Jackson, the military leader not known for political skill, took the helm. Like Jesus, Jackson "was in the world and the world knew him not." It was Jackson who carried democratic zeal forward. In the republican pantheon of saviors, Jefferson was the "intelligence" and Jackson "the moral courage and decision." In Jefferson and Jackson, Leland identified the true legacy of the American Revolution—

a legacy under attack that needed defense from those who understood that American democracy and Christian liberty were equally valuable and equally threatened. Of all challenges to liberty, two in particular worried Leland throughout his life. The first was "the Kings-Evil," which Leland described as "the lust of arbitrary power," including all "unjust" attempts to seize power, the deceitful designs to retain power, and the cruelties those in power inflicted on others. The second threat was "Priest-craft," or "the rushing into sacred work for the sake of ease, wealth, honor and ecclesiastical dignity." These distinct types of worldly ambition threatened what Leland saw as the legacy of the American Revolution.[13]

In Roger Williams, Leland identified the founding vision for American liberty, a view of church and state that respected the authority and independence of both. Speaking at a meeting of Democrats in Cheshire, Connecticut, an eighty-year-old Leland reflected on the legacy of Williams as the founder of "the first government, free from religious oppression" since Constantine. Williams paid the price for liberty, Leland asserted. Among the Puritans, Williams recognized the danger in erecting a so-called Christian nation, and he "manfully" revolted and suffered the consequences. Even though Williams did not fare well, his legacy did; the ideas that got him banished later formed the structure for the United States. "What an individual contended for against a host, and for which he was banished, is now become the supreme law of the whole United States," Leland asserted. The lesson of Williams for Leland was that witnesses for true freedom face conflict in every age. Even after the Revolution, with everyone advocating "liberty," the struggle for true liberty continued, facing attacks from all sides. "Democracy runs low in this state at present," Leland surmised, and for him this meant that support for President Jackson seemed to be waning in 1834. But just as Williams, an individual, fought for liberty against opposing forces, current advocates of liberty could see the tide turn in their direction. In hopes of reviving support for the democratic cause, Leland associated Williams's legacy with the full expression of liberty in the Jefferson and Jackson administrations: a newly proud United States, a nation with reduced debt and increased territories, a nation that far surpassed European countries in prosperity. Moreover, the United States had grown into a nation with "no king but *law*," with "no hereditary lords; no privileged orders in church or state," a land in which "we call no man master; we are all on a level, minding our own business, making our own bargains, and seeking our own happiness in our own chosen way." This democratic reality, for Leland, was "the genius of our institutions." It was also the legacy of Roger Williams, though it was a threatened legacy, even in the new nation founded on the principles of liberty.[14]

President John Quincy Adams and the "Character of Roger Williams"

If Leland, the Baptist advocate of Jefferson and Jackson, hailed Williams as a champion of liberty, President John Quincy Adams took the opposing view, arguing that Williams was more a troublesome heretic than a democratic hero. Here, the political division is clear between supporters and opponents of Williams's legacy. From Leland's perspective, it would have been only natural for President Adams to despise Williams's brand of liberty. The Adams administration was, in the view of Leland and other supporters of Jackson, the prototypical example of tyranny disguised as democracy. Much to the outrage of Jackson's supporters, Adams succeeded Monroe as president even though Jackson received more electoral votes—99 to Adams's 84, with the other votes divided between treasury secretary William H. Crawford (41) and speaker of the House Henry Clay (37). Because no candidate had a majority, the decision rested with the House of Representatives, which, under Clay's direction, selected Adams. Most suspiciously, Adams returned the favor by naming Clay the secretary of state. For Leland, this kind of politics was antithetical to the spirit of the American Revolution. If government does not represent "the will of the people, without awe or deception," it is not a just government. Anyone who promotes his own interests over the people's will "is a tyrant" and "a knave." "What will become of the United States, if such men are at helm?" Such political maneuverings were not the legacy of Roger Williams, a legacy realized by Jefferson and Jackson.[15]

In contrast, John Quincy Adams located in Williams not the founding of American liberty but its undoing. Writing in 1843, fourteen years after Leland's beloved Jackson had defeated him for the presidency, Adams reflected on Williams's legacy while preparing a speech for the Massachusetts Historical Society. By this time, Adams was in Congress, representing the state of Massachusetts, and in this speech, he was defending the history of Massachusetts against Williams's heroic reputation. The issue, as Adams saw it, was "the character of Roger Williams." A variety of historical admirers of Williams could not have agreed more. Although many of them did not know much of the details of his thought, they all praised his character as revealed through his benevolent integrity in representing others, his bravery in facing conflict for his convictions, and above all his prophetic patriotism—his willingness to suffer and fight for liberty long before 1776. This had been the refrain especially of Baptist historians, but also of George Bancroft, who praised Williams in his influential *History of the United States*.[16] Adams was well aware of this admiration of Williams. He knew that "it has in recent times become a sort of literary fashion to extol the character of Roger Williams by disparaging those of the Massachusetts (people) with whom he contended." Adams was particularly annoyed by his acquaintance Bancroft, with whom he frequently conversed on history, because Bancroft told the story of Williams "with extreme partiality," elevating Williams not only to the status of "a saint and a hero, but to a transcendent genius, a Newton, Kepler, or Copernicus." In this interpretation, Adams found much "injustice." The more he read, the more he believed that Williams came to America "sharpened for controversy, a polemical porcupine from Oxford, an extreme puritan, quilled with all the quarrelsome metaphysical divinity of the age." Soon after arriving in Massachusetts, he attacked the church because it was not separated from the English establishment, and he attacked the state because the king had overstepped his authority by seizing Indian lands without compensation. Given these insults, it was no wonder they eventually banished the radical. The real wonder of the story was not Massachusetts leaders' harshness but their leniency. Why did they not punish him more quickly and more severely than they did? Even Williams's conviction for religious liberty was an outrage—not because it was wrong (as a nineteenth-century American, Adams did not deny the importance of liberty of conscience), but because Williams himself violated it. No one was more intolerant than Williams. He was "the aggressor against the Massachusetts Colony from the day of his arrival." Far from being humble, he was proud and ambitious in his attempt to dethrone John Cotton "as the High-Priest of the Colony." He was seditious in refusing to swear an oath of allegiance to the government, and he was deceptive in denying that he had converted to "the Anabaptist denomination." In all these deceptions, he was intolerant of Massachusetts, its colony, and its church. He "excommunicated" them before they banished him. "Altogether," John Quincy Adams concluded, Massachusetts authorities "were amply justified in getting rid of him."[17]

"The Character of Roger Williams" Reasserted: Williams's Baptist Biographers

Much to John Quincy Adams's annoyance, Williams's reputation had grown to the point that many considered him a great man, a hero, even an admirable subject of full-length biographies. Predictably, the first full biographical treatment of Williams was the work of a New England Baptist. Published in 1834, James D. Knowles's *Memoir of Roger Williams, the Founder of the State of Rhode Island* was an exhaustive, 437-page narrative interspersed with primary sources, including a large sampling of Williams's extensive correspondence.[18] Knowles intended the work to be part biography, part reference work, and all dedicated to preserving the surviving evidence on Williams's life. The subtitle of the work is telling, because Knowles, a native of Providence, was nearly as interested in defending Rhode Island against the transgressions of Massachusetts historians as he was in defending Williams against the injustices of their Puritan founders. Knowles's book was a sturdy defense of Williams, following the lead of Backus, with ample accounting for Williams's status as a martyr for the cause of religious liberty and plenty of praise of Williams's character. Obviously Knowles recognized that Williams's reputation was on trial in the 1830s, but more importantly he believed that the United States was on trial as well, and he enlisted the memoir of Roger Williams to counteract disturbing trends in American society.

In the introduction to his biography of Williams, Knowles reflected his anxieties in the explosively productive American society of the early nineteenth century. His concern was that Americans of the day lacked the necessary connection to the past to strengthen their own self-identity. Focused as they were on "romantic visions" of "the future glory of their country," Americans tended to lose perspective.[19] Knowles had addressed similar concerns in his 1828 Fourth of July address, later published under the title *Perils and Safeguards of American Liberty*. The chief "peril" that worried Knowles was that the Revolutionary generation had largely died away, leaving a later generation of Americans who enjoyed the fruits of liberty but rejected its sacrifices. And knowledge only of the fruits of liberty without its costs had led to a leveled society demarcated only by wealth and the ambiguous pursuit of money.[20] Such avarice contributed to a decayed patriotism, an American selfishness, and an aversion to sacrifice for the nation.

Knowles's biography of Williams reflected these and other anxieties in the explosively productive American society. The early nineteenth century was a new world for many Americans, a radical reorientation of society with dramatic social, economic, cultural, and religious changes. The effect of these transitions on Knowles and many others was disorientation. In historian Gordon Wood's assessment, "everything seemed to be coming apart" during this period as "murder, suicide, theft, and mobbing became increasingly common responses to the burdens that liberty and the expectation of gain were placing on people."[21] One indicative factor was the consumption of alcohol. By 1820, Americans drank an average of five gallons of distilled spirits per person per year—an all time high, a rate three times that of today's rate of consumption. Much "to the astonishment of foreigners," Wood observed, "nearly all Americans—men, women, children, and sometimes even babies—drank whiskey all day long."[22] Hundreds of clergy responded by preaching and publishing on temperance, including Knowles, who published an address entitled *Spirituous Liquors Pernicious and Useless* in 1829.[23] For many Protestant ministers, including Knowles, the main culprit in all these social transformations and deformations was a misuse of liberty.[24] The American Revolution, it seemed, had liberated Americans from Britain but had also liberated them from all constraints of decency, leaving many Americans to question where liberty ended and anarchy began.

What America needed, Knowles asserted, was to remember its heroes. Americans needed to reacquaint themselves with the revolutionaries who knew the costs of freedom, who fought against tyranny with a "martyr-like firmness" that won the day. It was this patriotic character that Americans should celebrate on the Fourth of July, Knowles asserted, and Americans could only recapture this patriotic integrity by associating it with religion. The Fourth of July, therefore, should be "a religious duty"; Americans should transform this day of celebration into one of "the imperishable memorials of Zion." The only remedy for a flagging patriotism for Knowles was a resurgent Christianity that could school Americans in devotion to "pure political principles" and motivate virtuous men to political office. Such moves were necessary because without Christian principles, the nation would lose "the favor of God" and would even feel "his vengeance." In these sentiments, Knowles touched a consistent theme among evangelicals and particularly Baptists. As the denomination that saw itself best reflected in the national polity, Baptists were on the front end in defending national virtue. As reviewers of Knowles's address in *The American Baptist Magazine* stated, Knowles's advice was crucial in "touching the chords which harmonize the feelings of the Christian and the Patriot" in times of crisis.[25]

Knowles found in Roger Williams the "incitement to patriotism" that America needed. In a liberty-saturated society, when evangelicalism blended fluidly with republican thought, Roger Williams modeled the perfect combination of American hero and Baptist identity. In Williams's life, Knowles recognized the character needed to secure the principles of truth on which freedom should rest, safeguards that would protect society from degenerating into anarchy. Knowles's Williams defended the American cause by guiding America in its unique "responsibility" in handling liberty, a responsibility "which no other nation ever sustained." In Williams, Knowles found devout convictions for the freedom of individuals to rule themselves, and for the freedom of religion to speak powerfully, not only to individuals, but to society. What was needed, in Knowles's view, was religion that would speak "as the messenger of God, armed with his authority, and wielding his omnipotence," and "instead of leaning on the arm of the magistrate for support," the voice of religion "can enter the halls of legislation, the cabinets of rulers, and the courts of justice, to spread out her laws, and proclaim her eternal sanctions." Williams's witness, therefore, was needed at this "opportune," during "this crisis, when, both in America and in Europe, the public mind is strongly agitated by questions which affect both the civil and the religious rights" of individuals.[26]

Like Backus, therefore, Knowles found in Williams a prophetic figure, a sublime witness for principles that would later shape the United States. Yet there were significant differences. Backus's Williams was the vanguard for liberty, the first flowering of an American conviction for liberty that would flourish in the new nation. Knowles agreed; his Williams was equally patriotic, but in a different way. Unlike in Backus's day, the problem was not the lack of freedom but its overabundance. Americans had embraced the republican zeal for individual liberty, but they had neglected the republican virtue of self-sacrificial citizenship. Knowles found that Americans needed to recapture a patriotic wisdom to accompany the rampant patriotic fervor for individual liberty. For Knowles, then, Williams's primary character traits were his "spirit of self-sacrifice," his unselfish, "pure love of truth," and his "benevolent zeal for the welfare" of others. Williams, in his "benevolence towards the hapless savages," in "his patriotic and self-denying toils for the prosperity of his colony," asserted the right kind of patriotic piety, proving to be "one of the most disinterested men that ever lived." Despite the rampant confusion that liberty had ignited in the 1830s, therefore, Knowles found in Williams an optimistic vision. While Williams was dead, Knowles asserted that "his principles survive, and are destined to spread over the earth."[27] In this first among many American Baptists, Knowles found an American hero who embodied more than anyone the necessary pious character that accompanied any responsible vision of liberty. In Knowles's biography, Roger Williams, though not a Baptist for long, joined the Baptist side in a great controversy over the meaning of American liberty.

After Knowles's work, one of the most influential biographies of Williams, also written by a Baptist, was Daniel C. Eddy's *Roger Williams and the Baptists* published in 1861.[28] No biographer emphasized Williams's polemical value for Baptists more forcefully than Eddy, who was a Baptist minister who held a series of pastorates in New England and New York. He was also a politician, serving in the Massachusetts Legislature and speaker of the house in 1854, and he was a prolific author, publishing books on missions—focusing especially on women—along with fictional books on world travel for children, and a book on the afterlife.[29] Eddy's book on Williams was an exceptional example of denominational polemics. Though conciliatory in tone, Eddy was assertive in its argument for Baptist competitiveness in the American denominational marketplace. The book reprinted a lecture he had presented in a meeting of the Young Men's Christian Union meeting at the Hollis Street Church, a Unitarian congregation in Boston. Eddy's lecture was one in a series of presentations on denominations and their leaders. Eddy was the Baptist presenter, and his purpose was to defend Baptist views, and the witness of Roger Williams, in conversation and in competition with representatives of other traditions, including Catholicism, Methodism, Presbyterianism, the Christian Connection, Universalism, Unitarianism, and Congregationalism.

Although Eddy was never so fierce as James Robinson Graves and the Landmarkists in his polemical tone, he was no less convinced that the Baptists' best defense against denominational competitors was their ancient legacy. Even though Eddy tried not to assert anything "unkind or unjust to other sects," he asserted that "history and fact" defended the Baptist churches. As fervently as any Landmarkist, Eddy contended that the Baptist church was the ancient church, formed in the apostolic age, and traceable within various movements through the ages. Importantly, therefore, the Baptists were the one church never blemished by the papacy, emerging as they did from the apostolic church, not the later and corrupt rule of Catholic popes.[30] For Eddy, therefore, the argument for antiquity required an argument against postbiblical "founders." Accordingly, the argument against founders required some accounting for Roger Williams's importance. Eddy complied by asserting that Williams was no founder of the Baptist church, no Baptist equivalent to Wesley for Methodists, for instance. And yet Eddy did not marginalize Williams. Writing in New England, even as a Baptist pastor in Boston, Eddy valued the polemical value of Williams's Boston banishment. In Eddy's telling, therefore, Williams, though not a founder, was a hero among heroes, a representative of the best of the Baptist faith. In illustrating Williams's connection to the Baptist communion, Eddy retold a legendary story about Williams's grave. As Eddy recounted the story, the effort to erect a monument in Williams's honor required the exhumation of his remains. When the sextons uncovered his grave, however, they were surprised to find that Williams's remains were gone—not a bone was left. What they did find, however, was even more surprising: the root of a nearby apple tree had expanded into the grave and had perfectly traced the contours of Williams's skeleton. In this gruesome, mysterious mingling of human anatomy and vegetation, Eddy found polemical ammunition: "as that tree absorbed the body, flesh and bones, of that noble man, so did the great denomination whose views he adopted absorb his spirit and his remarkable genius, incorporating into its own living trunk and branches the principles that made him what he was, until strength was imparted to every fibre, and beauty to every leaf, and sweetness to every bud; and the essence of him who once struggled for soul liberty is merged in the immortality of the tenets for which he became an exile and a wanderer."[31] Gone from Eddy's account was any undue harping on the brevity of Williams's sojourn with the Baptists of Rhode Island. Such irrelevant facts paled in comparison to the stuff of legend, mystery, and especially principle. More impressive than the length of Williams's church membership, for Eddy, were the heroic character traits of Williams that later identified the Baptist witness.

Chief among Williams's character traits for Eddy was his witness for the truth at all costs, specifically his willingness to endure hardship and banishment in defense of his ideas. Soul liberty, for Williams, was not an abstraction; it was a hard-earned conviction. It was here that Williams was most polemically useful in denominational rivalries in the mid-nineteenth century. If Williams taught Baptists anything, he taught them that the fight was essential to the faith, that the truth of their convictions was worth the struggle, and that the struggle itself purified the witness. Williams's biography was as important as his ideas, therefore, which explains why Eddy devoted ample room in his narrative to detailing the value of Williams's suffering. The persecution that Williams endured was valuable currency in the denominational marketplace. As Baptists engaged competing denominations, they appealed to two characteristics of their unique claim to truth—antiquity and martyrdom, and the two were connected.

Not only could Baptists surpass any denomination, even Roman Catholicism, with the most primitive line of apostolic succession, but the truth of that Baptist apostolic line was verified with the constant suffering of its witnesses. Near the end of his lecture (and book), Eddy asserted these twin claims for Baptist supremacy: antiquity and martyrdom. Aware as he was that his lecture was one among many, that he followed a Roman Catholic in the program, and that others would have their say as well, Eddy asserted that his denomination "has an antiquity greater than the church of Rome, whose martyrs had held for truth long before Methodists, Quakers, Presbyterians, and Congregationalists were known, or heard of."[32] The martyrdom was the key to the defense of Baptist apostolic succession because it had always been the persecuted and never the persecutor. As Eddy asserted, the treatment of Baptists throughout the centuries is a history "written in blood" with "a long record of persecutions." As Baptists, Eddy confessed: "We hear the grating rack, the torturing thumbscrew, and the turning wheel. We see the bonfire, the expiring victim, and the flying exile. From the beginning the unselfish, non-persecuting Baptist element has met only with proscription and persecution."[33] The history of persecution was a critical mark of distinction between Baptist and Catholic claims to apostolic succession. Although Catholics could claim a line of succession, it was tainted by its constant violence and its persecution of heretics through its history. This succession of brutality tainted not only Catholics, but all Protestants who emerged out of Catholicism during the Reformation. Only Baptists could trace their lineage through a path of purity unstained with Catholic persecutions, therefore. As Eddy asserted to Episcopalians, "the apostolic succession you have came through Rome; the hands of the presbyters laid on you were red with the blood of the martyrs of ten centuries, and your line is lost in the bosom of that false church which you denounce as Antichrist."[34]

This graphic description of the martyrs' suffering was not only polemically acute; it also had a ring of appropriateness to it because Williams himself was so graphic in accounting for his own suffering and equally graphic in parallel descriptions of the suffering of many for religious convictions. Religious violence, for Williams, was a contemptible reality, and it had to be grasped before one could value religious liberty. It was Williams's awareness of the legacy of persecution and his acuity in analyzing it that set him apart and sealed his Baptist identity, in Eddy's view. At least as important as Williams's thought was his Americanness, his witness to the reality that persecution was not merely a European legacy left behind with the dawning of a new day in a new continent. Far from it: Williams ventured to America, and there found the "Bloody Tenet" manifested anew. Williams's calling was to expose this persecuting legacy in America, "to lift up the Baptist standard on this soil, and in the name of the denomination whose leading views" Williams represented. Williams above all others exposed the depth of religious persecution, just as he was the one who advocated most clearly the Baptist principles for which the true apostolic line of witness had suffered. In a new land of liberty, therefore, Williams set the tone, becoming the first individual to advance liberty's cause, and shaping a great "exhibition of moral heroism." It was this witness for liberty that made Williams the ultimate American symbol, and the ultimate American witness for Baptist convictions, the most American of denominations because of the Baptist advocacy for the American legacy of liberty. For their witness for soul liberty, Baptists earned a place within the "halo of glory" that includes Jefferson and Washington. Here, Eddy rehearsed the argument that Baptist principles for soul liberty influenced the republican freedoms embodied in the Declaration of Independence and the legacy of the United States. Just as Baptist convictions for freedom of conscience set the foundations for resistance to tyranny in all forms, the independent liberty of Baptist polity set the stage for American democracy.[35]

No Banishment, No Legacy: Henry Martyn Dexter's Assault on the Williams Tradition

The most sustained attack on the reputation of Roger Williams in the nineteenth century came from Congregationalist minister and historian Henry Martyn Dexter in 1876. The fact that Dexter devoted an entire book to dethroning Williams's status evidenced the importance of the conversation over Williams in a religious America that both heralded liberty in all forms and dealt with the results of free-ranging liberty in rampant denominational competition. Dexter's book stated the issue clearly in the title: *As to Roger Williams, and his 'Banishment' from the Massachusetts Plantation: with a few further words concerning the Baptists, the Quakers, and Religious Liberty*.[36] From the title alone, two issues are clear. First, Williams's reputation and the controversy surrounding it involved his life as much as his thought. The issue at hand was not so much Williams's novel ideas, but his supposed "banishment," the persecution he claimed to have suffered at the hands of the Massachusetts Bay authorities. It was this persecution as much as his thought that made Williams valuable for later polemicists. Second, the question of Williams's value was intensely denominational, specifically related to Baptists and their claims to be leading advocates for religious liberty. By the time Dexter published his book on Williams, he had already secured his reputation in the arena of denominational debate. In 1865, he published the first edition of *Congregationalism: What It Is, Whence It Is, How It Works, Why It Is Better than Any Other Form of Church Government, and Its Consequent Demands*, a book that defended Congregationalists not only as the polity that most closely matched the New Testament standard, but also the polity that most supports "a republican form of civil government." Tracing the genius of American republicanism through the Revolution to the Puritan founders in Massachusetts, Dexter declared Congregationalism to be "the mother of our civil liberties."[37] In his argument against Roger Williams, therefore, Dexter sought to safeguard the Puritan founders' legacy for American democracy. Most problematic for Dexter, the ascent of Williams had coincided with the descent of Massachusetts founders, as biographers hailed Williams as a prophet of liberty and chastised Massachusetts leaders as vile persecutors. In claiming the contrary point—that it was the Puritan founders and not Williams who pioneered American freedom—Dexter deftly recognized the denominational ramifications. To counter the reputation of Williams, he had to take on the Baptists, who were the primary architects of the Williams tradition.

Dexter's motivation to expose Williams's true reputation came in part from an 1874 petition on behalf of citizens of Sturbridge, Massachusetts, to lift the sentence of banishment against Williams. The petition bothered Dexter because its attempt to achieve "historical justice" for the persecuted committed a historical injustice against the founders of Massachusetts by branding them as tyrannical persecutors. The "slanders" against Massachusetts Puritans needed refutation, Dexter believed, and he hoped to set the record straight. For too long, Dexter argued, Americans had accepted the heroic portrayal of Williams by Baptist historians and biographers from Isaac Backus to the present. The Baptists, Dexter claimed, had "canonized" Williams, glorifying him "as their pet hero," and had done so on inaccurate historical grounds. In direct opposition to this errant tradition, Dexter launched what he called more accurate historical accounts of the trial, the alleged persecution, and most essentially "the character of Roger Williams."[38]

In comparing the modern exultation of Williams with seventeenth-century documents, Dexter asserted that several facets of the modern perspective were absurd. First, the Massachusetts authorities were hardly persecutors. Strictly speaking, they never even "banished" Williams at all. The term banishment was inflammatory rhetoric, claimed by Williams himself and repeatedly asserted by Baptists to reinforce the image of Puritan persecutors. Banishment, however, was not technically possible for the New England authorities at the time of the controversy with Williams. Only civil governments could banish citizens, Dexter asserted, and even then banishment required an act of Parliament. Banishment, therefore, was an act of government, and at the time of Williams's trial Massachusetts was merely a "company," not yet even a colony, with no authority to banish anyone and with little political clout with which to appeal to Parliament against a troublesome citizen. Second, the issue of Massachusetts's political standing—or lack thereof—was a critical issue in the Williams controversy. Even the Massachusetts charter was insecure, and threats to the company were serious. Not only were relations with indigenous peoples often unpredictable at best, but even more serious threats arose from the homeland. The early settlers of New England were never the favorites of King Charles I, and allowing them to colonize America was one way to distance himself from those who opposed "his tyrannous ends." Given the unstable situation, Massachusetts leaders were understandably sensitive to any threats to the stability of the company, especially any challenges to the legality of the charter itself and the just rationale of the settlement. Enter here Roger Williams, who posed exactly the kinds of threats that Massachusetts authorities feared. Faced with such "English hostility," Massachusetts could hardly tolerate dissension from within, especially the kind of dissension that Williams ignited, which focused on the legitimacy of the charter. Williams struck at the heart of the Massachusetts settlement. He disputed their rights to the land, arguing that it had been unjustly seized from the Native Americans. He called King Charles a liar for claiming that he was the first Christian ruler to "discover" the region. And he called English and Massachusetts leaders blasphemers for declaring that Christian nations still existed. No attacks could have been more serious on the viability of the immature settlement in New England. Here, Williams proved himself an anarchist, Dexter argued; Williams was a clear threat to the Massachusetts Bay Company and all those who believed in its future. "Our fathers," Dexter explained, were in a difficult situation with Roger Williams. They "felt themselves reluctantly compelled to choose between [Williams's] expulsion and the immediate risk of social, civil and religious disorganization."[39]

In this scenario, Dexter refuted the common notion that Williams was the innocent victim of Puritan persecution. The opposite was true, in

Dexter's view: Williams was "the aggressor." Massachusetts leaders never violated his liberty of conscience. They only required him to do no harm to their institutions. They did not require his agreement, only his restraint. They asked that he restrain himself "from attacking the fundamental basis on which all their institutions rested" in such a way that would "undermine the foundations of the social order." But Williams spurned their requests and launched headlong into a voracious attack on the society. What reasonable choice did they have but to remove him for their own protection? Even when Williams proved unreasonable, Massachusetts leaders were the epitome of reason and restraint. They delayed the trial, they restrained themselves from quick action in enforcing his departure once the verdict was in, and they gave him every opportunity to retract his offensive statements. They offered mercy; he refused on principle.[40]

Speaking of principle, what about Williams's famous principles, especially his advocacy of soul liberty? Here Dexter rejected not only Williams's banishment, but the supposed reason for it: Williams's fierce advocacy of modern views of liberty of conscience in an intolerant, premodern world. Contrary to the accepted view, Dexter asserted that Williams's expulsion from Massachusetts had little to do with his convictions for soul liberty. More to the point, Dexter noted that even Williams himself never asserted that soul liberty was central to his banishment. In a letter from 1651, Williams listed his convictions for liberty of conscience last among several reasons for his offense to Massachusetts authorities, behind more serious issues including his rejection of swearing oaths and requiring prayers in civil courts, his "separatism" or rejection of the Church of England as a true church, and his attacks on the charter and the English crown's rights to grant land in the New World. Given this list, Dexter concluded that Williams's treatment could hardly be blamed on his views on liberty of conscience. This principle was, at best, one among several causes and certainly not "*the* cause." With these revisions of the story of Williams's situation as it related to the Massachusetts court, Dexter rejected both of the key components of Williams's historical glorification: his persecuted status and his prophetic legacy for America. Technically, Massachusetts never banished Williams, and they certainly did not do so because of his views of soul liberty alone. Moreover, even Williams himself admitted as much. Here, Dexter stressed the irony that Williams himself "lived and died in humiliating ignorance of the fact which his biographers and eulogists have since discovered, that 'the *head and front of his offending*' consisted in his 'maintaining the great doctrine which has immortalized his name: *that the civil power has no jurisdiction over the conscience!*" This was an admirable principle, Dexter admitted, and Williams was ahead of his time for advocating it. Yet this principle was never the reason that New England Puritans could not tolerate his presence among them. His radicalism rested in his immature and rash attacks on the crown and all civil authority, not on his defense of the admirable idea of religious liberty. Williams was no prophetic thinker and, therefore, no harbinger of the modern age. He was, instead, more accurately described as President John Quincy Adams characterized him: as a "conscientiously contentious" character who promoted ideas that were "altogether revolutionary." In part, Dexter accounted for Williams's radicalism by attributing it to his immaturity. Williams was a young radical but he developed into a capable and admirable thinker and leader as he matured. It was this mature Williams that historians rightly admired, the "sweetness, wisdom, and true nobility" of Williams as he aged. But this mature, admirable Williams caused historians to forget that the youthful Williams exposed "great faults" in his character.[41]

As thoroughly as Dexter's book was an attack on the Williams reputation, it also leveled a glancing blow to Baptist historians. It was they who had exalted Williams's reputation beyond all recognition when compared to the historical Williams of the colonial era. Baptist historians, starting with Backus, had exalted the character of Williams and, as part of that process, they had overemphasized the importance of Williams's trial of banishment. Through their misrepresentation of the past, Baptist historians had inflated a minor squabble into a major trial and a significant event.[42] Given Dexter's attack on Baptist history, it is not surprising that some of the major defenders of Williams in the wake of Dexter's book were Baptists. In defending Williams's image, they were also defending their own legacy.

Williams as an American Christ: Thomas Armitage and the Apex of Williams's Baptist Image in the Late Nineteenth Century

Among the most thorough refutations of Dexter, and the most comprehensive integration of Williams's place in Baptist history, came in the monumental, nearly thousand-page *History of the Baptists* by Thomas Armitage, pastor of the Fifth Avenue Baptist Church in New York.[43] Born in England, Armitage became a Methodist minister before converting to Baptist views after coming to the United States. As Armitage transitioned from Britain to America and from Methodist to Baptist, his contemporary

William Cathcart observed that he "imbibed Republican doctrines."[44] Surely he did, for these Republican convictions affected Armitage's interpretation of Baptist history—and particularly his view of Roger Williams.

First published in 1887, Armitage's history innovated with a new perspective on the Baptist church and its distinctiveness amid America's denominational diversity. He rejected outright any attempts to trace a lineal succession of Baptist churches throughout history. Yet Armitage was as invested as any Landmarkist in securing ancient precedents for Baptist life. Armitage stated his view of the Baptist legacy in the full title of his book: *A History of the Baptists: Traced by their Vital Principles and Practices, from the Time of Our Lord and Saviour Jesus Christ to the Year 1886* (he would update the terminal year in successive editions). In rejecting a succession of apostolic Baptist churches in favor of a continuation of apostolic Baptist beliefs, Armitage developed a principle for history that suited perfectly prominent Baptist—and American—convictions in the late nineteenth century. In this denominationally competitive, individualistic, evangelistic, and democratic ethos, Armitage rejected an apostolic succession of churches as too Catholic, too dependent on the influence of tradition, and, accordingly, too independent of scripture. In Armitage's view, the Bible taught apostolic principles, not apostolic succession. The true church existed, therefore, whenever and wherever churches followed biblical principles and practices.[45]

True to the American spirit of individualism and the Baptist conviction for autonomy, Armitage heralded individual achievement in heroic witnesses for biblical truth. Christ never created a "mother church"; he never "established a law of Christian primogeniture" through a succession of faithful churches. Instead, Christ called a group of faithful individuals who followed his teachings. Christ was present in the world, therefore, not through a succession of "organic churches," traceable through apostolic succession, but through a succession of individuals "who have contended for the truth," often alone and always through struggle. As these heroic individuals struggled, enduring persecution, sometimes even martyrdom, their support came from within. They were individuals indeed, empowered directly from God, not from any external power, not even the church and its traditions. Moreover, these persecuted witnesses for truth were unique in another way—not only was their inspiration from within, but they witnessed to truths that the church did not see, truths that they alone perceived. In this way, also, they were unique in their prophetic insight into truths that were ahead of their time. It was not that their ideas were new—they were consistent with scripture—but they were neglected truths, lost in the mire of tradition and history. In recovering neglected apostolic truths, these heroic witnesses were "above the level of their age," but instead of receiving admiration, they had to "pay a large price in suffering for the purpose of blessing their race"—like Christ, they suffered for those who rejected them. The true succession of Christ's kingdom on earth, therefore, endured through the success of these individuals, not through a succession of a particular, visible church. Authentic Christianity "has been enwrapped in all who have followed purely apostolic principles through the ages." It is in this kind of succession that historians can locate "the purity of Baptist life"—in the witness of individuals, throughout time, who have suffered for apostolic truth.[46]

Armitage found the essence of Baptist history in these witnesses for apostolic truth. And no heroic witnesses for apostolic truth surpassed Roger Williams. In Armitage's view, Williams was the preeminent model of the persecuted prophet. And like Baptist historians before him, Armitage put as much emphasis on Williams's banishment as he did on his revolutionary ideas. Armitage discussed Williams most extensively in a chapter titled "The Banishment of Roger Williams"—an appropriate title, given that Williams's banishment experience was the lens through which Armitage interpreted his thought and his importance.[47] Moreover, writing after Dexter's polemic against the banishment interpretation of Williams, Armitage's emphasis on Williams's banishment was an appropriate response from a Baptist perspective. Any defense of Williams's relevance for America—and for Baptists—required a defense of his banishment, for Williams's banishment confirmed his character as a witness for American liberty.

In defending Williams's banishment, Armitage asked the same major questions that Dexter posed. Was Williams really a persecuted hero for the faith, or was he an anarchist, a political radical who Massachusetts Bay justly prosecuted? Did Massachusetts authorities have little choice but to expel Williams lest English authorities catch word of his anarchist views and punish the Bay Colony for tolerating him? Hardly, responded Armitage, because English authorities never viewed Williams as a political radical. To the contrary, evidence suggests Williams had more friends in Parliament than the leaders of the Bay Colony. Consider, for example, that the Massachusetts Bay charter seemed constantly under the scrutiny of English authorities. Meanwhile, Williams had little difficulty negotiating with Parliament to secure a patent for Providence Plantations. How, then, was Williams the radical? Also supporting Armitage's position was the nature of Williams's trial of banishment. Strictly considered, it was not a civil trial at all. "Not a witness was examined, no counsel was heard," as would have been necessary in any trial for "sedition or disturbance of the public peace," Armitage asserted. Instead, Massachusetts leaders enlisted Thomas Hooker, a Puritan minister, to dispute Williams, a move that clearly signaled that Williams's offenses were primarily religious. The fact that Williams suffered banishment for religious offenses only proved the convoluted and arcane nature of the Puritan regime that unjustly united church and state, punishing religious dissent with civil penalties.[48]

Williams was much more than a banished radical and, consequently, a Baptist hero in Armitage's history. He was a messianic figure, an American Jesus whose sacrifice for liberty resembled Christ's sacrifice for sin. "Since Jesus was sentenced to death," Armitage asserted, "a sublimer sight has not appeared . . . than that revealed in America on that crisp October morning in 1635" when the Puritans banished Roger Williams. In this scenario, the gospel reenacted itself in America when "Massachusetts did lay her political sins on [Williams's] head" as he became the "scapegoat," bearing his persecution "in the firmness of a martyr's will, in the resignation of a cavalier, in the calmness of a hero; for God was with him." Like Christ, Williams was "an illustrious exile," and the parallels between them were clear: as Christ sacrificed to redeem "the souls of men," Williams sacrificed "to give fifty millions of them soul liberty." In Williams's banishment, as in the crucifixion, "God overruled" the evil plans of men for redemptive ends. God's "eye rested on this wanderer in the New World, and his voice told him what to do and where to go." God was with Williams because God advocated the cause of freedom. "For that hour God brought [Williams] into the world," Armitage surmised. Williams, "nerved with a judicial love of liberty, fired with a hallowed zeal to liberate all the conscience-bound" and giving "life to a new age."[49]

In Armitage's history, therefore, Williams's story told of God's ultimate outsider, a Christ-like figure whose life prophesied future American freedoms and the patriotic costs required to secure them. And as Armitage narrated Williams's accomplishments, his heroic life spoke much louder than his published thoughts on religious liberty. Most important for Armitage was the heroic Williams in the wilderness who walked among "bronzed barbarians" who were "superstitious, ferocious and often treacherous." Even so, Williams's "sufferings touched the savage heart." Williams soothed "barbaric" Native Americans' savagery not with his brilliant ideals, but with his "sufferings," his sacrificial spirit. Though his sacrifices while among Native Americans were great, the rewards he achieved were greater still. In founding Providence, he launched American civil and religious liberty, laying "the foundation-stone of the freest city and State on earth; a republic of true liberty, a perpetual memorial to the unseen Finger that pointed out the hallowed spot." In verifying Williams's republican credentials, Armitage quoted from nonsectarian sources, including historian George Bancroft and Senator Henry B. Anthony's speech before the Williams memorial in the United States Capitol.[50]

Armitage enlisted such non-Baptist praise of Williams to support an important Baptist agenda. Williams was a famous Baptist who received acclaim from non-Baptist historians and politicians. As such, Williams was the perfect Baptist witness to America, and his contributions to the nation should be rightly credited to the Baptist tradition. Among all denominations in America, Baptists were unique in their solutions to the complex problem of holding fast to their specific doctrines and practices while defending just as fiercely the freedom of others to attack them. In this spiritual insight, Baptists had solved the American dilemma of denominational conflict and diversity in a distinctively patriotic way, supporting civil and religious liberty with religious zeal. Above all, it was in this spiritual insight that Baptists proclaimed themselves to be "the followers of Roger Williams."[51]

This legacy of Williams persisted in Baptist life long after he had left the Baptist church in Providence. Williams's departure from the Baptist church after a brief period, a fact that was so problematic for many Baptist historians, was no problem for Armitage. Ingeniously, Armitage even transformed this difficult, even embarrassing fact about Williams into a virtue. God led Williams to leave the Baptists, Armitage explained, so that Baptists would not "glory" too much "in his presence." Unlike many historians, who viewed Williams's departure from the Baptists as an indication of his inconsistent, radical spirit, Armitage blamed the Baptist church in Providence for Williams's departure. Specifically, Armitage suspected that Williams left the Baptist church because some of his Baptist colleagues were both hard to get along with and unorthodox in their theology. Even in departing from the Baptists Williams revealed his character as a Christ figure, a martyr for the faith. Williams's sacrifice of his Baptist identity only increased his Baptist relevance by broadening his Baptist witness into an American witness. The two legacies were inseparable; Williams's American legacy was intrinsically connected with his Baptist influence. The Baptists not only popularized Williams's witness and thought, they embodied it, manifesting Williams's influence for America. In illustrating Williams's importance for American life, Armitage joined Eddy in retelling the story of Williams's skeleton melding with the root of an apple tree. Armitage used this example to illustrate the dispersion of Williams's ideas. Just as the dust of Williams's decaying body joined with the seed of the tree and was dispersed through the land, so did Williams's witness—"political, literary, and religious"—spread widely to the point that it was "impossible to say how much of the national order and happiness is traceable to the memory and example" of Roger Williams. His influence on America was his fruit, just as his decomposing body spread through the fruit of the apple tree. Above all, Williams's influence was that of an outsider, a "weary pilgrim and exile" whose "sufferings and sacrifices" received "God's benediction" and blessing.[52]

Conclusion

Not all Baptists admired Roger Williams's contributions to Baptist life. Yet critics of Williams often honored him in spite of themselves. Consider, for instance, that one of the strongest indications of Williams's polemical authority in the nineteenth century came from James Robinson Graves, a Baptist who had little use for Williams's Baptist reputation. Born in Vermont and based in Nashville, Graves edited the influential *Tennessee Baptist* newspaper and founded the Landmark movement, which, as noted earlier, represented a network of ministers and churches that traced Baptist history through an unbroken line from the New Testament to the nineteenth century. As a Landmarkist, Graves had little use for Baptist "founders," because he was convinced that the true founder of the Baptist church was Christ. And Baptists in America had made so much of Roger Williams as the founder of the American Baptist tradition that Graves could tolerate no more. In opposition, Graves argued that the church Williams founded in Providence did not last long after he left it. Later another Baptist church formed in Providence, but it was a different community that falsely claimed the prestigious name of Roger Williams as its founder. What is more important, the church in Newport, under the direction of John Clarke, laid the lasting foundations for American Baptists, not Williams's abortive Providence church.[53]

But even as Graves downplayed Williams's Baptist authority, he never doubted Williams's republican credentials. For Graves, republican credentials mattered almost as much as Baptist identity; the two were intimately connected. Consider the prime example in Graves's massive attack on Methodism in 1857 titled *The Great Iron Wheel,* a metaphor that referred to the Methodist system of authorities—including bishops, elders, and conferences—a system that Graves viewed as illegitimate, in part because it trapped individuals within a confusing mechanism of authority that restricted their freedom and in part because it was an unbiblical invention less than a century old. Alongside Graves's title, *The Great Iron Wheel,* which attacked Methodism, was his important subtitle, *Republicanism Backwards and Christianity Reversed.*[54] Methodism was not only unbiblical, therefore, it was also un-American. In contrast, Graves would contend for the Baptist faith as both ultimately biblical and ultimately patriotic. If Methodism were "Republicanism backwards," the Baptist tradition was republicanism at its purest in polity, perfectly consistent with the freedoms of the nation. Accordingly, Graves dedicated his book: "To every American who loves our free institutions and scorns to be degraded or enslaved in church or state; to every Christian who loves the truth, and desires to serve no master but Jesus, and obey no king or lawgiver but Christ, this work is most confidently dedicated by its author, who here, most affectionately acknowledges his indebtedness for an ardent and early implanted love of republicanism, in civil and ecclesiastical government."[55] Graves recognized and admired these convictions in Roger Williams, who was a great American, even if he was not a great Baptist.[56] Williams suffered for his convictions, and he witnessed for the civil and religious liberty that made America great. Graves took pride in the fact that Williams's renown had spread around the world, and he stressed this point by quoting a German philosopher who gave Williams credit for establishing "perfect freedom in matters of faith" as well as a colony in which "the majority ruled in all civil affairs."[57] Williams was significant, Graves admitted. But Williams was great because he was a Baptist, though briefly. Baptists were not great because of Williams; Williams was great because of what he learned from Baptists.

When it came to engaging the Williams tradition, therefore, Graves was the exception that proved the rule. Though he did not admire Williams's Baptist witness, he was awash with it, to the point that he had to deal with it, if only to refute it. Yet even in refuting it, Graves affirmed Williams's greatness in his American legacy, a legacy that connected directly with the Baptist faith. In Williams, therefore, many American Baptists identified the ideal model for the Baptist witness to America. Like Williams, Baptists were outsiders, the persecuted minority who suffered for America's sacred principles of liberty long before they would form the basis for Revolution and a new nation. In this outsider witness, Williams and his Baptist successors became the ultimate Americans. In the nineteenth century, in the midst of denominational diversity and conflict, Baptists positioned themselves as the denomination best suited for America. They were the most republican of churches, empowered with a commitment to freedom that set the tone for the nation.

Notes

1. Williams's polemical works were reprinted in seven volumes with various editors in *The Complete Writings of Roger Williams* (New York: Russell & Russell, 1963). Included in this collection are the most important polemical treatises: *The Bloudy Tenent, of Persecution, for Cause of Conscience, Discussed, in a Conference Betweene Truth and Peace; Mr. Cottons Letter Lately Printed, Examined and Answered; Queries of Highest Consideration; The Bloody Tenent yet More Bloody; The Fourth Paper, Presented by Major Butler; The Hireling Ministry None of Christs;* and *The Examiner Defended in a Fair and Sober Answer.*

2. Historiographical treatments of Williams include James P. Byrd, *The Challenges of Roger Williams: Religious Liberty, Violent Persecution, and the Bible* (Macon, GA: Mercer University Press, 2002), chap. 1; Raymond D. Irwin, "A Man for All Eras: The Changing Historical Image of Roger Williams, 1630–1993," *Fides et Historia* 26, no. 3 (1994): 6–23; LeRoy Moore Jr., "Roger Williams and the Historians," *Church History* 32 (1963): 432–51; Nancy E. Peace, "Roger Williams: A Historiographical Essay," *Rhode Island History* 35, no. 4 (1976): 103–13.

3. Martha C. Nussbaum, "The First Founder: The American Revolution of Roger Williams," *The New Republic* 239, no. 4 (September 10, 2008): 24. See also Nussbaum, *Liberty of Conscience: In Defense of America's Tradition of Religious Equality* (Philadelphia: Basic Books, 2008).

4. Perry Miller, *Roger Williams: His Contribution to the American Tradition* (New York: Bobbs-Merrill, 1953); Perry Miller, "Roger Williams: An Essay in Interpretation," in *The Complete Writings of Roger Williams*, vol. 7, ed. P. Miller (New York: Russell & Russell, 1963), 5–25; Edmund S. Morgan, "Miller's Williams," *New England Quarterly* 38 (1965): 513–23.

5. R. Laurence Moore, *Religious Outsiders and the Making of Americans* (New York: Oxford University Press, 1986).

6. Mark A. Noll, *America's God: From Jonathan Edwards to Abraham Lincoln* (Oxford: Oxford University Press, 2002), 149.

7. Mark Noll cites Backus's republican arguments for religious liberty as

"a classic example of how a revivalist's alchemy could turn patriotic arguments against Britain into attacks on the establishment of religion in New England." Yet Backus's "rhetoric of republican civic humanism . . . remained the servant rather than the master of his theological vision." Backus's chief concern was with religious liberty, not political liberty. Noll, *America's God*, 151.

8. Isaac Backus, *A History of New England with Particular Reference to the Denomination of Christians Called Baptists*, vol. 1 (Newton, MA: Backus Historical Society, 1871), 113, 409.

9. Backus, *History*, 410, 118, 414.

10. John Leland, *The Writings of the Late Elder John Leland: Including Some Events in His Life* (New York: Printed by G. W. Wood, 1845), 172, 193. See also, Nathan O. Hatch, *The Democratization of American Christianity* (New Haven, CT: Yale University Press, 1991), 93–101 and Noll, *America's God*, 152–53.

11. Leland, *Writings*, 66, 592, 36.

12. Lyman H. Butterfield, "Elder John Leland, Jeffersonian Itinerant," *Proceedings of the American Antiquarian Society* 62 (1953): 214–19. See also Hatch, *Democratization*, 96.

13. Leland, *Writings*, 716, 484.

14. Ibid., 655.

15. Ibid., 522.

16. Bancroft's admiration of Williams drew largely from Baptist sources, including the work of Backus (already discussed) and Knowles (discussed later). See George Bancroft, *A History of the United States* (Boston: Charles Bowen, 1837), 68.

17. John Quincy Adams, *Memoirs of John Quincy Adams, Comprising Portions of His Diary from 1795 to 1848* (Washington, D.C.: J. B. Lippincott & Co., 1876), 376–77.

18. James D. Knowles, *Memoir of Roger Williams, the Founder of the State of Rhode-Island* (Boston: Lincoln Edmands, 1834).

19. Knowles, *Williams*, vii.

20. Massachusetts Baptist Missionary Society, "Review of James D. Knowles, *Perils and Safeguards of American Liberty*," *The American Baptist Magazine* vol. 8 (1828): 243.

21. Gordon S. Wood, *The Radicalism of the American Revolution* (New York: A. A. Knopf, 1992), 306.

22. Gordon S. Wood, *Empire of Liberty: A History of the Early Republic, 1789–1815* (New York: Oxford University Press, 2009), 339–40.

23. James Davis Knowles, *Spirituous Liquors Pernicious and Useless* (Boston: Printed by Lincoln & Edmands, 1829).

24. As Gordon Wood summarized the complaints of Samuel Mitchill, a contemporary New Yorker, America's problem was "that everybody wanted independence: first independence from Great Britain, then independence of the states from each other, then independence of the people from government, and 'lastly the members of society be equally independent of each other.'" Wood, *Radicalism*, 308.

25. Massachusetts Baptist Missionary Society, "Perils and Safeguards of American Liberty," 242–44.

26. Knowles, *Williams*, xiii–xiv.

27. Ibid., 388–89.

28. Daniel Clarke Eddy, *Roger Williams and the Baptists* (Boston: Andrew F. Graves, 1861).

29. For biographical information on Eddy, see *The Harvard Register* 3 (January–July 1881): 415; Eddy's books included *Angel Whispers; or, The Echo of Spirit Voices. Designed To Comfort Those Who Mourn* (Boston: Wentworth & Co., 1857); *Heroines of the Missionary Enterprise, or, Sketches of Prominent Female Missionaries* (Boston: Ticknor, Reed, and Fields, 1850).

30. Eddy, *Williams*, 5–6.

31. Ibid., 15–16.

32. Ibid., 133.

33. Ibid., 71–72.

34. Ibid., 68–69.

35. Ibid., 87–90, 122–25.

36. Henry Martyn Dexter, *As to Roger Williams and His 'Banishment' from the Massachusetts Plantation with a Few Further Words Concerning the Baptists, the Quakers, and Religious Liberty: A Monograph* (Boston: Congregational Publishing Society, 1876).

37. Henry Martyn Dexter, *Congregationalism: What It Is, Whence It Is, How It Works, Why It Is Better than Any Other Form of Church Government, and Its Consequent Demands* (Boston: Noyes, Holmes, 1874), 289–93.

38. Dexter, *Banishment*, 84, 1.

39. Ibid., 20, 24–27, 88.

40. Ibid., 30.

41. Ibid., 66–67, 79–88.

42. Ibid., 84.

43. Thomas Armitage, *A History of the Baptists: Traced by Their Vital Principles and Practices: From the Time of Our Lord and Saviour Jesus Christ to the Year 1886* (New York: Bryan, Taylor, 1890).

44. William Cathcart, *The Baptist Encyclopedia—Vol. 1* (Paris, AK: The Baptist Standard Bearer, Inc., 2001), 40.

45. As H. Leon McBeth observed, "Thomas Armitage introduced an important shift in Baptist historiography" in locating the historic truths of the Baptist tradition without arguing for successsionism, which he could not verify. McBeth, *The Baptist Heritage* (Nashville: Broadman, 1987), 58.

46. Armitage, *History,* 1, 3, 6–7.

47. Ibid., 627–40.

48. Ibid., 634, 638–39.

49. Ibid., 640–42.

50. Ibid., 642–43.

51. Ibid., 645.

52. Ibid., 660, 663, 648–49.

53. James Robinson Graves, *The Tri-Lemma: Or, Death by Three Horns . . . "Is Baptism in the Romish Church Valid?"* (Nashville: South-Western Publishing House, 1860), 124.

54. James Robinson Graves, *The Great Iron Wheel: Or, Republicanism Backwards and Christianity Reversed: In a Series of Letters Addressed to J. Soule, Senior Bishop of the M.E. Church, South* (Nashville: Graves and Marks, 1855).

55. Graves, *Great Iron Wheel,* dedication page. For an examination of Graves's *Great Iron Wheel* and its republican context, see Noll, *America's God,* 244–46.

56. For Graves's admiration for Williams "as a bold and powerful advocate of civil and religious liberty," see Samuel Adlam and James Robinson Graves, *Trials and Sufferings for Religious Liberty in New England; and, the Oldest Baptist Church in America Not the Providence Church* (Nashville: South-Western Publishing House, 1858), 214.

57. James Robinson Graves, *The Little Iron Wheel: A Declaration of Christian Rights and Articles, Showing the Despotism of Episcopal Methodism* (Nashville: South-Western Publishing House, Graves, Marks & Co., 1857), 51. Graves's quote was from Georg Gottfried Gervinus. See Gervinus, *Introduction to the History of the Nineteenth Century, from the Germ., with a Brief Notice of the Author* (London: Henry G. Bohn, 1853), 65.

4

E. Y. Mullins and the Siren Songs of Modernity

Curtis W. Freeman

Baptist Theology and the Perils of Modernity

Ancient sailors attempting to navigate the waters between present-day Italy and Sicily faced two seemingly impassable perils: Scylla, a massive rock that devoured hapless victims in its sharp teeth, and Charybdis, a whirlpool whose currents sucked helpless ships into its swirling vortex. Avoiding one danger meant succumbing to the other. The heroic journeys of the few who passed successfully were celebrated in epic tales. The Baptist heritage is full of paradigmatic stories worth telling through the generations. One such story is the theological pilgrimage of E. Y. Mullins, who like the sailors of old set out on a perilous voyage and made it safely home. His wise leadership and theological direction steered the Southern Baptist ship around the rocky waters of fundamentalism and past the swirling currents of liberalism. A key navigational tool for him, though not the only one, was "soul competency." Subsequent sailors in the Baptist fleet ventured into the powerful currents of modernity but did not make it through the straits so well, although that story must await another time to be told.

How is it that Mullins was successful when others guided by his theology were not as fortunate? One way of answering this question is simply *to state* the rules and principles of Mullins's theology. A more profound approach is *to show* the rules and principles of his theology at work.[1] The demonstration of Mullins's use of theological discourse will require a display of the Scylla and Charybdis that he perceived as well as the Siren songs that tempted him and shipwrecked others. It will further demand a demonstration of how Mullins used and quietly supplemented modern theology, narrowly escaping ruin himself.

The Rock of Reason

In the late eighteenth century, when evangelical Christianity and Enlightenment rationalism were not yet competing worldviews, few well-
educated Americans believed that there was a conflict between revelation
and reason. Moderate ideas associated with Newton and Locke, skeptical views represented by Voltaire and Hume, and even revolutionary notions stemming from Rousseau to Godwin had appeal to and influence
on early American social and political thought. But it was Scottish common sense philosophy, wedded to Baconian inductive science, that produced the grand American synthesis between faith and reason.[2] George
Marsden observes that in this account of faith and reason, "God's truth
was a single unified order and . . . all persons of common sense were capable of knowing that truth."[3] The "love affair" between evangelical religion and Enlightenment science dominated American academic thought
for most of the nineteenth century.[4] Yet as Perry Miller noted, in the two
or three decades after the Civil War, "the philosophy and the philosophers of Scottish Realism vanished from the American colleges, leaving
not even a rack behind, and were swiftly replaced by expounders of some
form of Idealism."[5]

Mullins was keenly aware of the common sense tradition in Baptist
theology. *The Elements of Moral Science* by Francis Wayland (1796–1865), a
Baptist minister and the president of Brown University for twenty-eight
years, was the first American textbook of moral philosophy. Its significance does not lie in its creative contribution to American philosophy, of
which it made none, but rather through its wide use in colleges and seminaries that both epitomized and popularized common sense realism in
nineteenth-century American intellectual life. For Wayland, ethics is a
science; moral laws are just as invariable as physical laws. Both denote the
order of sequence between cause and effect.[6] This confidence in the com-
patibility of science and faith simply mirrors the conviction of other evangelical Christians such as Charles Finney who insisted that producing a
revival of religion is no less scientific than yielding a crop of grain.[7] Wayland contended that the principles of morality are intuitively evident to
the moral sense of the conscience, just as the laws of science are immediately available to the common sense of the mind. Moral facts, like physical
objects, are directly apprehended. As the eyes are the faculties of physical
sight, so the conscience is the faculty of moral sight.[8] Wayland's moral
psychology shared the underlying individualism and atomism of Scottish

philosophy. Moral agents were believed to be equipped with a set of faculties ready for use in discerning right from wrong and acting on that knowledge. Moreover, at issue was *individual* human nature, and the conscience was simply a part of the human constitution. Like many others under the spell of Enlightenment rationality, Wayland was swept along in the cultural and intellectual currents of the early nineteenth century in which "the autonomous individual became for some the preeminent value to be preserved and served."[9]

Yet with his eighteenth-century Protestant forebears, Wayland recognized that human nature is not entirely capable of self-direction, for the conscience is an imperfect faculty and in need of additional light. "The precepts of natural religion," he wrote, must be supplemented by "the precepts . . . of the sacred Scriptures."[10] This harmony of reason and faith, however, is no mere coincidence as Wayland noted:

> The truths of revealed religion *harmonize* perfectly with those of natural religion. The difference between them consists in this—that the one teaches plainly what the other teaches by inference; the one takes up the lesson where the other leaves it, and adds to it other and vitally important precepts. Nay, so perfect is the harmony between them that it may safely be asserted that not a single precept of natural religion exists which is not also found in the Bible . . . So complete is this coincidence as to afford irrefragable proof that the Bible contains the moral laws of the universe; and hence that the Author of the universe—that is, of natural religion—is also the Author of the Scriptures.[11]

Thus for Wayland, the truth found in nature and in scripture form a unified whole which is directly available to be known by all individuals through the faculties of human rationality.

The theology of John Leadley Dagg (1794–1884) was also deeply influenced by the habits of mind associated with common sense rationality.[12] Dagg's *Manual of Theology*, a formative book among Southern Baptists, appears to be dependent on a simple biblicism, as he proposes to derive doctrine by going straight to scripture.[13] Yet, as Brooks Holifield observes, "religious conservatism in the Old South was always as much a matter of philosophical as of biblical considerations."[14] Dagg's *Theology* begins with the declaration that the "obligation that moves us to seek the knowledge of the truth . . . belongs to the constitution of human nature."[15] Implicit in this appeal to human nature are the common sense notions of morality and rationality. In effect, common sense provided a criterion for theological truth, and biblical revelation was congruous with human rationality. Thus for Dagg, no less than for Wayland, faith and reason were a seamless garment. Although his book follows an order traditional of Protestant orthodoxy (i.e., God, creation and providence, sin, Christ, the Holy Spirit, etc.), each doctrine is introduced by identifying a corresponding "duty" (i.e., to love God, to delight in the will and works of God, to repent, to believe in Christ, to live and walk in the Spirit, etc.). In effect, Dagg was suggesting that the truth of Christian doctrine was self-evident if measured by its commensurability with Christian morality and piety.

Common sense rationality made a deep and lasting impression on the theological tradition of Baptists in the work of James Petigru Boyce (1827–1888), the chairman of the faculty and first president of the Southern Baptist Theological Seminary. Although Boyce was influenced by Wayland as a student at Brown University, it was the Princeton theologians, especially Charles Hodge, who shaped his thinking. Theology for Hodge was a scientific discipline, and the view of science was Baconian: a strict induction of facts. The Bible provides the theologian with a "store-house of facts," and the theological task is "to ascertain, collect and combine all the facts which God has revealed concerning himself and our relation to Him."[16] For Hodge, these facts are directly apprehended by the mind through common sense.

Boyce followed Hodge in his description of theology as a science that investigates and arranges the facts that are propositionally set forth in the scriptures. Boyce similarly assumed—as Wayland, Dagg, and Hodge assumed—that the facts of the Bible are directly available to be known by means of common sense. Just as science describes the physical world as it is, so scripture simply describes God and God's ways as they really are.[17] That Mullins wisely saw that the course of common sense rationality was headed toward theological shipwreck is evident in the fact that the one and only reference to Boyce in *The Christian Religion*, the theological textbook at Southern Seminary for almost half a century, is in the dedication to his former teacher and predecessor in office.

The Whirlpool of Experience

While nineteenth-century evangelical Protestants in America were busy accommodating to the philosophy of common sense, Protestant theologians in Europe and Great Britain were occupied all century long with a rescue effort—saving the theological enterprise and Christianity itself from the threat of the Enlightenment. At the outset of the century, the problem was with the rationale and method of theology: "How is theology possible?" Claude Welch observes that the answers, though differently stated, shared "a decisive Socratic turn to the self."[18] Welch continues:

> It meant a new kind of self-consciousness and systematic recognition of the involvement of the religious subject—his point of view, his cognitive act, his interest, his willing and choosing, with which theological reflection has to begin. Consciousness of the truth of the religious object was peculiarly one with self-consciousness. An ineradicably subjective (though not subjectivist) viewing of the religious object emerged. Significant talk about God is talk in which the self is concerned. The religious object, God, is present for reflection only in and with the religious subject in his relation to God. Religious truth is not of a disinterested, neutral sort, but irreducibly involves the believer's being in the truth.[19]

Theology became "existential" or "experiential." Speech about God began with talk about the self. In short, theology became anthropology.

A decisive moment in this modern "turn to the subject" was the publication of Friedrich Schleiermacher's *Speeches on Religion* (1799), which offered a way to retain the traditional piety and language of the Christian faith, although recast to accommodate modern belief. Schleiermacher contended that religion cannot be reduced to a set of doctrines or ideas. It belongs to the realm of feeling or immediate self-consciousness. Consequently, the truth of the Christian religion is available, not in rationality or morality, but in affections. This feeling, however, is not just a consciousness of the self; it is a feeling of absolute dependence, a creature feeling toward the Creator, a sense of the Infinite. He explains: "To seek and find this infinite and eternal factor in all that lives and moves, in all growth and change, in all action and passion, and to have and to know life itself only in immediate feeling—that is religion."[20] When Schleiermacher expanded this definition of religion into a theological system, he proposed that "Christian doctrines are accounts of the Christian religious affections set forth in speech."[21] Thus, Schleiermacher mapped out a "public" place for theology where its warrants could be clearly stated and made intelligible outside the community of faith.

At a time when Baptists and most other Protestants in America were still following the paradigm of common sense realism, William Newton Clarke (1841–1912) began looking to the new theology of Europe for an alternative. Clarke's *Outline of Christian Theology* (1894) was America's (and Baptists') first systematic theology written from a liberal perspective. Like Schleiermacher, Clarke took religious experience as the starting point for theology. Religion was understood by Clarke, as by Schleiermacher, to be a universal, affectional faculty of human nature.[22] For Clarke, the intuitive sense of dependence and obligation corresponds to a higher power, and the reality of God is unknowable apart from experience.[23] Moreover, as Schleiermacher derived the second part of his doctrinal system from the consciousness of sin and grace, so Clarke defined theology as the expression of Christian experience, that is, "the saving of men and the renewing of their life."[24] Although Clarke's *Outline* shared much in common with Schleiermacher's *Glaubenslehre,* the account of religious experience in one is individualistic, whereas for the other it is communal. For Clarke, the experience of God is "private, personal, [and] esoteric,"[25] but for Schleiermacher, creature-consciousness is felt with all creation and the consciousness of sin and grace is shared with the church. Mullins followed Clarke as pastor of the Newton Centre Church and no doubt appreciated much about the theology of his elder colleague,[26] but it was the newly developing field of psychology that caught his attention.

As the twentieth century began, William James delivered his highly acclaimed Gifford Lectures on *The Varieties of Religious Experience* (1901–1902). There, James defined *religion* as "the feelings, acts, and experiences of individual men in their solitude, so far as they apprehend themselves to stand in relation to whatever they may consider divine."[27] He further explained that "the essence of religious experiences . . . must be that element or quality in them which we can meet nowhere else."[28] With James, experiential theology in America took a decidedly psychological turn. Unlike earlier evangelical and liberal theologians who spoke of religion as the perception of a single faculty and experience as a universal human capacity, James contended that religious experiences (e.g., particular instances such as conversion) are permutations of emotions, objects, and actions that possess a religious quality. These inner dispositions were, in his view, the province of individuals and had no essential connection with institutional aspects of religion. His concern in *The Varieties* was about "personal religion pure and simple."[29] Yet his point was not merely that institutions share no part in the essence of personal religion. As Nicholas Lash observes, this distinction expresses an underlying assumption that institutional expressions distort and threaten personal religion.[30] The privileging of individual over communal experience indicates James's view of corporate expressions as second-hand contaminations of first-hand experience. The religious experience that is the object of his investigation is that "which lives itself out within the private breast."[31] James helpfully delineates the difference between experiences (i.e., perceptual encounters with God) and experience (i.e., a theoretical construct disguised as a human faculty).[32] But the identification of personal with individual experience, as Lash rightly argues, cannot be sustained. Ritual acts and communal celebrations can and invariably do lead to personally transformational experiences with others and God.[33]

Shailer Mathews (1863–1941), dean of the Divinity School at the University of Chicago, enthusiastically embraced modernist theology and commended it to Northern Baptists. His book *The Faith of Modernism* was probably the most widely read book of American liberalism during the 1920s. Following Schleiermacher, Mathews asserted that "a theological pattern of unchanging content has never existed" because doctrines "imperfectly mirror experience."[34] Mathews continued that "the permanent element of our evolving religion resides in attitudes and convictions rather than doctrines. . . . Theology changes as banner-words change, but Christian experience . . . will continue."[35] Typical of the psychologized individualism that dominated American liberalism were the writings of Harry Emerson Fosdick (1878–1969), popular Baptist preacher and student of William Newton Clarke, who gave currency to the liberal motto: "abiding experience and changing categories."[36]

For Fosdick as for Mathews, "what is permanent in Christianity is not mental frameworks but abiding experiences that phrase and rephrase themselves in successive generations' ways of thinking and that grow in assured certainty and in richness of content."[37] Fosdick's claim that "the one vital thing in religion is first-hand, personal experience" has the distinct echo of William James, and his description of religion as "the most intimate, inward, incommunicable fellowship of the human soul" could have come right out of *The Varieties of Religious Experience*.[38] Personal religious experience as Fosdick conceived it was clearly individual and private, just as it was for James. Moreover, Fosdick, like Mathews, incorporated James's negative view of institutional religion. As Christianity grew more "organized, creedalized, ritualized," Fosdick declared that it became imperiled because it "took all the secondary and derived elements of Christianity, but often forgot that vital thing which all this was meant in the first place to express: a first-hand, personal experience of God in Christ. That alone is vital Christianity; all the rest is once or twice or thrice removed from life."[39] Liberals presupposed the priority of experience over belief. Furthermore, because the doctrine-making process was historically and socially conditioned, liberals ever sought to redefine doctrines so as to correlate with personal experience and comport with modern science. As William R. Hutchinson observed, the first and most visible characteristic of the liberal Protestantism was the "adaptation of religious ideas to modern culture."[40] Mullins was suspicious about so ebullient an accommodation to modernity, but he saw experiential theology as offering a more promising alternative than systems based on common sense rationality.

The Sirens of Modernity

The ancient Greeks told stories about the island of the Sirens. Their lovely voices could make sailors forget everything else. They offered beauty and wisdom, but in the end the sweet songs led to destruction. Moldering skeletons lay on the shore, emblematic of the destiny that awaited those who listened to the enchanting melodies of the singers. As Mullins charted the course of his theological pilgrimage, he recognized the twin perils of modernity. He perceived that, although theological liberals (e.g., Schleiermacher, Clarke, Mathews, and Fosdick) and conservatives (e.g., Hodge, Dagg, and Boyce) traveled different routes, they were on the same voyage. That both listened to the Sirens of modernity and were lured toward the same fate as the sailors of old is evident in at least two ways.

First, both adjusted their courses toward philosophical foundationalism by listening to the seductive voices of the Enlightenment. The melodies that conservatives and liberals followed may sound very different to an untrained ear, but they are in fact variations on a theme—foundationalism. As a theory of knowledge, foundationalism requires all beliefs to be justified by showing that they rest on some universal beliefs that need no support.[41] Karl Barth observed that Protestant theologians in the nineteenth century proceeded along the same lines of the eighteenth-century Enlightenment. In seeking to prove the possibility of faith, they made a prevailing philosophy the presupposition of their work. Although the various worldviews changed over the century (from Schleiermacher to Troeltsch), there were always capable theologians who took up the theological task in a new framework.[42] In his magisterial history of American theological liberalism, Gary Dorrien succinctly defines the essence of liberal theology as the conviction "that all claims to truth, in theology as in other disciplines, must be made on the basis of reason and experience, not by appeal to external authority."[43]

But liberals were not alone in the use of foundationalism. Conservatives also acquired the habit. For conservatives, the foundation is a common sense understanding of the self-evident facts of scripture. For liberals, the givenness of religious experience is a corollary to the existence of God and God's ways.[44] Both agreed, as Hans Frei observed, that "theology must have a foundation that is articulated in terms of basic philosophical principles."[45] Protestant theologians in America, and Baptists no less than others, accommodated to modernity by appealing to the foundations of reason or experience. To be sure, liberals and conservatives operated in different theological "paradigms" separated by an invisible wall. Thus the move from being a conservative to becoming a liberal requires a "paradigm shift."[46] That both liberals and conservatives, however, have adjusted their theologies to foundationalist theories of knowledge seems clear enough. The fate of this accommodation to modernity is now becoming apparent. The near consensus of the academy is that the Enlightenment project has run its course and with it the theological certitude once engendered by foundationalism is in question.[47] Without a firm foundation, liberal and conservative theologies have begun to founder as they approach the shoals of modernity.

A second indication that liberals and conservatives have listened to the modern Sirens is that the theological method of both reflects the turn to the subject. Barth noted that this focus on the human was the central concern, and in his judgment the key problem, of nineteenth-century theology. The theocentrism of the Reformation was displaced by the anthropocentrism of liberalism as the religious subject became the principal object of attention. Faith, rather than being understood as a response to God's actions and initiatives, was conceived in terms of human spirituality and self-awareness.[48] But anthropocentrism, like foundationalism, is not unique to liberalism. It is also at the center of modern conservative theology. Dagg, for example, assumed that human consciousness is an analog to God's knowledge of the world.[49] Welch observes that toward the end of the nineteenth century, there emerged in liberal theology "an attempt at an objective view of the religious subject" (viz. *Religionswissenschaft*).[50] The shift was from "my believing" to "my believing objectively considered." The objectification of the subjective had its counterpart in conservative theology (e.g., the Princeton theology); thus, following Hodge, Boyce insisted that theology is an objective science that "is concerned in the investigation of [biblical] facts."[51] This convergence has been nicely stated by Robert Roth, who writes that "liberals will not believe anything that cannot be proved historical, and conservatives want to prove as historical all that they believe."[52] In either case, it is the rational agent who is the measure of all things.

Mullins and the Modern Odyssey of Baptists

When Odysseus made his celebrated journey past the island of the Sirens, to resist their tempting calls, he plugged the ears of his crew with wax. Odysseus, however, was determined to listen, so he had himself bound to the mast. As they approached the island, all but Odysseus were deaf to the enchanting music. He longed to answer the alluring offers of wisdom but was held, as it were, against his will. Thus did he pass safely by the Sirens, although he only narrowly escaped destruction in the straits between Scylla and Charybdis, losing several members of his crew in the process.[53] As president of the Southern Baptist Theological Seminary, the Southern Baptist Convention, and the Baptist World Alliance, E. Y. Mullins (1860–1928), like heroic Odysseus, guided Southern Baptists on a middle course through the treacherous waters of the fundamentalist-modernist controversy.[54]

Mullins indeed personified what Bill Leonard has called the "Grand Compromise" of denominational loyalists who were committed to the programmatic and institutional unity in the SBC.[55] Yet Mullins contributed more than wise political leadership. He generated a new theological vision for Southern Baptists. It is precisely because of his importance as a theologian that Harold Bloom describes Mullins as the "re-founder" of the Southern Baptists.[56] Mullins, to be sure, rejected extreme liberal reformulations of Christian doctrine and defended such evangelical tenets as the virgin birth, the bodily resurrection, and the reality of miracles. But evangelical doctrines were merely the cords that bound him as he listened to the foundationalist and anthropocentric Sirens of modernity, passing perilously close to the Charybdis of experientialism.

Experience and God

The first issue of *The Baptist Review and Expositor* contained an article by the editor-in-chief, President E. Y. Mullins, titled "Is Jesus Christ the Author of Religious Experience?"[57] It began with a brief treatment of two works on religious experience by F. H. Foster and L. F. Stearns. Mullins had little quarrel with his theological colleagues and moved quickly to an examination of *The Varieties of Religious Experience* by psychologist William James. Although Mullins recognized that James's conclusions were "unsatisfactory" at many points, he nevertheless found them "extremely interesting" and "to be regarded as an advance towards Christianity." As he saw it, there is nothing to dispute about "the *reality* of religious experience" in James's account. The chief problem lay in the attribution of the *cause* of religious experience, about which James was vague. For Mullins, Christ was not the fulfillment of religious experience (as with Harnack) or its mediator (as for Schleiermacher) but rather the author who vitalizes faith. Mullins went on to make a case for Christ as the author of religious experience based on arguments from scripture, church history, Christian conversion, comparative religion, and human consciousness. He concluded that "the present direct relation to the Personal living Christ, the Author of the experience, finds explanation and confirmation at every point in the New Testament records of early Christian experience, and these in turn rest directly upon the words of the historic Christ."[58]

In his essay on "The Testimony of Christian Experience," Mullins declared that the discovery of the evidential value of religious experience has led to a Copernican revolution in theology. Unlike philosophy, which is an effort of humanity reaching up to God, "Christian experience is the effect of God reaching down" to humanity.[59] Theology is a correlative activity "wherein [hu]man[ity]'s upward soaring thought is met by God's descending revelation and love."[60] Yet for Mullins, the vector of theological correlation was from experience to God, not from God to experience as Karl Barth and (Mullins's own student) W. T. Conner would subsequently argue.[61] The revelation of God imparted in experience is intelligible because, Mullins asserted, there is a "seeing spot" in the human soul.[62] Barth argued that all the varieties of modern theology after Schleiermacher accept two cardinal principles: (1) the encounter with God is a human religious experience that can be established historically and psychologically, and (2) this experience is the actualization of the human religious capacity.[63] Mullins's account of religious experience fits Barth's description of modern theology in which the reality of God and God's revelation are known experientially, and experiential knowledge is foundational to theology.

Mullins's finest exercise in experiential theology, *The Christian Religion in Its Doctrinal Expression*, begins with the extravagant claim that "the experiential way of dealing with Christian doctrine has been employed in every vital and living system which has been produced since the New Testament times" and continues that "all theology must be vitalized by experience before it can become a real force for the regeneration of men."[64] William Mueller is certainly correct that Christian experience was the focal point of theological reflection for Mullins.[65] W. O. Carver similarly noted that Mullins simply made "explicit in reason that which is implicit in experience."[66] Indeed, he asserted that the existence of God, the reality of miracles, the deity of Christ, the freedom of the Christian, even the authority of the scriptures rest on the foundation of experience.[67] But as Fisher Humphreys correctly observes, Mullins did not integrate the experiential source into every doctrine.[68] Experience, Humphreys continues, often functions for Mullins more as an apologetic and corrective for the received body of evangelical doctrines rather than the source from which they are derived.

Others were not nearly so sanguine about such accommodation to modernity. Mueller is critical of Mullins for being "unduly influenced by Schleiermacher and James."[69] It is true that by describing the theological task as a display of the doctrinal expression of the Christian religion (i.e., experience), Mullins imitates the broad contours of Schleiermacher's theological method of "religious affections set forth in speech."[70] However, he did not follow Schleiermacher's revisionist ordering of doctrines but instead reproduced an outline more typical of evangelical theology. In addition to Schleiermacher and James, Mullins drew from the personalism of Borden Parker Bowne, which he suggested, "unifies the many elements of modern thought thus approximating very closely an evangelical Christian result," adding that "modern thought at no vital point contradicts the Christian view."[71]

Mueller's Southern Seminary colleague, William J. McGlothlin, characterized Mullins as "conservative as to position and progressive as to method."[72] But Mullins was not the first Baptist theologian to look to experience as the foundation of religious knowledge. William Newton Clarke, his friend and predecessor at Newton Centre, was the American pioneer of experiential theology. Yet the "experience" on which Mullins reflected was neither the romantic pietism of Schleiermacher, the psychological pragmatism of James, the self-consistent personalism of Bowne, nor the gentle mysticism of Clarke, but rather the evangelical revivalism familiar to Baptists south and north. But when he declared, "that which we know most indubitably are the facts of inner experience," it is clear that his account has resonances with the private experience of James and

Bowne.[73] With Mullins, then, the theological course through the deep waters of modernity was charted in a vector toward the Charybdis of experience. Succeeding generations followed the trajectory set by Mullins, though not all who came after him found it necessary to bind themselves with the cords of evangelical doctrine or to close their ears to the psychological Sirens.[74]

In 1924, Mullins wrote *Christianity at the Cross Roads* as a final attempt to defend supernatural Christianity from the assaults of modernity. There, he argued that religion is not subject to the principles of causality and rationality that govern science and philosophy. Rather it is guided by the principle of personality that can be confirmed only by "the immediate experience of God."[75] Mullins maintained connection with the Baptist theological heritage by defending the centrality of experiential religion (or experimental religion as earlier generations often called it). His understanding of Christian experience, as exemplified in his aunt's simple testimony to her conversion, is surely representative of Baptist religion.[76] Yet Mullins overreached the limits of Christian experience by treating it as if it were a philosophical foundation ne plus ultra—a knockdown defense against the onslaughts of modernity.

Fundamentalists, wary of liberal theology, were suspicious of Mullins's appeal to experience as a foundation for faith. Writing in the *Princeton Theological Review,* J. Gresham Machen argued, contrary to Mullins, that theology is grounded on scientific and philosophical facts. Indeed, Machen contended that personalism (i.e., experiential foundationalism) was a dangerous concession to modernity that, rather than saving Christianity, would result in its ultimate destruction in the whirlpool of experience as the historical events of God's revelation would ultimately become superfluous to their correlative religious feelings.[77] That Machen correctly described the liberal vector of Mullins and his successors should be noted; however, as Marsden has perceptively observed, Machen did not perceive that his own accommodation to common sense philosophy and Baconian science might shipwreck the Christian faith on the rock of rationalism.[78] The tragic consequences of fundamentalism are evidence of that trajectory.

The last decade has witnessed the revival of a version of Reformed theology among Baptists. The ascendant voices in this movement echo the older thesis of John Quincy Adams that Baptists were the only thorough Reformers.[79] One of the most vocal expressions of this resurgence is the Founders movement among Southern Baptists, which is committed to the etiological myth of Baptist Calvinism.[80] The Founders wonder how the doctrines of sovereign grace as embodied in the established orthodoxy of Dagg and Boyce became disestablished. Thomas Nettles answers that the culprit is "the gradual ascension of the liberal mentality" that "crept in the back door" of Baptist life.[81] E. Y. Mullins is identified as the bête noire of incipient liberalism, whose emphasis on experience accommodated Baptist theology to modernity. Nettles continues that "emphasis on human consciousness and experience so predominate in the totality of Mullins' theology that human decision and freedom eventually overshadow and crowd out effectual divine activity."[82] That Mullins is indicative of the adjustment of Baptist theology to modernity is surely correct. That he is the source or cause of this shift seems less likely.[83]

The movement away from the established orthodoxy of Dagg and Boyce is more easily explained by three broader cultural trends in nineteenth-century America. One is the gradual Arminianizing of popular religion by revivalism that modified the received Calvinism of the Puritans almost beyond recognition (e.g., Charles G. Finney).[84] A second determinant is the rise of populism and romanticism, whereby religious beliefs became increasingly democratized (e.g., Alexander Campbell).[85] A third factor is the displacement of common sense realism by some form of idealism or pragmatism in turn-of-the-century American academic life (e.g., Immanuel Kant and William James).[86] The force of these religious and intellectual currents was already changing the ethos and logos of Baptist theology. Mullins, like his contemporaries, simply adapted to these modern adjustments. But like Machen, the voices of the Founders movement fail to grasp the accommodation to the Enlightenment that permeates the theology of Boyce and Dagg, whose pursuit of an objective foundation for faith set them on a collision course with the Scylla of rationality.

Soul and Body

What is it that distinguishes Baptists from all other Christian bodies? Mullins answers: The competency of the individual soul.[87] He explains that "the competency of the soul in religion excludes at once all human interference," adding that "religion is a personal matter between the soul and God."[88] Here Mullins adopts from James both the view of corporate religion as a second-hand distortion of first-hand experience and the identification of personal with private religion. *Soul competency* means spiritual solitude. It asserts the inalienable right of every autonomous soul for direct and unmediated access to God. It establishes "the principle of individualism in religion."[89] Nowhere is this individualism more striking than in its meaning for biblical interpretation. Mullins writes: "Since the Reformation this axiom has found expression in nothing more than in the exercise of the individual's right of private interpretation of the Scriptures. It guarantees the right of examining God's revelation each man for himself, and of answering directly to God in belief and conduct."[90] No one can tell the competent soul how to interpret the Bible or how not to interpret the Bible. The same holds for the experience of conversion. It is unmediated, unassailable, and self-interpreted. Nobody but the competent soul can determine when or if the miracle of regeneration has occurred.[91]

No one was more enthusiastically supportive of Mullins's account of individualism than the archliberal Northern Baptist minister and University of Chicago Divinity professor, George Burman Foster. The year after the publication of *The Axioms of Religion*, he praised Mullins as one of the few scholars that was "seeking to recover the Baptist position of the autonomy of the human soul, for which our Baptist fathers fought, bled, and died." Foster continued that "while no man has any right to be pope for any other man, he must be his own pope." But he thought that moderates like Mullins stopped short of claiming the radical freedom of the Baptist heritage, invoking soul competency "in a context which usually denies what the phrase affirms."[92] Mullins quietly ignored Foster's exuberant praise, knowing instinctively that his support would likely do more harm than good among Baptists in the South.

Mullins would undoubtedly also recoil from the libertarian tangent of soul competency that takes it as a license for the anticreedal creed: "Ain't nobody but Jesus gonna tell me what to believe."[93] Such a claim quickly devolves into "Ain't nobody gonna tell me what to believe" as the "me" of this creed for all practical purposes becomes the exclusive arbiter of what Jesus is saying. Thus, soul competency mutates into sole competency. In view of the potential abuses of unrestrained libertarianism, Mullins might have done well to delineate the qualities of character that would constitute competency: the habits and skills that a competent soul would need to possess in order to read the Bible wisely. He could also have indicated the sort of community and spiritual formation that are necessary to initiate and sustain converted souls in the Christian life. Why the silence? Liberals and fundamentalists may contend it is because Mullins championed libertarian principles. But perhaps he says nothing because the safeguards of character and community were assumed, part of the evangelical consensus of his day, constitutive elements of the Baptist understanding of the Christian life that he thought needed no explanation to his readers. If so, the consensus of Mullins's generation has long since dissipated, and the usefulness of soul competency as a navigational tool is severely limited.

From whence does the axiom of soul competency arise? Mullins points to a confluence of three modern themes—Renaissance humanism, Anglo-Saxon individualism, and Reformed theology—although he contends that Baptists elevated these notions into "nobler forms."[94] But, in fact, Mullins seems to have derived the expression of soul competency as the individual's right of private interpretation from Francis Wayland (or at least from the same romantic zeitgeist). Wayland had championed "the absolute right of private judgment in all matters of religion."[95] On conversion, Mullins was in keeping with the new account of the "salvation experience" that arose as a result of evangelical revivalism.[96] Bloom goes so far as to suggest that Mullins "invented" the doctrine of soul competency, drawing on nineteenth-century notions of economic self-sufficiency and pragmatic versions of self-reliance, thus translating the apostle Paul into experiential, Jamesian terms.[97] That Bloom's account of Mullins lacks meticulous historical analysis and careful theological reflection is surely the case.

More judicious historians and theologians, however, share Bloom's basic critique of Mullins. In a more nuanced treatment of soul competency, historian Winthrop Hudson described it as a "highly individualistic principle" that "was derived from the general cultural and religious climate of the nineteenth century rather than from any serious study of the Bible."[98] James McClendon voiced a similar concern, and he grew increasingly cold to Mullins over the years. In the first edition of his *Ethics,* published in 1986, McClendon made a glancing critique of soul competency as not sufficient "to do justice to the shared discipleship that earlier baptists had embraced," but in the revised edition published in 2002, he characterized soul competency as "Mullins's anthropocentric motto" that "was framed too much in terms of the rugged American individualism of Theodore Roosevelt to do justice to the shared discipleship baptist life requires."[99]

In addition to these theological weaknesses, ascribing the theory of soul competency to the early Baptists is historically contested. A way of stating the matter more sharply might be to say that Mullins invented the myth of soul competency. Although the phrase *soul competency* as an anthropological concept does not appear in theological discourse before Mullins, it became for many the canonical reading of Baptist heritage: the rock on which all else stood. Indeed, it served as a metanarrative that supported the revisionism of the past that had located the roots of soul competency in earlier Baptist and primitive Christian soil, much as the myth of the trail of blood guided Landmarkers in their reading of the history of Christianity.[100] Mullins and his supporters like George Burman Foster continued to assert that soul competency was merely a restatement of such historic Baptist themes as soul liberty espoused by Roger Williams.[101] But was it so?

LeRoy Moore has exposed the faulty historiography at play in just such a romantic interpretation of Roger Williams that turns him into an enlightened secular democrat and a champion of liberal individualism.[102] Moore shows how the civil libertarian interpretation strips Williams of his theological concerns and "disclaims the whole theocentric structure of his ideas, opting for an enlightened, secular liberal who would hardly be recognizable to Williams himself."[103] This historical revisionism does not accurately represent the picture of earlier Baptist spirituality in either the British or American context. Moore simply states the theocentric and Christocentric premise of Williams (as opposed to the anthropocentric and romantic interpretations): "If Jesus Christ is king in his own kingdom, then it is presumptuous indeed for magistrates to assume his place and prerogatives."[104] By anthropologizing theology, Mullins turned the early Baptist Calvinism on its head and lost contact with the theocentric conviction Williams was living out by demanding that soul liberty is the presupposition of true theology.[105]

As problematic as this genealogy of soul competency as the animating principle of Baptist identity is, even more so is the fact that as a constitutive principle of theology, soul competency provides no basis for ecclesiology. Soul competency demands a one-on-one relationship between God and the individual soul. As Hudson succinctly stated it, "the practical effect of the stress upon 'soul competency' as the cardinal doctrine of Baptists was to make every[one]'s hat [their] own church."[106] It is not unimportant to note the absence of a chapter on ecclesiology in *The Christian Religion*. Humphreys may be correct to attribute this omission to pedagogical reasons at Southern Seminary: Ecclesiological matters were treated in a different course.[107] But perhaps Mullins realized that the church was not only beyond his assigned scope but his theological grasp as well.[108] Hudson is correct that the atomization of soul competency rendered ecclesiology all but impossible except as "the voluntary association of free individuals."[109] He thus approvingly quotes Strong, who wrote that such a description of the church as a voluntary association "is no more true than that hands and feet are voluntarily united in the human body for the purposes of locomotion and work."[110]

Bloom's deep suspicion is that this religious individualism constitutes a renewal of ancient gnosis.[111] That such a reading is not inappropriate may be seen by clarifying the meaning of the "soul" in soul competency. Mullins contends that human nature consists of two constituent parts: body and soul. Although in creation they are united, human existence nevertheless is essentially twofold. The body is merely the physical organism. The soul is the transcendent aspect of the human self, whose rational, moral, emotional, and volitional faculties resemble God.[112] In short, the "soul" in soul competency is disembodied. The soul can be saved.[113] The soul is free.[114] Mullins was neither the first nor the last to embrace a dichotomous anthropology or a disembodied psychology. Among American Baptist theologians, Dagg, Boyce, Clarke, and Strong held virtually the same view.[115] The first Baptist theologian explicitly to reject the prevailing dichotomy was H. Wheeler Robinson, who recovered the holism of Hebrew psychology. He displayed that, from a biblical point of view, it is correct to think of human existence as an ensouled body or an embodied soul.[116]

By reifying the dichotomy of soul and body in the theology of soul competency, Mullins opened up a chasm between salvation and history, just as by interpreting the gospel in terms of a transcendent history, ancient Gnosticism rendered immanent social history of no significance.[117] Carlyle Marney identified this sort of southern-fried gnostic individualism as one of the fundamental structures of racial prejudice, arguing that in "the warm, wet mothering womb of this vicious individualism, we find the most powerful breeding place of human prejudice."[118] With just such a gnostic and individualistic view of the self and salvation, Baptists in the South were ill-equipped to face the social evil of segregation with a gospel word.

For many like Douglas Hudgins, the pastor of the First Baptist Church of Jackson, Mississippi, soul competency justified a piety of indifference to the sufferings of black people and a politics of inaction toward the segregationist powers in the church and community. Hudgins asserted that the cross of Jesus Christ "has nothing to do with social movements or realities beyond the church; it's a matter of individual salvation."[119] Mullins would no doubt have been horrified by such an appeal to his theology as a rationale for the policies of Jim Crow racism, but he conceded that the church "cannot become the organ of social reform save *indirectly*."[120] In other words, Christian social ethics for Mullins was limited to regenerate individuals doing what they can to stand for righteousness. One way Mullins might have pushed the implications of soul competency toward righteousness was by attending to the gospel practices that are part of the being (not just the well-being) of the Christian social ethic (Matt. 25:31–46). Here, unfortunately, he was silent.[121]

Nevertheless, E. Y. Mullins was a courageous leader and a competent theologian who charted a course for the Southern Baptist ship of Zion through the waters of modernity. One way of accounting for how he negotiated a route through the narrow straits between the crushing rock of common sense rationality and the threatening swirl of experiential religion is that he made the journey on a calm day. The seas on which we sail, however, are more turbulent, and the currents are more treacherous. The consensus of evangelical doctrine with which Mullins bound himself has long since disappeared, and the value of soul competency as a navigational tool for averting danger seems limited. That successive generations of Baptist theologians did not sufficiently recognize the looming peril of the rising modern tempest or attempt to steer around the most dangerous streams of experientialism as Mullins tried to do cannot be simply attributed to his example. Nor should he be faulted for not having seen another way past the modern Scylla and Charybdis. But it may be instructive to recall that when Jason and the Argonauts were lured toward destruction by the sweet songs of the Sirens, Orpheus raised his lyre and played an even more beautiful melody, thus saving the Argo and its crew.[122] And so perhaps the way beyond modernity is not in resisting its voices by binding ourselves with the cords of evangelical doctrine or by closing our ears to its alluring theories, but by listening for the one(s) who would "sing the new, new song," of "the old, old story that [we] have loved so long."

Notes

1. James J. Buckley borrows from Hans Frei the difference "between *showing* the rules at work and *stating* the rules" to distinguish the profound from the mediocre interpretations of Karl Barth, in "A Field of Living Fire: Karl Barth on the Spirit and the Church," *Modern Theology* 10 (January 1994): 82.

2. Henry F. May, *The Enlightenment in America* (New York: Oxford University Press, 1976), xiv–xviii.

3. George M. Marsden, *Fundamentalism and American Culture* (New York: Oxford University Press, 1980), 14.

4. Marsden, *Understanding Fundamentalism and Evangelicalism* (Grand Rapids, MI: William B. Eerdmans, 1991), 122–52. On the relationship be-

tween common sense philosophy and religion, see Syndey E. Ahlstrom, "The Scottish Philosophy and American Theology," *Church History* 24 (1955): 257–72; and Mark A. Noll, "Common Sense Traditions and American Evangelical Thought," *American Quarterly* 37 (Summer 1985): 216–38.

5. Perry Miller, in the introduction to *American Thought: Civil War to World War I* (New York: Holt, Rinehart and Winston, 1965), ix.

6. Francis Wayland, *The Elements of Moral Science,* 4th ed. (1837; repr., Cambridge, MA: Belknap Press, 1963), 18–20.

7. Charles G. Finney, *Lectures on Revivals of Religion* (New York: Fleming H. Revell, 1868), 12–14.

8. Wayland, *The Elements of Moral Science,* 42.

9. Barry Alan Shain, *The Myth of American Individualism* (Princeton, NJ: Princeton University Press, 1994), 115. Whether individualism may be found at the origin of American identity is a matter of debate, but there can be no doubt it has become the prevailing contemporary notion of the self. Robert Bellah identified individualism as the culture that is shared by all Americans. But in pursuit of the goals of individualism, Bellah found that Americans have lost touch with the value of their interdependence with one another. Robert N. Bellah et al., *Habits of the Heart,* updated ed. (Berkeley: University of California Press, 1996); and Bellah et al., *The Good Society* (New York: Vintage Books, 1992). More recently, in his analysis of the National Survey of Youth and Religion, sociologist Christian Smith noted that "American youth, like American adults, are nearly without exception profoundly individualistic, instinctively presuming autonomous, individual self-direction to be a universal human norm and life goal. Thoroughgoing individualism is not a contested orthodoxy for teenagers. It is an invisible and pervasive *doxa,* that is, an unrecognized, unquestioned, invisible premise or presupposition." Christian Smith with Melinda Lundquist Denton, *Soul Searching: The Religious and Spiritual Lives of American Teenagers* (New York: Oxford University Press, 2005), 143.

10. Wayland, *The Elements of Moral Science,* 104.

11. Ibid., 123.

12. S. A. Grave distinguishes between the theoretical aspects of common sense philosophy and the more general habits of mind associated with it, in *The Encyclopedia of Philosophy,* ed. Paul Edwards, 8 vols. (New York: Macmillan, 1967), s.v. "Reid, Thomas," by S. A. Grave, 7:121.

13. John Leadley Dagg, *Manual of Theology* (Charleston, SC: The Southern Baptist Publication Society, 1857), 39–42.

14. E. Brooks Holifield, *The Gentlemen Theologians* (Durham, NC: Duke University Press, 1978), 125.

15. Dagg, *Manual of Theology*, 14.

16. Charles Hodge, *Systematic Theology*, 3 vols. (New York: Scribner, Armstrong, and Co., 1872–1873), 1:10–11.

17. James Petigru Boyce, *Abstract of Theology* (Philadelphia: American Baptist Publication Society, 1887), 3.

18. Claude Welch, *Protestant Theology in the Nineteenth Century*, 2 vols. (New Haven, CT: Yale University Press, 1972/1985), 1:59.

19. Welch, *Protestant Theology in the Nineteenth Century*, 2:68.

20. Friedrich Schleiermacher, *On Religion: Addresses in Response to Its Cultured Critics*, trans. Terrence N. Tice (Richmond, VA: John Knox Press, 1969), 79.

21. Schleiermacher, *The Christian Faith*, 2nd ed., trans. and ed. M. R. Mackintosh and J. S. Stewart (Philadelphia: Fortress, 1928/1976), sec. 15, 76–78.

22. William Newton Clarke, *An Outline of Christian Theology* (New York: Charles Scribners, 1912), 2.

23. Clarke, *An Outline of Christian Theology*, 118–26.

24. Clarke, *An Outline of Christian Theology*, 18–19; Schleiermacher, *The Christian Faith*, secs. 62–169.

25. Clarke, *An Outline of Christian Theology*, 125.

26. Clarke was pastor of the First Baptist Church of Newton Centre, Massachusetts before going to Colgate Theological Seminary (1890–1908). Mullins served the Newton Centre Church (1896–1899) during the time that Clarke's *Outline of Christian Theology* was published. Mrs. Mullins tells of Professor Clarke's personal support and friendship in the decision to leave Newton Centre for Louisville, in Isla May Mullins, *Edgar Young Mullins* (Nashville: Sunday School Board, 1929), 114.

27. William James, *The Varieties of Religious Experience* (New York: Collins, 1960), 50.

28. Ibid., 62.

29. Ibid., 49.

30. Nicholas Lash, *Easter in Ordinary* (Notre Dame, IN: University of Notre Dame Press, 1988), 52.

31. James, *Varieties of Religious Experience*, 328.

32. Thus, it would be correct to say "I have *experiences* with God" but not "I *experience* God."

33. Lash, *Easter in Ordinary*, 52–60.

34. Shailer Mathews, *The Faith of Modernism* (New York: The Macmillan Company, 1924), 72.

35. Mathews, *The Faith of Modernism*, 76. Here Mathews is less similar to other American liberals (like Clarke) and closer to Schleiermacher who re-

tained the doctrine of the Trinity in *The Christian Faith* despite the fact that it did not seem essentially related to the consciousness of sin and grace. See Schleiermacher, *The Christian Faith*, secs. 170–72, 738–51.

36. Harry Emerson Fosdick, *The Modern Use of the Bible* (New York: Macmillan, 1924), 97–130.

37. Ibid., 103.

38. Fosdick, *Christianity and Progress* (New York: Fleming Revell, 1922), 160.

39. Ibid., 163.

40. William R. Hutchinson, *The Modernist Impulse in American Protestantism* (Cambridge, MA: Harvard University Press, 1976), 2. Gary Dorrien similarly describes liberal theology as "mainly about adjustment and accommodation to the modern world," in Dorrien, *The Making of American Liberal Theology*, 3 vols. (Louisville, KY: Westminster John Knox, 2001), 2:389.

41. Rodney Clapp, "How Firm a Foundation: Can Evangelicals Be Nonfoundationalists?" in *The Nature of Confession*, ed. Timothy R. Phillips and Dennis L. Ockholm (Downers Grove, IL: InterVarsity Press, 1996), 81–92.

42. Karl Barth, "Evangelical Theology in the 19th Century," trans. Thomas Wieser in *The Humanity of God* (Atlanta: John Knox, 1978), 20–21.

43. Gary Dorrien, *The Making of American Liberal Theology*, 2:1.

44. Nancey Murphy, *Beyond Liberalism and Fundamentalism* (Valley Forge, PA: Trinity Press, 1996), 6–7, 11–35; and George Lindbeck, *The Nature of Doctrine* (Philadelphia: Westminster Press, 1984), 16–19.

45. Hans Frei, *Types of Christian Theology* (New Haven, CT: Yale University Press, 1992), 24.

46. Murphy, *Beyond Liberalism and Fundamentalism*, ix; cf. Thomas Kuhn, *The Structures of Scientific Revolution*, 2nd ed. (Chicago: The University of Chicago Press, 1970), 85.

47. For the most devastating critique of foundationalism, see Richard Rorty, *Philosophy and the Mirror of Nature* (Princeton, NJ: Princeton University Press, 1979).

48. Barth, "Evangelical Theology in the 19th Century," 24–27.

49. Dagg, *Manual of Theology*, 68. Liberal theologian William Newton Clarke argued similarly that "God and man are essentially alike in mental structure," in *An Outline of Christian Theology*, 191. Clarke further wrote that "Man has often been scoffed at for thinking that God is like himself, but instead of folly this is a beginning of wisdom," in *The Christian Doctrine of God* (Edinburgh: T.&T. Clark, 1912), 59.

50. Welch, *Protestant Thought in the Nineteenth Century*, 2:69.

51. Boyce, *Abstract of Theology*, 3; Hodge, *Systematic Theology*, 1:10–11.

52. Robert P. Roth, *Story and Reality* (Grand Rapids, MI: William B. Eerdmans, 1973), 66.

53. Homer, *The Odyssey,* XII, 153–259.

54. William E. Ellis provides an excellent account of the moderating influence of Mullins during the 1920s in *A Man of Books and a Man of People* (Macon, GA: Mercer University Press, 1985), 147–68, 185–208.

55. Bill J. Leonard, *God's Last and Only Hope* (Grand Rapids, MI: William B. Eerdmans, 1990), 29–31, 49–51.

56. Harold Bloom, *The American Religion* (New York: Simon and Schuster, 1992), 199. Bloom's claim that Mullins was the Southern Baptist equivalent of Calvin, Luther, or Wesley and pragmatically a more important theologian than Edwards, Bushnell, and the Niebuhrs is extravagant but not entirely unwarranted. In addition to the numerous works that became the theological standard for succeeding generations of Southern Baptist ministers, Mullins's most lasting contribution may be seen in the *Baptist Faith and Message* that was adopted as a confession of faith by the SBC in 1925.

57. E. Y. Mullins, "Is Jesus Christ the Author of Religious Experience?" *The Baptist Review and Expositor* 1 (April 1904): 55–70.

58. Ibid., 70.

59. Mullins, "The Testimony of Christian Experience," in *The Fundamentals,* 4 vols., ed. R. A. Torrey et al. (Los Angeles: Bible Institute of Los Angeles, 1917; reprint, Grand Rapids, MI: Baker Book House, 1980), 4:315.

60. Ibid., 317.

61. Karl Barth, *Church Dogmatics: The Doctrine of the Word of God,* vol. 1, pt. 1, trans. G. W. Bromiley and T. F. Torrance (Edinburgh: T. & T. Clark, 1936); W. T. Conner, *Revelation and God* (Nashville: Broadman Press, 1936). For Barth and Conner, there is no human *analogia entis* whereby like contemplates like. Rather, the starting point for Christian theology is the *analogia fidei* (Rom. 12:6)—not the givenness of human experience that correlates to God, but the gift of God in Jesus Christ by which God makes Himself known. See Barth, *Church Dogmatics,* vol. 1, pt. 1, 243–44; and Conner, *Revelation and God,* 99–100.

62. Mullins, "The Testimony of Christian Experience," 323.

63. Barth, *Church Dogmatics,* vol. 1, pt. 1, 193.

64. Mullins, *The Christian Religion in Its Doctrinal Expression* (Nashville: The Sunday School Board of the Southern Baptist Convention, 1917), 2–3. Although Mullins mentions Augustine, Clement of Alexandria, and Schleiermacher as exemplars of experiential theology, no effort is made to engage their methods as a pattern for his. Lindbeck has argued persuasively, however,

that three paradigms (i.e., propositionalism, experientialism, and cultural linguistics) not one have been operative in the history of Christian theology. See George A. Lindbeck, *The Nature of Doctrine* (Philadelphia: Westminster Press, 1984), 16–19. It is not unimportant to note that Mullins does not enter into any sustained conversation with theologians among the church fathers, protestant reformers (magisterial or radical), or even important Baptists such as Dagg, Boyce, or Strong. By contrast, he has multiple references to and discussions with modern theologians and theorists like Kant, Dorner, Ritschl, Schleiermacher, James, and Bowne.

65. William A. Mueller, *A History of Southern Baptist Theological Seminary* (Nashville: Broadman Press, 1959), 192.

66. Cited by W. Morgan Patterson in "The Southern Baptist Theologian as Controversialist," *Baptist History and Heritage* 15 (July 1980): 12.

67. Mullins, *The Christian Religion in Its Doctrinal Expression*, 7–12.

68. Fisher Humphreys, "E. Y. Mullins," in *Baptist Theologians*, ed. Timothy George and David S. Dockery (Nashville: Broadman, 1990), 339.

69. Mueller, *A History of Southern Baptist Theological Seminary*, 192.

70. Schleiermacher, *The Christian Faith*, sec. 15, 76–78.

71. Mullins, *The Christian Religion in Its Doctrinal Expression*, 195. For Borden Parker Bowne, see *Personalism* (Boston: Houghton Mifflin Company, 1908) and *The Essence of Religion* (Boston: Houghton Mifflin Company, 1910).

72. *Dictionary of American Biography*, ed. Dumas Malone (New York: Charles Scribner's Sons, 1934), s.v. "Edgar Young Mullins," by William J. McGlothlin, 7:322.

73. Mullins, *The Christian Religion in Its Doctrinal Expression*, 73.

74. In a book dedicated to Mullins, his "beloved teacher and honored colleague," Harold W. Tribble carried on the practice of theological reflection "in light of Christian experience," in *Our Doctrines* (Nashville: Convention Press, 1962), 4. For an example of the prominence of psychological voices in shaping the theology of Christian experience among Baptists, see Wayne Oates, *Anxiety and Christian Experience* (Philadelphia: Westminster Press, 1955); *The Religious Dimensions of Personality* (New York: Association Press, 1957); and *Christ and Selfhood* (New York: Association Press, 1961).

75. Mullins, *Christianity at the Cross Roads* (Nashville: Sunday School Board, 1924), 32, 56.

76. Mullins, *Talks on Soul Winning* (Nashville: Sunday School Board, 1920), 77–84.

77. J. Gresham Machen, "The Relation of Religion to Science and Philosophy," *Princeton Theological Review* 24 (January 1926): 38–66.

78. Marsden, *Fundamentalism and American Culture*, 216–17.

79. John Quincy Adams, *Baptists, the Only Thorough Reformers* (New York: Sheldon and Company, 1876). See Timothy George, "The Renewal of Baptist Theology," in *Baptist Theologians*, ed. Timothy George and David S. Dockery (Nashville: Broadman, 1990), 13–25.

80. See www.founders.org for *The Founders* online.

81. Thomas J. Nettles, *By His Grace and for His Glory* (Grand Rapids, MI: Baker Book House, 1986), 246–47. See also Nettles, "The Rise and Demise of Calvinism Among Southern Baptists," *The Founders Journal* (Winter/ Spring 1995): 17–19; and R. Albert Mohler, Introduction to *The Axioms of Religion*, by E. Y. Mullins (Nashville: Broadman and Holman, 1997). Nettles ascribes partial responsibility for the shift to the evangelistic method of L. R. Scarborough, but the influence of Mullins on Baptist theology was more pervasive.

82. Nettles, *By His Grace and for His Glory*, 247.

83. Bush and Nettles rightly caution against faulting Mullins as "the root source of the shallowness of experientialist theology among some Baptists," in L. Russ Bush and Tom J. Nettles, *Baptists and the Bible* (Chicago: Moody Press, 1980), 296.

84. Sidney E. Mead, *The Lively Experiment: The Shaping of Christianity in America* (New York: Harper and Row, 1963), 121–27.

85. Nathan Hatch, *The Democratization of American Religion* (New Haven, CT: Yale University Press, 1989), 67–81.

86. Perry Miller, Introduction to *American Thought*, ix–lii.

87. Mullins, *The Axioms of Religion* (Philadelphia: Judson Press, 1908), 53.

88. Ibid., 54.

89. Ibid., 92–94. Mullins is by no means alone in his individualistic interpretation of Baptist principles. His friend and colleague J. B. Gambrell identified the principle of individualism with the right of private interpretation, general human rights, the constitutional guarantee of religious liberty, and the priesthood of all believers, in "Obligations of Baptists to Teach Their Principles," in *Baptist Principles Reset*, ed. Jeremiah B. Jeter (Richmond, VA: The Religious Herald, 1901), 250–1.

90. Mullins, *The Axioms of Religion*, 94. Mullins' delineation of soul competency is historically false but could be corrected so as to read "Since the *Enlightenment*. . . ." Although "private judgment" is not a Reformation doctrine, it is well established in the political philosophy of John Locke. See, for example, *A Letter Concerning Toleration*, in which it occurs several times.

91. *Baptist History and Heritage* devoted an issue to "E. Y. Mullins and *The*

Axioms of Religion," Baptist History and Heritage 43, no. 1 (2008). My account of Mullins was cited by several of the authors. C. Douglas Weaver and Russell Dilday characterized my work as harshly critical of Mullins, whereas William Carrell described it as exposing genuine weaknesses in Mullins's theology. Weaver, "The Baptist Ecclesiology of E. Y. Mullins: Individualism and the New Testament Church," 31n4, and Introduction to *The Axioms of Religion*, ed. C. Douglas Weaver (Macon, GA: Mercer University Press, 2010), 26; Dilday, "The Significance of E. Y. Mullins's *The Axioms of Religion*," 93nn3, 5; and Carrell, "The Inner Testimony of the Spirit: Locating the Coherent Center of E. Y. Mullins's Theology," 35. These commentators may leave the impression that my view of Mullins is primarily negative. In response to similar characterizations of my work, I wrote: "Mullins retained the conversionist conviction that previous generations of Baptists had lived out, as well as the evangelical doctrines that his predecessors like J. P. Boyce had thought out. By adapting these convictions and doctrines to modern psychology and theology, Mullins believed he was protecting Christianity from the onslaughts of rationalistic philosophy and skeptical science. His aim was to move Baptists faithfully and effectively into the 20th century. In many ways he succeeded," in *The Baptist Standard*, May 15, 2000, 4.

92. George Burman Foster, *The Function of Religion in Man's Struggle for Existence* (Chicago: University of Chicago Press, 1909), 74–75, 132.

93. James M. Dunn, "No Freedom For the South With a Creed," in *Soul Freedom: Baptist Battle Cry* (Macon, GA: Smyth and Helwys, 2000), 83. Also Dunn's chapter in Everett C. Goodwin, ed., *Baptists in the Balance* (Valley Forge, PA: Judson Press, 1999); and James Dunn quoted by Kenneth L. Woodward in "Sex, Sin and Salvation," *Newsweek*, November 2, 1998, 37.

94. Mullins, *The Axioms of Religion*, 57.

95. See Wayland, *Notes on the Principles and Practices of Baptist Churches* (New York: Sheldon, Blackmon and Co., 1857), 132.

96. For an account of how the lengthy and communally guided conversion experience of Puritan theology was shortened into an instantaneous and self-interpreting conversion event, see Bill J. Leonard, "Getting Saved in America," *Review and Expositor*, vol. 82 no 1 (1985): 111–27; and Leonard, "Southern Baptists and Conversion," in *Ties That Bind*, ed. Gary A. Furr and Curtis W. Freeman (Macon, GA: Smyth and Helwys, 1994), 118–19.

97. Bloom, *The American Religion*, 206–14. Bloom alludes to the famous essay by Ralph Waldo Emerson, "Self-Reliance," in *The Complete Writings of Ralph Waldo Emerson*, 2 vols. (New York: Wm. H. Wise & Co., 1929), 1:138–52.

98. Winthrop S. Hudson, "Shifting Patterns of Church Order in the Twen-

tieth Century," in *Baptist Concepts of the Church*, ed. Winthrop Still Hudson (Philadelphia: The Judson Press, 1959), 215.

99. James Wm. McClendon Jr., *Ethics: Systematic Theology, Volume I* (Nashville: Abingdon Press, 1986), 30; *Ethics: Systematic Theology, Volume I*, rev. ed. (Nashville: Abingdon Press, 2002), 29.

100. J. M. Carroll, *The Trail of Blood* (Lexington: Ashland Baptist Church, 1931).

101. For example, William Roy McNutt, *Polity and Practice in Baptist Churches* (Philadelphia: The Judson Press, 1935); and Hershel H. Hobbs, *The Axioms of Religion* (Nashville: Broadman Press, 1978).

102. LeRoy Moore Jr., "Roger Williams and the Historians," *Church History* 32 (1963): 441–43. This romantic reading of history is what Barry Alan Shain has called "the myth of American individualism" in *The Myth of American Individualism*, 10–11 passim. Shain's thesis is that the misperception of individual liberty as the animating principle of American culture in time hardened into a libertarian myth.

103. LeRoy Moore Jr., "Roger Williams and the Historians," *Church History* 32 (1963): 443. Other important studies by Mauro Calmandrei and Alan Simpson call into question the established image among American historians of Williams as the icon of liberal democratic humanism. Alan Simpson, "How Democratic Was Roger Williams?" *The William and Mary Quarterly* 13, no. 1 (January 1956): 53–67, and Mauro Calamandrei, "Neglected Aspects of Roger Williams' Thought," *Church History* 21 (1952): 239–58. These "realists" stressed a historicized account that placed Williams more within the context of Separatist Puritanism in Old and New England.

104. Moore, "Roger Williams and the Historians," 444. For a fuller treatment of the liberal misappropriation of Williams, see my essay "Roger Williams, American Democracy, and the Baptists," *Perspectives in Religious Studies* 34, no. 3 (Fall 2007): 267–86.

105. Mullins recognized that soul competency, which is not understood as competency under God, is "like a rudderless ship driven by tide and tempest," in *Axioms of Religion*, 68–69. Thus, the first axiom is the freedom of God. Unfortunately, Mullins defined and defended this axiom, not theocentrically but anthropocentrically, by grounding God's sovereignty on human need, in *Axioms of Religion*, 83–86.

106. Hudson, "Shifting Patterns of Church Order," 216.

107. Humphreys makes the observation that ecclesiology was a part of the course on "Church Government and Pastoral Duties" not "Systematic Theology" in *Baptist Theologians*, 334. See Mueller, *A History of Southern Baptist Theological Seminary*, 113.

108. Mullins stated that discussion of the church was beyond the purview of his study in *The Christian Religion,* 425.

109. Mullins, *Baptist Beliefs* (Valley Forge, PA: The Judson Press, 1912), 65. The description of the church as a voluntary association has deep roots in the political philosophy of Locke, Jefferson, and Madison, see Mikael N. Broadway, "The Way of Zion Mourned: A Historicist Critique of the Discourses of Church-State Relations" (Ph.D. dissertation, Duke University, 1993), chap. 5.

110. Hudson, "Shifting Patterns of Church Order," 207.

111. Bloom, *The American Religion,* 207.

112. Mullins, *The Christian Religion,* 256–58.

113. Mullins, *Talks on Soul Winning,* 9–15.

114. Mullins, *Axioms of Religion,* 150–67.

115. Dagg, *Manual of Theology,* 149, 179–80; Boyce, *Abstract of Theology,* 200; Clarke, *An Outline of Theology,* 182–88; and Augustus Hopkins Strong, *Systematic Theology* (1889; repr. Philadelphia: The Judson Press, 2010), 486. Clarke goes so far as to claim that theology is not even concerned with the body in *An Outline of Theology,* 184.

116. H. Wheeler Robinson, "Hebrew Psychology," in *The People and the Book,* ed. Arthur S. Peake (Oxford: Clarendon Press, 1925), 362, 366.

117. Rowan Williams, *The Wound of Knowledge,* 2nd ed. (Cambridge, MA: Cowley Publications, 1990), 25.

118. Carlyle Marney, *Structures of Prejudice* (Nashville: Abingdon Press, 1961), 199.

119. Paraphrased by Charles Marsh in *God's Long Summer* (Princeton, NJ: Princeton University Press, 1997), 189–90.

120. Mullins, *Baptist Beliefs,* 77. Emphasis added.

121. In attempting to vindicate the Mullins legacy for social Christianity, Douglas Weaver rightly points out that as pastor of Lee Street Baptist Church in Baltimore and to a lesser extent during his ministry in the Newton Centre Baptist Church in Massachusetts, Mullins embraced "a moderate-type social gospel." The issue, however, is not whether Mullins personally acted in a socially responsible manner, which he did, but whether his theological individualism impels others to do so, which it does not. Weaver, introduction to *The Axioms of Religion,* 26–27.

122. Apollonius of Rhodes, *The Voyage of Argo,* trans. E. V. Rieu (London: Penguin Books, 1959), 171–72.

5

The Contested Legacy of Lottie Moon

Southern Baptists, Women, and Partisan Protestantism

Elizabeth H. Flowers

Background

When conducting an ethnographic study of Southern Baptist women a few years ago, I heard an ordained pastor involved with Baptist Women in Ministry speak of the "real Lottie Moon."[1] Having grown up in a Southern Baptist church and participated in the denomination's mission group for girls, Girls-in-Action, I was quite familiar with the late nineteenth- and early twentieth-century missionary to China. Her named Christmas offering, led by the Woman's Missionary Union (WMU), culminated my childhood church's yearly calendar. At ten, I proudly played one of her Chinese pupils in the annual Lottie Moon Christmas pageant. I had even heard Southern Baptists playfully referring to her as "Saint Lottie." But I had never heard the phrase, the "real Lottie Moon," and wondered who the imposters might be. As part of my research, I began asking women about their understanding of Lottie Moon. When visiting the WMU's archives, I also combed the offering's promotional material, uncovering a plethora of images and portrayals.[2] Some were expected; others were quite surprising.

As I discovered, Moon's actual biography was rather ambiguous. Although she was born in 1840 into a large, well-known, and slave-owning Virginian family, the Moon's wealth seemed to have dissipated by her adolescence and her father's untimely death in 1853. After the Civil War, Lottie taught school, eventually founding the Cartersville Female High School in Georgia. Then, at age thirty-three, she followed her younger sister Edmonia to China as a Southern Baptist missionary. Within a few years, Edmonia, for undisclosed reasons, returned home. Lottie, however, labored on. A prolific and talented writer, she sent hundreds of descriptive letters to family, friends, churches, and local women's mission circles, as well as Southern Baptist journals and papers—thereby making hers a Southern Baptist household name.

At this point, her story also became more open to interpretation. On the one hand, she appeared a forward-thinking maverick. At several points of local political unrest and rebellion, Moon refused to follow other missionaries to safer territory. After 1885, she abandoned the Southern Baptist compound and her teaching position in Tengchow to live as the sole Westerner in inner Pingtu province. Conforming to Chinese dress and lifestyle, she founded a church that attracted more than a hundred members. Writing home, she urged other women to join her in evangelizing the Chinese people. On the other hand, when Moon did return to the States on furlough, she embodied the Southern lady, following the gendered etiquette of addressing audiences of women only. More than once, male denominational officials failed in their attempts to hear her speak. Even more enigmatic, she initially accepted then turned down the proposal of the distinguished and controversial Southern Baptist theologian Crawford Toy. In 1912, fellow missionaries secured Moon's passage from China to Virginia, citing her frail health. She died aboard the ship as it docked in Japan. While the details remain unclear, the official cause of death was malnutrition.[3]

If Moon's narrative was somewhat imprecise, the success of her named offering has been incontrovertible. In 1918, the WMU's former corresponding secretary, Annie Armstrong, suggested using Lottie Moon's name for the organization's Christmas Offering for China.[4] Not only because its proceeds went to China, where Moon had served, but also because Moon had supported the WMU and died on Christmas Eve. WMU leaders accepted Armstrong's recommendation, though little about the promotion changed until, that was, the Southern Baptist Convention faced a debilitating budgetary crisis. In 1919, SBC leaders followed the fund-raising trends of other Protestant denominations and launched what they called the Seventy-Five Million Campaign to raise $75 million in five years. Much to church officials' surprise and delight, pledges exceeded the $75 million mark by more than $20 million. Agencies and boards, already strapped for cash, were quick to spend the anticipated funds against borrowed bank loans. Exuberance soon gave way to despair, however, as an agricultural recession hit the South, and only $58 million of the $98 million pledged came in. By 1924, the SBC faced financial ruin. Its agencies and boards were bankrupt. Feeling the crisis most acutely, the Foreign Mission Board proceeded to call many of its 324 missionaries from the field.[5]

In a story often repeated in Protestant circles, women saved the day. Distressed over the idea of bringing missionaries home, they turned to the Lottie Moon Christmas Offering and poured their energies into promoting it as the fitting legacy of their beloved missionary. While the previous Lottie Moon Christmas Offering (1923/1924) raised $49,000, the 1924/1925 Lottie Moon Christmas Offering reached an astounding $306,000.[6] The women never looked back. Soon, the Lottie Moon Christmas Offering funded anywhere from 40 to 50 percent of the Foreign Mission Board's budget. Within a quarter of a century, the Lottie Moon Christmas Offering transformed what had been a struggling mission body into the largest Protestant mission force worldwide. By 2009, it had raised more than $3 billion for Southern Baptist missions, advancing what some viewed as an empire.[7]

Argument

This chapter examines how the WMU and the SBC shaped and reshaped the image of Lottie Moon to fit their fund-raising purposes and experienced such phenomenal financial success. For most of the twentieth century, WMU women skillfully promoted an image appropriate to the time. The first transformation, Moon as a self-sacrificing martyr, dominated during years of financial hardship and depression. The next, Moon as Southern belle, captured the postwar period of wealth and prosperity. As one image morphed into another, the WMU balanced numerous interpretations of Moon's life and work, often emphasizing one aspect of her life over another, imaginatively retelling stories and anecdotes for a particular audience or age. This strategy of negotiation and compromise, which prioritized monetary and structural efficiency over any theological exactitude, provided a model to denominational officials. It also proved crucial to expanding the SBC and its mission enterprise.[8]

After 1979, though, self-described conservatives began to wrestle control of the SBC from moderates in power. Historians have referred to the ensuing two-decade conflict as the "Baptist battles." Multiple tensions erupted, including the one over women's roles and behaviors. This was hardly surprising as the struggle was fought amid the rise of feminism, the campaign for the Equal Rights Amendment, and ultimately the 1980s and 1990s culture wars. Moreover, as the conflict progressed, conservatives elevated women's submission to male authority as the "test for fellowship," thus making it a primary criterion for acceptance or nonacceptance in denominational life.[9] In this chapter, I argue that initially Lottie Moon's legacy proved fairly malleable. In the post-1979 conflict, however, the varied images of Moon collided, pitting some women's revolutionary "she-preacher" against others' domesticated "cookie lady." As a result, Southern Baptists' beloved missionary functioned as one of the denomination's most divisive symbols.

The story of Moon's conflicted legacy is significant. First, by presenting it as the illustrative subplot of the SBC and its post-1979 battles, we find that women's power, like Moon herself, was more complicated than often portrayed and open to varied interpretations. On the one hand, WMU leaders used traditional gendered understandings of women as nurturers and caretakers to legitimize their active roles in mission education and giving. In this sense, the WMU empowered women in practical ways, enabling them to assume authority as public speakers, educators, and administrators.[10] On the other hand, missions also reiterated their secondary status by placing boundaries and limitations on their ecclesial roles and performances, as did the very images of Moon as a Southern belle that they used to justify their church work as women. When women attempted positions of leadership outside the realm of missions, sensing a call to preach from the pulpit, for example, they encountered tremendous resistance and tension.[11] Second, and relatedly, this story points to the changing place of women in American and Southern society, particularly in the postwar period. The SBC both influenced and was influenced by broader cultural impulses to rethink women's roles. Certainly the most sweeping movement here was feminism. Afterward, women's call to ordained ministry could only be seen as a bid to equality with men. This posed a challenge, because throughout the 1970s, conservative evangelicals linked feminism and women's liberation with abortion, homosexuality, and secular culture.[12] As a result, Southern Baptists ultimately fought their battles as part of the wider culture wars, with the denomination's conservatives finding a prominent place in the religious right.

Finally, then, the contest over Moon also tells us something about the South's and Southern Baptists' distinct role in the culture wars. As the region became increasingly vital to the burgeoning national economy after World War II, it experienced unprecedented growth and financial triumph. Moon's historical transformation after the 1940s embodied Southern Baptists' newfound middle-class status. But the acceleration of change also produced internal anxieties, and some Southerners began to protest what they felt to be an infiltration of liberal thinking and practices. Coming full circle, many of these ideas involved women. They also invoked race. The two were interrelated. Southern society had long rested on a white patriarchal and class order. As hardened concepts of race fell out of favor during the civil rights movement, Southern Baptists sought a more constrained view of women and their ministries.[13]

To understand the scope of change within Southern society and among Southern Baptists, it is necessary to start with the WMU's initial rendering of Lottie Moon. Somewhat ironically, this image was far less traditional than future portrayals.

Action, Martyrdom, and Self-Sacrifice

Like other Protestant women organizing for missions, Southern Baptist women founded the WMU as a means to greater "usefulness," asserting in 1888, women's natural "right for service."[14] At the same time, because Southern Baptists were uncomfortable with the independence of Northern women's mission organizations, women established the WMU as an auxiliary dedicated to educating women and children about Southern Baptist missions and raising money for the SBC's home and foreign mission boards. In fact, the former was most often viewed as the means to the latter. As the preamble to the WMU's constitution read: "We, the women of the churches connected with the Southern Baptist Convention, desirous of stimulating the missionary spirit and the grace of giving among the women and children of the churches, and aiding in collecting funds for missionary purposes, to be disbursed by the Boards of the Southern Baptist Convention, and disclaiming all intention of independent action, organize."[15] Still, there was one problem with their declared intent. The women who crowded the WMU's local circles were of low to moderate means. In fact, the majority of Southern Baptists during the first half of the twentieth century were not much different from the scratch farmers who populated the churches at the SBC's 1845 founding.[16] In terms of education and income, Southerners certainly trailed Northerners, and Southern Baptists also fell well behind their Southern Presbyterian and Methodist neighbors. At first glance, Southern Baptist women were perhaps the least capable of all white Protestant mission women when it came to "aiding in collective funds."

To achieve usefulness in monetary matters, the WMU's leaders emphasized an active form of self-sacrifice, urging members toward "work, self-denial and inventive genius in the department of financial transactions for sacred ends."[17] Spurning such one-time fund-raising events as the Methodist women's bake sales, bazaars, and ticket dinners, the WMU instructed its women to practice individual and systematic weekly giving. Rural women, it suggested, might pledge their egg money toward missions, whereas city women might allot a certain amount from their household budget. As the WMU's longtime president Fannie Heck proclaimed, "We have been given the joy of sacrificing for Christ. To have the privilege of giving is much; to have the privilege of giving up is more."[18] The contrast between "giving" and "giving up" was crucial as the latter appealed to women of limited means, for whom an offering frequently meant significant denial for themselves and their families. Heck was clearly trying to show that a monetary contribution toward missions was not simply for those in a position of abundance.

The program material for the 1924 Lottie Moon Christmas Offering promoted the ideals of the "joy of sacrificing" and the "privilege of giving up" in active ways. For a full week before taking the offering, WMU women and girls held daily prayer services. During these services, they read the story of Lottie Moon's life. One of these prayer-service narratives, seemingly aimed at children, claimed that "Miss Moon" was "like Christ in that she was constantly showing forth compassion." In China, she aided hurt animals, took in abandoned children, and tended to hungry and sick adults. Moreover, she "was as brave as a lion." Not only did she live "alone" among the Chinese, but when other missionaries fled the terrifying 1911 revolution, the "heroine Miss Moon" remained "happy in service" amid lawless disorder.[19] According to another story, Moon transformed a missionary life she initially felt "hard to bear" into a "time of opportunity," with, said the author Eliza Broadus, the help of WMU offerings. This tale, directed at adults, concentrated on her death. Her sympathies, it claimed, "were so stirred by the need of the [Chinese] people that she could not and would not eat enough to sustain life." Moon's martyrdom, then, was a radical act of self-sacrifice, not a passive form of suffering. To add urgency to the SBC's 1924 context, the story also suggested that "the debt of the Foreign Board weighed upon her also."[20]

For the week's climactic "in-gathering service," the WMU instructed its local circles to provide a "boat receptacle immediately after reading aloud 'Miss Lottie Moon's Life.'" Members would come forward to place their offerings in the miniature boat, intended to be a "reminder of China."[21] Because the WMU taught that the Christmas offering should follow a tithe, most Southern Baptist women in 1924 must have doubted their abilities to "give up." The focus on Moon's self-sacrifice was designed to check such thinking. Placing their offering into this symbolic boat signified to women that they were re-enacting Moon's martyrdom through their own giving up. For the next twenty years, ones of economic depression and war, the WMU perpetuated its rhetoric of active self-sacrifice and giving up. Even as the Lottie Moon Christmas Offering's promotional materials began to incorporate stories of other missionaries and countries of service, the WMU highlighted Moon as a martyr for the Chinese people. In fact, she proved most Christ-like in her death.

On one level, in its cultural resonances, the language of self-sacrifice buttressed the WMU's status as an auxiliary to the SBC, assuaging denominational leaders' constant fears that women might overstep their proper boundaries. In practical terms, however, WMU women did not interpret auxiliary, self-sacrifice, or giving up as full submission to male authority, particularly as it related to missions. Moon's sacrificial death, they showed, was the culmination of a life of remarkable—and sometimes radical—action. In following Moon's example of self-sacrifice through giving up, WMU women raised incredible amounts of money, achieving a phenomenal feat, and legitimized active roles for themselves and for women missionaries. Notably, their fund-raising accomplishments made the WMU essential to Southern Baptist missions at exactly the time other women's mission organizations were losing power. First, it salvaged the Foreign Mission Board from the rubble of the Seventy-Five Million Campaign. Then, in 1927, after the Foreign Mission Board's treasurer embezzled the agency's financial holdings, the Lottie Moon Christmas Offering returned sixty missionaries to the field. During the Depression, the WMU provided up to 76 percent of the Foreign Mission Board's revenues. By the mid-1930s, the Lottie Moon Christmas Offering consistently surpassed all other foreign mission donations. And in 1945, it hit the $1 million mark.

Success gave Southern Baptist women leverage. Quite controversially, the WMU went against the male-led mission board and insisted on allocating the Lottie Moon Offering. Although the WMU did not function as a sending agency, it had started a women's training school as early as 1907. Allocation ensured that the training school's graduates secured missionary appointments as well as pressured the SBC to do the WMU's bidding. On behalf of mission education and mission giving, women also gained access to the local pulpit and church classroom. In responding to the charge that Paul bid women to keep quiet to hear the men speak, the WMU asked from the pages of its monthly periodical, "We wonder how many husbands could tell us very much about missions and mission work and missionaries."[22] In 1929, the WMU's president, Ethlene Boone Cox, delivered the organization's report from the convention podium, signifying the first time that a woman addressed the annual convention. After trying to silence Cox, a group of men left in protest. In many ways, women were following the example of the "heroine Miss Moon," pushing the boundaries of women's proper place in their "right for service."

There were, nevertheless, limits. When the Nineteenth Amendment was ratified in 1920, thereby giving women the vote, WMU president Minnie James declared that the "time has come when we must widen yet further the widening work of our WMU."[23] In 1921, the WMU attempted to "widen yet further" its work by submitting a resolution to the convention mandating that nine WMU women be appointed to the SBC Executive Committee and twelve women, also WMU members, to each of the SBC's five boards.[24] The WMU included several justifications for its women's request. As the resolution stated, "a large part of the work of each Board is planned for women, is supported by women through the Woman's Missionary Union and . . . could not be done without women." It also highlighted the fact that women were "the majority of the active adult members of our churches." It then drew attention to the "large gifts of the Union" as "evidence" of the "loyalty and fidelity of our constituency to the great works of the Boards." And it concluded by emphasizing women's "desire to see the Woman's Missionary Union grow along with the Convention in usefulness, in power, in vision."[25] SBC officials quickly tabled the suggestion. As women discovered, they gained public voice in ecclesial and denominational life only when directly related to the WMU's original purpose of mission education and fund-raising. When they pushed this boundary to "widen yet further" their active roles, they experienced resistance. In addition, as the male-led SBC moved into a period of bureaucratic growth and financial stability, women saw their authority diminish despite the fact that they continued to raise the bulk of money for Southern Baptist missions. To maintain success, they transformed Moon into a more traditional and less active heroine, ironically reinforcing their secondary role culturally in order to give legitimacy to their own efforts and those of women missionaries. The nature of her sacrifice likewise changed as one more befitting a wealthy Southern belle.

Privilege, Wealth, and the Southern Belle

The South benefited enormously from the post–World War II economic boom.[26] Offering cheap land and nonunionized labor, the region found itself at the center of the burgeoning industrial military complex. By all historic accounts, the earnings gap between Southerners and non-Southerners began to lessen significantly, and with their newfound purchasing power, Southerners became a leading consumer market in the growing national economy. Urbanization was a natural result of industrialization. In 1940, 65 percent of Southerners lived in rural areas and 35 percent in urban ones. By 1960, more than half, 57 percent, claimed urban residence. The 1970 figures almost reversed the 1940 ones: 64 percent resided in urban areas while 36 percent were in rural areas.[27] In less than a few decades, it seemed, the once isolated South had transformed itself into the newer "New South" or the burgeoning Sunbelt.[28]

Southern Baptists followed this general pattern. In terms of both education and income levels, they became solidly middle class. As if to flaunt their status and respectability, in a dramatic reversal of previous periods, Southern Baptists' general offerings overflowed the church coffers. Having established a central headquarters and executive committee in Nashville, the postwar SBC was able to recreate itself into a thriving bureaucratic institution. It expanded its institutions and agencies, created an array of age-appropriate programs for its local congregations, and promoted greater unity and uniformity with a denominational calendar that filled the year. Massive membership drives, evangelism campaigns, and church plants enabled exponential growth.[29] Moreover, some Southerners had followed job opportunities north and west in the years before and during the Depression and World War II, and they had carried their Southern Baptist heritage with them. After the war, geographic boundaries between regions became more porous as relocation across states and regions for educational and business purposes increased. The new interstate highway system further promoted transregional travel and communication. By 1955, the SBC was the largest denomination in the country, and in 1961, it reported churches in every state. If the SBC was the Catholic Church of the South, as recognized by some historians, it had also become a symbol of national expression.[30]

The WMU celebrated the SBC's success, growing alongside the denomination. At the same time, its role as a fund-raiser for Southern Baptist missions shifted. Most significantly, the Lottie Moon Christmas Offering no longer served to keep the Foreign Mission Board afloat but rather to extend its programs and personnel. Long banners, colorful offering envelopes, glossy posters, and enticing press releases advanced the Lottie Moon Offering and publicized its yearly theme. As the WMU transformed the offering into a churchwide event, it encouraged Southern Baptists to promote it during their regular Wednesday and Sunday services. For postwar Southern Baptists, the Lottie Moon Christmas Offering was as integral to December as Advent for more liturgical traditions. And Lottie Moon herself became a veritable cottage industry. Lottie Moon plays, pamphlets, musicals, picture books, and even a cookbook—something catering to every age and interest—poured from the WMU's press.[31] Still, despite vast changes in the age, particularly the Americanization of Dixie, the portrayal of Moon harkened back to a previous time.

During this period, the WMU increasingly stressed Moon's genteel Southern upbringing, readily identifying her with the classic Southern lady of moonlight and magnolias. One play, for example, opened with a playful young Lottie in the "great hall at Viewmont, an old southern mansion," which seemed somewhat akin to Tara in *Gone with the Wind*.[32] Early scenes of a mischievous girl in an aristocratic South contrasted with later scenes of a toiling older missionary in an impoverished China. Another similar short dramatic piece has Moon spurning the love of a handsome, young Confederate officer.[33] Biographic pamphlets spoke of "Miss Moon" as a "daughter of the Old South," as one who was "reared in the finest tradition of Christian culture, wealth, and educational advantages."[34]

A popular and often-cited juvenile book from the late 1950s and early 1960s, Helen Monsell's *Her Own Way: The Story of Lottie Moon*, elaborated Moon's privileged Southern upbringing in the "Big House," complete with a stereotypical black "mammy," often fussing with Lottie, the irritable slave cook "Aunt Sukey," and "black Negro children" playing happily on Viewmont's ground. The crude dialect of the black slaves obviously contrasted with that of the elite Moon family.[35] In one scene, the house servant Tom announced, "The soldiers a' coming! They burn Charlottesville now. Marse Jim's old home is ablazing. They're going t'be here 'most any minute!"[36] Lottie and her sisters quickly wrapped the silver and buried it under one of Viewmont's many trees. As it turned out, Tom, a stock hysteria-prone black character resembling Prissy in *Gone with the Wind*, has confused local fireworks for Yankee explosives. At the expense of Tom, the Moon sisters' scrambling to bury the silver served as comedic relief amid the hardships of war. At many points, the book elaborated on the Civil War's "sad ending for the people of the South" and the "cause for which they had fought."[37] Monsell devoted most of her book to Moon's childhood and youth at Viewmont, leaving only the last pages to her China years.[38] The title, *Her Own Way*, referred as much to the affluent young Lottie, a girl accustomed to having her own way, as to the adult missionary, though Monsell was obviously highlighting the connection. In addition, Monsell never attributed Moon's death to starvation, only briefly mentioning that she suffered a severe illness.

As a result of such depictions, girls born and raised into the WMU could imagine the young Moon as a precocious Scarlett O'Hara–like character.[39] This characterization had two implications. First, Moon's self-sacrifice entailed the giving up of an elite existence for the squalor and loneliness of a missionary's life. And second, her early life as a Southern belle involved a strict racial order. Moreover, as the literature made clear, Moon did not reject the ideology governing Southern privilege and order. Overall, her missionary calling simply denied her the comforts of her born status rather than posed any moral questioning. Southern Baptists moving up the social ladder measured the cost of Moon's sacrifice in terms of their own middle-class lifestyles. If most white Southerners, including the bulk of Southern Baptists, had been scratch farmers with no slave-owning heritage, a new generation was experiencing unprecedented prosperity. Proud members of the South's new elite, Southern Baptists clearly read themselves back into the privileged past of Southern plantation life.

The promotional material thus indicated that most Southern Baptists were not called to give up what was, in reality, their newfound lifestyle—wealth and the creature comforts of a middle-class existence. Even though God called only a few, like Moon, to give up their material status, God did, nevertheless, call all Southern Baptists to support their missionaries' sacrifices. In emphasizing the divide between the life of a Southern belle and that of a missionary, the WMU drew attention to the gulf between Southern Baptist prosperity and Third World poverty, between white America and the foreign other. As one year's Lottie Moon Christmas Offering theme expressed it, "Because We Have Been Given Much," much had to be given by Southern Baptists. The WMU still appealed to sacrificial giving, but it more readily spoke of a "thank you offering," "love-gift," "sharing of blessings," or "sharing possessions." In one creative monologue, a WMU woman presented herself as a typical Southern Baptist wife and mother. At first, she was excited and animated in talking about her previous year's Christmas preparations. She then turned quite somber as she recounted how Christ had appeared to her on Christmas morning, carrying in his nail-scarred hand her contribution to the Lottie Moon Christmas Offering. That ten dollar bill, which she had crammed into the offering envelope at the last minute and in great haste, paled in comparison to the hundreds of dollars she had spent for her husband and children in carefully wrapped gifts, new toys, and an elaborate holiday meal. Feeling the shame of Christ's visit and revelation, she urged other WMU women to treat the offering with the same thoughtfulness, even extravagance, that they would devote to their families this Christmas season.[40]

The WMU's message of "sharing possessions" yielded results. In 1945, the Lottie Moon Christmas Offering reached $1 million, and it doubled every five years until 1965, steadily increasing afterward. Its continued success had a tremendous impact on missions. In 1940, the SBC reported 455 missionaries in thirteen countries. Within ten years, these figures had also doubled. Throughout the 1970s, the SBC boasted three thousand missionaries in ninety-five countries and claimed another title as the largest Protestant denominational mission force worldwide. The WMU buttressed this force because its Lottie Moon Christmas Offering still served as the Foreign Mission Board's largest monetary source.

And yet, despite the WMU's tremendous accomplishment here, its women largely resisted any claims to power. This new Lottie Moon as Southern belle in some ways functioned as a throwback to concepts of womanhood that earlier WMU women in their pursuit of usefulness and service had actually resisted. It also should be viewed as a more overt version of the subtly submissive image of Moon they had promoted in the prewar era, one of "sacrifice" and "giving up," stances deemed appropriate to women. Submission had, after all, defined both the racially and gendered order of the old South.[41] Jim Crow extended the duration of this order with its mandate of racial segregation. Moreover, the domestic ideology of the 1950s celebrated the role of women as wives and mothers in ways that once again reinstated male authority.[42] Over the 1960s, as this prevailing order, first in terms of race and then in relation to gender, began to unravel, women avoided what many Southerners and Southern Baptists felt to be the threat of change, carefully reaffirming the status quo through a very traditional imaging of Lottie Moon.[43]

As for race, throughout the 1950s, hard-line segregationists dominated the region and its institutions, including the SBC. The civil rights movement of the 1960s obviously posed a challenge to the Jim Crow regime. At first, Southerners rejected racial change, and the WMU's depiction of Moon reflected their resistance. But a new generation expressed embarrassment by what increasingly seemed not only an outdated but morally problematic ideology. In a dramatic shift, by the 1970s, few white Southern politicians actually admitted any lingering opposition to desegregation and civil rights legislation. The same could be said for those in SBC leadership.[44] Racism persisted but certainly not as openly. In addition, it was seen more as a nationwide rather Southern phenomenon.[45]

The WMU's reinterpretation of Moon as Southern belle signified this shift. Another juvenile biography, for example, Jester Summers's *Lottie Moon's Life* replaced Monsell's *Her Own Way*.[46] Summers's book followed the basic narrative of Monsell's but downplayed stereotypical representations of plantation life. It expunged the black dialect and avoided Monsell's more extreme stereotypes and stock black characters, referring to house slaves as "maids." Lottie's "mammy" even became "Mandy," and the relationship between Lottie and Mandy far more restrained. But the racially subordinate structure of the story remained basically the same, even if, in the story, after the war, Summers had Lottie exclaim that "no-one should make slaves of other men and women." It is noteworthy that Summers was careful to present the Civil War as a "war between the states" rather than a war over slavery. This way, the life of Moon could also reflect and soothe both the anxieties and hopes of the slowly changing racial order in the South.

As with race and civil rights, the WMU was initially guarded over feminism. In light of both Southern Baptists' overall conservatism and the WMU's power, it appeared that the WMU wanted to quell any possible connection between itself and the rising women's liberation movement. According to the WMU's executive secretary, Alma Hunt: "The Lottie Moon Christmas Offering is . . . not designed to promote particular objectives of Woman's Missionary Union, but rather to undergird the total missionary effort extended in foreign lands." Hunt appealed to an enduring theme in Moon imagery and SBC women's expression of their roles, concluding: "The greatest glory of Woman Missionary Union is that she does not seek her glory, but rather undertakes to reinforce a worldwide ministry of love."[47] When asked, in 1966, about women's ordination, only two years after the first Southern Baptist church ordained a woman, the WMU's president, Marie Mathis, claimed not to know any Southern Baptist woman who would aspire to the church pastorate.[48]

Well into the 1970s, the WMU made few, if any, comments on feminism and refused to involve itself in the campaign for the Equal Rights

Amendment. They were not only silent. During the 1950s and 1960s, WMU leaders also relinquished some of their more active and controversial roles. First, they handed over allocation of the Lottie Moon Christmas Offering to the male-led Foreign Mission Board. Then they transferred ownership of their training school to the SBC. Last, many state WMU organizations ceded ownership to their state conventions. While these moves might have eased some of the administrative burdens of WMU, they significantly diminished women's power in denominational life.[49]

Like their male counterparts, a genteel oligarchy who ruled the SBC by compromise, national WMU leaders wanted to squelch any possible controversy. Overall, they felt that for the sake of missions, denominational loyalty should precede any partisan politics. For the most part, they ruled in tandem with their male counterparts. During the 1970s, however, denominational unity began to erode. With the nationalization of Dixie and the end of Jim Crow, many Southerners and Southern Baptists felt the subsequent invasion of alien ideas and practices. Cultural tensions invoked doctrinal disputes, and Southern Baptists began to argue over a whole host of issues. One of these issues involved the biblical interpretation of women's roles and practices. In reaction to feminism, some Southern Baptists began to insist on a more constrained view of women's ministry, even in missions.[50] Once again, the legacy of Moon underwent a transformation. This time around, though, women in the WMU and Southern Baptists more generally could not find a consensus that balanced the power of tradition and resistance to it (or bending of it), and the image of Moon became mired in controversy.

WMU, Women, and the Southern Baptist Battles

In 1979, two events dramatically and irrevocably changed the direction of Southern Baptist life. First, more than fifteen thousand messengers gathered at the SBC's annual June convention to elect the young, charismatic mega-church preacher Adrian Rogers as the denomination's next president.[51] To the dismay of church officials, Rogers stood outside the traditional network of leadership, and he defeated several elder Southern Baptist statesmen for the SBC's most powerful office. Even more significantly, his victory represented the beginning of a two-decade struggle between self-described conservatives such as Rogers and the denominationalists, now "moderates," that his opponents represented. As for the second event, that same summer a little-known independent Baptist preacher from Virginia launched a campaign against America's first "born-again" president.

Accusing the Southern Baptist Jimmy Carter of abandoning his religious heritage for secular causes, Jerry Falwell and his Moral Majority laid the foundation for the new religious right that helped Ronald Reagan sweep into the Oval Office. Shortly afterward, the religious right declared itself in a political culture war for America's moral soul. Although some historians have distinguished the Baptist battles from the larger culture wars, seeing the former as a conflict or skirmish over theological and ecclesial concerns, Southern Baptist conservatives were largely victorious in the denomination because they linked these concerns to the issues espoused by the Moral Majority. The two events and conflicts, then, were closely connected. The religious right attacked feminism vehemently, claiming that the movement promoted homosexuality, divorce, and sexual promiscuity.[52] To culture warriors, feminism represented a full-scale attack on the nuclear family, which was, they held, the moral bulwark of American society. As feminism became increasingly threatening, Southern Baptist conservatives then focused much of their rhetoric of inerrancy on women's roles, drawing tight boundaries to control their behaviors and practices.[53]

Like many other evangelical groups, SBC conservatives held women's authority over men as a violation of scripture. As early as 1984, they passed a convention resolution that "encourage[d] the service of women in all aspects of church life and work other than pastoral functions and leadership roles entailing ordination."[54] If tensions over women's roles functioned as one of multiple divisive issues, by the mid-1990s it had become a primary driving determinant. In 1998, conservatives amended the historic *Baptist Faith and Message,* the SBC's confession of faith, by adding an article on the family. The most discussed passage highlighted the role of men and women in marriage. A husband, it stated, "has the God-given responsibility to provide for, to protect, and to lead his family." In contrast, "a wife is to submit herself graciously" to his "servant leadership" as the "church willingly submits to the headship of Christ."[55] In 2000, conservatives amended the *Baptist Faith and Message* once again. Their changes were more far-reaching this time; one of the more substantive came in the article on church. Similar to the 1984 Kansas City resolution, the revision stipulated: "While both men and women are gifted for service in church, the office of pastor is limited to men as qualified by Scripture." As a result of these amendments, and sometimes in elaborately staged ceremonies during which seminary professors signed the revised confession, conservatives made certain that the SBC's executive officers, agency heads, seminary presidents, theologians, and appointed missionaries affirm the revised *Baptist Faith and Message,* ensuring that they would promote the doctrine of male authority and female submission as part of their Christian faith and witness.[56]

Although the WMU initially refused to take any official side in the controversy, it could not help getting involved in the debate over women's roles in church and marriage. Two issues proved sticking points. The first involved women's ordination. From 1964 to 1974, eight Southern Baptist women underwent ordination. By the early 1980s, nearly two hundred had been ordained.[57] Two Southern Baptist seminaries, Southern and Southeastern, had hired women to their theology departments and were opening their doors more widely to women pursuing ministerial degrees. To be sure, few of these women found Southern Baptist church placements, and their ordinations took place in a limited network of churches. Still, conservatives viewed the numbers with alarm. Before it was too late, they needed to stop a tiny trickle from becoming a steady stream, or even, as they saw with other mainstream Protestant denominations, a deluge.

As for the WMU's role in this conflict, many ordained women and seminarians cited the women's mission organization and its language of call as the major influence in their journey. In addition, a new generation of women had assumed the WMU's reins. Unlike the previous generation, many of these WMU officials were seminary-trained with career experiences outside of missions. In 1978, they had the WMU host a conventionwide conference on women in church-related vocations. If the phrase *church-related vocation* was vague, those present translated it to include ordained ministry. Catherine Allen, the WMU's associate executive director and the consultation's steering committee chair, reported afterward that ordination was the "hottest topic of the consultation." According to her report, it "repeatedly came up. People wanted to talk about it. Obviously women are hearing calls from God which in various ways come to involve ordination. Churches are ordaining them. Some are pursuing comfortable and successful careers. Some are having troubles."[58] With the success of the conference, at the 1982 SBC's annual convention meeting, the WMU more boldly sponsored what it called a "women in ministry" dinner. It then provided the seed money and meeting space for Southern Baptist Women in Ministry, an organization dedicated to supporting Southern Baptist women seeking ordination and a pastoral vocation.

The second issue between the WMU and SBC conservatives involved administrative control of the women's organization. Ironically, while every Southern Baptist agency, board, and seminary fell to conservative control, because the WMU was an auxiliary to the SBC and not an official agency or board, conservatives could not designate the historic women's group's trustees or leaders, assume its headquarters, or touch its finances. For this reason alone, the WMU survived the 1980s intact. Then, in 1992, it published mission materials for the newly formed Cooperative Baptist Fellowship, a moderate organization or group that functioned as a shadow denomination to the conservative-controlled SBC. The WMU's decision drew considerable ire from conservatives. Morris Chapman, president of the SBC Executive Committee, announced that "if the women's group continues on its present course, the SBC leadership might consider starting its own women's group." Chapman stressed that the SBC "needs to know" where WMU planned to direct its resources, "whether those contributions would be channeled to its [the SBC's] mission programs or elsewhere." Moreover, he questioned the validity of the WMU's auxiliary status, maintaining that "when an organization gets a program of its own, it ceases to be an auxiliary" and "becomes its own entity."[59] To make matters worse, the WMU refused the subsequent "invitation" from the SBC to become one of the denomination's official agencies or boards. Adrian Rogers immediately denounced the "feminization of missions" among Southern Baptists. He declared that the WMU should be "hard-wired" into the Convention's structure and argued that mission promotion be led by both male pastors and the Brotherhood Commission.[60] Clarifying his position, he stated, "We need to put male leadership back where it belongs," which was, as Baptist Press interpreted him, "in supporting, promoting and leading out in missions. When men take their rightful place in supporting missions then women and children also will be involved."[61]

Tensions between the WMU and the SBC finally reached their peak over money. The Lottie Moon Christmas Offering supplied more than 50 percent of the Foreign Mission Board's budget, ensuring the status of SBC missionaries as the largest Protestant denominational force worldwide. The Annie Armstrong Easter Offering, though earning about half the amount as the Lottie Moon Christmas Offering, served a similar purpose for the Home Mission Board. In 1994, the Virginia state WMU discovered that the SBC was attempting to trademark the name Lottie Moon.[62] When the national WMU protested, the SBC backed away and the two negotiated legal settlements over both offerings. The settlements stipulated that the WMU owned the named trademarks. But the WMU agreed that all funds raised through its named offerings would be used exclusively for the work of the SBC's mission boards. In the end, then, the SBC and the WMU remained dependent on one another. But who, now, was Lottie Moon?

She-Preacher versus Cookie Lady

During this embattled period the image of Moon moved in contrasting directions. At first, she underwent a radical transformation, emerging as a traveling evangelist and preacher. Up to this point, most of the literature on Moon as Southern belle had portrayed the young Lottie as a feisty, strong-willed prankster, the Scarlett O'Hara who underwent a conversion and gave herself to God. But a short dramatic piece from the 1970s in a new and more direct way emphasized the adult Moon as a "radical" of her day: "a radical" who "believed that women should be treated as people with important contributions," "a radical" who "believed people should question," "a radical" who "believed a person should follow that path which seemed the proper one for her, no matter how peculiar in the eyes of society." As it asserted, "There was nothing traditional about Lottie Moon, not as a child, not as a young woman, and not as a mature servant of God." Although the piece stopped short of naming any specific radical act, it certainly hinted toward a new vision of Moon, asking, "Do you feel you have heard her story before?" and cautioning, "Don't be so certain." Crucially, as with the more overtly traditionalist Southern belle of the immediate postwar years (compared to images of Moon before the war), this "radical" Moon not only promoted practical changes for women but directly confronted prevailing Southern Baptists traditions about women. "The new things you hear might not be easy to live with," stated one unnamed woman character, as another then acknowledged, "changing isn't always easy."[63]

In 1980, the Baptist Sunday School Board published Catherine Allen's biography of Lottie Moon, *The New Lottie Moon Story*. Commissioned by the WMU to write the book, Allen covered many facets of Moon's life, including her years in Pingtu province. If much of Allen's story followed the traditional narrative, it did not shy from challenging the predominant understanding of Moon's mission work as a teacher to women and children only. Even as Allen acknowledged Moon's continued struggle to negotiate traditional Southern expectations of women from afar, she held that laboring alone in harsh conditions, Moon eventually taught a Bible class to men, led them in devotions, conducted worship, and performed baptisms. Allen also wrote that when it came to the "woman question" back home,

"Lottie was irked to hear people in comfortable pews theorizing about the proper role of women in the church."[64] A juvenile book, *Lady of Courage: The Story of Lottie Moon* by Ann Hughes, accompanied Allen's study, announcing that Moon "broke Chinese and American custom by teaching men as well as women. She could not turn anyone away who came to her to hear the gospel."[65] Unlike Monsell, Hughes focused on Moon's feats in China, rather than her plantation childhood and youth.

Despite purported strong sales, in 1994, the Baptist Sunday School Board withdrew Allen's biography. The WMU then republished it. In her revised introduction, Allen focused on the recent opening of China and her guided tour to Moon's towns and village of teaching, ministry, and work. Allen noted that subsequent Southern Baptist–related tour groups to Tengchow had encountered a Chinese woman pastoring in the Monument Street Church building attributed to early Baptist missionaries, including Moon. "What would Lottie have thought," asked Allen, "after all her years of pretending not to lead or teach in public or among males."[66] Allen subtly questioned the Baptist Sunday School Board's decision to withdraw the book by stating that "*The New Lottie Moon Story* was accurate in 1980 and is accurate in 1997."[67]

If Allen never directly called Moon a preacher, the "new" Lottie Moon energized some women who recognized her as such. One Baptist Women in Ministry (formerly Southern Baptist Women in Ministry) participant, who also defined herself as an ordained minister, chaplain, and grandmother, lamented that Allen's biography came so late. Reflecting on her own childhood and youth, she stated that "I only wish that she [Moon] could have been written about more clearly." When asked after the meaning of Lottie Moon, she stated that Moon "was a foremother to many of us, an independent who listened to God despite the men telling her 'no.'"[68] A young nineteen-year-old Southern Baptist woman desiring ordination and attending a related Women in Baptist Life conference wrote that Moon "was clearly a preacher, a minister of God's love to his people. This makes me laugh because someone who is honored by all Southern Baptists was a woman and a preacher. The irony strikes me."[69] She was not alone. Other women had taken to calling Moon a preacher. On its website, Baptist Women in Ministry described Lottie Moon as being censured by the Foreign Mission Board for "preaching in the countryside."[70] In the hearts and minds of many ordained women professing a Southern Baptist history and heritage, God had transformed Lottie Moon's initial call to missions, much like theirs, into a ministry of evangelism and preaching.

Soon, though, as this image of Moon as preacher began to inspire some women, another, more domesticated Moon also emerged—and this time, under the auspices of the WMU.

By the mid-1990s, the WMU was struggling for survival. Conservative churches were dropping the historic women's mission organization for new women's ministry to women programs, which were heavily supported by the SBC's Sunday School Board. Moderate churches were leaving the SBC. For many contemporary women, conservative and moderate alike, the WMU seemed dated. After a period of engagement, the WMU, once again, sought compromise and seemed to work more closely with the International Mission Board (formerly the Foreign Mission Board) in publicizing the Lottie Moon Christmas Offering. Not surprisingly, the portrayal of Lottie Moon underwent a taming.

Along with this taming came another change, as the era of the Lottie Moon cottage industry had for the most part ceased. Stories of contemporary SBC missionaries in their countries of service now replaced those of Moon and China. But biographic pamphlets and sketches on Moon still described her as the missionary personality behind the offering's name. One 1997 pamphlet called Moon the "mother of North China" and emphasized that "Chinese custom and Baptist tradition kept her from ministering directly to the Chinese men." While the pamphlet acknowledged that "her network of relationships transcended race, gender, religion, culture, age and denomination," it followed conservative "women to women" ministry programs by emphasizing that "Chinese women became Lottie's personal mission strategy."[71] The most widely circulated pamphlet after 2000 celebrated Moon for following God's call to the point of sacrificing the comforts of home, re-emphasizing a traditional gendered theme. Acknowledging that men sometimes eavesdropped while she taught, it nonetheless presented her solely as a teacher to women and children. The pamphlet also devoted a section to her nickname "cookie lady," a name given to Moon because her sugar cookies drew Chinese children to her home and school.[72] The story had often appeared in the literature, even in Allen's account, but at this point, it could only have seemed a domestication of her more radical image.

As late as 2010, the contest over Moon persisted. In December 2009, Southwestern Baptist Theological Seminary announced that an alumnus had purchased from China the house of Lottie Moon and was donating it along with other historic Moon artifacts to the seminary. Paige Patterson, who is generally perceived as the architect of Southern Baptist conservatism and also Southwestern Baptist Theological Seminary's president, praised Moon and explained her worth "in the aftermath of the conservative renaissance of the convention." According to Patterson, Moon "saw very clearly, the close connection between a high confidence in the Word of God and the success of her missionary endeavor in China." Her refusal to marry Crawford Toy, said Patterson, was based on the knowledge that Toy had "imbibed historical-critical thinking." Patterson claimed further that Moon "feared that liberal theology would undo the positive impact she had made among the Chinese people for Christ."[73] In the moderate publication *Baptists Today,* Catherine Allen responded with a scathing critique of Patterson's interpretation of Moon under the title "Lottie Moon Legacy Not Captured in Texas." In it, she insisted that Patterson used Moon to "promote his particular bias" and noted that "personally, I do not believe a word of the claims Dr. Paige Patterson has been making about Lottie Moon for years." She also drew attention to the woman, Pastor Wang Xia, who now pastored Pingtu Christian Church and traced the current congregation to the one Moon had established. Comparing Wang to Moon, Allen declared: "I am eager for Southwestern to spotlight the model of women pastors who are willing to pump a bicycle 60 miles to officiate at the Lord's Supper in rural villages, to care for the sick, and to preach the Gospel in all conditions."[74] To advance Allen's point, one letter to the editor questioned the conservative direction of the SBC and the International Mission Board and asked, "Would Lottie Moon be appointed today?"[75] That would, of course, depend on which Lottie Moon was being appointed: martyr, Southern belle, she-preacher, or cookie lady.

Conclusion

For most of the twentieth century, the WMU's reshaping of Lottie Moon to fit the changing context of Southern Baptists' lives demonstrated the power of compromise that had shaped the growing denomination. But this tradition of compromise failed in the 1970s and 1980s. In the years after World War II, Southern Baptists had moved off the farm, the Jim Crow South had largely disappeared, and some women had even moved into the pulpit. Dixie nationalized and Southern Baptists not only experienced commercial success, greater mobility, and higher education rates, but a bewildering pluralism of social movements, theological doctrines, scientific ideas, and gendered understandings. In response, the Southern Baptist battles and the culture wars erupted.

Other Southerners and evangelicals experienced the same changes and fought over them. The SBC, then, was only one of many denominations and church-related organizations to fight and fragment over whether women could enter the pulpit, preach, perform baptisms, and assume authority over men in congregational and domestic matters. It was, nevertheless, the largest. And its struggle over Lottie Moon demonstrates how women's roles in everyday life as well as their imagined portrayals and performances functioned as fiercely contested sites of meaning in both the denomination and larger culture.

Yet, despite outside perceptions of dominantly male-driven narratives, women were hardly passive in this process. Southern Baptist women actively shaped, reshaped, and fought over the "real Lottie Moon" because she affirmed their greatest hopes and aspirations, sometimes emphasizing traditional roles and other times challenging them. For nearly a century, thousands of girls had moved through the WMU's ranks. Although few Southern Baptist women remained active in the WMU into the twenty-first century, some still claimed Lottie Moon as their ideal Christian woman. They engaged her legacy because, as with preceding generations, in resisting, affirming, and reconstructing Moon, they discovered their own calling. Only this time around, their callings moved between opposing poles and tensions, furthering the fragmentation of their former world. Moon's image continued to serve as a source of consensus only so long as Southern Baptist women incorporated an overarching traditionalist interpretation of it, challenging tradition to legitimize practical new roles for women in the WMU and the mission fields, but affirming images of women as "sacrificing" and "giving up." As a spritely "Southern belle," Moon could serve as a source of unity. But with the women's movement of the 1960s and 1970s, and as some SBC and evangelical women began to move into pulpits, hard-line conservatives rejected this compromise. So too did some women, refusing the traditionalism that had always come with Moon. A genuinely feminist image of Moon, even a missionary evangelical feminist, could not serve as a source of unity. The power of the image had always depended on a compromise with tradition. The culture wars and denominational battles made Moon into a curiosity.

In short, the "gold" for us as historians studying the legacy of Moon lies not in who won her name, the prevailing image, nor even the billions of dollars that came with her offering. The real gold is the significance of the conflict itself and what it tells us about women, gender, and Protestant Christianity in the South, among Southern Baptists and throughout an increasingly divided and partisan religious America.

Notes

1. I would like to thank my mentor, Grant Wacker, for his continued interest in my work as demonstrated by his enthusiasm and wise counsel regarding this project. I would also like to thank William Katerberg, Rebecca Sharpless, and the two anonymous reviewers for *Fides et Historia* for their comments and critiques, which strengthened this chapter. Finally, I appreciate the generous financial assistance of Texas Christian University. Monies provided by TCU's Research and Creative Activities Fund made travel to the Southern Baptist Historical Library and Archives possible while its Junior Faculty Summer Research Program gave me time to write.

2. The WMU Archives are located in the Alma Hunt Library of the WMU's national office and headquarters in Birmingham, Alabama. I would like to thank the WMU's librarian and archivist at that time, Amy Cook, and the library assistant, Dianne Baker, for their help in directing me to sources and locating materials.

3. While somewhat dated, the most scholarly biography remains Irwin T. Hyatt Jr., *Our Ordered Lives Confess: Three Nineteenth-Century American Missionaries in East Shantung* (Cambridge, MA: Harvard University Press, 1976), 65–138. A more celebrated portrayal of Moon's life, Catherine Allen's *The New Lottie Moon Story* (Nashville: Broadman, 1980) still counts as a painstakingly researched and scholarly work. Una Roberts Lawrence's *Lottie Moon* (Nashville: Sunday School Board of the SBC, 1927) is a hagiographic yet detailed depiction of Moon. Until Allen's 1980 account, the WMU's promotional material primarily pulled from Roberts's work. See also Keith Harper, ed., *Send the Light: Lottie Moon's Letters and Other Writings* (Macon, GA: Mercer University Press, 2002); Alan Neely, "Saints Who Sometimes Were: Utilizing Missionary Hagiography," *Missiology: An International Review* 27, no. 4 (1999): 441–57.

4. Annie Armstrong stepped down as corresponding secretary in 1906, afterward maintaining a careful distance from the organization that she helped found until her death in 1938. Her suggestion regarding the offering represented one of the few times that she intervened in WMU affairs.

5. For a history of the Seventy-Five Million Campaign, see Jesse C. Fletcher, *The Southern Baptist Convention: A Sesquicentennial History* (Nashville: Broadman and Holman Publishers, 1994), 134–39.

6. While connecting it to the previous Christmas, the WMU initially held the Lottie Moon Christmas Offering and its accompanying Week of Prayer the first week in January. In 1926, it moved both to early December.

7. Two helpful historical overviews of the Christmas Offering include Catherine Allen, *A Century to Celebrate: History of Woman's Missionary Union* (Birmingham, AL: Woman's Missionary Union, 1987), 147–55; Bobby Sorrill, "The History of the Week of Prayer for Foreign Mission," *Baptist History and Heritage* 15, no. 4 (1980): 28–35. Allen appears to be the only scholar to recognize the transition in promotion. She also states that an SBC-wide debt relief campaign helped account for the extraordinary 1924/1925 increase. Still, the WMU's records for the following ten years show the Christmas Offering's revenues as falling anywhere between $170,000 and $246,000, a far cry from 1923/1924's $48,000.

8. The WMU Archives hold a folder on promotional material for each annual Lottie Moon Christmas Offering. In writing this chapter, I consulted these folders.

9. See Elizabeth H. Flowers, "Varieties of Evangelical Womanhood: Southern Baptists, Gender, and American Culture" (Ph.D. dissertation, Duke University, 2006).

10. Patricia R. Hill makes this argument in *The World Their Household: The American Woman's Foreign Mission Movement and Cultural Transformation* (Ann Arbor: University of Michigan Press, 1985).

11. I want to recognize the noted historian Donald G. Matthews for pushing me to recognize more fully this other side of the story.

12. See Seth Dowland, "'Family Values' and the Formation of a Christian Right Agenda," *Church History* 78, no. 3 (September 2009): 606–31.

13. See again Flowers, "Varieties of Evangelical Womanhood."

14. "Organized!" *Baptist Basket*, June 1888, 100; WMU Organizational Minutes, May 11, 1888, WMU Archives. For a history of the term *usefulness* in connection to women's missions, see Dana Robert, *American Women in Mission: A Social History of Their Thought and Practice* (Macon, GA: Mercer University Press, 1997) as well as Hill, *Their World Their Household.* Though dated, Ann Firor Scott addresses this understanding of usefulness among nineteenth- and early twentieth-century Southern women. Scott, *The Southern Lady: From Pedestal to Politics, 1830–1930* (Chicago: University of Chicago Press, 1970). In relation to Southern Baptist women, see Carol Holcomb, "Mothering the South: The Influence of Gender and the Social Gospel on the Social Views of the Leadership of the Woman's Missionary Union, Auxiliary to the Southern Baptist Convention, 1888–1930" (Ph.D. dissertation, Baylor University, 1999); Laine Scales, *All that Fits a Woman: Training Southern Baptist Women for Charity and Mission, 1907–1926* (Macon, GA: Mercer University Press, 2000).

15. "Organized!," 104.

16. As late as 1922, for instance, the Sunday School Board located nearly 85 percent of Southern Baptist churches in rural areas with populations of less than a thousand. Overall, approximately 90 percent of Southern Baptists lived in similar agricultural and small-town settings. See James J. Thompson Jr., *Tried as by Fire: Southern Baptists and the Religious Controversies of the 1920s* (Macon, GA: Mercer University Press, 1982), 36; J. Wayne Flynt, "Southern Baptists: Rural to Urban Transition," *Baptist History and Heritage* 16 (1981): 24–34.

17. *A Lesson in Stewardship* (Baltimore: Woman's Missionary Union, 1889).

18. Heck, Annual Address, WMU Annual Report, 1893.

19. T. W. Ayers, *Miss Lottie Moon—As I Knew Her* (Birmingham, AL: Woman's Missionary Union, 1924).

20. Eliza S. Broadus, *The Life of Miss Lottie Moon* (Birmingham, AL: Woman's Missionary Union, n.d.). The pamphlet can be located in the mid-1920s scrapbook, WMU Archives.

21. Lottie Moon Christmas Offering Ingathering Program, with general program notes, January 7, 1925, Lottie Moon Christmas Offering 1924/25 folder, WMU Archives. The Lottie Moon Christmas Offering folders hold nothing labeled "Miss Lottie Moon's Life." It seems, however, that "Miss Lottie Moon's Life" referred to *The Life of Miss Lottie Moon* by Eliza S. Broadus, particularly as the latter is found in the WMU's mid-1920s scrapbook.

22. "How to Keep Silent in the Churches," *Royal Service*, September 1923, 14.

23. Allen, *A Century to Celebrate*, 338.

24. A copy of the resolution can be found in the minutes, annual WMU meeting, May 12, 1921, WMU Archives.

25. Minutes of annual WMU meeting, May 12, 1921.

26. For an overview of economic change, see Gavin Wright, *Old South, New South: Revolutions in the Southern Economy since the Civil War* (New York: Basic Books, 1986). Two significant works from the 1980s explore the decline of Southern agriculture: Gilbert C. Fite, *Cotton Fields No More: Southern Agriculture, 1865–1980* (Lexington: University Press of Kentucky, 1984); Jack Temple Kirby, *Rural Worlds Lost: The American South, 1920–1960* (Baton Rouge: Louisiana State University Press, 1987). Studies that focus on industrialization include James C. Cobb, *The Selling of the South: The Southern Crusade for Industrial Development, 1936–1990*, 2nd ed. (Urbana: University of Illinois Press, 1993); Bruce J. Schulman, *From Cotton Belt to Sunbelt: Federal Policy, Economic Development, and the Transformation of the South, 1938–1980* (New York: Oxford University Press, 1991).

27. Thomas H. Naylor and James Clotfelter, *Strategies for Change in the*

South (Chapel Hill: University of North Carolina Press, 1975), 223; Charles P. Roland, *The Improbable Era: The South since World War II* (Lexington: University Press of Kentucky, 1975), 23–25. The Bureau of the Census classifies areas with 2,500 or more residents as urban and areas with less than 2,500 residents as rural.

28. Scholars of the South have debated endlessly the issue of postwar continuity and change. Early scholars emphasized continuity in change. John Shelton Reed became a leading spokesperson for this position. He argued that Southern localism, Southern violence, and Southern religion forged a single culture. Differences between Southerners and non-Southerners persisted because Southern distinctions did not rest on tangible dissimilarities with other regions. Reed, *The Enduring South: Subcultural Persistence in Mass Society* (Chapel Hill: University of North Carolina Press, 1972). Charles P. Roland likewise argued the paradox of continuity in change. Roland linked the South's endurance to the stories and myths it told itself—stories of the Romantic South, the Tragic South, the Fundamentalist South, and the Benighted South. Moon as Southern belle certainly tapped into these myths. As Roland admitted, the South that spun such stories was solidly white. And the widely used term *Solid South* referred both to the white South's one party politics and its Jim Crow segregation. Roland, *The Improbable Era: The South since World War II* (Lexington: University Press of Kentucky, 1975). As these systems collapsed, some scholars welcomed a newer New South. See, in particular, Ernest M. Lander and Richard J. Calhoun, eds., *Two Decades of Change: The South since the Supreme Court Desegregation Decision* (Columbia: University of South Carolina Press, 1974); Donald R. Noble and Joab L. Thomas, eds., *The Rising South: Changes and Issues* (Tuscaloosa: The University of Alabama Press, 1976). By the 1980s and 1990s, most historians had become less optimistic. As Numan V. Bartley observed, sweeping change had occurred, but during the 1970s, a national recession hit, and the South's glory days ended. Consequently, old economic and racial problems resurfaced. Bartley, *The New South, 1945–1980* (Baton Rouge: Louisiana State University Press, 1995). In *Lost Revolutions: The South in the 1950s* (Chapel Hill: University of North Carolina Press, 2000), Pete Daniels likewise explored the radical potential for change that had been squandered. Other scholars focused on the continuity of racism in reactionary politics. See Earl Black and Merle Black, *Politics and Society in the South* (Cambridge, MA: Harvard University Press, 1987); Dan T. Carter, *From George Wallace to Newt Gingrich: Race in the Conservative Counterrevolution, 1963–1994* (Baton Rouge: Louisiana State University Press, 1996). For more recent works, see notes 30 and 43.

29. See H. Leon McBeth, *The Baptist Heritage* (Nashville: Broadman Press, 1987), 609–75.

30. Here, I am referring primarily to the ways in which the SBC followed other Protestant denominations in adopting a more corporate or business model of church to achieve growth, expansion, and financial stability. Seemingly overnight, the SBC emerged as something of a bureaucratic superpower in American Protestant life. See Fletcher, *The Southern Baptist Convention*, 179–218. Some scholars have argued more for the Southernization of America than the nationalization of the Dixie. One of the first was John Egerton, *The Americanization of Dixie: The Southernization of America* (New York: Harper's Magazine Press, 1974). Egerton claimed that as Southerners moved north and west, they took a distinct worldview and religious sensibility with them. The Americanization of the South led, in turn, to the Southernization of American Christianity and culture. See more recently, James N. Gregory, *The Southern Diaspora: How the Great Migrations of Black and White Southerners Transformed America* (Chapel Hill: University of North Carolina Press, 2005). In *Resurgent Evangelicalism in the United States* (Columbia: University of South Carolina Press, 1996), Mark Shibley both refined and questioned Egerton's thesis. Shibley argued that whereas Southern religion has undoubtedly influenced American culture, Southern religion has also been irrevocably changed in the process, and certainly more than Egerton acknowledged—or could have foreseen. Consult also note 45.

31. For a detailed description of this industry, see Hyatt, *Our Ordered Lives Confess*, 127–36. Hyatt notes that after 1950, the "sensuous impact" of the legend took precedent over the "actual events" of Moon's life. In my own exploration of the promotional material, her death was not discounted, but the nature of her sacrifice changed.

32. Miriam Robinson, *Faithful Unto Death* (Birmingham: Woman's Missionary Union, n.d.)

33. Lucy Hamilton Howard, *Her Lengthened Shadow* (Birmingham: Woman's Missionary Union, 1964).

34. See, for example, *Biographical Sketch of Lottie Moon* (Birmingham: Woman's Missionary Union, 1960).

35. Helen A. Monsell, *Her Own Way: The Story of Lottie Moon* (Nashville: Broadman Press, 1958).

36. Monsell, *Her Own Way*, 97.

37. Ibid., 103.

38. The term *Southern belle* refers to a woman of marriageable age. I apply the term to the Moon of this postwar period because works like Monsell's fo-

cused on Moon as a young woman. Her sacrifice was measured in terms of the privileged life anticipated by a Southern belle.

39. Catherine Clinton explores the myth versus the reality of Scarlett, Tara, *Gone with the Wind,* and plantation life in her work *Tara Revisited: Women, War, and the Plantation Legend* (New York: Abbeville Press, 1995). She also considers the role of *Gone with the Wind* in popular Southern culture.

40. This monologue was an annual Christmas tradition in my childhood church and, as later explained to me, had been passed down by WMU women from the 1950s and 1960s. I have found no reference to it in the official WMU promotional material.

41. There has been much scholarly work on the relationship between gender and race in the antebellum South. In her groundbreaking study *Within the Plantation Household: Black and White Women of the Old South* (Chapel Hill: University of North Carolina Press, 1988), Elizabeth Fox-Genovese tied Southern gender constructions to the slave system. Other scholars then built on her thesis. See Jean E. Friedman, *The Enclosed Garden: Women and Community in the Evangelical South, 1830–1900* (Chapel Hill: University of North Carolina Press, 1999); Margaret Ripley Wolfe, *Daughters of Canaan: A Saga of Southern Women* (Lexington: University of Kentucky Press, 1995); as well as Bertram Wyatt-Brown's earlier work on Southern chivalry and male honor; *Southern Honor: Ethics and Behavior in the Old South* (New York: Oxford University Press, 1982).

42. For a study of the new domesticity of the 1950s, see William Chafe, *The Paradox of Change: American Women in the Twentieth Century* (New York: Oxford University Press, 1991); Elaine Tyler May, *Homeward Bound: American Families in the Cold War Era* (New York: Basic Books, 1988); Steve Mintz and Susan Kellogg, *Domestic Revolutions: A Social History of the American Family* (New York: The Free Press, 1988). These works set the postwar domestic ideal within cold war politics and anxieties.

43. As for the question of continuity and change in regard to Southern religion, or more specifically white Southern Protestantism, Samuel S. Hill first claimed that white evangelical Protestantism promoted the conservative status quo, thereby abetting white supremacy. The failure of white evangelical piety to address racism and its inability to sustain change underscored the crisis motif in the historiography of Southern religion. Hill, *Southern Churches in Crisis* (New York: Holt, Rinehart and Winston, 1967). Later scholars, though, questioned this motif. Beth Barton Schweiger challenged Southern religious history's "preoccupation" with "establishing the South's uniqueness." Schweiger, as quoted in Hill, *Southern Churches in Crisis Revisited* (Tuscaloosa: The

University of Alabama Press, 1999), xxi. See also her contribution in "Forum: Southern Religion," *Religion and American Culture* 8, no. 2 (Summer 1998): 161–66. David L. Chappell challenged the crisis motif as well by claiming that white supremacy did not muster the religious support needed to overcome change. Chappell, *A Stone of Hope: Prophetic Religion and the Death of Jim Crow* (Chapel Hill: University of North Carolina Press, 2004).

44. As for change among Southern Baptists, Mark Newman outlines three distinct periods: First, from 1945 to 1954, "Baptists continued to support segregation but argued that African Americans should be given equal opportunities for change." Second, after *Brown* in 1954, "their primary commitments began to push Baptists, however reluctantly and incrementally, towards an acceptance of change." Third, with the passage of the Civil Rights Act of 1964, "more and more Baptists abandoned their commitment to segregation and repudiated racism as unchristian." Newman, *Getting Right with God: Southern Baptists and Desegregation, 1945–1995* (Tuscaloosa: The University of Alabama Press, 2001), 22. See also E. Luther Copeland, *The Southern Baptist Convention and the Judgment of History: The Taint of an Original Sin* (Lantham, MD: University Press of America, 2002), 17–32; Walker L. Knight, "Race Relations: Changing Patterns and Practices," *Southern Baptists Observed: Multiple Perspectives on a Changing Denomination*, ed. Nancy T. Ammerman (Knoxville: The University of Tennessee Press, 1993), 165–81; Alan Scott Willis, *All According to God's Plan: Southern Baptist Missions and Race, 1945–1970* (University Press of Kentucky, 2005). Willis looks more carefully at the WMU's record on race, noting that at times, WMU leaders were more progressive than their male counterparts. Depending on the actual author, depictions of the "foreign other" in the WMU's mission literature sometimes reinstated Southern notions of ethnicity, and therefore racial inferiority, while at other points questioned underlying concepts.

45. As for the role of the South in the persistence of racism, scholars first argued that a top-down Republican "Southern strategy" produced the Reagan era. Republican Party strategists exploited a white Southern backlash against ongoing civil rights legislation to create a Republican majority among white Southern voters. See Joseph A. Aistrup, *The Southern Strategy Revisited: Republican Top-Down Advancement in the South* (Lexington: University Press of Kentucky, 1996); Peter Applebome, *Dixie Rising: How the South is Shaping American Values, Politics, and Culture* (New York: Harcourt Brace, 1996); Carter, *From George Wallace to Newt Gingrich*. Others have more recently held that a subtler race- and class-oriented suburban strategy masked as color-blind economic conservatism linked white middle-class Southerners to Republi-

cans nationwide. Matthew D. Lassiter outlined the latter theory in *The Silent Majority: Suburban Politics in the Sunbelt South* (Princeton, NJ: Princeton University Press, 2006). See also David Lublin, *The Republican South: Democratization and Partisan Change* (Princeton, NJ: Princeton University Press, 2004); Bruce J. Schulman, *The Seventies: The Great Shift in American Culture, Society, and Politics* (New York: Free Press, 2001).

46. Jester Summers, *Lottie Moon of China* (Nashville: Broadman Press, 1979).

47. "Sharing Possessions," Alma Hunt folder, WMU Archives.

48. In 1964, the Watts Street Baptist Church in Durham, North Carolina, ordained Addie Davis to the gospel ministry. Her ordination preceded many mainstream, even liberal, Protestant denominations. For her story, consult Keith E. Durso and Pamela R. Durso, "'Cherish the Dream God Has Given You:' The Story of Addie Davis," *Courage and Hope: The Stories of Ten Baptist Women Ministers*, ed. Pamela R. Durso and Keith E. Durso (Macon, GA: Mercer University Press, 2005), 17–30. For Mathis's comment, see "Southern Baptists Tell Why 'Ministry Is for Men Only,'" *Detroit News*, May 24, 1966.

49. For a more in-depth consideration of the allocation issue, see Allen, *A Century to Celebrate*, 154–55; as well as Sorrill, "The History of the Week of Prayer for Foreign Mission." As for the training school, see Allen, 279–81; Scales, *All that Fits a Woman*. Finally, see Allen's assessment of the transfer of ownership to the state conventions, 294–99.

50. Several recent historians claim that white Southern evangelicalism shifted its gaze from race to gender. See Seth A. Dowland, "Defending Manhood: Gender, Social Order, and the Rise of the Christian Right in the South, 1965–1995" (Ph.D. dissertation, Duke University, 2007); Glenn Feldman, "The Status Quo Society, The Rope of Religion and the New Racism," *Politics and Religion in the White South*, ed. Glenn Feldman (Lexington: University Press of Kentucky, 2005), 287–352; Paul Harvey, *Freedom's Coming: Religious Culture and the Shaping of the South from the Civil War through the Civil Rights Era* (Chapel Hill: University of North Carolina Press, 2005).

51. The SBC chose the term *messengers* rather than *delegates* purposefully, arguing that although designated by their churches, messengers attended the convention as individuals who might possess "messages" from their churches but still did not function as representatives or delegates of an institutional body with a formal agenda and set of instructions. See Paul Harvey, *Redeeming the South: Religious Cultures and Racial Identities among Southern Baptists, 1865–1925* (Chapel Hill: University of North Carolina Press, 1997), 7.

52. See again Dowland, "'Family Values' and the Formation of a Christian Right Agenda."

53. The post-1979 conflict has been analyzed by insiders and outsiders alike. For a moderate perspective, see Grady C. Cothen, *What Happened to the Southern Baptist Convention* (Macon, GA: Smith and Helwys, 1993); his sequel *The New SBC: Fundamentalism's Impact on the Southern Baptist Convention* (Macon, GA: Smith and Helwys, 1995); Walter B. Shurden, ed., *The Struggle for the Soul of the SBC: Moderate Responses to the Fundamentalist Movement* (Macon, GA: Mercer University Press, 1993). These works basically regarded the conflict as a doctrinal and biblical dispute with wide-ranging institutional consequences. Bill J. Leonard, *God's Last and Only Hope: The Fragmentation of the Southern Baptist Convention* (Grand Rapids, MI: William B. Eerdman's Publishing Company, 1990); and David T. Morgan, *The New Crusades, the New Holy Land: Conflict in the Southern Baptist Convention, 1969–1991* (Tuscaloosa: The University of Alabama Press, 1996) considered theological, institutional, and cultural concerns, though they prioritized theology. Conservatives joined the conversation with Robison B. James and David S. Dockery, eds., *Beyond the Impasse: Scripture, Interpretation, and Theology in Baptist Life* (Nashville: Broadman Press, 1992); James C. Hefley, *The Truth in Crisis: The Controversy in the Southern Baptist Convention*, 5 vols. (Hannibal, MI: Hannibal Books, 1989–1990); Jerry Sutton, *The Baptist Reformation: The Conservative Resurgence in the Southern Baptist Convention* (Nashville: Broadman and Holman Publishers, 2000). Moving beyond insider accounts, Emery Farnsley explored denominational polity and politicking in *Southern Baptist Politics: Authority and Power in the Restructuring of an American Denomination* (University Park: Pennsylvania State University Press, 1994). Both Nancy Ammerman, *Baptist Battles*, and Barry Hankins, *Uneasy in Babylon: Southern Baptist Conservatives and American Culture* (Tuscaloosa: The University of Alabama Press, 2002) cited the debate over women in what they interpreted to be a sociocultural struggle among Southern Baptists.

54. "Resolution No. 3—On the Ordination and the Role of Women in Ministry," *Annual of the Southern Baptist Convention Nineteen Hundred and Eighty-Four* (Nashville: Executive Committee, Southern Baptist Convention, 1984), 65.

55. For the amendment and its accompanying commentary, as presented in the resolution, see *Annual of the Southern Baptist Convention Nineteen Hundred and Ninety-Eight* (Nashville: Executive Committee, Southern Baptist Convention, 1998), 78–81.

56. By this time, moderates had formed a shadow organization to the denomination called the Cooperative Baptist Fellowship. As a sign of difference between itself and the SBC, the Cooperative Baptist Fellowship featured

women as ministers in its literature, annual meeting, and related worship functions.

57. The exact numbers are difficult to pinpoint. During the early 1980s, in its newsletter *FOLIO*, Southern Baptist Women in Ministry regularly reported about two hundred. The 1983 "Statement of Resolution on Women," a resolution penned by Southern Baptist Women in Ministry advocate Linda Stack Morgan, personal papers of Reba S. Cobb, also referred to two hundred. Certainly, then, this number was the perception.

58. Catherine Allen, "Background Information—Consultation on Women in Church-Related Vocations," Consultation on Women Collection, Southern Baptist Historical Library and Archives, Nashville. While Allen's four-paged "Background Information" was typed, a handwritten note marked the date as September 25, 1978—three days after the consultation ended. The Southern Baptist Historical Library and Archives holds a collection of information and material from the convocation, which I also consulted. I would like to thank the library's director, Bill Sumners, and its archivist, Taffey Hall, for bringing the collection to my attention and directing me to other materials related to Lottie Moon and her named offering.

59. *Christian Century*, February 17, 1993, 168. The article appears to summarize Chapman rather than quoting him directly. See also "Chapman: SBC Needs Clarification from WMU," *Baptist Press*, December 11, 1993, 3.

60. *Christian Century*, April 21, 1993, 424.

61. "Rogers is Critical of Persons Speaking for Him," *Baptist Press*, March 11, 1993, 7.

62. The agreement was recorded in numerous Southern Baptist state newspapers. See also Catherine B. Allen, "Shifting Sands for Southern Baptist Women in Missions," *Gospel Bearers, Gender Barriers: Missionary Women in the Twentieth Century*, ed. Dana L. Robert (Maryknoll, NY: Orbis Books), 118.

63. Carol Tomlinson and Doris Standridge, *It Cannot End at Kobe: How Moon Loves in Missions in the 1970s* (Birmingham, AL: Woman's Missionary Union, n.d.).

64. Catherine B. Allen, *The New Lottie Moon Story* (Nashville: Broadman, 1980), 186.

65. Ann Keltner Hughes, *Lady of Courage: The Story of Lottie Moon* (Birmingham, AL: Woman's Missionary Union, 1987).

66. Catherine B. Allen, foreword to *The New Lottie Moon Story* (Birmingham, AL: Woman's Missionary Union, 1997). The foreword is not paginated.

67. Ibid.

68. Karrie Oertli, written questionnaire, July 6, 2004.

69. Anonymous, written survey, Women in Baptist Life Conference, First Baptist Church, Oklahoma City, March 2005. Several other women in surveys from this conference or in related interviews concerning Southern Baptist Women in Ministry referred to Moon as a preacher.

70. Baptist Women in Ministry, [home page text], www.bwim.info, July 21, 2009. (The website has since been redesigned.)

71. "Lottie Moon: Shaper of Foreign Missions" (Shawnee, OK: Woman's Missionary Union and the Southern Baptist Historical Society, 1997).

72. "Lottie Moon: Incredible Life, Remarkable Gift," (Nashville: International Mission Board, 2000). The pamphlet has been published in several forms.

73. "Lottie Moon's Belongings Unveiled," *Baptist Press*, December 22, 2009.

74. Catherine Allen, "Lottie Moon Legacy Not Captured in Texas," *Baptist Today*, March 2010, 32.

75. "Appreciates Lottie Moon Article," *Baptists Today*, April 2010, 25.

6
Walter Rauschenbusch and the Second Coming
The Social Gospel as Baptist History
Christopher H. Evans

In his 1912 book, *Christianizing the Social Order,* Walter Rauschenbusch made a passing comment in response to a pamphlet that critiqued his first major book, *Christianity and the Social Crisis.* The pamphlet in question was written by prominent northern Baptist clergyman I. M. Haldeman. Haldeman not only enjoyed status as the pastor of the First Baptist Church, New York, but his ministry reflected the growing prominence among Baptists of dispensationalist theology and a harsh criticism of social gospel leaders like Rauschenbusch.[1] Haldeman's pamphlet embodies a theology that one commonly associates today with what later became known as fundamentalism, in particular, his defense of biblical inerrancy. Yet the central theme undergirding Haldeman's argument is not simply that Rauschenbusch's interpretation of scripture was wrong. It was that Rauschenbusch had been caught in the snare of substituting the human discipline of history in place of the divine power of the Bible. "Church history is, and always must be, a peril to the student for the ministry," Haldeman asserted. "If he can pass through it, if he can assist at the process of doctrine making, and still hold faith in the integrity of Holy Scripture, he may be congratulated on his escape, and will be worth listening to as a preacher, not of critical guesses, but divine certainties."[2] Rauschenbusch's response to Haldeman sums up the larger divide occurring within several Protestant denominations in the early twentieth century. "If any one will read the book [*Christianity and the Social Crisis*] and the pamphlet side by side, he will face two kinds of Christianity and can make his choice."[3]

Studies on the social gospel movement in the United States tend to navigate around three modes of inquiry. The earliest scholarship in the 1930s, and extending through the 1960s, examined the social gospel as a response to late nineteenth-century industrial capitalism. A second direction examined the social gospel more as a continuation of certain impulses of evangelical Protestantism emanating from a variety of churches and social movements prior to the Civil War. These scholarly traditions have led to further studies that have looked at the social gospel in relationship to issues of race, gender, and class.[4] Finally, more recent scholarship on the social gospel has offered a nuanced analysis of the movement's theology, in particular, seeing the social gospel as a unique outgrowth of American liberal theology.[5] Regardless of the path one pursues, all roads to studying the American social gospel lead to Walter Rauschenbusch. At the same time, studies on the relationship between Rauschenbusch's theology and his Baptist roots deserve further inquiry.[6]

Although some scholars have noted the importance of Rauschenbusch's Baptist heritage on his theology, the majority of studies on Rauschenbusch tend to see that influence in a somewhat secondary fashion. On one hand, this is understandable given his irenic posture toward a variety of Christian traditions, as well as the fact that, at points, Rauschenbusch could be a harsh critic of Baptists. However, every aspect of Rauschenbusch's thought—from his elevation of religious ethics, his calls to "democratize" American churches, and his views on the kingdom of God—all relate to his Baptist identity.

Because Rauschenbusch was so ecumenical in his outlook, it is easy to overlook his indebtedness to Baptist sources. It is true that Rauschenbusch drew on an eclectic range of sources, and much of his grounding in theological liberalism came from non-Baptist theologians (in particular, his fidelity to important figures of German liberalism such as Albrecht Ritschl and Adolf von Harnack). However, although Rauschenbusch was clearly a theological liberal, he was a Baptist liberal, and if he had to choose between these two identities, he would have unequivocally identified himself as a Baptist. What is frequently forgotten about Rauschenbusch is that for all the acclaim and scorn heaped on him in the years following his death in 1918, his legacy was largely shaped during the final ten years of his life, when his work enjoyed a significant level of public notoriety. Before *Christianity and the Social Crisis* was published in 1907, however, Rauschenbusch labored in relative obscurity within a range of social networks primarily confined to northern Baptist constituencies. The majority of his career, from his theological education, to his time as a pastor of a German-Baptist congregation in New York and as a seminary professor, occurred within a Baptist prism. It was to this audience that the bulk of his published work before 1907 was addressed. Rauschenbusch's ideas were never stagnant, and his formative books and writings between 1907 and his death in 1918 reflect important evolutions in his thinking. By the same token, significant themes within Rauschenbusch's theology, including his concept of the kingdom of God, were highly formulated before he became well-known, and it was for Baptist audiences that his arguments were crafted and honed.

Rauschenbusch's Baptist identity comes through in the role that most suited him as a teacher, minister, and writer: church historian. Despite the fact that later generations viewed him as a theologian, he identified himself vocationally as a church historian. Henry Bowden notes that Rauschenbusch was one of the first Americans to embrace the study of Christian history as a critical discipline, and his historical methodology can be seen in many of his major writings.[7]

Yet Rauschenbusch was also a Baptist historian, who not only wrote as an apologist for a tradition that he loved, but sought to counter those voices antithetical to his kingdom vision. In particular, Rauschenbusch worried about the rising popularity of premillennial dispensationalism in northern Baptist circles, and he hoped that his voice might stave off its influence.

The lion's share of theological analysis on Rauschenbusch usually centers upon his doctrine of the kingdom of God. Rauschenbusch took this strongly Protestant concept and applied it not merely as a model for political engagement (embodied through his support of democratic socialism), but as a means to understand God's relationship to the church and to the world. As Rauschenbusch noted early in his ministry, "the best way to get the self ready for Heaven . . . is to get this world ready for God."[8]

Yet what made Rauschenbusch's understanding of the kingdom ideal so compelling was that he tied it to his belief that God was actively involved in history, working through individuals and communities to bring about a vision of justice and social transformation. Rauschenbusch never questioned that dispensationalism was a form of Christianity. However, it was a truncated form of belief that needed to be countered by a more positive eschatology that affirmed that humans, working in partnership with God, could change the course of history.

Part of the importance of Rauschenbusch in American religious history is that he represented an era in which Protestants labeled by later generations as "liberal" and "conservative" were still to a degree in conversation with one another.[9] While theological debates and heresy trials were starting to tear churches apart, there was still a certain bond among Protestants of cultural, if not theological, unity. Yet as many representatives of what became known as the "Protestant establishment" proclaimed the importance of spreading the gospel throughout the world, and the necessity to build an institutional structure equal to the task, the power of dispensationalism was sweeping through American denominations, including many Baptist congregations, leading to an emerging network of dispensationalist-leaning institutions by the early twentieth century.[10]

Dispensationalism was not the only movement of evangelicalism to emerge in the late nineteenth century, nor was it the only incantation of what would today be referred to as theological conservatism. However, it represented one of the strongest grassroots movements to come out of the nineteenth century.[11] As an active participant in the affairs of what was occurring within northern Baptists (and among Protestants, in general), Rauschenbusch recognized the appeal of dispensationalism and was cognizant of the challenge that it presented to Protestants as a whole, and Baptists in particular. Rauschenbusch wrote only a few articles dealing directly with dispensationalism. However, his work repeatedly argued not only against an otherworldly apocalyptic interpretation of Christianity, but frequently tied his vision of Christian hope around his Baptist interpretation of church history. Although Rauschenbusch prided himself on his ecumenism, he never backed down from claiming his love for the Baptists and their central role in the future of American Christianity. Even though Rauschenbusch was not shy about affirming the uniqueness of Baptists, one of his worries about dispensationalism was that it fostered a spirit of religious sectarianism—the exact opposite of what was needed if the nation's Protestant churches were to be united in a common mission of kingdom building.

Rauschenbusch's response to popular dispensationalist preachers like I. M. Haldeman was more than an effort to defend what became known as "the social gospel." It is a prime example of what Grant Wacker has called "the dilemma of historical consciousness."[12] For Rauschenbusch (and other liberals), Christianity was not simply a religion shaped by historical forces (and more than a mere recitation of names and dates); it required persons to make critical judgments about how churches succeeded, or failed, in carrying out what Rauschenbusch believed were the prophetic biblical and theological mandates for the kingdom of God *in* history. In arguing against dispensationalism, and related forms of premillennialism, Rauschenbusch was arguing against sectarianism in his own denomination and among American churches. In part, to be a Baptist was to embrace a unique tradition (a tradition that Rauschenbusch believed was preferable to any other form of Protestantism), but it also meant being on a faith journey that pointed *beyond* the theological and ecclesiastical confines of that tradition. On one level, Rauschenbusch's life helped shape a distinctive legacy within twentieth-century Protestantism, but the extent to which his legacy has become central to Baptist identity in the twenty-first century remains open to debate.

Walter Rauschenbusch in Late Nineteenth-Century Baptist Context

A scholar might be disappointed if she chose Rauschenbusch as a primary subject to learn about the major doctrinal controversies influencing Baptists in the late nineteenth and early twentieth centuries. Rauschenbusch rarely made explicit references to Baptist doctrinal debates, such as Landmarkism, and at times his references to Baptists, when compared to other American churches, might give an impression that he devalued his Baptist heritage. By the same token, the majority of Rauschenbusch's writings dealt with theological themes that were hotly contested by Baptists (and most Protestants) at the end of the nineteenth century. These themes included questions of biblical inerrancy, the church's mission, and the relationship of apocalyptic thought to contemporary theology. One of the overarching themes throughout his writings is that Rauschenbusch identified himself as part of a wider legacy of Christian tradition, embracing his Baptist tradition but also transcending it. "I do not want to make Baptists shut themselves up in their little clam-shells and be indifferent to the ocean outside of them," he noted in 1906. "I am a Baptist, but I am more than a Baptist. . . . The old Adam is a strict denominationalist; the new Adam is just a Christian."[13] Rauschenbusch was not engaging in hyperbole. Rather, he reflected his desire that any Christian, no matter how fond he was of his own church or denomination, was indebted to a wider heritage that transcended his birth tradition.

Although scholars rightly emphasize the importance of Rauschenbusch's Hell's Kitchen ministry on his thought, the impact of his lifetime connection to Rochester Theological Seminary cannot be overstated. For all the ways that this school identified itself with a strong Baptist tradition of Reformed Calvinism, the school's ethos contributed to many of Rauschenbusch's theological views, including a degree of ecumenical openness to both historical and modern sources of Christian tradition.[14]

Rochester Theological Seminary (RTS) was founded in 1850 out of a desire to train an educated Baptist ministry. By the end of that decade, in addition to its main theological school, it had established an additional department to educate a growing German immigrant population in the United States. The seminary, located in the heart of western New York's famous "burned over" district, reflected a unique theological heritage, even in its early years. The seminary built a huge endowment (including significant financial support later in the nineteenth century from John D. Rockefeller) and developed a strong reputation for academic excellence and for training a range of important leaders in church, society, and academia. (Francis Bellamy, the author of the "Pledge of Allegiance," was an RTS alum, as was George Burnam Foster, one of the most significant religion scholars, who helped shape Chicago School liberalism at the University of Chicago.) Much credit for the seminary's success needs to be attributed to the leadership of Augustus Hopkins Strong. Born into a prominent Rochesterian family, Strong traced his conversion to a revival held in the city by Charles G. Finney. After graduating from Yale College and RTS, Strong served a series of Baptist pastorates (including serving as John Rockefeller's minister in Cleveland) before becoming president of RTS in 1872. For forty years until his retirement in 1912, Strong solidified the seminary's position as a school that both promoted a learned ministry and a theological worldview that, on the surface at least, affirmed a deeply rooted European and North American Baptist tradition of Reformed theology.

Although displaying a passion for the Reformation heritage, and affirming fidelity to certain historical confessions of faith, Strong was not a hard-line Calvinist (especially in comparison with his contemporary at Princeton Seminary, Benjamin Warfield). Nor, like other conservatives, was he interested in the "Bible Prophesy" movement of the late nineteenth century that gave rise to dispensationalism. His theology was consistent with many Protestant evangelicals who came of age in the antebellum era. They saw the church's mission in terms of preaching personal conversion, believing that one day the church would foster conditions for the return of Christ. Although millennial speculation was not at the heart of his theology, his view of the church was basically one of postmillennialism, the dominant strand of evangelicalism before the Civil War, stressing that as the church engaged in evangelism, social conditions would improve.[15]

Yet there was another side to Strong's theology that greatly benefited Rauschenbusch's development. Although he carried a public reputation for being theologically orthodox, his demeanor reflected an openness to new theological currents of the mid- and late nineteenth century. While Rauschenbusch was a student at RTS between 1883 and 1886, he was the beneficiary of some of these influences, reading a range of theological sources, including those in what was then known as "the new theology," or theological liberalism (one of Rauschenbusch's papers written for Strong was a critique of Horace Bushnell's doctrine of the atonement).[16] Years later, Strong was responsible for a thorough redefinition of the RTS faculty hiring a spate of prominent Baptist liberals including Rauschenbusch, Conrad Moehlman, and Cornelius Woelfkin. Famously, when the seminary's board of trustees called for the firing of Rauschenbusch after the publication of *Christianity and the Social Crisis* in 1907, Strong staved off his board by telling them in no uncertain terms that if Rauschenbusch were fired, he would resign as the seminary's president.

There were marked similarities and differences between Strong and his friend and colleague in the seminary's German department, Walter Rauschenbusch's father, August. A fifth-generation German-Lutheran clergyman, August emigrated to the United States in the 1840s, and, finding within Baptist communions what he believed to be the true essence of the primitive church, underwent baptism by immersion in 1850. After a stint with the American Tract Society and a pastorate on the Missouri frontier, August became the head of RTS's German department in 1858, three years before Walter's birth in 1861.[17]

Walter Rauschenbusch's relationship with his father was one of both admiration and dread. While admiring his father's pietism and his leadership resolve (which helped secure the financial position of the German department in the 1860s and 1870s), there was a distance between the two that was only partially a product of their growing theological differences. Even though August did not display the same irenic qualities as Strong toward theological liberalism, many of Walter's later interests in history, including his father's interest in Anabaptism, helped shape Rauschenbusch's vision for his own ministry. He shared his father's intense pietism and saw personal pietism as a central component to Baptist identity. "Experimental religion is necessarily free and voluntary," Rauschenbusch noted in 1905. "Men can compel attendance at the mass. They can compel subscription to a creed. They can not compel an inner experience. It has to be free and spontaneous."[18]

Even during his New York City ministry in the 1880s and 1890s, Rauschenbusch passed on several offers from Strong to join the RTS faculty (including one to replace his father as head of the German department). It was only after Rauschenbusch became fully aware of the limitations of his hearing loss (a condition that plagued him from his mid-twenties until the end of his life) that he finally became open to the possibility of a move to Rochester. The circumstances of his teaching career, as much accidental as planned, had a tremendous impact on Rauschenbusch's life and on the future of what became known as the social gospel.

Rauschenbusch as Baptist Historian

Despite the fact that Rauschenbusch identified strongly with the field of church history, he would have hesitated to call himself a "professional" historian. Unlike several of his Baptist colleagues associated with the growth of the University of Chicago, Rauschenbusch's passion for church history did not come through advanced graduate study, but was formed amid the chaotic pace of his ministry in Hell's Kitchen, New York, in the 1880s and 1890s. Even after Rauschenbusch returned to Rochester in 1897 to join the faculty of his alma mater, his teaching was initially confined to the school's German department, where he taught German immigrant students the rudiments of theological study as well as American history and civics that would aid these pastors in their acculturation to the United States. His appointment in 1902 to the English faculty as a professor of church history was made possible only after a colleague's death. Even after this appointment, however, he frequently complained to his colleagues that he considered himself a "pedagogic hack" in the classroom, worrying that he lacked sophistication as a teacher and scholar.[19] Rauschenbusch's concern about his own fitness as a historian is borne out by the fact that he never published any original historical scholarship.

Yet one of the reasons why Rauschenbusch would emerge as such a brilliant theological apologist for the social gospel was that he approached history, like theology, from a practical perspective. As Henry Bowden observed, "Rauschenbusch's importance as a church historian lies in his theological and social perspective rather than his brilliance as an independent researcher."[20] Although Rauschenbusch often questioned his scholarly competency, he was well versed on contemporary historical scholarship.[21] Even though books like *Christianity and the Social Crisis* were identified later on as works of theology, their method was decidedly historical, reflecting many themes that he had honed through his church history lectures in Rochester. Rauschenbusch took his audience through a view of history that discussed how the early church lost focus on Jesus's mission as the arbiter of the kingdom, replacing it with a priestly form of institutionalized faith represented by medieval Catholicism. Even though he looked with favor to developments of the sixteenth-century Reformation, he placed great emphasis on the modern era as a time when Christianity was "rediscovering" aspects of early Christianity's ethos on Jesus's radical teachings on the kingdom of God.

Rauschenbusch frequently lamented what he saw as a popular indifference to the discipline of history, and he often noted that this was a major problem within his own denomination. "Americans are less historical in their thinking than older nations," he remarked. "Baptists also have taken less interest in history than older bodies. Our thought would be enriched, and we should understand our own position and mission better if we studied history more."[22] As he articulated his vision for the contemporary church, he never strayed far from his Baptist identity.

In 1905 and 1906, Rauschenbusch published a series of articles under the heading, "Why I am a Baptist." These articles do more than reflect on his Baptist beliefs; they flesh out many of the salient points on Rauschenbusch's view of church history. Rauschenbusch defined his fidelity to Baptist beliefs around four principles (analogous to the four freedoms historically practiced by Baptists): experiential religion, the absence of formal ecclesiastical creeds, the democratic conception of the church, and the centrality of scripture. For Rauschenbusch, the Baptists represented the prime movers of religious liberty in America, a tradition that sought to bring the best aspects of biblical Christianity to the forefront of its churches. What made Baptists unique was not fidelity to certain doctrines, but religious experience. "I am a Baptist, then, because in our church life we have a minimum of emphasis on ritual and creed, and a maximum of emphasis on spiritual experience, and the more I study the history of religion, the more I see how great and fruitful such a position is."[23] Rauschenbusch's stress on personal experience was not antinomian, nor was it necessarily "liberal," in the sense that experience was merely subjective. Rather it was the means by which Baptists supported religious liberty and voluntarily affirmed faith in Jesus Christ, expressed through believer's baptism. He asserted that "baptism of believers is an outward act plus an inward experience. Infant Baptism, we believe, is an outward act *minus* any inward experience, and we will have none of it."[24]

Yet Rauschenbusch's interest in religious liberty went beyond a fidelity to believer's baptism. The Baptist genius was that it was formulated around personal and communal liberty that captured both the ethos of the New Testament *and* the spirit of a modern democratic world. As he reflected, "It takes a trained mind to understand the fine distinctions of the creeds. It takes a good deal of historical information merely to understand the ritual and symbols of some of the old churches. . . . The intellect is aristocratic; human love and religious faith are both democratic."[25] Part of the tension that one finds in Rauschenbusch's thought is for all the stress that he placed on the knowledge gained through the study of church history, he returned to a religious populism that saw personal experience as the chief criterion for church membership.

Rauschenbusch has been criticized at points for lacking a clearly developed ecclesiology, and in some way, these articles on Baptist identity support those assertions. Like much of his work, they castigate church traditions that stressed more formal liturgical traditions and were nondemocratic in fostering religious liberty. The Roman Catholic Church and the Anglo-Catholic wing of the Episcopal Church came in for especially rough treatment from Rauschenbusch for the ways they fostered a "priestly class" and took away power from the people in the congregation. Although it is true that at times Rauschenbusch's work displayed a harsh attitude toward more creedal and liturgical traditions, in part this emanated from a concern that Baptists not follow the example of these traditions—confining theological and ecclesiastical truths to one exclusive path. He warned his readers about the dangers to Baptists of a sectarian faith through the following story: "A near-sighted child was taken to the Zoo and stood in front of the lion's cage. The lion's tail was hanging down through the bars. 'But I thought the lion was different,' said the child, 'it looks like a yellow rope.' So there are Baptists who have hitherto discovered only the tail-end of our Baptist ideals and convictions, and it is no wonder that they turn out as narrow as the tail they devoutly believe in."[26]

Baptists were vital to the future of Christendom not simply because they practiced a particular form of baptism or adhered to certain confessions of faith. They were important in that the tradition pointed the way to a church free of personal and communal tyranny, standing for the liberty of every Christian—principles that Rauschenbusch saw as essential toward his theology of the kingdom.

Rauschenbusch displayed his father's fascination with the history of European Anabaptism, seeing the tradition's fidelity to believer's baptism and their battles against government coercion as a model for the contemporary church. Yet his theology of the church had far more in common with the heritage of Calvinism than with any of the representatives of sixteenth-century Anabaptism. As Donovan Smucker notes, Rauschenbusch was well aware of the historical argument of whether Baptists and Anabaptists were historical kin, and, much as Winthrop Hudson argued in the 1950s, he reflected a view that saw the two traditions as separate.[27]

Like Hudson, Rauschenbusch identified the first Baptists in America as radical Puritans. For Rauschenbusch, the cherished American ideal of the separation of church and state was not for the purposes of isolating the church from society. "Some Baptists seem to think that this separation is based on the idea that the spiritual life has nothing to do with the secular life," he asserted. "I utterly deny that assertion and think it a calamitous heresy."[28] Far from being sectarian, the greatness of the Baptist heritage was how it translated into the social fabric of America. It was this reality that did not make Baptists necessarily superior to other American churches, but showed how Baptists ideals of religious freedom and religious democracy (epitomized for Rauschenbusch by Roger Williams) became part of the larger fabric of American Christianity. Rauschenbusch certainly was laudatory toward the history of Anabaptists; however, he admired Anabaptists for their example of religious liberty, *not* their sectarianism.

Rauschenbusch saw church history as an indispensable tool that enabled one to see how churches were working toward the practical attainment of the kingdom of God. Yet as Henry Bowden notes, Rauschenbusch took a chastened view toward the church, seeing church history as a chronicle of the church's successes *and* failures.[29] While church history revealed the worst aspects of human nature, it also reflected the best aspects of human moral achievement. Rauschenbusch observed that history "records . . . the moral life of the race; but morals depend on religion. Religion is the axis of history."[30] Rauschenbusch's historiography owes much to historians and theologians such as Ritschl and Harnack, especially as he sought evidence in history of the church's efforts to realize the theological truths of the kingdom ideal. However, he spent a considerable amount of time wrestling with what he saw as the ambiguities of church history, especially in terms of examining the successes and failures within the nascent field of American church history. In this regard, Rauschenbusch saw the democratic ethos of his Baptist identity as a means to lead American churches to a greater union, not so much expressed by formal ecclesiastical merger, but through concerted ethical action.

There is no doubt that Rauschenbusch carried forth a largely Reformed Protestant perspective of the church, predicated on a belief that the church's influence over time would "transform" society.[31] His thought contained strong elements of Christian perfectionism (a tradition with strong roots in a number of nineteenth-century evangelical movements, including many Baptist movements). This theme of perfectionism was important to Rauschenbusch not simply as a means to justify ethical action, but also in terms of how it reminded Christians of God's actions in history. For Rauschenbusch, this spirit of Christian activism did not bring "only sweet peace," but served as "the leaven of social unrest."[32] Rauschenbusch's stress on Christian perfection at points came precariously close to a "work's righteous" theology. "A life of service is a holy duty," he wrote in 1898. "So much to be done, and as yet so little accomplished. I want to work, to serve in the redemption of the world from wrong, to help my Master save humanity."[33] Yet for all the ways that Rauschenbusch saw the kingdom of God as a means to apply the ethics of Jesus to the social problems of the late nineteenth and early twentieth centuries, systemic change in America would not occur without lives sanctified by God's love. He wrote: "I fear lest my life pass away and I have not slaked my thirst for the service of God. This life can be so full, so noble, so blessed to us, so useful to others. And so often it is empty, vapid, trivial, discontented, useless. Which is the real privilege, to serve or to idle? Which is the real burden, to live for self or to live for the Kingdom of God?"[34] It was not that the Baptists had a monopoly on Christian virtue or holy living (and the way that he pulled from numerous Protestant and Catholic sources in this regard is a reflection of this fact). Yet the theological and historical genetic code of Baptists fit well into what Rauschenbusch identified as the twofold mission of Christianity's mission. "It is to create and foster the religious life in the individual; it is to build up the kingdom of God in all humanity."[35]

Ironically, for all the ways that Rauschenbusch prided Baptists for their historical witness—from standing up to state tyranny to affirming religious liberty to witnessing (in some cases) against societal evils such as slavery—his assessment of the early twentieth-century American church held out the highest praise for two non-Baptist denominations: the Episcopal Church and the Methodist Church. Despite the fact that both churches centralized authority around bishops (and Rauschenbusch's disdain for the Anglo-Catholic wing of the Episcopal Church), he conceded that these bodies were taking a leading role in the social awakening of the early twentieth century. Although the Episcopal Church took little active engagement in social witness for much of the nineteenth century, it played a major role in the modern social awakening of the late nineteenth and early twentieth centuries. Rauschenbusch was especially laudatory toward the Methodists not just because of that tradition's commitment to social justice (noting that body's role in crafting the social creed of the churches, adopted by the Federal Council of Churches at its founding in 1908), but ironically he conceded the effectiveness of their polity to the American context. As he noted in 1912, "They combine the democratic spirit of the Congregationalist group with a much stiffer and more centralized organization."[36]

However, what was key for Rauschenbusch was not simply the question that these non-Baptist churches were succeeding. It was his affirmation that these churches were displaying the sentiment of a democratized Christianity that he perceived was sweeping American Protestantism. Rauschenbusch was aware that America contained a religious vibrancy missing from many European nations. Yet while later historians of American religion saw religious diversity in the form of sectarian growth, Rauschenbusch viewed democratized religion as a force working *against* sectarian sentiment (in some way, anticipating an argument that would be used by many American church historians by the mid-twentieth century).[37] For Rauschenbusch, a democratized church was not simply predicated on a particular form of church government (even though he rather admired the efficiency of the Methodist itinerant system, in which bishops controlled clergy deployment). It was a reflection of how churches moved away from otherworldly speculation to embrace a wider theological vision of Christianity's role in creating conditions of social equality in America. The fact that Rauschenbusch could take such a praiseworthy stance toward the Episcopal and Methodist traditions was not because he preferred their polity, but because they each had seized on the substance of Jesus's teachings on the kingdom and revealed through their actions, the ethos of a democratized faith. One of his repeated warnings was that when a church enshrined a particular form of polity, it forgot that any form of church government was only useful when it served churches as a means to a greater end. As Rauschenbusch noted to a Baptist gathering in the early 1900s, "The fact is, I think, that the conception of a divinely revealed church polity and the emphasis on it, are both the product of a debased Christian life; of an age when the spirit of Christ was being choked under ecclesiastical forms; when evangelical faith was being petrified into theological dogmatism; when the primitive equality of Christians was changed into a clerical despotism; and when the creative freedom of the Spirit gave way to legalism and servile reverence for precedent. We Baptists have owed allegiance to spiritual liberty. We should scrutinize closely an hypothesis which is the product of legalism and ecclesiasticism."[38]

Part of why Rauschenbusch's legacy has been so strong is that he balanced an imperative for social justice with a deep-seated spiritual discernment. Yet he displayed an impatience with many forms of Christianity that focused too much on asceticism (such as forms of mysticism), and that put ecclesiastical questions related to church government, worship, and sacraments in front of ethical mandates. His final book, *A Theology for the Social Gospel,* has rightly been identified as a cornerstone in the development of American liberal theology. Yet it says practically nothing about questions of "proper" ecclesiastical life.[39] As Rauschenbusch's articles on Baptist identity indicate, he believed that questions of ethics trumped questions of ecclesiology. To be a Baptist was partly to be open to the range of social forces that moved churches to embrace this common goal of Christian unity, expressed through concerted social action.

Part of what characterized the social gospel was the way that its proponents viewed the relationship between Christian theology and social reform in a systemic fashion. This did not mean, however, the abandonment of an individual's personal faith. Yet Rauschenbusch repeatedly argued that the trouble with a Christianity based only on individual salvation was not only its limited view of salvation, but that it demonstrated the worst aspects of Christianity historically, mainly, its reliance on asceticism, otherworldliness, and apocalyptic worldviews.

In many respects, Rauschenbusch shared with dispensationalists an eschatological vision that the kingdom of God would not occur without tremendous suffering and sacrifice of the faithful. Yet he also believed that dispensationalism embodied the worst characteristics of theological and ecclesiastical sectarianism that needed to be eradicated if Baptists, and other Christians, were to achieve their goal of a democratized church.

Rauschenbusch against the Rapture

Part of what characterized Rauschenbusch's era in American Protestantism was that he came of age at a time when many figures later identified by historians as "conservative" and "liberal" could still sit at a shared table of fellowship. As a young minister in the 1880s, Rauschenbusch wrote enthusiastically about his experiences attending Dwight Moody's summer conference at Northfield, Massachusetts, and unlike later twentieth-century liberals, Rauschenbusch never shied away from identifying himself as an

evangelical. Yet Rauschenbusch was clearly alarmed by the growing popularity of premillennialist thought within northern Baptist circles, and his
critique of these movements became an important undercurrent in his
writing.

Along with many of the original social gospelers such as Josiah Strong
and Washington Gladden (as well as conservatives like Augustus Strong),
Rauschenbusch's perspective on millennialism had much in common with
an earlier evangelical doctrine of postmillennialism. Part of the significance of Rauschenbusch's theology was the emphasis that he placed on
systemic social analysis and social change, stressing that salvation was not
merely about individual conversation, but on altering the collective behavior of society. By the same token, aspects of his thought continue to
echo themes of an earlier nineteenth-century evangelicalism that believed
that the more people who embraced Christianity, the better the world
would become. However, what characterized Rauschenbusch's view of social progress was not a sense of gradualism, but that progress emerged
only as Christians engaged in concerted work of kingdom building. What
Rauschenbusch garnered from church history was not so much a theology
that the church would realize the kingdom through a smooth linear pro-
gression; church history showed him that successes came at a cost, emerging out of moments of victory and defeat (as the church's struggle over
slavery revealed). At its core, what made dispensationalism aberrant for
Rauschenbusch was not just that its interpretation was wrong, or too focused on the individual, but that it lacked any grounding in historical
analysis.

This theme emerged in a series of articles by Rauschenbusch entitled,
"Our Attitude toward Millenarianism" published in *The Examiner,* a prominent northern Baptist periodical, in 1896. Although these articles represent one of Rauschenbusch's few direct repudiations of dispensationalism,
these essays reflect themes that he would return to in his later writings.

What is interesting about these articles was that he did not accuse dispensationalists of not being Christian; rather, he believed they displayed
an undeveloped form of Christianity that was formed by a narrow view
of eschatology. "They try to round this Cape Horn of theology with all
sails set, but little of the ballast of historical knowledge in the hold," he asserted.[40] Rauschenbusch was clearly well versed in the fine points of dispensationalist theology, including its views on the rapture, the tribulation,
and the movement's tendency to give preferential treatment to the biblical
books of Daniel and Revelation. While Rauschenbusch disdained dispen-

sationalists for what he considered their selective proof-texting, this was not the primary substance of his critique, nor was he completely bothered by dispensationalism's stress on an apocalyptic theology. Rather, it was dispensationalism's ahistorical interpretation of these apocalyptic themes in scripture. As he said it, "The passages of Scripture are to them not portions of a living organization of thought, belonging to one man of a certain age and a certain nation, to be handled reverently and to be understood only in connection with the other thoughts of that man and his time. They are rather adamantine pieces of dead matter, bits of glass distributed in boxes, which are to be arranged in a mosaic by the cunning workman in prophecies who has found the key, as if it was all a gigantic puzzle devised by the Almighty."[41]

Although Rauschenbusch always downplayed the apocalyptic themes in the New Testament, he acknowledged that apocalyptic theology was useful when it led to an awareness of social injustice, leading toward a desire to work for justice, as opposed to an otherworldly faith. On one hand, an abandonment of apocalyptic thought enslaved Christianity historically to a priestly faith (embodied by the medieval Catholic Church). Yet dispensationalism went too far in the other direction, turning Christianity into a pessimistic otherworldly faith that placed the message of Jesus outside the realms of this life. By 1912, as the impetus of the social gospel appeared to be winning the day in most American Protestant traditions, Rauschenbusch recognized that dispensationalism's appeal remained strong. For all of his hopefulness by 1912 that American churches were embracing the social hope of the kingdom of God in their ministries, he appealed to dispensationalists to forsake the narrowness of their vision. Thus, "the apocalyptic hope has always contained ingredients of religious force and value, but its trail through history is strange and troubled reading. It has been of absorbing fascination to some Christian minds, but it has led them into labyrinths from which some never emerged. It has been the inspiration of earnest Christian men in some lines of Christian activity, but it has effectively blocked their minds with strange prejudices against other important lines of work."[42] Like many late nineteenth-century liberals, Rauschenbusch's reading of the Bible centered upon his interpretation of the historical Jesus. To rediscover Jesus's mission in its first-century context was to recover what he saw as the "social hope" in Christianity, predicated on the ways in which the significance of Jesus's ministry could be seen through the lens of the modern era.

Rauschenbusch came down strongly on the side of a modernist worldview, stressing the importance of historical and social scientific tools toward analyzing the scriptures. At points, he came precariously close to suggesting that if conservatives were to embrace these tools, then their minds would be opened to the truth of Christianity. Yet, the struggle against dispensationalism was not just seen by Rauschenbusch as a social scientific problem but a theological one. Rauschenbusch affirmed that many dispensationalists were concerned about many of the same things as he was, mainly, justice for the poor, an alleviation of human suffering, and an ultimate eschatological vision of justice and peace. Yet he emphatically rejected what he saw as dispensationalism's theology of pessimism that from his perspective encouraged personal selfishness, at the expense of sacrificial Christian love. The conclusion to his 1896 article series directly makes that point: "Faith in salvation by catastrophe cuts the nerve of action, but only in the unselfish pursuits of life. . . . I have yet to see proof that those who believe in the imminence of Christ's coming are indifferent to the security of real estate titles, the length of leases, the education of their children, and other things that involve a long look ahead. . . . The question is, which will do more to make our lives spiritual and to release us from the tyranny of the world, the thought that we may at any moment enter into the presence of the Lord, or the thought that every moment we are in the presence of the Lord?"[43]

Rauschenbusch and other social gospelers came in for especially rough treatment at the hands of later twentieth-century theologians for being too progressive in their orientation toward social progress. Yet this accusation against Rauschenbusch is fundamentally unfair and misreads how he viewed history. For Rauschenbusch, history was not simply a quest for church unity, nor a quest of churches to achieve something called the kingdom of God. It was a chronicle of the churches' successes and failures in that quest. In 1912, Rauschenbusch remarked that "history is the sacred workshop of God."[44] He was not simply commenting on the fact that God acted through individuals in history, but that the affairs of humans were tied together around a larger vision of eschatology that kept Christians hopeful, even amid times of failure. What made his social gospel "progressive" was that it built on the best attributes of Christianity historically. "It is true that the social enthusiasm is an unsettling force which may unbalance for a time, break old religious habits and connections, and establish new contacts that are a permanent danger to personal religion. But the way to meet this danger is not to fence out the new social spirit, but to let it fuse with the old religious faith and create a new total that will be completer and more Christian than the old religious individualism at its best."[45]

Needless to say, dispensationalist leaders remained unconvinced. Rauschenbusch was well acquainted with northern Baptist leaders like I. M. Haldeman and William Bell Riley. He had engaged in some theological sparing with both men throughout his ministry, and the publication of *Christianity and the Social Crisis* in 1907 gave Haldeman an opportunity to fight back. Haldeman's response to Rauschenbusch's theology was far more caustic than Rauschenbusch was to dispensationalists like Haldeman. On one hand, Haldeman did point out a central weakness of the social gospel that later generations of liberals and neo-orthodox theologians recognized, mainly, Rauschenbusch's tendency to gloss over Pauline sources, which were critical to earlier Reformation movements. Yet Haldeman echoed themes that would characterize dispensationalist arguments against liberalism to this day, mainly, liberalism's denial of biblical inspiration, its over emphasis on human reason, and, in particular, its positive view of God's plans for human history that Haldeman believed devalued the claims of scripture. Although Haldeman did concede that Rauschenbusch's concern for the poor was laudable, he considered Rauschenbusch's work dangerous to the church's mission. "Its subtle denial of inspiration, its discount of New Testament integrity, and the unmiraculous Christ in whose name it comes, make it a dangerous bit of reading to unformed faith, and to minds swayed by sentiment rather than a 'thus saith the Lord.'"[46]

Rauschenbusch's personal correspondence toward dispensationalist ministers, like Haldeman and William Bell Riley, mostly displayed an irenic posture. However, his later writings displayed less tolerance toward those who carried an apocalyptic outlook. Perhaps he grew tired of the personal attacks. Yet, by the publication of his last major work, *A Theology for the Social Gospel,* there was even less tolerance for any sort of apocalyptic theology in the church. Even as other liberals began to revisit earlier assertions concerning the apocalyptic nature of Jesus's teachings, Rauschenbusch continued to insist that Jesus's teachings were rightfully interpreted through a movement beyond personal religion. As he noted in *A Theology for the Social Gospel,* "Jesus was neither ascetic nor other-worldly. . . . He believed in a life after death, but it was not the dominant element in his teaching, nor the constraining force in his religious life."[47]

However, by the time that he wrote these words in 1917, Rauschenbusch's focus had moved far away from the Baptist context that formed the basis for his series of articles on millennialism in 1896. His lifetime mirrored what was to be institutionalized within American Protestantism in the 1920s and 1930s, as increasingly denominations split both theologically and organizationally. The sad irony is that Rauschenbusch, an individual who truly sought to embody a "big tent" theology akin to individuals like Dwight Moody, would find himself an outcast, not only among conservatives but also, in many ways, among liberals.

Conclusion: Where Have You Gone, Walter Rauschenbusch?

H. Richard Niebuhr noted in his classic work, *The Kingdom of God in America*, that Walter Rauschenbusch was an important example of a mediating tendency within some traditions of theological liberalism that balanced a belief in sin with an ability to overcome sin. Niebuhr noted that Rauschenbusch stressed a faith whereby "the reign of Christ required conversion and the coming kingdom was crisis, judgment as well as promise. Though his theory of the relation of God and man often seemed liberal he continued to speak the language of the prophets and St. Paul."[48] Even though Niebuhr's characterization is accurate for many exponents of theological liberalism, it is no accident that many diverse Christian communities look with renewed interest today to Rauschenbusch. Over the last several years, Rauschenbusch's work has been analyzed from just about every angle—his historical place in American Christianity, his view of "social salvation," and even from the perspective of contemporary liberation theology. By the same token, Baptist communities since Rauschenbusch's death have struggled to define his place within their heritage. Depending on where one sits today, Rauschenbusch is either responsible for saving Christianity from otherworldly futility or tampering with the time-honored traditions of the past. Both perspectives are extreme views and do not do justice to Rauschenbusch's theological nuances.

The common perspective on Rauschenbusch among many liberal Protestants (including Baptists) is that he stood as a great social prophet that helped save Christianity from otherworldly simplicity. Nobody has given a more articulate defense of this posture than the prominent historian (and Baptist) Winthrop Hudson in his important work, *The Great Tradition of the American Churches*. Hudson saw Rauschenbusch's intellectual impact on American Protestantism not simply as a proponent of the social gospel, but as the embodiment of a faith that was attentive to the realities of modern culture while staying grounded in the historic mission of Protestantism as an evangelical movement. "To the end of his life, he was an evangelical in an era when evangelicalism as a dynamic movement had quite disappeared."[49] Even though Hudson grasped the essence of how Rauschenbusch viewed his mission, he failed to see that Rauschenbusch was not the only evangelical Protestant in the early twentieth century calling for the renewal of the church. In the formative years of his career, Rauschenbusch was well aware of the emergent theological realities that were competing for the hearts and minds of American Protestants, and a significant part of his ministry was to present a compelling alternative to these movements.

Rauschenbusch's desire to halt the spread of dispensationalism, and his confident posture toward the end of his life that the movement would disappear, has proved shortsighted. Yet this reality is not the remarkable part of this story. What is remarkable is that at the time that Winthrop Hudson wrote about Rauschenbusch's historical contribution to American Protestantism in the penultimate chapter of his book, Rauschenbusch's impact on Protestants, including among his beloved Baptists, was at its nadir.

In 1942, Dores Sharpe, a prominent denominational leader in the Northern Baptist Convention, published the first full-length biography on Walter Rauschenbusch. Even though the book is chock-full of anecdotal accounts of Rauschenbusch's life (many derived from Sharpe's own first-person accounts when he served as Rauschenbusch's secretary while a student at Rochester Theological Seminary), the book reads more like a nostalgic memoir than a critical biography.[50] Sharpe was an unequivocal defender of Rauschenbusch's legacy, prone at points to overstate his mentor's impact. Yet he understood that Rauschenbusch was an evangelist who saw part of his mission to rouse his beloved Baptists to be the leaven that would lead to a more vibrant form of American Christianity. As Sharpe summarized, "he was a piece of ecclesiastic nebulae thrown off by the Baptist denomination as it moved through time in its orbit of complacency. He woke it up."[51]

Yet by the time that Sharpe's biography appeared, Baptists (and Protestants in general) had already started to lose sight of Rauschenbusch's place in their histories. In part, this ambivalence can be explained by the fact that many Baptists, consistent with most mainline Protestants, were caught up in debates over neo-orthodoxy, associated with the popularity of Reinhold and H. Richard Niebuhr. Yet it is also a reflection of the fact that dispensationalism was a powerful grassroots feature of Baptist life, even as many of its critics underplayed its role.

From the standpoint of the intellectual history of American religion, it is appealing to see Walter Rauschenbusch's legacy, as Winthrop Hudson did, as part of the "great tradition of the American churches." Yet there were clear signs during Rauschenbusch's lifetime that this tradition was being challenged by those like I. M. Haldeman who saw religious authority not through the "modern" creation of church history, but through the time-tested Reformation view of the centrality of the Bible. In response to another Baptist social gospeler, Shailer Mathews, Haldeman voiced a sentiment that has undergirded many dispensationalists' (and other conservatives') views of liberalism since the late nineteenth century. One cannot help but notice the contrast between Haldeman's vision of Baptist theology with that of Walter Rauschenbusch's.

As I see the so-called Christian nations becoming as Scripture long ago foretold, "wild beast" nations, and whole races slipping down into the depths of intellectual ferocity; as I see the genius of man engaged, not in construction, but destruction until his figure looms forth the incarnation of ruthless havic; . . . as I see the very things taking place which the New Testament in unfeigned and unfigured speech forewarned, and know by reason of its hitherto unfailing forecast what is yet to come, I am hoping and intensely praying for the return of the Lord in my day and generation to put an end to this suicide of nations, this butchery and blasting, solace the hearts that are breaking, hush the lamentation, wipe away the tears of wives, of mothers and orphans, illumine with the sunlight of His presence the threshold of blackened homes, relight and warm with His love the frozen hearthstones and bring in the Kingdom of the everlasting peace.[52]

Despite the fact that Rauschenbusch sought at points to strike an irenic tone toward dispensationalism, his observation about Haldeman in 1912 that opened this chapter was closer to the mark. Protestantism was increasingly becoming a choice between at least two distinctive genres of Christianity. Although the Northern Baptist Convention at least initially avoided some of the theological rupturing that occurred in other Protestant denominations during the 1920s,[53] Baptists today are very much a house divided, in ways that reflect the differences articulated by Rauschenbusch and Haldeman a hundred years ago.

Today, dispensationalism, a movement that the social gospel sought to eradicate, is alive and well, and worthy of as much serious historical scrutiny, as historians have given to the heirs of the social gospel. Although most twentieth-century American religious historians tended to see dispensationalism, and other apocalyptic movements, as aberrant, one needs to acknowledge that the otherworldly beliefs of these movements have been far more successful on a grassroots level than Rauschenbusch's social gospel. This discussion goes beyond common historical labels such as fundamentalist and modernist, but reflects the truth of more recent data on American religion that suggest that belief in divine judgment and an apocalyptic end to history lay just beneath the surface of many contemporary Americans.[54]

Baptist history represents an especially compelling illustration of this trend, and whereas one trajectory of Baptist history moves neatly from Walter Rauschenbusch to Harry Emerson Fosdick to Walter's own great-grandson, Paul Raushenbush, another track moves from I. M. Haldeman to Jerry Falwell to John Hagee. Both heritages are important to Baptists; however, for more liberal and progressive Baptists, it is difficult to admit that the Rauschenbusch legacy, at least on a popular level, was not as prominent as they would like to believe.

Ironically, however, some conservative Baptists (and other conservative Protestants), heirs to the very tradition championed by I. M. Haldeman, have found it difficult to dismiss Rauschenbusch as an annoying obstacle to their theological worldview. In recent years, a wide cross section of conservative evangelical groups have started to acknowledge that there is more to Rauschenbusch than what Haldeman was able to see a hundred years ago. Although some evangelicals acknowledge their difficulty with aspects of Rauschenbusch's theology, they have also started to develop an appreciation for many of the themes behind his social gospel. In a hundredth-anniversary edition of *Christianity and the Social Crisis,* Tony Campolo noted that for many evangelicals, "Rauschenbusch offers us a clear and pronounced alternative to any attempt to place the kingdom of God solely in another world after this life is over. . . . It has taken Evangelicals like me far too long to come around to embracing Rauschenbusch's kind of holistic gospel that not only promises eternal life to individuals but also offers hope for dramatic positive changes in our present social order."[55] Campolo's assertion does not signal that some of the age-old divisions over millennialism and biblical inerrancy that have divided liberals and conservatives will be ending anytime soon. But it might very well reflect that elements of the evangelical community are beginning to see part of their own tradition in the life of Walter Rauschenbusch.

Yet many liberals are equally guilty of a false reading of Rauschenbusch's legacy. Even though it may be theologically appropriate to connect Rauschenbusch's theological ideals to more contemporary incantations of theology, especially liberation movements, such an interpretation in its own way is ahistorical and denies the fact that Rauschenbusch was a historical figure who had, from the perspective of our time, feet of clay. Some liberals bemoan his Victorianism, decry his conservative views toward women, or his lack of engagement with American racism, and decide that he has nothing of value to contribute to the contemporary church. This selective historical proof-texting serves no useful purpose, other than to satisfy one's desire to believe that somehow our knowledge and wisdom of the present exceeds the achievements of the past.

There is a sad irony that Walter Rauschenbusch is in many ways a prophet without honor within his own denominational family. As a wide range of Baptist communities seek to define themselves theologically, and while debates rage about the nature of the historical Baptist freedoms, the essence of a true church, and the historical relationship between Baptists and Anabaptists, Rauschenbusch's name does not leap out as someone who models how best to be a Baptist. Perhaps this is consistent in some way with Rauschenbusch's own desire that the beauty of the Baptist heritage is that it leads beyond itself toward a greater awareness of the whole of Christian tradition. But it does raise a legitimate question of not only what Rauschenbusch can say to Baptists today, but why it is important to understand that Rauschenbusch's social gospel would not have emerged had he not been a Baptist.[56] This question is critical not simply for Baptists interested in assessing Rauschenbusch's place in their stories, but also for anyone interested in pondering how an individual who labored most of his life in relative obscurity came to achieve an iconic status in American Christianity.

Notes

1. *Dispensationalism* refers to a theological movement stating that scripture should be read as a series of specific epochs, or dispensations, that point believers to the conclusion that the world is on the verge of God's apocalyptic actions to end human history and to inaugurate God's reign on earth. Associated largely with the teachings of John Nelson Darby in Ireland, dispensationalism emerged as a powerful theological force in American Protestantism by the 1870s and 1880s, and its influence as a popular movement in evangelical theology remains strong to this day.

Even though many different traditions of dispensationalist theology have emerged since the time of Darby, these theologies stress at least three central points: (1) a literalistic interpretation of the Bible, with particular emphasis on the apocalyptic themes associated with the books of Daniel and Revelation; (2) a belief in a final dramatic (and often violent) judgment of God on human history, and (3) a premillennial theology. As opposed to the evangelical heritage of postmillennialism that stressed that Christians work for the improvement of social conditions before the Second Coming of Christ, premillennialism tends to view history as part of the larger tragedy of human sinfulness that could only be rectified by the saving grace of God through Jesus Christ. For most dispensationalists, these beliefs centered on faith in "the rapture," a reference to I Thessalonians 4:17 that states that true believers would suddenly disappear from the earth, setting the stage for a series of confrontations between God and the Antichrist (often referred to by dispensationalists as "the tribulation"), Christ's Second Coming, a thousand years of peace (Rev. 20), and the final defeat of Satan. For further discussion, see Timothy P. Weber, *Living in the Shadow of the Second Coming: American Premillennialism, 1875–1925* (New York: Oxford University Press, 1979); and Paul Boyer, *When Time Shall Be No More: Prophesy Belief in Modern American Culture* (Cambridge, MA: Belknap Press, 1992).

2. I. M. Haldeman, *Prof. Rauschenbusch's "Christianity and the Social Crisis"* (New York: Charles C. Cook, n.d.), 34.

3. Walter Rauschenbusch, *Christianizing the Social Order* (New York: Macmillan Company, 1912), 56n1.

4. For a summation of the scholarship related to these two historiographical trends, see Ralph E. Luker, "Interpreting the Social Gospel: Reflections on Two Generations of Historiography," in *Perspectives on the Social Gospel*, ed. Christopher H. Evans (Lewiston, NY: Edwin Mellen Press, 1999), 1–13. On the social gospel and race, see Ralph E. Luker, *The Social Gospel in Black and White* (Chapel Hill: University of North Carolina Press, 1991); and on gender issues, see Carolyn DeSwarte Gifford and Wendy J. Deichman Edwards, eds., *Gender and the Social Gospel* (Urbana: University of Illinois Press, 2003).

5. See, for example, William McGuire King, "'History as Revelation' in the Theology of the Social Gospel," in *Harvard Theological Review* 76, no. 1 (1983):109–29, and King, "An Enthusiasm for Humanity: The Social Emphasis in Religion and Its Accommodation in Protestant Theology," in *Religion and Twentieth Century American Intellectual Life*, ed. Michael J. Lacey (Cambridge: Cambridge University Press, 1989); Gary Dorrien, *Soul in So-*

ciety: The Making and Renewal of Social Christianity (Minneapolis: Fortress Press, 1995); and Dorrien, *The Making of American Liberal Theology: Idealism, Realism, & Modernity, 1900–1950* (Louisville, KY: Westminster John Knox Press, 2003).

6. Since the early 1920s, Rauschenbusch has been the subject of hundreds of articles and scores of monographs. For a good primer on his life, as well as access to bibliographies on Rauschenbusch's thought, see Paul Minus, *Walter Rauschenbusch, American Reformer* (New York: Macmillan, 1988); and Christopher H. Evans, *The Kingdom Is Always but Coming: a Life of Walter Rauschenbusch* (Grand Rapids, MI: William Eerdmans, 2004).

7. Henry Bowden, "Walter Rauschenbusch and American Church History," *Foundations* 9 (July–September 1966): 234–50.

8. Evans, *Kingdom Is Always but Coming*, 90.

9. See Grant Wacker, "The Holy Spirit and the Spirit of the Age in American Protestantism, 1880–1910," *Journal of American History* 72 (June 1985): 45–62.

10. Even though the theological "institutionalization" of dispensationalism is often seen as an outgrowth of the fundamentalism-modernist controversy in the 1920s, dispensationalism was well on its way toward organizing itself on a transdenominational level by the end of the nineteenth century. See Glenn T. Miller, *Piety and Profession: American Theological Education, 1870–1970* (Grand Rapids, MI: William B. Eerdmans, 2007), 179–200.

11. On the emergence of dispensationalism, and its ongoing impact on American religion, see Paul Boyer, *When Time Shall Be No More.*

12. See Grant Wacker, *Augustus H. Strong and the Dilemma of Historical Consciousness* (Macon, GA: Mercer University Press, 1985).

13. Rauschenbusch, "Why I am a Baptist: Postlude," *Rochester Baptist Monthly,* copy in the Rauschenbusch Scrapbook, Vol. 2, Ambrose-Swasey Library, Rochester, N.Y., 51.

14. For a history of Rochester Theological Seminary, see LeRoy Moore Jr., "The Rise of American Religious Liberalism at Rochester Theological Seminary, 1872–1928" (Ph.D. dissertation, Claremont Graduate School, 1966).

15. On Strong's theology, see Wacker, *Augustus Strong and the Dilemma of Historical Consciousness.*

16. See Evans, *Kingdom Is Always but Coming*, 39–40.

17. On August Rauschenbusch, see Carl E. Schneider, "Americanization of Karl August Rauschenbusch, 1816–1899," *Church History* 24 (March 1955): 3–14.

18. Rauschenbusch, "Why I am a Baptist: My First Reason," in Rauschenbusch Scrapbook, Vol. 2, 41.

19. Evans, *Kingdom Is Always but Coming*, 145.

20. Bowden, "Walter Rauschenbusch and American Church History," 237.

21. Rauschenbusch, "Introduction to the Study of Church History," in Rauschenbusch Scrapbook, Vol. 3, Ambrose-Swasey Library, Rochester, N.Y., 68.

22. Rauschenbusch, "Introduction to the Study of Church History," 71.

23. Rauschenbusch, "Why I am a Baptist: My First Reason," 41.

24. Ibid., 40.

25. Ibid., 41.

26. Rauschenbusch, "Why I am a Baptist: Prelude," 38.

27. Donovan E. Smucker, *The Origins of Walter Rauschenbusch's Social Ethics* (Montreal: McGill-Queen's University Press, 1994), 34–36. Winthrop S. Hudson, "Who were the Baptists?" *The Baptist Quarterly* vol. 16 (July 1956): 303–12.

28. Rauschenbusch, "Why I am a Baptist: My Second Reason," 44.

29. Bowden, "Walter Rauschenbusch and American Church History" and Bowden, *Church History in the Age of Science: Historiographical Patterns in the United States, 1876–1918* (Chapel Hill: University of North Carolina Press, 1971), 170–95.

30. Rauschenbusch, "Introduction to the Study of History," 70.

31. In this regard, I equate Rauschenbusch's understanding of the church as analogous with H. Richard Niebuhr's "Christ transforming culture" paradigm. See Niebuhr, *Christ and Culture* (New York: Harper, 1951).

32. Cited in Walter Rauschenbusch, *Christianity and the Social Crisis in the 21st Century: The Classic That Woke Up the Church*, ed. Paul Raushenbush (New York: HarperOne, 2007), 113.

33. Quoted in Winthrop Hudson, ed., *Walter Rauschenbusch: Selected Writings* (New York: Paulist Press, 1984), 100.

34. *Walter Rauschenbusch: Selected Writings*, 100.

35. "Why I am a Baptist: My Second Reason," 42.

36. *Christianizing the Social Order*, 23.

37. See, for example, Winthrop S. Hudson, *The Great Tradition of the American Churches* (New York: Harper & Brothers, 1953).

38. Rauschenbusch, "Does the New Testament Provide a Definite and Permanent Church Polity?" Rauschenbusch Scrapbook, Vol. 2, 36.

39. In fact, only one short chapter in *A Theology for the Social Gospel* deals with explicitly ecclesiastical issues, on the sacraments. See Rauschenbusch, *A Theology for the Social Gospel* (New York: Macmillan, 1917).

40. "Our Attitude Toward Millennarianism," quoted in Hudson, ed., *Walter Rauschenbusch: Selected Writings*, 80.

41. "Our Attitude," 89.

42. *Christianizing the Social Order*, 55–56.

43. "Our Attitude," 94.

44. *Christianizing the Social Order*, 121.

45. Ibid., 122.

46. Quoted in Evans, *The Kingdom Is Always but Coming*, 225.

47. Rauschenbusch, *Theology for the Social Gospel*, 157.

48. H. Richard Niebuhr, *The Kingdom of God in America* (New York: Harper, 1937), 194.

49. Hudson, *Great Tradition of the American Churches*, 242.

50. Dores Robinson Sharpe, *Walter Rauschenbusch* (New York: Macmillan, 1942). Even though the book would not pass muster today as a work of history, Sharpe presents a touching account of Rauschenbusch that clearly is indicative of the affection with which he was held. If Sharpe is guilty of hagiography, he nevertheless captures the theological and personal appeal of Rauschenbusch during the heyday of the social gospel in America.

51. Dores Robinson Sharpe, "Walter Rauschenbusch—a Great Good Man," *Colgate-Rochester Divinity School Bulletin*, December 1939, 3.

52. I. M. Haldeman, "Professor Shailer Mathews' Burlesque on the Second Coming of Our Lord Jesus Christ" (pamphlet, n.p., n.d.), 36–37.

53. For a summary of the historical and theological themes that have divided Baptists during the twentieth century, see Bill J. Leonard, *Baptist Ways: A History* (Valley Forge, PA: Judson Press, 2003), 390–421.

54. The apocalyptic undercurrents in contemporary American religion are revealed in a number of recent surveys on American religion. See, for example, the Pew U.S. Religion Landscape Survey at http:/religions.pewforum.org/.

55. Rauschenbusch, *Christianity and the Social Crisis in the 21st Century*), 75.

56. Although Martin Luther King Jr.'s indebtedness to Rauschenbusch is well-known, one of the first "recoveries" of Rauschenbusch's theology on the eve of the Civil Rights movement was the work of another African American Baptist, Benjamin Mays. See Mays, ed., *A Gospel for the Social Awakening* (New York: Association Press, 1950).

7

"I Am Fundamentally a Clergyman, a Baptist Preacher"

Martin Luther King Jr., Social Christianity, and the Baptist Faith in an Era of Civil Rights

Edward R. Crowther

To some, the sound was that of a truck backfiring; the Reverend Ralph David Abernethy initially thought *"Firecracker?"* Charlie Stephens, a tenant in Bessie Brewer's rooming house on South Main Street, knew it was a gunshot, as did a Memphis fireman, George Loenneke, who was observing the scene through field glasses at nearby Fire Station No. 2. Faster than the sound of the report could be heard, a 30.06 slug fired from the Brewer's Boarding House bathroom had traveled at 2,760 feet per second, tearing into the right cheek of Dr. Martin Luther King Jr., then into his spinal column, before tumbling down the left side of his chest. The heavy round from the Remington Gamemaster model 760 slammed King, who was leaning forward over the railing of the second floor balcony of the Lorraine Motel, violently backward onto the second floor concrete balcony. His colleagues quickly understood that King had been shot and rushed to his side, finding him barely breathing. It was 6:01 P.M., April 4, 1968. After medical personnel removed King to an ambulance, observers on the scene noted that the pattern formed by the blood that pooled under King's back and arms looked eerily like a cross. Interpreting the event, Reverend James Lawson and other movement leaders would thenceforth refer to his murder as a "crucifixion."[1]

Interpreting King as a person and as a public figure has occupied the attention of scholars, parishioners, and pundits, since he first garnered national notability in December 1955, for his role in the boycott of city buses in Montgomery. Some contemporaneous commentators viewed him as the epitome of Americanism; others saw him as a communist-inspired agitator. Within the various elements of the movement for African American liberation, he was at once lionized and dismissed derisively as "De Lawd."

Among his fellow African American Baptist ministers, King both won the support and earned the ire of pillars among the pastors, most notably Reverend Joseph H. Jackson. Whether and how to commemorate him after his murder led to divergent discussions among his former colleagues and his widow. Mrs. Coretta Scott King, the King Center, and Congressman John Conyers of Michigan spearheaded a successful but controversial effort to create a King national holiday. Indeed, when the 98th Congress debated the bill to create King National Holiday in 1983, contentious theater erupted on the floor with North Carolina Republican Senator Jesse Helms raising the issue of King's association with communists, before withdrawing his words from the record. South Carolina's Strom Thurmond, the former Dixiecrat, voted in favor of the bill, whereas Arizona Senator John McCain voted against it. But Arizona did not observe the day as a paid state holiday until 1992, and South Carolina did not until 2000.[2]

Historians have painted a favorable image of King as a civil rights leader, as a figure in world history, as an American. In describing King as a man and measuring his historical significance, scholars have focused on his words and their sources, his relationship to Gandhi and nonviolence in a century fraught with world wars and the threat of nuclear holocaust, and his influence in confronting the massive historical context of racism and racial violence. Scholars of African American religion discuss King's theology of liberation and his ministerial style as an exemplar of the prophetic tradition within African American Christianity. His myriad biographers dwell on King's own avowed "personalism," finding in his belief of a transcendent yet active God the psychological and religious underpinnings of his remarkable courage and extraordinary equanimity. More recently, scholars have returned to the ecclesiastical and theological context in which King came of age, locating him in the broad and eclectic tradition of social Christianity. King did indeed embrace and exemplify many elements of the social gospel of American Christianity and especially its protean Baptist and African American Baptist expressions. Contextually comforting to him and familiar, it provided the vehicle for King to act out his personal theology and his Baptist faith.[3] Moreover, King's social activism drew from a deep spring of social Christianity, rooted in consistent application of core biblical teachings he had encountered as a young man to the challenging social conditions he experienced as a public person. He returned to these same ideas and beliefs repeatedly, using them as a vehicle for social transformation.

That King saw himself as a Baptist preacher is hardly a novel concept.

In 1965, King had said: "In the quiet recesses of my heart, I am fundamentally a clergyman, a Baptist preacher. This is my being and my heritage for I am also the son of a Baptist preacher, the grandson of a Baptist preacher and the great-grandson of a Baptist preacher." To introduce and elucidate King, Professor Clayborne Carson, the long-time and distinguished senior editor of the Papers of Martin Luther King Jr. project, selected those words of King's to begin volume one of the King Papers, as opposed to a reference to King's illustrious "I Have a Dream" speech or his "Been to the Mountaintop" impromptu. Since the release of volume one, Carson has consistently located King the Baptist within the social gospel of American Christianity.[4]

More recently, the Papers of Martin Luther King Jr. project released a trove of newly discovered King documents titled *Advocate of the Social Gospel, September 1948–March 1963*, in 2007. This volume shows how King's homiletic style evolved, but, even more, it shows how his concepts of an activist, applied Christianity developed early and were adapted to the needs of the nascent civil rights movement of the 1950s and the vast social unrest of the 1960s. More tellingly, the volume shows how King's ideas preached to the black church were sanitized by white editors to make them palatable to white liberals in King's *Strength of Love*, which appeared in 1963. One of the volume's coeditors, Troy Jackson, subsequently published his splendid *Becoming King: Martin Luther King and the Making of a National Leader*. This volume has earned acclaim for explaining the relationship of King and the Women's Political Council in launching the bus boycott and the sometimes contentious interactions among movement leaders in Montgomery, but it also advances the argument of King's Baptist social gospel outlook that helped to shape, and evolved during, the bus boycott. Indeed, Jackson describes King's personal faith and social gospel approach to Christianity as "sustained theological underpinnings that help explain why King and the influence and following that he did." Both these volumes show King's involvement in actual civil rights events as melding his thoroughgoing commitment to a socially relevant and personally meaningful Baptist faith to a real-world application in Montgomery and finding institutional expression in the creation of the Southern Christian Leadership Conference in 1957. Its stated mission, characteristic of its nature as a ministerial alliance in support of social Christianity, was "to redeem the soul of America."[5]

These volumes propagate a growing scholarly awareness between King's private convictions and his moving public articulation of ideas, revealing

King's consistent and thoroughgoing commitment to a prophetic ministry rooted in social Christianity. To be persuasive to a congregation as a Baptist minister and, increasingly, as a public figure, King often advanced his ideas in powerful language. But he sought to cultivate common cultural and religious terrain and, hence, eschewed larger ideological and theological implications for his views and critiques. He consistently asserted his civil rights claims in the language of foundational documents such as the Declaration of Independence and Constitution, and in the biblical cadences of Old Testament prophets such as Amos: "But let judgment run down as waters, and righteousness as a mighty stream." Later in his public career, as the locus of the civil rights movement and King's public role shifted from de jure segregation in the South to de facto segregation in northern metropolises like Chicago, King's public pronouncements moved to a broader critique of domestic materialism at home and inhumane warfare abroad, most notably in his April 4, 1967, "Beyond Vietnam" address at Riverside Church in New York City's upper west side. King's critique of capitalism as morally and spiritually bankrupt shocked many who had not heard King preach and, as a public figure, he appeared to be growing toward political and theological extremism in response to bloated body counts and bigots' brick bats.

The evolving public King theme is eloquently and judiciously depicted in Harvard Sitkoff's *King: Been to the Mountaintop*. Though noting King's longstanding personal "radicalism . . . that has been airbrushed out of the historical picture" especially about social issues, he portrays a public King who until very late in his career eschewed rhetoric beyond his withering critiques of the Jim Crow South that might threaten his alliances with white liberals, especially those in the White House. And their negative and retaliatory responses to his later broad pronouncements shows that Sitkoff's King understood the fragile nature of his partnerships with the white power structure all too well. King's public auditors, therefore, might have understandably seen him to have been developing almost a new theology and concept of Baptist ministry in the face of events of the mid-1960s.

Yet King's private writings from his student days at Morehouse College and Crozer Theological Seminary reveal a powerful theological and moral consistency that questioned dominant economic, cultural, social, and religious norms in the United States, all couched in his role as a Baptist minister who adhered to the social gospel. For example, King had written in 1952 that capitalism was no longer a relevant system and its concentration of wealth robbed poor people of the necessities of life. That is, King's public rhetoric moved, powerfully, in response to a growing awareness of the deep-seated racism and violent imperialism, but his ideology and his understanding of his ministerial duty as a socially engaged Christian to speak out against and to work to change questionable social norms had long been in place.[6] He articulated these ideas in scholarly papers, personal notes, and private correspondence. In a letter to Coretta Scott, his future spouse who had presented him with Edward Bellamy's utopian classic, *Looking Backward* (1887), King held forth about his basic endorsement of the ideas it contained:

> There can be no doubt about it. Bellamy had the insight of a social prophet as well as the fact finding mind of the social scientist. I welcomed the book because much of its content is in line with my basic ideas. I imagine you already know that I am much more socialistic in my economic theory than capitalistic. And yet I am not so opposed to capitalism that I have failed to see its relative merits. It started out with a noble and high motive, viz., to block the trade monopolies of nobles, but like most human systems it fell victim to the very thing it was revolting against. So today capitalism has outlived its usefulness. It has brought about a system that takes necessities from the masses to give luxuries to the classes. So I think Bellamy is right in seeing the gradual decline of capitalism.[7]

As he continued his argument, he contended that capitalism, having run its moral course, was headed for the ash can of history, although he noted it could take a long time for its dénouement. Two further points from this missive bear commentary: He outright rejected Marx's materialism as a solution, a theme his critics forced him to revisit again and again, but also other Utopian structures as well, because fundamentally "man is a sinner" and cannot reform himself "until he submits his life to the Grace of God." That is, the problem humanity faced was "theological." In short, the world needed religious rejuvenation, not humanistic nostrums, a recommendation rooted in a Christian analysis of social ills. Furthermore, he addressed his duty as a minister to engage in social Christianity: "[R]eligion [can] so easily become a tool of the middle class to keep the proletariat oppressed. Too often has the church talked about a future good 'over yonder,' totally forgetting the present evil over here. As a theologian and one deeply convinced that the way of Christ is the only ultimate way to man's salvation, I will try to avoid making religion what Marx calls the 'opiate of the people.'" Rather, said King, "Let us continue to hope, work, and pray that in the future we will live to see a warless world, a better distribution of wealth, and a brotherhood that transcends race or color. This is the gospel that I will preach to the world." King the young, budding black Baptist minister, was also King the Social Gospeler.[8]

Indeed, his long-standing social Christianity and understanding of his ministerial role, not a new anger and alienation, composed the core of his famous address at Riverside Church in 1967. He began by asserting his ministerial role. Not only did he identify himself as a "preacher," he also noted his duty to speak out on subjects that impacted his "moral vision." He asserted that his ministerial path begun in Montgomery had brought him, twelve years later, to New York, but he could have also noted how his address fulfilled his early promise of the type of gospel he wished to preach. Intoning in his characteristic ringing baritone cadence, King called for "a radical revolution in values" in the United States, urging a movement from a "thing-oriented society to a person-oriented society." "When machines and computers, profit motives and property rights, are considered more important than people, the giant triplets of racism, extreme materialism, and militarism are incapable of being conquered," he said, challenging his congregation to move not merely toward more just outcomes, but toward a "restructuring" of a wealthy society that still systematically manufactures poor people, one where "capitalists" mine the wealth in the Third World "with no concern for the social betterment of the countries." Because it "continues to spend more money on military defense than on programs of social uplift," the United States was "approaching spiritual death." Although the themes that he was addressing in 1967, especially those related to the Vietnam War, were not in King's imagination in 1952 when he wrote to Coretta Scott, his sense of his proper role as a Baptist minister who engaged the eternal and the temporal issues of the secular world was already well-formed.[9]

The foundations of King's consistent Baptist social Christianity rested on the powerful bedrock of the social traditions of African American Christianity, exemplified by his father and grandfather, but also by African American mentors such as Benjamin Elijah Mays, Howard Thurman, and George Dennis Sale Kelsey. In addition, as Clayborne Carson and Keith Miller have demonstrated so thoroughly and convincingly, King was influenced by and borrowed freely from a slew of white social gospel ministers and theologians, ranging from nationally known Walter Rauschenbusch, Harry Emerson Fosdick, and Reinhold Niebuhr to popular but lesser-known preachers such as James Wallace Hamilton. But, as Carson and Miller have noted, King borrowed their words, but delivered them in the cadence of his own Afro-Baptist faith, and he often rejected certain of their ideas, or as Miller phrases it, "King succeeded largely because he resisted numerous ideas proffered by his professors and the Great White Thinkers." And, as Carson notes, rather than a tension between the two sources of theology, King was able to "combine elements of African-American and European-American religious traditions," not only because he was a great borrower and synthesizer, but because his African American mentors were themselves "products of predominantly white seminaries and graduate schools."[10]

For example, Adam Daniel Williams (1863–1931), King's maternal grandfather, known as A. D., was a self-educated, sometimes itinerant minister in Georgia. A "pioneering advocate of a distinctive African-American version of the social gospel," one which blended the economic self-help of Booker T. Washington with W. E. B. DuBois's focus on civil liberties, Williams helped organize "the Georgia Equal Rights League," to challenge white-supremacist electoral practices in Georgia. He mixed political and social activism with business opportunism and, as pastor of Atlanta's Ebenezer Baptist Church, he oversaw its growth in membership from 400 in 1903 to 750 in 1913. The following year, his ten-year-old daughter, Alberta Williams, mother of Martin Luther King Jr., was baptized. Still, his commitment to social Christianity was central to his ministry and, in 1917, he helped Walter White establish an Atlanta branch of the National Association for the Advancement of Colored People. Williams was already a member of the national NAACP. He then worked with a committee to overturn a decision by the Atlanta School Board to terminate the seventh grade for African American children in order to construct a new junior high school for white Atlantans. A. D. Williams was subsequently elected branch president of the Atlanta NAACP, where he continued to advocate for voting rights and fair distribution of local tax dollars.[11]

In 1920, A. D. William's daughter, Alberta, met Michael King (1897–1984), who had come to Atlanta to obtain an education and make something of himself. He married Alberta in November 1926, and he began to study for the ministry at Morehouse College. The couple's famous son, and second child, was born just over two years later in January 1929. The young King grew up under the influence of his father's "social-gospel Christianity that combined a belief in personal salvation with the need to apply the teachings of Jesus to the daily problems of their black congregations." Indeed, "King Sr.'s activism shaped his son's understanding of the ministry and presaged King Jr.'s own career," setting forth for King Jr. the ideal of an "educated, politically active ministry."[12]

Dr. Benjamin Elijah Mays (1894–1984) had served as the dean of the School of Religion at Howard University and earned a Ph.D. from the University of Chicago, before coming to Morehouse College at its president from 1940 to 1967. While King attended Morehouse (1944–1948), he was an indifferent student but a required attendee at Mays' Tuesday morning lectures. From Mays, King heard that he should seek "contact with people who demonstrate in their person the fact that religion counts." "Religion which ignores social problems will in time be doomed," he intoned. In language that would have shocked a white audience, Mays told his captive audience that neither communism nor fascism were appropriate ends, but neither was "capitalistic individualism." Mays recalled that King was more than a passive attendee; he would debate Mays. King would later list Mays as a "great influence."[13]

Mays was part of a generation of African Americans who began to acquire the accoutrements of majority culture professionalism, including professional degrees. Animated by the concept of "uplift," in which fortunate African Americans were to assist those who were less able, Mays was perhaps the most influential African American educator in the South. In *The Negro's God as Reflected in His Literature,* he asserted that African American "ideas of God . . . are chiseled out of the very fabric of the social struggle. Prior to 1860, the Negro's idea of God developed around slavery. After the Civil War, they grew out of the wrongs of Reconstruction. Since 1914, they are inseparable from the social and economic restrictions which the Negro meets in the modern world." The social context of Jim Crow and racism explained the current plight of African Americans. Restrictions left them in a position of having to cope and such conditions restricted their views of religion and concept of God. The "Negro group has produced great preachers but few theologians." King and his Morehouse peers found themselves in a position to develop a healthy understanding of God and ample direction to apply Christianity to improve the social and religious conditions of fellow African Americans.[14]

Howard Thurman (1899–1981) had attended Morehouse College with King's father, and his wife and King's mother had been classmates at Spelman College in Atlanta. Later, Thurman came to Boston University, during King's final year in residency, as dean of Marsh Chapel. In Thurman's recollection, he and King had only watched the "World Series on Television" in 1953, before Thurman visited King in New York in 1958, after King had been stabbed by Izola Ware Curry, a deranged forty-two-year-old woman. Thurman suggested that King extend his recovery time so that he could determine best how he could serve the civil rights movement. But Thurman's influence was much more direct than his humble memoirs reveal. Thurman was the author of the classic statement of early liberation theology, *Jesus and the Disinherited,* which appeared in 1949. Journalist Lerone Bennett would later claim that King traveled with a well-worn copy of this volume. Whether Bennett's claim was literally true or not, King had come to know Thurman's ideas through his father and through Mays. At its core, Thurman's beliefs advocated for a Christian gospel sided with the poor, oppressed, and depressed, and he laid out ideas of resistance to unjust systems. King's emphasis on loving the oppressor is remarkably similar to Thurman's idea of transformative and redemptive love. Thurman wrote: "The religion of Jesus says to the disinherited: 'Love your enemy. Take the initiative in seeking ways by which you can have the experience of a common sharing of mutual worth and value. It may be hazardous, but you must do it.' For the Negro it means that he must see the individual white man in the context of a common humanity." King's sermon "Death to Evil Upon the Seashore" contains similar verbiage to Thurman's *Deep River; Reflections on the Religious Insight of Certain of the Negro Spirituals,* especially in describing the horrors of slavery, specifically the sexual exploitation by white masters of African American women. Thurman and Mays shared another important bond besides the tie to Morehouse College; both men traveled to India and met Gandhi, giving King a vicarious connection with the exemplar of nonviolent resistance, long before activist Bayard Rustin began to tutor King in the essential Gandhi.[15]

Although King was a mediocre student at Morehouse, George Kelsey (1910–1996) inspired him intellectually, and King earned his only undergraduate A from him. Kelsey completed his Ph.D. in philosophy from Yale in 1946, during King's tenure at Morehouse. King admired Kelsey's philosophical rigor and his belief that Christianity held the key to addressing racial issues in society. Anticipating ideas of human evil trumping human perfection that King would later encounter with Reinhold Niebuhr, Kelsey wrote that the potential of a Kingdom of God on Earth, a goal associated with the white social gospel, would go unrealized because of human sin. King also credited Kelsey with helping him reconcile the biblical text with King's doubts about its literal truth and, hence, its usefulness.

Behind the stories were "profound" truths. The King Papers' editors assert that this understanding reopened the path for King, whose intellectual awakening was leading him toward skepticism, to enter the ministry.[16]

King's African American mentors believed not only that Christianity promised eternal rewards, but that it must also be relevant to the real spiritual and material needs of African Americans in the Jim Crow era. King's white influences, who developed their social gospel against the backdrop of class inequality, poverty, vices associated with urbanization, and the recognition of the need to address the lack of educational opportunity in the backwoods, likewise agreed that Christianity must address the earthly condition of people. Walter Rauschenbusch (1861–1918) was perhaps the leading advocate of the social gospel movement in the early twentieth century. It remains unclear whether King first learned of Rauschenbusch at Morehouse, whose President Mays edited an anthology of Rauschenbusch's writing published in 1950, but King studied Rauschenbusch intensely at Crozer Theological Seminary with Professor George Washington Davis. Kenneth Smith, another of King's professors at Crozer, recalled King saying that he was heavily influenced by Rauschenbusch. King scholars debate this contention and Keith Miller simply dismisses the claim, demonstrating that when King claims to quote Rauschenbusch in the "Pilgrimage to Nonviolence" chapter in *Stride Toward Freedom*, he was really quoting Harry Emerson Fosdick. No doubt that King knew a great deal about Fosdick and about Rauschenbusch and his misattribution could have simply been sloppiness.[17] Given the audience of *Stride Toward Freedom*, and Fosdick's criticisms of both segregation and fundamentalism, King may simply have shied away from Fosdick's name: King's focus was on a common theme found in both figures of the social gospel and he likely used the name of the one with less cultural baggage for a white audience. Were his target audience exclusively African American, he might have used his father, Mays, or even Vernon Johns as his authority for the social gospel. The point remains that the force of the social gospel was strong in Martin Luther King Jr.

Harry Emerson Fosdick (1878–1969) exerted a strong influence on King, apart from King's use of his words. Fosdick held many pulpits in New York, earning fame—and infamy in some circles—for his sermon "Shall the Fundamentalists Win." He served the Riverside Church, which was dedicated to a social gospel ministry, and in whose building—construction of which was funded by John D. Rockefeller Jr.—King would preach in April 1967. At Crozer, King used Fosdick's ideas developed in *A Guide to*

Understanding the Bible (1938) and *The Modern Uses of the Bible* (1942), notions commonly termed *progressive revelation,* to square the stories in the Bible with the findings of modern science. References to Fosdick read blandly in King's seminary papers, because he had already learned to distinguish the spiritual teachings of the Bible from strict textual literalism in his Morehouse classes with Professor Kelsey. In order to complete a seminary paper, he simply used a Fosdick citation as authority for what he had already come to believe. It was Fosdick's sermons, not his writings that moved King. In part, Fosdick was well-known in King's day. And, in part, Fosdick's social Christianity allied with King's own. Hence, as Professor Keith Miller has thoroughly demonstrated, King's *Letter from Birmingham Jail,* written without access to a library, expropriates Fosdick's notions of Christians as God's imperialists, including a biblical reference from James Moffatt's plain English translation of Philippians 3:20 used by Fosdick in *Hope of the World,* rather than the more familiar King James, which describes Christians as "a colony of heaven upon the earth," rhyming with the references to Christians as "leaven" in the dough of humanity. Fosdick had to justify a claim for socially active Christianity in the 1920s and 1930s. King justified his ministerial role during the dark spring of 1963 against the challenges of white ministers in part by borrowing Fosdick's powerful argument, including the use of a not-so-commonplace translation of the Bible, and King did it from memory, a measure of King's familiarity with and willingness to employ Fosdick.[18]

Reinhold Niebuhr (1892–1971), along with Paul Tillich, was perhaps the best-known theologian in the United States, and King had a long acquaintance with Niebuhr's neo-orthodoxy or Christian realism. Although King likely learned of Niebuhr at Crozer, he did not appear to engage Niebuhr's ideas until he matriculated to Boston University where he used Niebuhr's ideas to critique "liberal theology," including the excessive optimism found in some elements of social Christianity. King appreciated Niebuhr's struggle with the moral and Christian implications of "the appalling injustices evident in modern industrial civilization, and particularly by the concentration of power and resources in the hands of a relatively small wealthy class." King, however, found Niebuhr's realism essentially denied the possibility of social amelioration. Currently, government was necessary because Christian principles, which King termed *agape,* had not infused the world, but King suggested that Niebuhr had considered the possibility that the Christian gospel could have a globally transformative effect. The following fall, however, King appropriated Niebuhr in explicating Jeremiah 17:5: "It seems to me that one of the great services of neo-orthodoxy, not withstanding its extremes, is its revolts against all forms of humanistic perfection. They call us back to a deeper faith in God. Is not this the need of the hour? Has modern man placed too much faith in himself and to [sic] little faith in God?"[19]

James Wallace Hamilton (1900–1968), a Canadian-born Methodist social gospel preacher based in Florida, whose recorded sermons sold well in the 1940s and 1950s, made such a theme a major component of his preaching. His sermon, "The Drum Major Instinct," written and likely first delivered to the congregation of Pasadena Community Church in 1949, and most likely encountered by King in its published form in 1952, provided much of the inspiration and verbiage for King's own sermon by that name delivered in 1968, not long before his death. As Keith Miller has painstakingly shown, both King's and Hamilton's versions of the sermon show how the longing for dominion produces social evil. For Hamilton, human hubris produces Mussolini and fascism. For King, it was the threat of nuclear war and the actual war in Vietnam. King borrowed Hamilton's evocation for Lincoln's explaining to an auditor that kindliness toward the South might end the Civil War in his own sermon "Loving Your Enemies." Like King, Hamilton eventually preached at Fosdick's Riverside Church.[20] King's use of Hamilton reflects less a systematic study of Hamilton's theology, but rather the fact that Hamilton's homilies were filled with examples of Christian concern for others influencing human relations and the social order.

As a preacher, King indulged himself in the common convention and, given his increasingly busy schedule, necessary practice of homiletic pilfering. Black and white ministers routinely cannibalized one another's sermons. To build up support for the Southern Christian Leadership Conference, King delivered as least as many sermons away from his storied pulpits at Dexter Avenue Baptists Church and Ebenezer Baptist Church as he did at his home churches, speaking at the Detroit Lenten Series, major northern pulpits such as Detroit's Central Methodist Church, and ecumenical Chicago Sunday Evening Club. He borrowed freely in these northern sojourns from white pastors and preachers to speak the language of his largely white audiences, just as he borrowed from Mays, Thurman, and his father in sermons on home turf. Kenneth Miller's point is sound, then, that King as a theologian or a philosopher is at best derivative because of his use of borrowed homilies, rather than his developing original exposition of great works of theology or novel theological or philosophical discourse of his own authorship. But it is not splitting hairs to say that King did have a personal theology rooted in the social gospel, and he borrowed only those homilies that fit his conception of applied Christianity.[21]

Indeed, in his less hectic student days, King drafted a welter of sermons and took personal notes on a range of biblical topics, particularly choosing to record reflections and ideas related to Christian social justice that appeared repeatedly in his speeches and sermons later in his career. Before he was King, the national figure, he often fleshed these ideas out into sermons whose words were largely his own. When he became a national figure, he did frequently borrow rhetoric from fellow ministers that aligned with his own conception of social Christianity, but with predictable frequency returned to his own Q sources to ground and articulate his conception of the social gospel. In the fall of 1952, as a doctoral student, King took personal notes on Amos 5:21–24. "God is a God that demands justice rather than sacrifice," King wrote. "Unless a man's heart is right, Amos seems to be saying, the external form of worship means nothing." A card labeled "Social Ethics" gleaned from Amos reads: "Amos' emphasis throughout seems to be that justice between man and man is one of the divine foundations of society. Such an ethical ideal is at the root of all true religions. This high ethical notion conceived by Amos must always remain a challenge to the Christian Church." There is not a direct reference in these cards to Amos 5:24, which King made famous: "Let justice roll down like water and righteousness like a mighty stream," but here he clearly was reflecting deeply on what the man who "was among the herdmen of Tekoa" might be saying about social conditions in the twentieth-century United States. Given the later use to which he put Amos 5:24, he was likely reflecting on Amos through the lens of the social gospel at the time of his note taking.[22]

Likewise, King read and studied Psalm 72. "The whole Psalm is a plea for social justice," wrote King, who, no doubt examining verse four continued: "There is expressed a deep concern for needy and the oppressed. The oppressor is looked upon with scorn. He is to be crushed." King shifted focus from the specific psalm to the message of social justice in the whole Bible and the Christian gospel:

> This emphasis found its greatest expression, excluding the fine work of the prophets, in the teachings of Jesus. Throughout his ministry, he manifested a deep concern for the poor and oppressed people of his day. While somewhat extravagant, there is a healthy warning in this statement, Christianity was born among the poor and

died among the rich. Whenever Christianity has remained true to its prophetic mission, it has taken a deep interest in social justice. Whenever it has fallen short at this point, it has brought about disastrous consequences. We must never forget that the success of communism in the world today is due to the failure of Christians to live to the highest ethical tenets inherent in its system.[23]

Likely he took these notes as part of his required reading for Professor L. Harold DeWolf's class, "Religious Teachings of the Old Testament" but they nonetheless reflect King's own belief that biblical religion demanded social concern.

In a sermon he delivered at Second Baptist Church in Detroit, just before he arrived at Dexter Avenue Baptist Church, "Rediscovering Lost Values," King developed the connection between inner spirituality and the social order in the world: "The greatest problem facing modern man is that the means by which we live, have outdistanced the spiritual ends for which we live. . . . [W]e've made the world a neighborhood . . . we've failed to make it a brotherhood." He concluded: "The real danger confronting civilization today is that atomic bomb, which lies in the hearts and souls of men, capable of exploding into the vilest of hates and into the most damaging selfishness."[24]

To some in the tense years of the Cold War, King's insistence on social duty could be read as a devotion to doctrinaire communism. The charge that King was really a communist was part of the campaign by J. Edgar Hoover's Federal Bureau of Investigation to discredit him. King's social opponents readily gravitated toward such an accusation, because he and his message could be dismissed as both godless and un-American. King's criticism of the materialism in capitalism and the close alignment of his ideas with socialism and social democracy appeared to give credence to these charges in those already disinclined to dismiss King's religious and social message. Yet, King had already privately announced the godless materialism underlying socialism could not be reconciled with Christianity and in his "Communism's Challenge to Christianity," he reasserted his belief that communism and Christianity were incompatible as belief systems. Communism made no place for "God and Christ" and dismissed revealed religion as an opiate for the masses. It pursued its goals by inhumane and immoral means. It crushed human liberty. "We must try to understand Communism," he preached, "but never can we accept it and be true Christians." He conceded that communism did nobly attempt to eliminate race and class exploitation and privilege. Borrowing his words from Robert J. McCracken, senior pastor at Riverside Church from 1947 to 1967, King emphasized, "With this passionate concern for social justice Christians are bound to be in accord. Such concern is implicit in the Christian doctrine of the Fatherhood of God and the brotherhood of man." Regaining his own words, "The Christian ought to begin with a bias in favor of a movement which protests against unfair treatment of the poor, for surely Christianity is itself such a protest."[25]

The Jim Crow South provided King an ample arena for protest animated by applied Christianity. In a sermon entitled "A Religion of Doing," a splendid homiletic exercise in which he referred specifically both to Fosdick and Thurman, King elucidated the implications of Mathew 7:21 to his new congregation at Dexter Avenue Baptist Church: "Not everyone that saith unto me, Lord, Lord, shall enter the kingdom of heaven; but he that doeth the will of my Father which is in Heaven." In themes he revisited again and again, King noted that there was "no true divorce between belief and action. . . . The ultimate test of a man's sincerity in crying Lord, Lord, is found in his active doing of God's will." Were all of the seven hundred million Christians in the world to live the faith they claimed, "the condition of this world would be better than it is." The purveyors of racial violence, economic injustice, and the "strongest advocators of segregation in America also worship Christ." About this Christ, King asserted: "Let us be assured amid our beautiful churches, and our lovely architecture, that Christ is more concerned about our attitude toward racial prejudice and war than he is about our long processionals. He is more concerned with how we treat our neighbors than how loud we sing his praises. Christ is more concerned about our living a high ethical life than our most detailed knowledge of the creeds of christendom."[26]

Before the eruption in December 1955 of the Montgomery Bus Boycott, public opinion focused on the brutal murder in August 1955, of Emmett Till, a fourteen-year-old African American youth, killed by Roy Bryant and J. W. "Big" Milam not simply, as it has often been reported, for his conversation with Bryant's wife ("Don't be afraid, I've been with white women before"), but for refusing to show fear to white men after Bryant and Milam had apprehended him. In the trial of Bryant and Milam that followed in Sumner, Mississippi, in September 1955, the jury quickly acquitted both men who, given the protection of double jeopardy, confessed their crime to journalist William Bradford Huie. At the end of September, King's Sunday sermon to his congregation referred specifically to Till. In his homily, a recounting of Jesus's parable of the Pharisee and the Publican, in which the traditional trope calls for humility before God, not ceremonial religion, King riveted his attention on the social implications for society when the religion of social norms stands in place of the sacrificial religion exemplified by Jesus, and in a manner that presaged his later public proclamations that linked vicious racism with acquisitive imperialism:

> Jesus condemned this over-emphasis on the ceremonial, because he knew the ominous effects . . . it could lead to. He saw that it could be the springboard of a religion which substitutes emotions for moral [action?]. That is what we are seeing in the world today—countless millions of people worshipping Christ emotionally but not morally. Great imperialistic powers, like Britain, France, and Holland, which have trodden and crushed Africa and Asia with the 'iron feet of oppression' worship Christ. The white men who lynch Negroes worship Christ. That jury in Mississippi, which a few days ago in the Emmett Till case, freed two white men from what might be considered one of the most brutal and inhuman crimes of the twentieth century, worships Christ. The perpetrators of many of the greatest evils in our society worship Christ. These people, like the Pharisee, go to church regularly, pay their tithes and offerings, and observe religiously the various ceremonial requirements [of Christianity]. . . . They cast his ethical and moral insights behind the gushing smoke of emotional adoration and ceremonial piety.[27]

Although King knew that his auditors and the larger society might not rise to the challenges implicit in the text as he elucidated it, he was certain of God's wrath. Returning to Amos, chapter five, King quoted: "Take away from me the noise of thy songs; for I will not hear the melody of thy viols. But let Judgment run down as waters and righteousness as a mighty stream." Concluding, "This is always God's response to those who would make ceremonial piety a substitute for genuine religious living."[28]

Six months later, as King was swept up in and gave prophetic voice to the Montgomery Bus Boycott, he turned his attention to the decision by The University of Alabama to expel Autherine Lucy, an African American graduate student in library science, in February 1956, on the grounds that her presence was violently disruptive and the university was unwilling to guarantee her physical safety. (The university also suspended the white ringleader of the egg-and-rock-throwing opposition to her presence, Leonard Wilson.) The white community rejoiced once Lucy left the campus, calling it a return to peace. King, a consistent advocate of nonviolent injustice, selected Matthew 10:34–36, in which Jesus claimed, "I came not to send peace, but a sword." In King's hermeneutics, the text required a rethinking of what constituted peace and what thing was a sword. The peace reigning at Alabama, now that Lucy was gone, one which subverted the rule of law and genuine democracy, was "obnoxious . . . the type of peace that stinks in the nostrils of God." "Peace," said King, "is not merely the absence of some negative force—war, tensions, confusions but it is the presence of some positive force—justice, goodwill, the power of the kingdom of God." To secure such an outcome, it requires that "every true Christian is a fighting pacifist" in a "spiritual war" to realize social justice. Concluding with his baritone crescendo, and applying his ideas to the present crisis of the bus boycott and the conditions of African Americans generally, King thundered:

> If peace means accepting second class I don't want it. If peace means keeping my mouth shut in the midst of injustice and evil, I don't want it. If peace means being complacently adjusted to a deadening status quo, I don't want peace. If peace means a willingness to be exploited economically, dominated politically, humiliated and segregated, I don't want peace. In a passive non-violent manner we must revolt against this peace. Jesus says in substance, I will not be content until justice, good will, brotherhood, love yes, the kingdom of God are established upon the earth. This is real peace. Peace is the presence of positive good.

In his final point, presaging his final pronouncement in Memphis on April 3, 1968, at Monument Temple Church, King returned to the transcendent notions in his own religion that steeled him in the nonviolent war for civil rights: "[N]ever forget that there is an inner peace that comes as a result of doing God's will."[29]

King's social gospel required the practice of ideals in daily living. As a pastor, King was quick to link soaring rhetoric of Christian duty with his own shepherding role at Dexter Avenue. His initial sermon at Dexter cited Luke 4:18, a text his father had used on many occasions. King parroted Jesus, who was addressing the synagogue in Nazareth and had invoked Isaiah 61:1: "The Spirit of the Lord GOD is upon me; because the LORD hath anointed me to preach good tidings unto the meek; he hath sent me to bind up the brokenhearted, to proclaim liberty to the captives." In applying his preaching mission to his new pastoral mission, King shortly prepared written directions for his church. His instructions mixed the practical and ordinary—apportioning his members into birthday month clubs to raise money for the building fund, committees to welcome new members and to fund scholarships for high school graduates, men's groups, women's groups—with the social gospel applied to the real world of race. He not only called for the creation of a "social service committee" to channel in a more efficient manner money given to assist the "sick and needy," he also created a "Social and Political Action Committee." In a remarkable intersection of King and the preexisting movement, this committee's suggested membership included Mary Fair Burke, as chair, and Jo Ann Gibson, cochair, faculty members at Alabama State College and leaders of the Women's Political Council, who would actually launch the Montgomery Bus Boycott, forcing male ministers, including the initially reticent King, to become even more thoroughgoing social Christians. But King's own language in creating the committee illustrates how social gospel beliefs might make creative tensions between Jim Crow and African American social Christianity in the capital of the "Heart of Dixie" a virtual inevitability:

> Since the gospel of Jesus is a social gospel as well as a personal gospel seeking to save the whole man, a Social and Political Action Committee shall be established for the purpose of keeping the congregation intelligently informed concerning the social, political and economic situation. This committee shall keep before the congregation the importance of the NAACP. The membership should unite with this great organization in a solid block. This committee shall also keep before the congregation the necessity of being registered voters. Every member of Dexter must be a registered voter. During elections, both state and national, this committee will sponsor forums and mass meetings to discuss the relative merits of candidates and the major issues involved.[30]

King's activist social Christianity moved him from a vigorous pulpit ministry to the forefront of the larger quest of social justice in the 1950s and 1960s. He drank deeply from the surging wellsprings of the social gospel. It seems, then, that the social component of King's faith is clear and its many manifestations easy to demonstrate. But what did *Christian* mean to

King? His three conversion experiences shed light on King's evolving belief in a real God and personal savior. It is well-documented that the teen-aged King had come to doubt, indeed to have been embarrassed, by the literal biblicism of his father. As a Morehouse student, he might best be described as a doubter, but under the influence of Professor Kelsey, King found that he did not have to choose between what is logical and what the literal words of the biblical text said. Indeed, he could use his fine mind and increased learning to uncover the deeper moral truths of God and apply them to the task of living. So he abandoned his earlier direction to distance himself from his father's church, perhaps to be a medical doctor or a university professor, and to follow his father's calling into the Baptist ministry. As King wrote on his application to Crozer Theological Seminary, "My call to the ministry was quite different from most explanations I've heard. This decision first came about in the summer of 1944 when I felt an inescapable urge to serve society. In short, I felt a sense of responsibility which I could not escape." This growing awareness of a mission of Christian service constituted King's first conversion.[31]

King came of age in an important time in the development of African American Christianity. Though one cannot accurately generalize about any movement as broad as the black church, in the early twentieth century, many of its churches and ministers reflected the impoverished social conditions in which they lived. Thus, the church was, largely, a community in which the faithful endured the "nadir of race relations" in the United States, looking for King Jesus to lead them to a new promised land, in hortatory styles of "whoops," emotionalism, and raw feeling. Learned pastors were few and the religious orientation of most parishioners was compensatory, otherwordly. King, and many of his generation, could not find comfort in that folk faith with their higher education and, thus, "theological study became the means by which . . . [he] reconciled his desire to pursue a social gospel ministry with his deep seated distrust of the emotionalism that sometimes accompanied Baptist religious practices." It, of necessity, drew King from his southern African American moorings to the not-so-familiar harbors of northern seminaries and universities, because as a late as 1950, there were but two African American seminaries accredited by the American Association of Theological Schools.[32]

In this northern environment, King underwent a second conversion, one that has attracted a welter of scholarly attention. He first rejected the humanistic optimism of "liberal" theology and the pessimism of Niebuhr's neo-orthodoxy, in which evil seemed always the victor. As a student at

Crozer and then at Boston University, King gravitated toward a theology of "personalism," as expounded by Boston University Professor Edgar S. Brightman. Clayborne Carson and his fellow editors of the King Papers write that personalism "strengthened his belief that experience as well as intellectual reflection could be the basis of religious belief." For King, this helped solve the problem of evil in a world presumably overseen by an omnipotent God. "God's power is finite, but his goodness is infinite," that is, there could be no real goodness, if God simply compelled morally good behavior. This "is the only adequate explanation for the existence of evil. . . . It establishes the Christian idea of sacrificial love on metaphysical grounds. . . . Theistic absolutism fails" to account for the necessity of choice, without which there could be no goodness, but also fails to explain how a good God could allow evil, which necessarily follows if God binds himself to allow people to choose good or evil. Beyond this, King's personalism, according to Harvard Sitkoff, "led one to judge a state or a law by its effect on a person. Any violation of the worth of an individual was evil. Thus, segregation, which debased personality, and caused people to be treated as things, was evil."[33]

King understood all too well how racism and segregation could devalue and humiliate a person. Returning by bus from Dublin, Georgia, as a teenager in 1944, King was ordered to give up his bus seat by a white driver; ironically, King had just delivered an address entitled "The Negro and the Constitution." Recalling that event, King noted that it was the "maddest" he had ever been in his life. Later, in January 1956, King received a direct death threat: "Listen, Nigger, . . . We gonna blow your brains out and blow up your house." Three days later, King's house was bombed. Amid that pressure, King underwent his third conversion, in the form of what he believed was Jesus saying that King should "stand up for righteousness" and that He would always personally be with King. With this third conversion experience, King made the omnipresent Jesus an intimate part of his psychology, in the way that personalism was his theology, and social Christianity was his means of applying his beliefs. In this way, the God, whose kingdom King was trying to establish on the Earth, became part of King's inner life.[34]

In Dexter's pulpit on November 20, 1955, King gave a powerful exegesis of a core text in Christianity, the parable of the Good Samaritan, which Jesus uttered in response to a question "from a certain lawyer. . . . Master, what shall I do to inherit eternal life," or "be saved" in contemporary Christian parlance. Like most good rhetoricians handling an exceedingly familiar theme, King's literary device in explaining this core text was that most people had interpreted it wrongly. And in King's hands, the text became a clear message to become neighbor as the answer to the question, highlighting King's social gospel as relevant and revolutionary.[35]

In the narrative, a man heading down the road to Jericho was beaten nearly to death, robbed, and left stranded and naked on the roadside. In the wake of this violence, a Levite and then a priest, much too busy to tend to the needs of the wounded man, passed by. But the socially despised Samaritan rendered aid. King suggested that Jesus told the story for a specific purpose and earlier expositors had erred by reading the passage so as to reduce Christian responsibility simply to the requirement of opportunistically doing good deeds. He even asserted that the priest and Levite might have actually been in a hurry to discharge extremely important social justice responsibilities. That is, there was a "case" to be made for their passing by on the other side of the roadway. Indeed, in King's reinterpretation, not just the priest and the Levite, but also the Samaritan all demonstrated "shortcomings." They dealt with immediate circumstances, something King said was important but not enough to discharge the totality of their moral charge as Christians. Because the Samaritan "sought to sooth the effects of evil, without going back to uproot the cause," he had not done his full duty: "Like the good Samaritan we must always stand ready to descend to the depth of human need. The person who fails to look with compassion upon the thousands of individuals left wounded by life's many roadsides is not only unethical, but ungodly. Every Christian must ply [play?] the good Samaritan. But there is another aspect of Christian social responsibility which is just as compelling. It seeks to tear down unjust conditions and build anew instead of patching things up. It seeks to clear the Jericho road of robbers as well as caring for the victims of robbery."[36]

Delivered just three weeks before Mrs. Rosa Parks's arrest would catalyze a movement, King's Good Samaritan sermon should be read in the context of his working with a congregation of relatively comfortable African Americans, many of whom had the best jobs that the racist Jim Crow South permitted blacks to have. They faced material risks, were they to put King's ideas into practice. King hoped to awaken his parishioners to a deeper sense of responsibility, which is the significant challenge for applying Christianity. No one knew that the boycott was soon to ensue. King was not alone in the 1950s and 1960s in his ministerial struggle with other Christians about what that religion might require of the faithful in a country seemingly at ease in a Zion of racial apartheid.

Many African Americans, best exemplified by Reverend Joseph H. Jackson, pastor of Olivet Baptist Church in Chicago and long-time president of the National Baptist Convention, advocated a priestly gospel of gradualism and spoke critically of King's subsequent campaigns of creative tension and nonviolent resistance of Jim Crow. That is, Martin Luther King's black social gospel did not enjoy universal support among African American Baptists. King's theology was much more akin to that of white Methodist Ed King, a native of Vicksburg, Mississippi, and chaplain of Tugaloo College, whose radical version of Christianity—one writer calls it "countercultural"—mixed a thoroughgoing social gospel with a personal belief in the real, transcendent presence of a personal Christ. This white King won the ire of mainstream Methodists in Mississippi for attempting to integrate worship services, in 1964, in a series of "visitations." King's Mississippi Methodist brethren constructed a Christianity resembling that of E. Douglas Hudgins, pastor of First Baptist Church, Jackson, Mississippi, and long-time leader of the Mississippi Baptist Convention, whose Christian ideology made no place for the social gospel. Christianity consisted of responding to Christ's invitation of salvation through faith; it assuredly did not entail ameliorating the social conditions of humanity beyond those minimally necessary to permit individuals to hear and respond to the gospel. Hence, in this view, a Christian ought actively to oppose communism, because its godless materialism did not allow Christian preaching. But Jim Crow was another matter. Whatever its evils, under Jim Crow, a vibrant African American Christianity obviously thrived. Perhaps, in time, more and more Christians would find interracial brotherhood through a recognition of a common humanity made possible by an awareness of their common faith, but the church was not to make such an outcome a goal of its ministry.[37]

Martin Luther King's social gospel stood as a powerful dissent to the more conservative articulations of the Baptist faith, white and black. It consisted of a call to patrol the menacing highway of life, rendering aid and reconfiguring the social order so that fewer and fewer people were in need of material and moral aid. As King told his auditors at Riverside Church in April 1967: "True compassion is more than flinging a coin to a beggar. . . . It comes to see that an edifice which produces beggars needs restructuring."[38]

After a whirlwind career that saw the creation of the Southern Christian Leadership Conference; movements in Albany, Birmingham, Selma, and Chicago; designation as *Time* magazine's "Man of the Year" in 1964;

and attainment of the Nobel Prize, by late 1967, King, the Southern Christian Leadership Conference, and other civil rights groups prepared for the Poor People's Campaign, which would include a massive march on Washington and the establishment of a large tent city on the National Mall to call attention to the need for economic redress, something in King's estimation a so-called Christian nation was obliged to do.

On February 1, 1968, Echol Cole and Robert Walker, two Memphis sanitation workers, were crushed to death when a malfunctioning garbage compacter into which the men had crawled to escape a driving rainstorm, had activated. The settlement for the victims' families did not even cover funeral costs. Within a week, the fledgling Memphis Local Number 1733 of the American Federation of State, County, and Municipal Employees, the sanitation workers' union, struck. Once invited to lend assistance, King believed that he had to go to Memphis, despite the pressing need to work on the Poor People's Campaign, because as he had said from the dark cell in Birmingham, "Injustice anywhere is a threat to justice everywhere." He hoped to show that a nonviolent demonstration could yield amelioration for poor workers in Memphis and demonstrate its viability as an option elsewhere. It was another expression of his consistent social Christianity.[39]

King first came to Memphis on March 18, 1968, addressing a mammoth crowd at the Mason Temple Church. He expressed admiration for the simple slogan adopted by the strikers: "I AM A MAN," which King understood to be their essential assertion of humanity. They were human beings, not things. He noted that in their standing up, they were making it more difficult for others to oppress them: "A man is hard to ride unless his back is bent." Impromptu, he returned to the various themes he had articulated throughout his public career, themes deeply seated in the concepts of the social gospel. "You are demonstrating that we are all tied in a single garment of destiny and that if one black person suffers, if one black person is down, we are all down," he said, before returning to his restructuring ethic, "that it is a crime for people to live in this rich nation and receive starvation wages. . . . It is criminal to have people working on a full-time basis and a full-time job getting starvation wages." Concluding that theme in a conversational reference to Matthew 25:40, he noted that: "This may well be the indictment on America." It had built massive infrastructure and stockpiled wealth but ignored the command of Jesus: "If you do it unto the least of these, of my children, you do it unto me."[40]

The nonviolent demonstration was to have occurred on March 22, but a snowstorm of biblical proportions struck Memphis, requiring the cancellation of the protest and, given King's schedule, it had to be put off until March 28. When it finally commenced, poor planning and the infusion of a police riot created a media nightmare for King, the strikers, and the movement supporters in general. King's advisors removed him from the scene and checked him into the Rivermont Hotel. King's critics lampooned him as an agitator who scurried for cover in a palatial hotel while police were left to deal with the disorder King has instigated. The white power structure worked to link the failed march in Memphis with the imminent march on Washington, hoping to compel its cancellation. Mississippi's Senator John Stennis insisted that the likely violence required a court injunction to stop the march and West Virginia Senator Robert Byrd denounced King as a "self-seeking rabble-rouser." Stung by the criticism of cowardice, wearied by the accusation of instigator, King was determined to return to Memphis, stage a peaceful demonstration, and, for his image's sake, to stay at the Lorraine Motel, an intention the media widely reported. King was even filmed by local television entering Room 306 on his return to the city on April 3.[41]

King planned to spend the evening of April 3 working on the Poor People's Campaign, but when Ralph David Abernethy and other King aides arrived at Monument Temple to speak to supporters of the Memphis movement, the building strained with the throngs who had braved a powerful thunderstorm and desired to hear King, the son of thunder, himself. He was telephoned and soon arrived to give an address. He did not know that it would be his last public utterance, but to many, it was his best public speech, filled with the cadences of the African American church and buttressed by a philosophy of Christian activism that he had encountered, embraced, and nurtured throughout his life. He noted that nonviolent unity was the key to success in Memphis. The movement for social, economic, and political liberation was growing worldwide and Memphis was a part of that larger struggle in which human beings were now having to

> grapple with the problems that men have been trying to grapple with through history, but the demand didn't force them to do it. Survival demands that we grapple with them. Men, for years now, have been talking about war and peace. But now, no longer can they just talk about it. It is no longer a choice between violence and nonviolence in this world; it's nonviolence or nonexistence. That is where we are today. And also in the human rights revolution, if something

isn't done, and in a hurry, to bring the colored peoples of the world out of their long years of poverty, their long years of hurt and neglect, the whole world is doomed.[42]

He praised his fellow ministers particularly for their role in leading this movement, using those same biblical references that were emblematic of his own social preaching: "Who is it that is supposed to articulate the longings and aspirations of the people more than the preacher? Somehow the preacher must be an Amos, and say, 'Let justice roll down like waters and righteousness like a mighty stream.' Somehow, the preacher must say with Jesus, 'The spirit of the Lord is upon me, because he hath anointed me to deal with the problems of the poor.'"[43]

Continuing with the theme of social Christianity, King noted: "I'm always happy to see a relevant ministry. It's all right to talk about 'long white robes over yonder,' in all of its symbolism. But ultimately people want some suits and dresses and shoes to wear down here. It's all right to talk about 'streets flowing with milk and honey,' but God has commanded us to be concerned about the slums down here, and his children who can't eat three square meals a day. It's all right to talk about the new Jerusalem, but one day, God's preachers must talk about the New York, the new Atlanta, the new Philadelphia, the new Los Angeles, the new Memphis, Tennessee. This is what we have to do."[44]

King then described strategies for unity and organized activity, including boycotts, to pressure the economic system for redress. The practical activist King was also King the Baptist preacher and, regaining his religious tack, he retold the parable of the Good Samaritan. Adding a reference to Martin Buber, King initially followed the same development of the ideas he had expressed some thirteen years earlier in Montgomery at Dexter Avenue Baptist Church, but he twisted the teaching point to suit the needs of the moment. The priest and Levite did not stop because they were hurrying on their way to deal with the root causes of Jericho Road violence, but then King mused, "It's possible those men were afraid." They too might be robbed, so they hurried on their way, thinking, "If I stop, what will happen to me?" In King's retelling of the story, the Good Samaritan reversed the question: "If I do not stop, what will happen to him?"[45]

King concluded his explication of the dangerous civil rights road in Jericho and in Memphis. And, perhaps, his final words—"Mine eyes have seen the glory of the coming of the Lord"—referred to his belief that his brand of social Christianity might actually realize the Kingdom of God on the Earth. James Earl Ray's slug cut short the opportunity to obtain direct evidence from the preacher King. But he left behind a solid explanation of what took him to the mountaintop of ministerial care, of his Baptist pilgrimage in the challenging racial and economic times of the mid-twentieth century. As a first-semester student at Crozer, King wrote: "Above all, I see the preaching ministry as a dual process. On the one hand, I must attempt to change the souls of individuals so that their societies may be changed. On the other I must attempt to change the societies so that the individual soul will have a change. Therefore, I must be concerned about unemployment, slums, and economic insecurity. I am a profound advocate of the social gospel."[46]

Notes

1. Hampton Sides, *Hell Hound on His Trail: The Stalking of Martin Luther King Jr., and the International Hunt for his Assassin* (New York: Doubleday, 2010), 145, 153, 165–71; Michael K. Honey, *Going Down Jericho Road: The Memphis Strike, Martin Luther King's Last Campaign* (New York: W. W. Norton, 2007), 450.

2. Don Wolfensberger, "The Martin Luther King Jr. Holiday: The Long Struggle in Congress, An Introductory Essay," pp. 2, 7. Seminar on "The Martin Luther King Jr. Holiday: How Did It Happen?" Woodrow Wilson International Center for Scholars, Monday, January 14, 2008, accessed April 20, 2011, http://www.wilsoncenter.org/events/docs/King%20Holiday-essay-drw.pdf; Francis Romero, "A Brief History of Martin Luther King Day," *Time*, January 18, 2010, accessed April 20, 2011, http://www.time.com/time/nation/article/0,8599,1872501,00.html.

3. The list of excellent King biographies is delightfully long. Key is David J. Garrow, *Bearing the Cross: Martin Luther King and the Southern Christian Leadership Conference* (New York: William Morrow, 1986). In addition to recent treatments cited in the text, see Adams Fairclough, *To Redeem the Soul of America: The Southern Christian Leadership Conference and Martin Luther King Jr.* (Athens: University of Georgia Press, 1987), and his *Martin Luther King Jr.* (Athens: University of Georgia Press, 1990); Stewart Burns, *To the Mountaintop: Martin Luther King Jr.'s Sacred Mission to Save America, 1955–1968* (San Francisco: HarperCollins, 2004), esp. 53–56 on King's "personalism"; David L. Lewis, *King: A Biography* (New York: Praeger, 1970). On King and personalism, see also "Introduction," and Martin Luther King Jr., "Final Answers, Personalism," January 1952, in *Papers of Martin Luther King Jr.*, vol. 2: *Rediscovering Precious Values, July 1951–November 1955*, ed. Clayborne Carson et al.

(Berkeley: University of California Press, 1994), 2–10, 112. Professor Peter J. Paris employs a typology for African American ministers in the twentieth century: priestly, prophetic, political, and nationalist. See his insightful *Black Religious Leaders: Conflict in Unity* (Louisville, KY: Westminster/John Knox Press, 1991), 17–28. A welter of scholarly material on the social gospel also exists. A splendid and succinct introduction to the scholarly literature, especially in its Baptist context, is Keith Harper, *The Quality of Mercy: Southern Baptists and Social Christianity, 1890–1920* (Tuscaloosa: The University of Alabama Press, 1995), 1–12.

4. Clayborne Carson, "Martin Luther King Jr., and the African-American Social Gospel," in *African-American Christianity: Essays in History*, ed. Paule E. Johnson (Berkeley: University of California Press, 1994), 159–77.

5. Clayborne Carson et al., eds., *Papers of Martin Luther King Jr.*, vol. 6: *Advocate of the Social Gospel, September 1948–March 1963* (Berkeley: University of California Press, 2007), esp. 40–41; Troy Jackson, *Becoming King: Martin Luther King and the Making of a National Leader* (Lexington: University Press of Kentucky, 2008), xiv–xv, 11–12, 144.

6. Harvard Sitkoff, *King: Pilgrimage to the Mountaintop* (New York: Hill and Wang, 2008), xi; King to Coretta Scott, July 18, 1952, in *Advocate of the Social Gospel*, 123–26.

7. King, "To Coretta Scott," *Advocate of the Social Gospel*, 123–26.

8. Ibid.

9. Martin Luther King Jr., "Beyond Vietnam: Address Delivered to the Clergy and Laymen Concerned about Vietnam, at Riverside Church," April 4, 1967, pp. 2, 9, pdf file, *A Call to Conscience: The Landmark Speeches of Martin Luther King Jr.*, Martin Luther King Junior Papers Project, Stanford University, accessed April 20, 2011, http://mlk-kpp01.stanford.edu/kingweb/publications/speeches/Beyond_Vietnam.pdf.

10. Keith D. Miller, *Voice of Deliverance: The Language of Martin Luther King Jr., and Its Sources* (New York: The Free Press, 1992), 2–8; Carson, "King Jr., and the African American Social Gospel," 159. An excellent summary of King's formal education, its sources, and impacts, is Taylor Branch, *Parting the Waters: America in the King Years, 1954–1963* (New York: Simon and Schuster, 1988), 27–104.

11. Clayborne Carson et al., eds., *Papers of Martin Luther King Jr.*, vol. 1: *Called to Serve, January 1929–June 1951* (Berkley: University of California Press, 1992), 4–18.

12. Ibid., 18–26, 33. Having traveled to Germany and been inspired by Martin Luther, Michael King Sr., legally changed his name and that of his

second child and namesake, to Martin Luther King. Some of King's acquaintances thus continued to call King Jr., "Mike," but he was often called "ML" by some intimates, especially during his days in Montgomery, and "Martin" by his ministerial friends.

13. Ibid., 37–39.

14. Benjamin E. Mays, *The Negro's God as Reflected in His Literature* (New York: Russell and Russell, 1938), 255.

15. Howard Thurman, *With Head and Heart: The Autobiography of Howard Thurman* (New York: Harcourt Brace & Co., 1979), 254–55; Howard Thurman, *Jesus and the Disinherited*, reprint ed. (Boston: Beacon Press, 1996), 100 and see esp. introduction by Vincent Harding; Miller, *Voice of Deliverance*, 120–21.

16. *Called to Serve*, 42–43; Drew University Library, *George D. Kelsey Papers, 1932–1996—Finding Aid*, accessed April 20, 2011, http://www.drew.edu/depts/library.aspx?id=13207.

17. *Called to Serve,* 55; Miller, *Voice of Deliverance,* 54–58; Ralph E. Luker, *The Social Gospel in Black and White: American Radical Reform, 1885–1915* (Chapel Hill: University of North Carolina Press, 1991), 319–22.

18. Martin Luther King Jr., "How to Use the Bible in Modern Theological Construction," *Called to Serve,* 251–56; Miller, *Voice of Deliverance,* 164–65. In inscribing a copy of *Stride Toward Freedom* for Fosdick, King wrote: "If I were called upon to select the greatest preacher of this century, I would choose your name." Quoted in *Advocate of the Social Gospel,* 30.

19. Martin Luther King Jr., "Reinhold Niebuhr's Ethical Dualism," May 9, 1952, in *Papers of Martin Luther King Jr.,* vol.2: *Rediscovering Precious Values, July 1951–November 1955,* ed. Clayborne Carson et al. (Berkeley: University of California Press, 1994), 55, 142, 146–47, 150. Jeremiah, in *Rediscovering Precious Values,* 166. Jeremiah 17:5 reads: Thus saith the Lord; Cursed by the man that trusteth in man, and makes flesh his arm, and whose heart departeth from the Lord." See Miller, *Voice of Deliverance,* 104–8, for a demonstration of how few of Niebuhr's ideas show up in King's homiletics.

20. Miller, *Voice of Deliverance,* 2–3, 90–92, 190; East Carolina University, Special Collection Guides, *Preliminary Inventory of the J. Wallace Hamilton Collection, ca. 1963–1977,* accessed April 21, 2011, http://digital.lib.ecu.edu/special/ead/findingaids/0970/0970.pdf.

21. Miller, *Voices of Deliverance,* 69–71.

22. Martin Luther King Jr., "Note Cards," September 1952–January 1953, in *Rediscovering Precious Values,* 165.

23. Ibid., 167.

24. Ibid., 249. In subsequent sermons, King often suggested that bombs were a poor substitute for divine love in dealing with social problems. See his "Questions that Easter Answers," April 21, 1957, ibid., 292.

25. Martin Luther King Jr., "Communism's Challenge to Christianity," August 9, 1953, in *Advocate of the Social Gospel,* 147–49. Apart from the sermon itself, here King is borrowing from a white minister in a sermon to the black congregants at Ebenezer Baptist Church. On King and the communist accusations, see Garrow, *Bearing the Cross,* 360–63 and Sitkoff, *King,* 15, 142–43.

26. Martin Luther King Jr., "A Religion of Doing," July 4, 1954, in *Advocate of the Social Gospel,* 171, 173. A marvelous outcome of the effort by Clarence Carson and his fellow editors at the King Papers project in the published King volumes shows how the demands of civil rights activism affected King's preaching preparation. This sermon was written out in full; by the spring of 1955, King's sermons are largely outlines.

27. Martin Luther King Jr., "Pride Versus Humility: The Parable of the Pharisee and the Publican," September 25, 1955, in *Advocate of the Social Gospel,* 231–32. For Emmett Till, see Stephen J. Whitfield, *A Death in the Delta: The Story of Emmett Till* (Baltimore: The Johns Hopkins University Press, 1988); William Bradford Huie, "The Shocking Story of Approved Killing in Mississippi," *Look* 20 (January 24, 1956): 46–49, accessed April 22, 2011, http://www.pbs.org/wgbh/amex/till/sfeature/sf_look_confession.html.

28. King, "Pride Versus Humility," *Advocate of the Social Gospel,* 232.

29. Martin Luther King Jr., "When Peace Becomes Obnoxious," March 18, 1956, in *Advocate of the Social Gospel,* 258–59. King's recitation of the goal of realizing the Kingdom of God on the Earth is standard social gospel fare. Walter Rauschenbusch wrote about the church's real mission: "It is not a matter of getting individuals to heaven, but of transforming the life on earth into the harmony of heaven." *Christianity and the Social Crisis* (New York: MacMillan & Co., 1913), 65. In his "Been to the Mountaintop" finale, King proclaims, "I just want to do God's will," as an antidote for the fear he faced as a leader in the civil rights movement. For Autherine Lucy, see William Warren Rogers, Robert David Ward, Leah Rawls Atkins, and Wayne Flynt, *Alabama: The History of a Deep South State* (Tuscaloosa: University of Alabama Press, 1994), 569, 572.

30. Martin Luther King Jr., "Recommendations to the Dexter Avenue Baptist Church for the Fiscal Year 1954–1955," *Rediscovering Precious Values,* 287–94; Jackson, *Becoming King,* 38; Clayborne Carson et al., "Introduction," *Advocate of the Social Gospel,* 19. The vast literature on the Montgomery Bus Boycott illustrates how no one person made the movement; indeed, in so many de-

monstrable ways, the boycott made King, but as I am trying to argue here, he had prepared himself to be made. Jackson's splendid *Becoming King,* and his fellow Papers Project alumnus Stewart Burns's *To the Mountaintop,* 3–155, detail this rich intersection. Robinson's memoir, *The Montgomery Bus Boycott and the Women Who Started It* (Knoxville: University of Tennessee Press, 1987) is de rigueur for anyone addressing this question, as is Mary Fair Burks, "Trailblazers: Women in the Montgomery Bus Boycott," in *Women in the Civil Rights Movement: Trailblazers & Torchbearers, 1941–1965,* ed. Vicki L. Crawford, Jacqueline Anne Rouse, and Barbara Woods, reprint ed. (Bloomington: Indiana University Press, 1993). The larger context is thoroughly treated in a manner that demolishes any attempt to tell the story of Montgomery as a simple black-white morality play in J. Mills Thornton's magisterial *Dividing Lines: Municipal Politics and the Struggle for Civil Rights in Montgomery, Birmingham, and Selma* (Tuscaloosa: The University of Alabama Press, 2002), 1–140.

31. Carson et al., "Introduction," *Call to Serve,* 42–43.

32. Carson et al., "Introduction," *Rediscovering Precious Values,* 2–3; Ira de Augustine Reid, *The Negro Baptist Ministry: An Analysis of Its Profession, Preparation, and Practices,* report of a survey conducted by the Joint Survey Commission of the Baptist Inter-Convention Committee: The American Baptist Convention, The National Baptist Convention, The Southern Baptist Convention (n.p.: Baptist Inter-Convention Committee, 1951), 20–21.

33. Clayborne Carson, "Introduction," *Rediscovering Precious Values,* 3–4; Martin Luther King Jr., "Final Examination Answers, Philosophy of Religion," January 9, 1952, in *Rediscovering Precious Values;* Sitkoff, *King,* 17.

34. Garrow, *Bearing the Cross,* 89; Sitkoff, *King,* 38. Interestingly, King's juvenile speech followed the same rhetorical structure of his famous "I Have a Dream" speech of August 1963. King began his address with the promise of the Declaration of Independence and noted that "Black America still wears chains," an eerie foreshadowing of "One hundred years later the Negro is still not free." Martin Luther King Jr., "The Negro and the Constitution," May 1944, *Called to Serve,* 109–11.

35. Luke 10:25–37. Martin Luther King Jr., "The One-Sided Approach of the Good Samaritan," November 20, 1955, *Advocate of the Social Gospel,* 239–40.

36. King, "The One-Sided Approach of the Good Samaritan," 239–40.

37. Joseph H. Jackson, *Unholy Shadows and Freedom's Holy Light* (Nashville: Townshend, 1967), 94–182; For Ed King and Hudgins, see Charles Marsh, *God's Long Summer: Stories of Faith and Civil Rights,* reprint ed. (Princeton, NJ: Princeton University Press, 2008), 82–151.

38. Howard Zinn, *The Power of Nonviolence: Writings by Advocates of Peace* (Boston: Beacon Press, 2002), 122.

39. Honey, *Going Down the Jericho Road,* 96–102. Garrow, *Bearing the Cross,* 575–624.

40. Honey, *Going Down the Jericho Road,* 296–99.

41. Ibid., 362–71.

42. Martin Luther King Jr., "I've Been to the Mountaintop," April 3, 1968, p. 2, pdf file, *A Call to Conscience: The Landmark Speeches of Martin Luther King Jr.,* Martin Luther King Junior Papers Project, Stanford University, accessed April 24, 2011, http://mlkkpp01.stanford.edu/kingweb/publications/speeches/I%27ve_been_to_the_mountaintop.pdf.

43. Ibid., 4.

44. Ibid.

45. Ibid., 5–6.

46. Martin Luther King Jr., "Preaching Ministry," September 14–November 24, 1948, *Advocate of the Social Gospel,* 72.

III
Historiography

8
"Written that Ye May Believe"
Primitive Baptist Historiography
John G. Crowley

A denomination with *Primitive* in their title proclaims a deep commitment to the principle of *ad fontes* and, therefore, a profound commitment to the past, at least as they understand it to have been. Two factors hamper their investigations. First, most Primitive Baptist history is purely oral or recorded in unpublished church minute books or brief associational minutes, which often conceal more than they reveal. Though seldom read, the manuscript church minutes are carefully guarded, at least until they pass into the hands of descendants of members who throw them out with the trash. The history known to the average Primitive is an oral tradition that extends with some accuracy for about three generations.[1]

Reading old records can have an alarming effect on the brethren. Perhaps the most dramatic effect of the resurfacing of old records occurred in the Bennett Faction of the Alabaha River Association. While some members of the association pondered their ancient ban on receiving "missionary" baptism, a meddling historian, who shall remain nameless, pointed them to the 1765 minutes of the Philadelphia Association. Smith's Creek Church queried the association "whether it be proper to receive a person into communion who had *been* baptized by *immersion* by a minister of the church of England, if no other objection could be made?" The association answered "Yea, if he had been baptized on a profession of faith and repentance." The Alabaha concurred, and the shock waves disrupted church fellowship across a large reach of southeastern Georgia and caused the complete disintegration of the woefully misnamed "Peace" faction of the Union Primitive Baptist Association.[2]

Another barrier to Primitive Baptist historiography lies in their widespread suspicion of religious literature as a futile infringement on the prerogative of Almighty God. In this vein, the authors of the 1832 *Black Rock Address,* the very *Magna Carta* of the Old School, condemned extreme claims made for religious tracts as "charg[ing] God with folly; for why has he given us the extensive revelation contained in the Bible, and given the Holy Spirit *to take of the things of Christ and show them to us,* if a little tract of four pages can lead a soul to the knowledge of Christ." Likewise, the Black Rock Convention condemned the idea of denominational schools, because it "implies that our distinct views of church government, of gospel doctrine and gospel ordinances, are connected with human sciences, a principle which we cannot admit: for we believe the kingdom of Christ to be altogether a kingdom not of the world."[3]

In spite of their suspicion of worldly wisdom and uninspired writings, Primitive Baptists' strong identification with the Baptist past inevitably led a few of them into writing history of a sort. I define *Primitive Baptist history* as writing on historical themes by Primitive Baptists for Primitive Baptists. I propose to examine four such writings.

Joshua Lawrence: *The American Telescope* (1825)

Elder Joshua Lawrence was a leading figure in the Kehukee Association of North Carolina, one of the most influential anti-missionary bodies. After tolerating missionary activity in their membership for several years, the Kehukee declared nonfellowship with Missionism in 1827, one of the earliest associations to do so. Lawrence led the opposition to missions.[4]

Born in North Carolina in 1778, Lawrence had little formal education, but a powerful mind and eloquent pen, and no small stock of information for a largely self-educated bivocational Baptist preacher in the pine barrens and pocosins of Eastern North Carolina.[5] His *The American Telescope,* published under his usual pen name, "A Clodhopper of North Carolina," was a tract of twenty-four pages that relied heavily on historical references.[6]

Lawrence's chief concern stemmed from the difference between a spontaneous, genuine "revival" and what he saw as a spurious excitement gotten up by human agency. Lawrence knew many who had experienced the Great Awakening and had himself witnessed the Great Revival. He contrasted the dependence on financial support of the modern missionary with the figures of the past: "How unlike the prophets, John the Baptist, Jesus Christ, the apostles, a Luther, a George Whitfield, a Wesley, a Dow, and a thousand others who are ornaments to the free gospel of Christ; all impressed with the worth of souls; and who go forth taking up their cross, denying themselves, and devoting themselves to the work of God, for the good of men: dependant on God, without begging or being shamefully backed by monied societies."[7] In light of the narrow sectarianism that came to characterize many Primitive Baptists, Lawrence's appreciation of so many non-Baptists and even nonpredestinarians is impressive, as is his apparent view of the Baptists as being in the mainstream of classical Protestantism.

Lawrence believed the slow and paltry results of missionary effort constituted another proof of divine disapprobation. He found missionary work in India a sad contrast to that of God-sent evangelists of old, having read unimpressive reports "that about three hundred persons have been, at last, persuaded to renounce *cast* and turn Christian, after fifteen or twenty years' labour, when a single Peter, a Paul, a Luther, a Whitefield, a Wesley, and others, being sent of God, have done more in a few days or weeks, without the aid of self-created societies, and monied institutions, and numerous beggars not sanctioned by the word of God, nor found in the pages of the New Testament."[8]

As might be expected from one born in the midst of the American Revolution, Lawrence feared mixing of money and religion boded ill for liberty and the separation of church and state. After mentioning the results of Constantine's establishment of Christianity, and Henry VIII's establishment of royal supremacy, he warned: "And does it not show us, as a beacon, on our own coast, how we should endeavor to keep the church apart from any influence of the men of this world; for they know not the things of the spirit, and hence their influence is always bad. But the clergy want to get hold of their fat purses, and this is the way they have taken to do it: to build a sort of National Church, and let them come into it for pay, having a fixed price for members, directors, and presidents for life, and so they make a sort of half-brothers of the rich men of this world."[9] Lawrence praised the constitution of North Carolina, which banned clergymen from seats in the legislature.[10] He concludes by citing the Crusades, the St. Bartholomew's Massacre, and the Anglican persecution of the Baptists of Virginia as typical results when carnal methods are applied to religious aims.[11] Keenly aware of the temptation power offers to fallen human nature, the antimissionaries feared not only the spiritual futility of the benevolences, but also the threat offered to liberty by concentrations of power and wealth. The Black Rock Convention conceded that one benevolence, the Bible Society, seemed "calculated to meet the approbation of all those who know the value of the sacred Scriptures."[12] However, under this plausible guise, the American Bible Society presented a frightening "combination of worldly power and influence lodged in the hands of a *few*, render[ing] it a dangerous engine against the liberties, both civil and religious, of our country, should it come under the control of those disposed so to employ it."[13] They believed all the other benevolent organizations equally dangerous.[14]

Although Lawrence's opposition to missions was intense, it did not indicate any yawning theological chasm. The next example of Old Baptist historiography differs considerably. Lawrence wrote at the beginning of the schism, Benjamin Griffin wrote at its conclusion, when many things once indifferent had become set in stone.

Benjamin Griffin: *History of the Primitive Baptists of Mississippi* (1853)

The schism looming in 1825 was all but complete in 1850. In that year, the Primitive Baptist Association of Mississippi appointed Benjamin Griffin of Holmes County, a prosperous farmer, to write a history of the Mississippi Primitive Baptists.[15] His association had been organized in 1839 expressly in opposition to the doctrine of universal atonement and the missions movement. In 1840, the association declared the reception of "missionary" baptism to be disorder, which usually signaled the final, irrevocable break into separate denominations.[16]

Griffin intended "not only to set forth the History of the Primitive Baptists of Mississippi, but also to show to all concerned that they now occupy the same platform of principles that the Primitive or Regular Baptists have ever done as far back as their history can be traced."[17] Griffin prefaces his work by a review of the chain of supposed Baptist antecedents extending through the "Novations [*sic*], the Paulicians, the Paterines, and the Waldenses" to the Apostolic Church. He apparently knew that many of these groups bore little resemblance to one another, not to mention contemporary Baptists. He avoided the difficulty with the ingenious observation that titles such as *Protestant* and *Baptist* cover a multitude of variants, and, therefore, the true believers of old, persecuted and hidden, passed through the centuries under a multitude of names, unnoticed in a company of dissenters that often varied from them in belief and practice.[18]

Perhaps aware of the shaky foundations of this pedigree, or merely exhibiting Old Baptist suspicion of human learning, Griffin then declared, "Church history, except what little can be gleaned from the inspired writers, is, at best, nothing more than the traditions of men."[19] He further observed, "Though God has no doubt reserved to Himself, in all ages of the Gospel day, a people who have never bowed the knee to Baal, yet, to say that the legitimacy of his visible church depends on proving a regular succession from the days of the Apostles, would be laying an unnecessary burden upon the household of faith." With this caveat stated, Griffin quotes at length from Jones's *Church History* on the Waldenses.[20] He continued on to the Anabaptists and used the same argument of multiplicity of opinion under a common name to distance the Baptists from some of the extravagances and heresies of the early rebaptizers. Johan Lorenz Mosheim was his chief resource in this section and highly valued because of his supposed Lutheran animus against the Anabaptists.[21] He then skipped lightly to the English Baptists and after briefly noting the mere existence of the General Baptists, hails the 1689 Particular Baptist Confession as "in substance the same as those of the Primitive, or Old School Baptists of this day."[22] The ensuing chapter consisted entirely of excerpts from the most thoroughly Calvinistic chapters of the Century Confession: "Of God's Decree," "Of Divine Providence," "Of Effectual Calling," "Of Good Works," and "Of the Perseverance of the Saints." "The foregoing is deemed amply sufficient to portray the distinguishing features in the articles of faith of the Particular Baptists of that day."[23]

Andrew Fuller (1754–1815) represents the embodiment of false doctrine to American Primitive Baptists and to English Strict and Particular Baptists, especially those of the Gospel Standard connection. The dominant Baptist writing theologian of the eighteenth century was the fabulously learned John Gill (1697–1771) whose voluminous works set forth such high predestinarian views that his successor Charles Haddon Spurgeon called him the "Coryphaeus of the Hyper Calvinists."[24] Although himself converted under the "hardening, refrigerant, soporific, hyper-Calvinistic, Antinomian" doctrine then in vogue among the Baptists, Fuller largely rejected Gill's theology and popularized a modified Calvinism setting forth an "indefinite" atonement rather than the view that Christ suffered for a definite number of particular persons and them alone. Fuller also taught that humanity's inability to perform any spiritual good was not "proper or physical, but only figurative or moral" and that ministers ought to give "the most unlimited invitations to unconverted hearers of the gospel." He further argued that parts of his doctrine might be "inconsistent with the doctrines of grace" but that both were "scriptural and therefore true."[25] Fuller's doctrine reflected the emotional, antirationalist aspect of the romantic era, as opposed to the careful definitions and logical balance of John Gill and other children of the age of reason.[26] The circulation of his views in England and America caused an enormous uproar among the Baptists, with missions and the other benevolences seen by many as the logical offspring of Fuller's hypo-Calvinism. The Noxubee Primitive Baptist Association of Mississippi stated this in their constitutional documents: "We ... contend that the system was originated in Arminianism, and to act consistent, they are obligated to preach a doctrine equivalent to it."[27]

Not surprisingly, Griffin drew attention to the London Confession's contradiction of Andrew Fuller's doctrine of an indefinite atonement: "The Lord Jesus, by his perfect obedience and sacrifice of himself, which he, through the eternal spirit, once offered up unto God, hath fully satisfied the justice of God, procured reconciliation, and purchased an everlasting inheritance in the Kingdom of Heaven, for all those whom the Father hath given unto him."[28] Speaking of Fuller's doctrine of the atonement, Griffin denied any intention to "sift the abstruse disquisitions of Mr. Fuller on this subject." After a few quotations and biblical texts offered in response, Griffin declared Fuller's views on atonement "so refined and obscure, that most of his followers suppose him to be in favor of a general atonement—while those who do understand him, can occupy a position between the Arminian and Predestinarian, and cozen the former on the atonement, and the latter on the application."[29]

After notice of Fuller's theology, Griffin advanced to criticize the institutions growing from it. Quoting Fuller's comment, "There was a great responsibility attached to us who began the business," Griffin drily concurred that Fuller "no doubt uttered a profound truth." On the subject of missions in general, Griffin observes that their principal text, "Go ye into all the world," seems to have been fulfilled in the days of the New Testament, citing Colossians 1:23 and Romans 10:18. To further distinguish the duties of modern preachers from the apostles, he quoted from the 1847 circular of the Primitive Baptist Association to the effect that the apostles were also commanded to work miracles.[30] In succeeding chapters, Griffin reproduced testimonies to the often luxurious, tyrannical, and duplicitous behavior of missionaries in India, Africa, Polynesia, and the West Indies.

Missions in America he excoriated for their emphasis on money, their courting of the "world," and their watering down of historic Baptist theological and disciplinary standards to further their cause. Like most Old Baptists, Griffin feared the rise of a powerful union of religious auxiliaries that would in time constitute a new establishment of religion and tyrannize the consciences of Americans. He quoted a Boston newspaper with similar concerns: "We never had any doubt but there were some who supported religion from the best motives; but we believe that many support it with about the same object that the multitude had when they followed Jesus—namely for 'the loaves and fishes.'" Further, "we find tract societies established, charitable institutions set on foot; new plans devised to meliorate our condition: new buildings erected; new laws devised; new improvements suggested; and when we follow them up and see them organized, we shall find the pious, humane, and totally disinterested projectors filling the lucrative places of presidents, scribes, agents, clerks, printers, etc.,—a son here, a brother there, and religion is made to answer the purpose of private gain, under the specious pretext of public good."[31] Griffin then cites the description (and cost) of an elaborate "Missionary" Baptist church in a northern city, and then asked, "Is it possible that these people, who make such a lavish expenditure of money, for such purposes, do, in the sincerity of their hearts, believe that that money could have been made instrumental in saving souls from perdition?"[32]

After spending about one-fourth of his volume laying a foundation in the blood of Fullerism and its works, Griffin at last turns to the history of the Baptists in Mississippi. Because he was born in Mississippi about 1808, only a few years after it passed into undisputed American sovereignty, Griffin was probably related to many of the first planters of the Baptist faith in that region. He related that "prior to 1785" a few South Carolinians, Baptists among them, had removed to Spanish territory at Natchez, fleeing the tumults of the Revolution. Their attempts at Baptist worship met with harassment from Catholic authorities until the cession of Natchez in 1795, when they organized a church.[33] In 1807, a sufficient number of churches existed to organize the Mississippi Association, with articles of faith as Calvinistic as any Primitive Baptist could desire.[34] Griffin then follows the rather cumbersome plan of narrating the history of each separate association, mainly by copious extracts from their minutes. He concentrates on associations ancestral to the later Primitive Baptists and to the Primitive Baptist associations themselves. As a narrative of the rise and course of the mission division in Mississippi, his work is partisan but copious and firsthand. Besides the bête noire of Missionism, he also noted other issues such as freemasonry, Parkerism, and Campbellism. The "two seed" doctrine of Elder Daniel Parker spread widely among the antimissionary Baptists. Parker taught the existence of an eternal, uncreated Satan, and the souls of the nonelect as his "seed." The souls of the elect were the "seed" of Christ. Any effort to turn the one into the other he held to be alike futile and blasphemous. Various forms of this doctrine agitated the Primitive Baptists for generations.[35] The Campbellites, or Restorationists, followed Alexander Campbell in his attempts to heal sectarian divisions by reducing doctrine to extreme free will and practice to baptismal regeneration. The Campbellites succeeded only in founding yet another acrimonious sect, particularly parasitic on the Baptists.[36]

Griffin noted with dismay the laws passed in the aftermath of the Missouri controversy forbidding blacks their own separate churches, but excused it because "the course pursued by the northern people, led on by talented fools, has been such that personal safety to the white race, had rendered it necessary to clip the privileges of the black race, little by little, till now they are not even permitted to hold worship by themselves."[37]

After years of backbiting and maneuvering, the missionary and antimissionary parties began to divide in Mississippi. Griffin relates eyewitness reports of the schism in the Yalobusha Association at Loosacoona Church in 1839. A missionary preacher set out to show that antimissionaries were Roman Catholics in disguise, and the entire proceeding was summed up by one participant thus: "I have never in all my life been a witness to such a scene among professors of religion, much less among people calling themselves Baptists." The antimissionaries withdrew from the Yalobusha and formed the Loosacoona Regular Baptist Association.[38] Against the charge of tyrannizing over their members' consciences in the manner of Catholics, the Noxubee Association cleverly observed that "As regards our being opposed to every man using his money as he pleases— we answer that every man has a legal right to use his money as he may think proper, if it be to lay it out for ardent spirits, upon which he drinks himself to death, and brings his family into distress and degradation. . . . who can blame us for trying to . . . impress upon him his moral obligation, in abstaining from the abuse of his legal privileges."[39]

Griffin's own association, however, explicitly denied a position that later became a major rallying point for the Primitives: the denial that the preached gospel is the usual means through which the souls of the elect are born again. "It has been reported by some, and believed by others, that we discard the idea of God's using means or instruments for the accomplishment of his divine purposes. This charge is gratuitous and untrue. Although we do most positively deny the supposed power or efficacy of humanly devised means, to facilitate the salvation of lost sinners, in the manner the doctrine is preached, believed and acted upon in the present day, yet we most freely admit and firmly believe, that the all wise and glorious God has appointed instruments by which he will accomplish his ador-able purposes."[40]

Other Primitive Baptists opined that their opponents were "fast tend-ing to a law religion, and leading to a union (or what is still worse, if pos-sible, a collusion) between church and state."[41]

Griffin concluded his own history with an acidulous review of David Benedict's recently published *History of the Baptist Denomination,* not-ing "if [it] is no more reliable generally than that portion which treats of the Primitive Baptist Association in Mississippi, it is unworthy of the name."[42] Benedict claimed the Old School Baptists had provided him few materials from which to write their history, which Griffin disputed with a series of quotations and references from letters and other information submitted to Benedict at his request by leading Old Baptists. If the let-ter of Christopher Serch was typical, Benedict might be forgiven for not quoting them. Quoth Brother Serch: "If you have not been 'born again,' we cannot make you understand the kingdom of God, if we should reason with you till doomsday." In reply to Benedict's argument that the missions dispute only concerned the "modus operandi" of the spread of the gos-pel, Griffin rejoined that "when they meet their opponents on baptism, why, then, the 'modus operandi' is of the utmost importance."[43] Griffin marshals a series of damning admissions from the *History:* "But doctri-nal matters have been at the bottom of all the troubles, and predestina-tion has been the bone of contention. The anti-mission party, as near as I can learn, without any exception, are high or hyper-Calvinists, and are so tenacious of the old theory of particular atonement."[44] And even more to his delight: "Our old ministers in this region, half a century since, would have denounced as unsound in the faith, the great mass of our community of the present day, both in Europe and America, Fuller and Hall among the rest."[45]

Griffin bade his fellow historian farewell with a couple of typical Hard-shell Parthian shots. Benedict apparently still wished to claim the antimis-sionaries as brethren and considered the missions dispute a "family mat-ter." Griffin wished Benedict "to understand that we repudiate all such insinuations—our mothers are no more alike than Sarah and Hagar, and our fathers are still less alike."[46] Benedict also predicted the demise of the antimission movement before his book reached its remotest subscribers. Griffin sneered that "his book has been published several years, and the Old School Baptists still exist, and are in at least as prosperous a condition, and as strongly opposed to Missionism, as when the above prophecy was made," thus branding Benedict a false prophet, unless perchance some of his books never reached their remotest subscribers.[47]

Cushing Biggs Hassell and Sylvester Hassell, *History of the Church of God* (1885)

Towering above all other Primitive Baptist sallies into historiography is the notable work known among Primitive Baptists as "Hassell's History." When the late Turner Lassetter of Atlanta devoted his retirement to re-printing a small number of essential Old Baptist books, he chose Hassell, along with forty of Philpot's Sermons, and Gill's *Exposition, Divinity,* and *Cause of God and Truth.* Elder Jeff Harris told me that he presented each of a group of foreign preachers interested in the Primitive Baptists with two books, John Gill's *Body of Doctrinal and Practical Divinity* and Cush-ing Biggs and Sylvester Hassell's *History of the Church of God.* G. W. Pas-chal, author of *A History of North Carolina Baptists,* called Hassell's his-tory "the very best piece of historical work ever done in North Carolina."[48] This was high praise from one who characterized Hassell's beloved Kehu-kee Association as "a real blight of hyper-Calvinism."[49] Elder R. H. Pitt-man claimed Spurgeon said that "Hassell's History contained less error than any book he ever read."[50] I rather doubt this, but anything is possible.

The Kehukee Association, the fourth oldest Baptist association in America, has always been very conscious of its history. In 1803, Elders Lemuel Burkitt and Jesse Read compiled a history of the first fifty years of the association, and in 1833, the association commissioned Elder Joseph Biggs to continue Burkett and Read's work. In 1876, the association ap-pointed Cushing Biggs Hassell, a Primitive Baptist minister of national standing, planter, merchant, and moderator of the association from 1857 until his death, to write a history of

> some 500 pages, giving an abridged but faithful and impartial his-torical account, reaching as far back into the past as reliable his-tory casts its light, of the faith and government or discipline of the Baptist Church; especially that body of them known as "par-ticular" in England, who composed and constituted the Philadel-phia, Charleston, and Kehukee Associations . . . From thence giv-ing a sketch of the Kehukee Association down to the great division which took place . . . and here give a faithful, impartial and unpar-tisan account of the true causes that produced these unhappy divi-

sions, viz., change in doctrine and practice, Fullerism, Missionism, and then follow the foot-prints of old Mother Kehukee down to the present time.

After his death in 1880, his son Sylvester succeeded him both as associational moderator and author of the history, which he expanded to twice the limits planned by his father or the association.[51] C. B. Hassell planned to use only Jonathan Edward's *History of Redemption* for the general history section of the book.[52] Both father and son made a discovery common among the writers of large books: "No one who has not written a careful and conscientious history of thousands of years has any adequate idea of the enormous labor of such an undertaking. Both my father and myself were greatly mistaken, both before and after the beginning of the preparation of this work, as to the time that would be required for its completion."[53]

Sadly, the limits of a chapter scarcely provide scope for the enormous and diverse nature of this book. Opening it at random, one always finds interesting matter. Among the minority of Primitive Baptists who read anything beside the Bible, its influence is still strong. It is about as "impartial" as one would expect. C. B. Hassell began his account of the Kehukee by calling it "one of the most remarkable bodies of Christians in America." He then reproduced verbatim the entire London Baptist Confession, that the Kehukeeites might "know that they stand where their brethren in London stood."[54] The elder Hassell cultivated a wide acquaintance among the Primitive Baptists and provided a survey of "Predestinarian Baptists of Canada and the United States," which is a truly valuable source of historic information. He writes with the grumpy straightforwardness of Benjamin Griffin and had sufficient education to deprive him of the fine old ruffian style of his older contemporary and friend, Joshua Lawrence. However, when he had "Missionaries" in his sights, he unloaded with the best of them. Believing that the Missionary Baptists embraced a doctrine of salvation based on conditions that must be fulfilled by human beings in order to be saved, Cushing Hassell placed them in the same category as Roman Catholics and others who believe that good works are essential to salvation. "The constant tendency of the Missionaries," he thundered, "is *from* the doctrine of *predestination and election as set forth in the Bible* to the doctrine of a *Conditional Salvation*, made sure only by man; . . . they have abandoned the true church of Christ, and made a confederacy with the daughters of Babylon and of Papal Rome; and ... the Mother of Harlots herself has as good a doctrine to preach to the millions of her deluded followers as have a large number of Missionary Baptists, so-called, either of Europe or America."[55] Sylvester Hassell wrote that he had never met his father's equal "in self control and evenness of temper."[56]

Sylvester Hassell graduated with honors from the University of North Carolina with a degree in classical languages, and studied the New Testament in Greek. He owned a personal library of five thousand volumes and corresponded extensively with a score of eminent church historians while writing his magnum opus. His portion of the book is remarkably acute compared to other Old Baptist productions. Without departing from their fundamental beliefs, Hassell nevertheless recognized and tried to address the rising tide of scientific and critical research. Although denying that the origin of life could have been happenchance, and also deriding Darwinism, he did recognize that geology posed difficulties in regard to the biblical creation account, and was willing to entertain "days" of indeterminate length, as well as a localized flood.[57] He detested not only the "higher" criticism of the German schools, but even the textual criticism underlying the Revised Standard Bible. He assured his readers that "there are very few of the [textual] variations that are not trivial and worthless."[58]

More specifically on the historical realm, he recognized the limitations imposed by his dependence on secondary sources: "It would require not only great intellectual and spiritual ability, but a long lifetime spent diligently in the great libraries of Europe, to write the history of the church as it ought to be, but never has been written."[59] Although dated, his conceptions are seldom far from the mainstream Protestant scholastics of his time. He doubtless introduced many Primitive Baptists to a great many people, events, and ideas they had never previously encountered.

Hassell clearly recognized that no solid evidence existed for a formal "apostolic succession" connecting the Baptists with the apostles. He embraced the skeptical conclusions of Protestant and Agnostic historians in regard to the earliest history of the church. If the Baptists had no unbroken chain of provable succession, he would allow none such to the Catholic, Orthodox, or Anglicans:

As for a nominal, natural, outward, or mechanical succession, the God of providence and grace, eighteen centuries ago, forever buried all such claims in the dark, impenetrable gulf of the *speculum obscurum,* or obscure age, immediately succeeding the death of the leading Apostles and the destruction of Jerusalem, A.D. 70, and extending to A.D. 100, as freely acknowledged by the ablest scholars of Europe; the irreconcilable inconsistencies and contradictions of the leading Roman Catholic authorities in regard to the pretended Romish succession during this period furnish a sufficient illustration of this fact. According to the entire tenor of the New Testament Scriptures, what we are to look for is, *not such outward succession, but a spiritual* succession *of principles, of inward, vital, heartfelt religion.* Names are nothing, principles are everything, in the true kingdom of God.[60]

In this, he concurs with the editorial of Gilbert Beebe on "Ecclesiastic History and Church Creeds" printed as an appendix to his own work.[61] Beebe wrote, "The question with us now is not or should not be, What was believed and practiced in the church one hundred or a thousand years ago? But rather, What was the faith which was once delivered to the saints? We are not now to ask, Are our ministers by succession of ordination, through the dark ages of papal abominations traceable to the Apostles? But rather let it be asked, are they such men as the Holy Ghost commanded the church to separate to the work whereunto He had called them?"[62]

On the other hand, Hassell seems to have suffered from a sort of schizophrenia on the subject of succession. He quoted a remark of Cardinal Hosius, a member of the Council of Trent: "If the truth of religion were to be judged of by the readiness and cheerfulness which a man of any sect shows in suffering, then the opinions and persuasions of no sect can be truer or surer than those of the Anabaptists, since there have been none for twelve hundred years past that have been more grievously punished."[63] Then in another place, he speciously attempted to make this an admission by Hosius that the Anabaptists had continuously existed since the time of Constantine, rather than having been the most persecuted of all the sectaries in the last twelve centuries, which Hosius obviously meant.[64]

Hassell grudgingly admits in a footnote that the continental Anabaptists did not immerse, and worse, did not apparently hold to predestination. "Thus we see that even those who ably and strenuously advocate the doctrine of salvation by sovereign grace alone may be in great darkness on other important subjects; and in the case of the conditionalist 'Anabaptists' and 'Mennonites' we also see that persons may be in mental darkness in regard to the glorious doctrine of grace, and yet may be blessed with heavenly light on other spiritual subjects of great importance."[65] In short, if there were always people who claimed to be Christians and did not baptize infants, the Baptists are home free on the succession question, never mind that a Primitive Baptist of Hassell's day would have had more fellowship with a horse than some of these early "Baptists."

The organization of the book is essentially chronological, but two crucial issues are dealt with in chapters nine and ten, "Twelve Marks of the Apostolic Church," and "The Doctrine of Grace and Missions." Not surprisingly, the twelve marks pointed out the Primitive Baptists and no others, and the doctrines of grace were inconsistent with modern missions. However, these are possibly the best and most profitable parts of the book, and certainly sum up the Old School belief in a small compass.

The *History* handled references to predestination, and its relationship to sin and evil very gingerly. Although Primitive Baptists were often stigmatized as "Hyper-Calvinists," they entertained differing views on the extent of the decrees, and sinister rumblings shook the denomination as the Hassells were writing. Some Primitive Baptists had long questioned the doctrine of absolute predestination of all things. Fearing that a moral inertia would stem from this belief, and influenced by the improvement mania of the Progressive era, a group of younger Primitive Baptist ministers developed the doctrine of "conditional time Salvation." Even though the eternal salvation of the souls of the elect had been absolutely predestined, there yet remained an experience of fellowship with God, a "timely salvation," that could be gained by obedience and good works and lost by disobedience and rebellion. This new teaching was at first closely linked with the "Progressive" movement, which opposed associational authority, advocated more financial support for ministers, and tolerated the use of organs in worship. By 1910, Primitive Baptists had divided into "Progressive" and "Old Line" factions over the use of the organ. In the decades after the publication of the *History*, a major schism erupted between Absolute Predestinarian Primitive Baptists and those who contended for a "conditional time salvation."[66] Nonetheless, Hassell included Gilbert Beebe's editorial "Absolute Predestination of All Things" at the request of his sons and to satisfy the partisans of Beebe's periodical *The Signs of the Times*. Hassell mentioned this in an editorial aside, in which he also exonerated the *Signs* from anything in his book, especially any use of the word "permission" in respect to the decrees of God.[67]

One issue the *History* addresses only briefly is the issue of the "use" of the preached gospel. Perhaps the greatest gulf between most modern Primitive Baptists and other Calvinistic parties lies in the common Primitive belief that the regeneration of the soul is solely the work of the Holy

Spirit without any instrumentalities such as preaching or scripture. All Primitive Baptists do not believe in the noninstrumental theory of regeneration even to this day, and considerably more held to the instrumental view in the nineteenth century. The writings of Lawrence and Griffin are quite absent of much sense of this. By the 1880s, however, opposition to Missionary Baptist emphasis on the spread of the gospel had led the majority of Primitive Baptists to deny "gospel means," the belief that preaching is the "means" the Holy Spirit uses to save the elect.[68] Cushing Biggs Hassell wrote, "Believing, as [an Old Baptist] does, in the sovereignty of God's grace, in the perfection of Christ's redemption, in the omnipotence of the Holy Spirit, and in the freeness and fullness of God's salvation toward all who will be saved, he cannot for a moment suppose that any human means have ever sent, or ever will send, a single soul to glory."[69] Sylvester Hassell quotes with approval Elder Thomas P. Dudley of Kentucky: "Experience and observation of more than fifty years have satisfied me that where Andrew Fuller's system, attempting to harmonize Divine sovereignty and human free agency, a general atonement and special application, salvation by works and salvation by grace, prevails, it has only widened the flood-gates of error, making the preacher the *instrument*, and the preached gospel the *means* of the salvation of our apostate world. I, however, have not so learned Christ."[70] In a biographical sketch of Elder Wilson Thompson, Sylvester Hassell very clearly stated the majority view. "In regard to the use and effect of the preached gospel, Elder Thompson held, with the majority of the Old School Baptists, that it is not the means of imparting spiritual life to the dead sinner; that as no means can be used to give life to one literally dead, even so no means can be used to give life to those who are dead in sins; that, as all temporal means are used to feed, nourish, and strengthen living subjects, and not dead ones, so the preaching of the gospel is the medium through which God is pleased to instruct, feed, and comfort His renewed children, and not by which He gives life to the dead sinner whom the *Spirit alone* can quicken."[71]

One of Sylvester Hassell's most petty and irritating practices was the minute care that he took to always place words like *baptism, bishop,* or *church* in quotes when referring to the actions or organization of other denominations. On the other hand, he could be remarkably broadminded, given his theological mindset. Although he viewed Catholicism in general as the Antichrist striving to regain world domination, he acknowledged that there was "true spiritual religion among a few Catholics of South Germany," and "among some of the aged, poor and ignorant Catholics of

Ireland," and even concedes some "spiritual worshippers of God" among all the various bodies of Protestants. "There may be more or less darkness in the head, while at the same time grace exists in the heart."[72] Given his attitude toward most mission programs, it is surprising to find him warmly commending the Moravian missionaries who worked with their hands among the poorest nations.[73]

E. I. Wiggins, *A History of the Mount Enon Association Holding to the Doctrine of Absolute Predestination* (1921)

The few Primitive Baptists with literary pretensions do not in some ways represent the great "silent majority" of simple, unadorned, die-hard believers, the true "Old-Line Hardshells." Occasionally a letter to a periodical, a written conversion experience, a passage in associational or church minutes will let their voices come through to later times. Such a jewel is E. I. Wiggins's *History of the Mount Enon Association.*[74] It is not a scholarly work, certainly not a history in the academic sense, but it passionately states the belief of a decided Absolute Predestinarian Primitive Baptist, a child of the earliest white settlers of the South Florida frontier, and the founders of the Primitive faith there. It reads like a cross between the Gospel of Mark and an Icelandic Saga, written in pellucid Cracker.

After invoking the doctrine as his muse, Wiggins begins with the genealogy of his family, the core membership of the first Primitive Baptist church in south Florida. Originally from South Georgia, they moved to Columbia County, Florida, where they sided with the Primitives during the Missionary controversy. After the Seminole War, his Raulerson, Wiggins, and Thomas kindred moved to the neighborhood of Tampa. Most of the settlers in that area were stockmen, living miles apart. Wiggins paints an idyllic picture of pioneer life.

> Then they commenced clearing and fencing in land and penned their cattle on their land at night in order to protect them from the wild beasts: while it made their land rich and they were soon having nice gardens and plenty of sweet potatoes and rice. As for milk, butter and wild honey, they had more than they could consume and as for meat, it was no object. Wild turkey and deer were in abundance and plenty of fish. Their hogs, and cattle were fat and increased, while the bear, panther, and wolves caught some of the young stock, they protected them pretty well with their dogs and old flint and steel rifles. They soon had good size fields and making plenty of corn

and sugar cane. They cut down live oak and sawed blocks off and put them up in a frame and turned out mill rollers and ground their cane on wooden mills.

The people fitted the land: "Most of the old men had on the old-fashion flint and steel britches and old-fashion hunting shirts and home-made shoes and hats. There were not any 'big I's or little you's' among them."[75]

But every Eden must have its serpent, and with an increase of settlers after the end of the Third Seminole War, Missionary Baptists began to infiltrate the country, establish churches, and attempt to subvert the Old Baptists. The Primitives had no minister among them and held no services, but Wiggins's father

> was pretty well informed in the scriptures and took the *Signs of the Times* and was ready for them. It didn't take him long to put them to flight. They would get mad and say to him: "If it is like you say, then God is an unjust God," then they would flirt off and leave him, but they would not give it up, they would send others to see him to persuade him to join in with them. They told him that he was in the way, that he was keeping others from joining, but if he would join, a good many others would join, but they would get their dose and go off mad. I have seen him follow them to the front gate and preach to them as far as he thought they could hear him, but they would go right on and never look back.[76]

By the time of the Civil War, their children had grown to adulthood and never heard the Primitive doctrine advocated except when their elders argued with the proselytizers: "But the Lord, God of Heaven had not forgotten those old brethren that had dwelt in the wilderness for twenty years tempted of the Devil through Missionarism." In 1864, a septuagenarian Primitive preacher, James Moseley of Alabama, became burdened to travel south. Having no family, he piled his few belonging into an old buggy with a top made of raw deerskins, and set out as his mind led him. A popular preacher, many Primitive Baptist communities invited him to settle with them, but his burden for the south would not leave him. Eventually he reached country in Florida where there were no Primitive Baptists, but he still felt impelled to travel further south. In Hernando County, he heard that the few Hardshells in that country were dead. Heartsick at that news, he still pressed on, until a stranger directed him to the farm of John Thomas, a Primitive Baptist. Here he felt the first glimmer of hope since he had left Alabama that his long journey might be at an end. After nearly deciding he had taken a wrong turn, he finally arrived at the Thomas place. John Thomas cordially invited him in, the first man in Florida to do so. "Well, I am hunting old Hardshells," Elder Moseley announced. When Thomas learned his visitor was a Primitive Baptist preacher, "they grabbed each other by the hand again and greeted each other with kisses from the heart." As soon as the small community of Old Baptists knew a preacher of their faith had arrived among them, they secured a log chapel built by the Missionary Baptists and held their first Primitive Baptist service in twenty years. Along with the Primitives came many neighbors who were curious to hear a Primitive Baptist, and even a few Missionaries. The Primitive Baptists were so overcome that they lost all sense of decorum and called out through Moseley's sermon, endorsing his doctrine.[77]

Making the Thomas and Raulerson households his headquarters, Moseley preached throughout the region. His hearers built a meetinghouse for him where they held services and received and baptized members. When Elder Andrew Kicklighter from Bulloch County, Georgia, moved into the community in 1867, they organized the Mt. Enon Primitive Baptist Church.

Elder James Moseley died in 1868, aged eighty. Wiggins wrote of him:

> I don't reckon any man ever suffered any more persecution than he did outside of Paul and if it had not been for the laws of our land he would have been stoned and cast into prison. He was called all kinds of disrespectable names compared to a dog, accused of preaching a dangerous doctrine; said he ought to be drummed out of the country and was threatened to be stoned with rotten eggs at one time if he came back there and preached such stuff again; they would not let their children go hear him preach; said he preached infants into hell, but he went right on with his old raw hide buggy top and filled all his appointments and wherever he was sent for he never spoke a harm word against anyone, and if they did not like his doctrine he could not help it. He never preached to please man; he declared the whole truth of our God, regardless of man.

The cause prospered, and by 1871, five Primitive Baptist churches had been organized in Hillsborough and nearby counties. In the fall of that year, they organized the Mt. Enon Primitive Baptist Association. Wiggins remembered "how it was at father's house on Saturday night. He had a large double pen log house and took all the house room for the women and children. The men and boys took blankets and quilts and slept on the porches in the woods, and corn cribs, but everyone seemed to be lively and enjoyed the meeting. I never had such a time helping feed horses. . . . I think there were about 45 or 50 heads of horses to feed that night. They preached after supper was over. I think of the old white headed brethren who sat up and talked very near all night."[78]

The Missionaries were not the only worldly trouble the young association faced. In the late 1870s, post-Reconstruction melanophobia took a toll when two elders, Andrew Kicklighter and J. W. Keen, refused to fellowship an African American named Isaac Berry who inquired if he could join the church. Kicklighter and Keen "cut loose from the association" with several churches. The association ruled with true "southern Christian" magnanimity that "they had no right to reject any nationality of people regardless of color and if a negro came to the church with the evidence that he had received a hope in Christ, they would receive him and baptize him into the fellowship of the church and give him free access to the ordinances of the church and treat him as a brother in the spirit but not socially as a man which is contrary to the laws of our country."[79] So much for Jas. 2:9.

A greater conflict lay ahead. In the 1890s, some elders "began to find fault with the signs of the times, said it advocated a two seed doctrine or a doctrine that made God the author of sin and a good many travelling preachers came through preaching that churches would not prosper under doctrine preached to them all the time; said you might preach doctrine to a church until it became dormant and lost all zeal and go down to nothing."[80]

The controversy over unlimited predestination as opposed to "conditional time salvation" arrived in the Mt. Enon Association.[81] Wiggins, a die-hard Absoluter, described in excruciating detail several years of procedural maneuvering between the "Conditionalist" and "Absoluter" factions. The crux arrived at the 1906 association, when the Absoluters forced an endorsement of the London Confession, and were thrown out of the house by the Conditionalist church hosting the association, which divided at this point.

Wiggins concluded his account with words that capture the true Primitive Baptist stance: "Dear Brethren, I feel that the lord has purged his floor and found out all the chaff throughout Old Mt. Enon Association which refines it to only seven small churches and three orderly preachers. . . . Yet we are not discouraged because the promise is to the remnant. We do not know where else to go, for the doctrine of God's unlimited predestination is the only doctrine under heaven that gives God all the honor, glory and praise."[82]

Notes

1. John Crowley, *The Primitive Baptists of the Wiregrass South: 1815 to the Present* (Gainesville: University Press of Florida, 1999), 143–44.

2. A. D. Gillette, ed., *Minutes of the Philadelphia Baptist Association from A.D. 1707 to A.D. 1807, Being the First Hundred Years of Its Existence* (Philadelphia: American Baptist Publication Society, 1851), 95; John Crowley, "The Story of Primitive Baptists: 'Alien Immersion' among Primitive Baptists," *The Baptist Studies Bulletin* 3, no. 8 (August 2004), accessed December 20, 2011, http://www.centerforbaptiststudies.org/bulletin/2004/august.htm; Alabaha River Primitive Baptist Association [Bennett Faction], *Minutes*, 2003, 4; Union Primitive Baptist Association [Peace Faction], *Minutes*, 2003.

3. *The Feast of Fat Things* (Salisbury, MD: The Signs of the Times, n.d.; reprint, Middletown, NY: G. Beebe's Son, n.d.), 7, 19.

4. Cushing Biggs Hassell and Sylvester Hassell, *History of the Church of God from the Creation to A.D. 1885; Including Especially the History of the Kehukee Primitive Baptist Association* (Conley, GA: Old School Hymnal Co., 1973; repr., Middletown, NY: Gilbert Beebe's Sons, 1886 [with some additional matter]), 736–743.

5. Ibid., 783.

6. [Joshua Lawrence], *The American Telescope, by a Clodhopper of North Carolina* (Philadelphia: Joshua Lawrence, 1825), Documenting the American South, accessed December 20, 2011, http://docsouth.unc.edu/nc/lawrence/menu.html.

7. Ibid., 4–5.

8. Ibid., 10.

9. Ibid., 13–14.

10. Ibid., 17.

11. Ibid.

12. *Feast of Fat Things*, 11.

13. Ibid., 13.

14. Ibid.

15. Benjamin Griffin, *History of the Primitive Baptists of Mississippi, from*

the First Settlement by the Americans up to the Middle of the XIXth Century. Containing a Brief Allusion to the Course, Doctrines, and Practice of the Christian Church from Jerusalem to America; Also the Doctrine and Practice of Modern Missionaries from the Days of Andrew Fuller, and a Brief Notice of D. Benedict's late History of the Baptists; Concluded with a General Address to the Reader by Benjamin Griffin of Holmes County, Miss. (n.p.: J. R. Holder, B. D. Bryant, Wiley Sammons, n.d.; orig. publ. Jackson, MS: Benjamin Griffin, 1853), 1, 175; 1850 U.S. Census, Holmes County, Mississippi, population schedule, Lexington Police Beat, p. 462 (penned), p. 232 (stamped) dwelling 55, family 55, Benj. Griffin; digital images, *Ancestry.com,* accessed August 10, 2009, http://www .ancestry.com.

16. Griffin, *Primitive Baptists of Mississippi,* 155–62, 163.

17. Ibid., 221.

18. Ibid., 8.

19. Ibid.

20. Ibid., 9–13.

21. Ibid., 15.

22. Ibid.

23. Ibid., 16–23.

24. Quoted in Iain Murray, *Spurgeon v. Hyper-Calvinism: The Battle for Gospel Preaching* (Edinburgh: Banner of Truth Trust, 1995), 127. A "Coryphaeus" is the leader of the chorus in a Greek play.

25. Hassell, *History,* 337–38.

26. For a corrective to Iain Murray and a critique of Andrew Fuller from a modern and very warm high predestinarian, see George Ella, *Law and Gospel in the Theology of Andrew Fuller* (Eggleston, England: GO Publications, 1996).

27. See the "Prospectus" in *Signs of the Times* 1 (November 28, 1832):1; Griffin, *Primitive Baptists of Mississippi,* 189.

28. Griffin, *Primitive Baptists of Mississippi,* 23.

29. Ibid., 23–24.

30. Ibid., 27–29.

31. Ibid., 57.

32. Ibid., 58–59.

33. Ibid., 63–64.

34. Ibid., 66–68.

35. Ibid., 99; See John M. Watson, *The Old Baptist Test* (1867) for a good treatment of Parkerism.

36. For a hilarious send-up of the jarring sects in the West, with particular attention to Campbell, see Walter Brownlow Posey, *Religious Strife on the*

Southern Frontier (Baton Rouge: Louisiana State University Press, 1965). Posey's views on Baptist Calvinism are extremely weak and ill informed, however.

37. Griffin, *Primitive Baptists of Mississippi*, 132.

38. Ibid., 153–54.

39. Ibid., 187.

40. Ibid., 164–65.

41. Ibid., 187.

42. Ibid., 196.

43. Ibid., 204–5, 199.

44. Ibid., 201.

45. Ibid., 202.

46. Ibid., 204.

47. Ibid., 218–19.

48. G. W. Paschal to Sylvester Hassell, December 5, 1924, quoted in Hassell, *History*, x. (Perhaps more of a comment on North Carolina historiography than a compliment to the Hassells.)

49. George Walsh Paschal, History of North Carolina Baptists (Raleigh, NC: The General Board, North Carolina Baptist Convention, 1930), 270–71.

50. Hassell, *History*, 1013. The book reviews of the *Sword and Trowel* ought to be searched for any verification of this remark.

51. Ibid., 746, 796–814, 820.

52. Ibid., 549.

53. Ibid., 819n.

54. Ibid., 661, 663.

55. Ibid., 749–750.

56. Ibid., 930.

57. Ibid., 32–34, 56.

58. Ibid., 615–16.

59. Ibid., vi.

60. Ibid., 18; Hassell's emphasis.

61. Ibid., 654, 934–36; *Feast of Fat Things*, 4. Gilbert Beebe (1800–1881) was founder and editor of the *Signs of the Times*, the oldest and one of the most influential Primitive Baptist periodicals. He also coauthored the *Black Rock Address*, and Sylvester Hassell believed that "there has been no scriptural uninspired teacher superior to the late Elder Gilbert Beebe, of Middletown, New York." Hassell, *History*, 654, 934–36.

62. Hassell, *History*, 937–38. On this topic, see also W. J. Berry, *Tracing the True Worship of God* (Elon College, NC: Primitive Baptist Library, 1971).

63. Hassell, *History*, 504.

64. Ibid., 440.

65. Ibid., 505–6.

66. Crowley, *Primitive Baptists of the Wiregrass South*, 135–46; Julietta Haynes, *A History of the Primitive Baptists* (Ann Arbor: University Microfilms International, 1989), 255.

67. Hassell, *History*, 942–43.

68. Crowley, *Primitive Baptists of the Wiregrass South*, 112–15.

69. Hassell, *History*, 337.

70. Ibid., 557–58.

71. Ibid., 633–34.

72. Ibid., 583.

73. Ibid., 586.

74. E. I. Wiggins, *A History of the Mount Enon Association Holding to the Doctrine of Absolute Predestination* (Lake Panasofkee, FL: Donald E. Martin, 2006; reprinted with addendum of 1921 ed.).

75. Ibid., 1–2, 7.

76. Ibid., 2.

77. Ibid., 4.

78. Ibid., 7, 8.

79. Ibid., 8.

80. Ibid., 9.

81. Crowley, *Primitive Baptists*, 135–36.

82. Wiggins, *Mt. Enon*, 17.

9

Reframing the Past

The Impact of Institutional and Ideological
Agendas on Modern Interpretations of
Landmarkism

James A. Patterson

The modern historical enterprise assumes a close relationship between
memories of the past and the present-day identities of both individuals
and organizations. In other words, one of the widely acknowledged benefits of historical consciousness is that it sharpens memory and thus can
contribute to an enhanced sense of personal or group character. At the
same time, memory is not a perfect instrument for reconstructing what
exactly took place in the past; nor do simple remembrances of bygone people,
events, or eras necessarily guarantee sound explanations or interpretations
of them. In recent musings about earlier periods in his life, *First Things*
editor Joseph Bottum wisely counsels against placing too much of a premium on memory: "Memory may be our best tool for self-understanding,
but only when we remember how weak a tool it really is: prone to warping
under the narrative drive of storytelling, vulnerable to self-interest, susceptible to outside influence."[1] Although Bottum directs these remarks
primarily toward autobiographers, his caveats should likewise be heeded
by those who research and write about Christian movements and denominations—especially their own.

As if to reinforce Bottum's warnings, religious historian Lynn Neal
adroitly illustrates that some skewed approaches to the past produce re-
framed, renarrated, and reenvisioned history with some unintended moral
consequences.[2] Although the Wake Forest professor focuses on the visual
and verbal power of Pillar of Fire Church publications in early twentieth-
century America, her portrait of imaginative memories that shaped a
mythical past surely suggests broader applications. Indeed, both Bottum
and Neal testify to regrettable abuses of history on the popular level that be-

tray myopic and sometimes palpable agendas. Those who filter the past in these ways inevitably distort, confuse, or otherwise manipulate it.

Nineteenth-century Landmarkers undoubtedly exemplified some of the worst features of a popularized history-as-apologetics approach to the question of Baptist origins. In short, they seriously misused history to justify their distinctive ecclesiology and to posit a "trail of blood" that allegedly verified the perpetuity of Baptists all the way back to apostolic times. After all, successionists argued, local Baptist churches—like First Baptist of Jerusalem—were the only true ones. Jesus himself prophesied that the gates of Hades would not prevail against his church (Matt. 16:18); hence, Baptist congregations had to exist in an unbroken chain since the first century of the Christian era. Successionist history radically reworked the contours of Baptist history, allowed historical memory to be held captive to ideology, and jumbled the issues pertaining to denominational identity.[3]

At the same time, professional historians have not been entirely immune from apologetic mistreatments of the historical record. What is not readily acknowledged is that the historiography of Landmarkism, especially since the middle of the twentieth century, has been prone to more subtle historical reconstructions. Even some of the most insightful accounts of the rise and development of Landmarkism have at times succumbed to the projection of twentieth-century debates and interests back into the nineteenth century. While the Landmarkers creatively fashioned a fictional Baptist heritage, their cultured despisers have attempted to fit them into suspect interpretive schemes that actually blur their historical identity. As three of the following sections of this essay will demonstrate, some Baptist historians who have written about the Landmarkers share with them a susceptibility toward flawed or selective historical memories. The shortcomings of the historical scholars have not been of the same magnitude as the fantasies of Landmark successionist folklore; all the same, the more recent interpreters have sometimes set forth inadequate elucidations of the controversial nineteenth-century movement.

Nineteenth-Century Landmarkism

Landmarkism emerged in the mid-South during the 1850s largely as an effort to set boundaries between Baptists and other Christian denominations in the context of intense rivalry on what was then the American frontier. Landmarkists, moreover, sought to impart to the Southern Baptist Convention, which was launched in 1845, a distinct ecclesiological identity during its formative years. The movement's founder, James Robinson Graves (1820–1893), was a transplant to Tennessee via Vermont, Ohio, and Kentucky. As the editor of the *Tennessee Baptist,* a post that he assumed in 1848, Graves became increasingly troubled by the successes of groups such as the Methodists and Alexander Campbell's disciples in areas of the South such as his own base of Nashville; he also fretted that many of his fellow Baptists—including editors of some other denominational newspapers—apparently lacked the fortitude to engage their religious competitors in vigorous debate about church polity, ordinances, and doctrine.

The birth of Landmarkism as a noteworthy faction in Southern Baptist life is usually traced to a meeting that Graves organized in Cotton Grove (near Jackson), Tennessee, in 1851. Baptist historian Joe Early Jr. has aptly summarized the significance of this event: "The tenets of Landmarkism were first defined, the organization of the Landmark movement began, and J. R. Graves was elevated from Baptist editor to denominational spokesman and champion."[4] The resolutions that were adopted at Cotton Grove and later approved by several Baptist associations in Arkansas, Alabama, Tennessee, and Texas essentially declared that non-Baptist "societies" could not be classified as true or genuine churches. Pastors or elders of such organizations likewise could not be recognized as valid gospel ministers, which meant that pulpit exchanges between Baptist and non-Baptist preachers were illegitimate. Finally, the Cotton Grove gathering concluded that it was inconsistent to "address as brethren those professing Christianity who not only have not the doctrine of Christ and walk not according to his commandments but are arrayed in direct and bitter opposition to them."[5] Thus, Graves and his supporters signaled a strongly militant and aggressive posture in their defense of Baptist principles; these Landmarkers staked out clear boundaries and well-defined enemies.

Landmarkist ideology soon gained wide distribution through articles in the *Tennessee Baptist* and Graves's annual *Southern Baptist Almanac and Register,* as well as in other books and tracts printed by his publishing houses—first in Nashville and later in Memphis. Graves gained a valuable collaborator for promoting his cause in 1852 when he persuaded James Madison Pendleton (1811–1891), pastor of the First Baptist Church in Bowling Green, Kentucky, to deny the validity of immersions done by non-Baptists. At Graves's request in 1854, Pendleton wrote a series for the

Tennessee Baptist in which he argued that pedobaptist clerics could not be regarded as bona fide gospel ministers. The preacher from the Bluegrass State, moreover, dealt critically with pulpit affiliation and additional fraternal practices that might blur the differences between Baptists and other denominations. Graves soon published Pendleton's articles in pamphlet form with the title *An Old Landmark Re-Set,* which supplied the budding movement with its characteristic name. Three years after the publication of his tract, Pendleton accepted a position as theology professor at Union University in Murfreesboro, Tennessee, and also served for a time as a joint editor of the *Tennessee Baptist.* Although Pendleton disagreed with Graves on some matters, including successionism, he was Landmarkism's most noteworthy theologian.[6]

Amos Cooper Dayton (1813–1865), another important ally of Graves, contributed a work of fiction to the Landmark cause. A transplanted Yankee like Graves, Dayton held various positions with the Bible Board, the Southern Baptist Sunday School Union, and the *Tennessee Baptist* in Nashville during Landmarkism's seminal decade of the 1850s. His novel, *Theodosia Ernest,* was first serialized in Graves's newspaper in 1855 and appeared in book form the following year. The heroine of the story was a young Presbyterian who became a Baptist after determining that she had found the "true church"; in this manner, she mirrored the author's own pilgrimage. Dayton's melodramatic flair ostensibly appealed to some who were not directly convinced by the more straightforward polemics of Graves or Pendleton.[7]

The classic, perhaps definitive statement of Landmark ecclesiology, however, was Graves's *Old Landmarkism: What Is It?* Originally published in 1880, when the Landmark patriarch was living in Memphis during a mellower stage of his career, this volume nonetheless represented Graves's fully developed and most immovable ecclesiological views. In addition to reiterating the Cotton Grove strictures on pulpit affiliation and non-Baptist "societies," Graves utterly rejected any notion of an invisible, universal, national, or provincial church by underscoring his conception of the New Testament *ecclesia* as wholly visible, local, and independent: "The primitive model was a single congregation, complete in itself, independent of all other bodies, civil or religious, and the highest and only source of ecclesiastical authority on earth, amenable only to Christ, whose laws alone it receives and executes. . . . This church acknowledges no body of men on earth, council, conference or assembly as its head, but Christ alone, who is invisible, as 'head over all things' to it."[8] For Graves, this ecclesial arche-type derived from Jesus himself and thus was not subject to alteration or compromise.

Indeed, Graves avowed, only the Baptists had strictly and consistently preserved a biblical understanding of the church through the long epochs of Christian history. The reference to *Old* Landmarkism in his title surely intimated that church successionism constituted a fundamental compo-nent of his ecclesiology. Though rejecting "apostolic succession" and omit-ting a full-blown proof for Baptist perpetuity, he nevertheless linked the kingdom established by Christ in the first century to the aggregate of "true and uncorrupted" Baptist congregations that could be found in every age.[9] Graves's stress on historical continuity even led him to put forward the conjecture that specifically *Landmark* Baptists could be located from the first century to his own day in geographical regions as far east as Russia and as far west as North America. Furthermore, he identified Baptist fig-ures such as William Kiffin, John Clarke, Isaac Backus, and Jesse Mercer, who belong to earlier generations, as "Old Landmarkers."[10] Hence, both an atypical theology of the kingdom and an apologetic use of history func-tioned as essential buttresses for Graves's version of Landmarkist ecclesi-ology.

Old Landmarkism also summarized Graves's principles regarding the two New Testament ordinances: baptism and the Lord's Supper. First, the Baptist editor assigned the authority and responsibility for administer-ing them solely to the local church. Second, he reaffirmed his longstand-ing antagonism to "alien" immersion (i.e., believers' baptism performed by non-Baptist clergy); he insisted that a valid baptism required the cor-rect mode, the jurisdiction of a local Baptist church, and a properly bap-tized administrator. Finally, he defended at length a tight fencing of the communion table, a posture that had not characterized his early ministry. As Graves, however, developed the logical implications of his ideas about pulpit affiliation, alien immersion, and congregational autonomy, he ulti-mately accentuated the Lord's Supper as a strictly local church ordinance and reserved it exclusively for the immersed members of a local body.[11]

Between the 1850s and 1880s, then, Graves shaped Landmarkism into a consistent, albeit unyielding system that fixed precise borders between Baptists and other Christians. While many Southern Baptists subscribed to his paper and read his books, they did not necessarily endorse every plank in his platform. Graves himself remained loyal to the Southern Baptist Convention, but some of his more extreme disciples packaged his local church ecclesiology and warnings against centralized denominational structures (e.g., mission boards) into sectarian separatism.[12]

At the same time, Landmarkism established a sizeable constituency within the SBC that was known for expressing itself in contentious and bellicose ways; intradenominational discord, in fact, was unexceptional among nineteenth-century Southern Baptists. Graves himself jousted regularly with editors of other Baptist state papers and, in the late 1850s, even engaged in what appeared to some observers to be a personal vendetta against his own pastor, R. B. C. Howell of First Baptist, Nashville. This latter controversy spilled over into the 1859 SBC meeting in Richmond, where Graves attempted to block Howell's reelection as convention president, as well as to challenge the role and operation of the Foreign Mission Board.[13] Although Graves appeared to be much more supportive of convention causes after the Civil War, some SBC leaders deemed Landmarkism a major obstacle to a strong and vigorous denominational structure.

Overall, the passionate polemics between Landmarkers and non-Landmarkers worked at the outset against serious or evenhanded historical explanations of Landmarkism. Indeed, what historian Bill J. Leonard later wrote about Baptists in general fit nineteenth-century Landmarkers especially well: They were "messy, controversial, divisive, and energizing."[14] Even after Landmarkism ceased to be a principal source of debate in the SBC, Baptist historians still struggled to deal with the movement's problematic legacy. During the twentieth century, the following three significant interpretive perspectives emerged, none of which did full justice to the various renditions of Landmarkism and all of which showed understated institutional or ideological agendas that inhibited historical clarity.[15]

Landmarkism as a "High-Church" Movement

One of the most widely accepted designations in modern Baptist historiography is that Landmarkism represented a "high-church" impulse in nineteenth-century denominational life. The first Baptist historian to apply this label was probably William Wright Barnes, who was a professor of church history at Southwestern Baptist Theological Seminary from 1913 to 1953. In his 1934 study of Southern Baptist ecclesiology, he suggested some parallels between Roman Catholic and Baptist views of succession, at the same time noting a distinction: "The Roman succession of bishops assures the continuity of the body; the Baptist succession of the body assures a continuity of pastors (bishops in the New Testament sense) . . . The idea of succession furnishes the ecclesiological background of theory for the organization that results from practical tendencies. It gives authority to power, spirit to form, soul to body."[16] Barnes, thus, seemed to be implying that a successionist ecclesiology led directly to a strong emphasis on the institutional church as an end in itself. Although he shared with the Landmarkers a profound zeal for the autonomy of local congregations, he judged that Landmarkism was "more interested in stressing the fact that the Commission was given to the churches than in stressing the obligation upon the churches to give the gospel to the world." He concluded from this that Landmarkism's influence on the SBC, particularly in reference to the dispute over how churches were represented in the convention, actually diminished missionary fervor.[17] For Barnes, then, Landmarkism ironically contributed to some "Catholic" tendencies in the SBC that detracted from its purportedly voluntary basis of membership.

Two decades later, Barnes clarified and expanded his earlier assessment of Landmarkism with a much more explicit discussion of its "high-church" traits. In a commissioned bicentennial history of the SBC—which was delayed in publication—the Southwestern research professor categorized the Landmarkers with other nineteenth-century groups that were searching for a sufficient and ancient authority base. He found in Landmarkism a "formal, high-church emphasis" that was more commonly associated with the Roman Catholic and Protestant Episcopal communions. Barnes, for example, drew this comparison: "Within the Protestant Episcopal Church, high-churchism put the emphasis upon the church (in the general use of the term) as the body of Christ. The Baptist counterpart began by putting the emphasis upon the church (in the local use of the term) as the apostolic institution on earth which had had a continuity of existence since the days of the apostles."[18] According to Barnes, Landmarkism, in general, and J. R. Graves, in particular, took on the features of high churchism by combining historical successionism and an altogether local church ecclesiology.

In fact, the official SBC historian referred to Landmarkism's high-church character no less than ten times in a nine-page section of his chapter, "The Convention and Internal Conflicts"; in three of the citations he employed the adjectives "formal" or "rigid" to describe Baptist high churchism and six times he put the Landmark system side by side with either Roman Catholicism, Episcopalianism, or both.[19] In one context, he even contended that Landmark high churchism, with its outright rejection of alien baptisms, went beyond the Catholic or Anglican varieties.[20] Barnes's overall evaluation of Landmarkism in two books clearly disclosed an aversion to its successionism, inflexibility, and desire to turn the SBC into an ecclesiastical entity composed of churches. He further intimated that the SBC's "great advance" beginning around 1900 became possible because the denomination's generally negative response to the Landmarkers' agenda "developed a sense of unity and corporate consciousness" and likewise caused the extreme party in the movement to leave the convention.[21]

Why did Barnes insist on depicting Landmarkism as a high-church bloc in Southern Baptist life? He did not appear to be insinuating that Graves and his followers promoted ritual or elaborate ceremony in worship, which is the meaning that most Baptists today would attach to the term *high church*. To be sure, Landmark churches probably differed from non-Landmark congregations only in degree when it came to worship practices. The reason for Barnes's central focus on high churchism, therefore, might well be found in Michael Williams's comment that Barnes, like onetime Southern Baptist Theological Seminary president E. Y. Mullins, "believed that the key Baptist distinctive was soul competency."[22] If so, the Southwestern educator likely perceived Landmarkist ecclesiology as contrary to the principles of voluntarism and noncoercion that he linked closely to the notion of soul competency. In other words, Barnes— like many Baptists both before and after his time—placed a high premium on religious, ecclesiastical, and political freedom. Traditions such as Catholicism and Anglicanism, particularly with their oppressive state churches, historically had threatened liberty and individual conscience in part because they disavowed soul competency. For Barnes, the Landmarkers shared this ethos because of their dogmatism and alleged rigidity. Hence, they could appropriately be labeled as high church.

Although Barnes's analysis had some merit, especially in recognizing the role that successionism played in Landmark ideology, it unfortunately overlooked two important matters that raise questions about his understanding of Landmarkism as a high-church movement. First, he appeared to be oblivious of the fact that Landmarkers had been accused of high churchism as far back as 1853. William W. Hill, editor of the *Presbyterian Herald* in Louisville, Kentucky, indicted Graves and Pendleton for being high church because he made the mode of baptism "an essential element of a true church" and then "unchurched" those groups that did not properly immerse believers. He then compared this to high-church Episcopalians who mandated a particular form of ordination. Graves, who relished debates with editors from other denominations, naturally defended a position on non-Baptist "societies" that had already been included in the Cotton Grove Resolutions. The Landmark journalist's reply to the charge of high churchism, however, remained ambiguous. After critiquing Hill's attempt to "fix the odium of 'high churchism' and bigotry upon us" for policies that the Presbyterians themselves practiced, Graves subsequently arrived at a qualified acquiescence in his rival editor's allegation:

> Mr. Hill is welcome to use upon us the phrase of "high churchism," if the above principles [i.e., on baptism and church polity] render us obnoxious to the charge—and "*exclusive*," also, if he please. But we will remind him that the Church of Christ is one—he gave but one form of government—not a score of different and necessary [*sic*] antagonistic organizations; but one character of membership, but one form of church ordinances, and doctrine, and if strictly conforming to these in our churches exposes us to the odium of the world, the sneers of men, or the hatred of devils, we must suffer, if we would be accepted of Him. [23]

Barnes perhaps may have welcomed Graves's argument here as primary evidence of Landmarkist rigidity and high churchism. On the other hand, Hill applied the high church moniker in a different context and for a different reason than Barnes did. In addition, there is no unmistakable evidence that Graves ever fully endorsed the idea that Landmarkism represented a high-church posture.

A more serious shortcoming with Barnes's high-church interpretation of the Landmark movement is that he completely ignored the reality that its founder pushed a "freedom" agenda of his own. For instance, Graves vehemently opposed the high churchism of the Roman Catholic and Episcopal traditions partly because he connected them to ecclesiastical tyranny. Furthermore, republican rhetoric thoroughly permeated his *Tennessee Baptist*, especially during the pivotal decade of the 1850s. As Notre Dame scholar Mark Noll has remarked, "American republican language returned consistently to two main themes: fear of abuses from illegitimate power and a nearly messianic belief in the benefits of liberty."[24] Landmarkism's founding father frequently addressed those topics, sometimes with an eloquence that echoed the patriots of the Revolutionary era. Although endorsing Orchard's successionist history, for example, Graves employed a lofty style to commend the superiority of historic Baptist polity: "Through the influence of our [i.e., Baptist] religious principles, and the example of our form of Church government, Republicanism and republican institutions have already bequeathed to half the world, and are now rocking the other half to its centre, crumbling the thrones of its tyrants, and arousing and energizing oppressed humanity, to assert its rights, and overthrow its oppressors."[25] By and large, Graves combined his local church ecclesiology with nineteenth-century republican individualism to wield an effective polemical weapon against any ecclesiastical system that harbored clerical "despotism," "absolutism," or "hierarchism." His extreme localism consequently functioned to some extent as a safeguard against tyranny.[26]

Barnes, however, and most other modern Baptist historians have missed this dimension of Graves's thought. One notable exception is Wake Forest dean and professor Bill Leonard, who provides this handy summary of the Landmarkers' commitment to the value of freedom in his overview of Baptist history: "Amid its biblical and theological conservatism, Landmarkism reflected a solid democratic idealism. Graves, Pendleton, and others advocated radical freedom of the Christian in the liberty of the free state. They were outspoken opponents of establishments, secular or religious, that would undermine the freedom of conscience and religious liberty. In its aggressive emphasis on the autonomy of the local congregation, Landmarkism reflected democratic sentiments of post-Revolutionary American life."[27] Although Leonard does propose elsewhere that the Landmarkers established "their own form of catholicity" in the midst of nineteenth-century denominational pluralism, he avoids the term *high churchism* in describing that impulse.[28] In light of the radicalism that he ascribes to Landmarkism, his terminology seems more scrupulous and less confusing than that used by W. W. Barnes.

All the same, Barnes's high-church model continued to influence a line of Baptist historians, particularly those who succeeded him on the church history faculty at Southwestern Seminary. Robert Baker, who completed his own survey of SBC history in the early 1970s, backed off from Barnes's high-church label and generally measured Landmarkism in a more impartial manner than his mentor had. At the same time, he retained Barnes's inclusion of the Landmarkers in the mid-nineteenth century search for authority, and also reiterated his colleague's point concerning the Landmarkist stance on the composition of Baptist conventions. Finally, Baker at least hinted that the weakening of Landmarkism as a movement in the twentieth century was a good thing: "A strong Landmark undercurrent would have rendered impossible what took place in Southern Baptist organizational life between 1917 and 1972."[29] Thus, both Barnes and Baker tended to depict Landmarkism as essentially detrimental to the longer-term institutional interests of the SBC.

It was left to Baker's student, Leon McBeth, to return more openly to the Barnes paradigm for understanding Landmarkism. The pejorative language of his lengthy textbook on Baptist history actually went well beyond Barnes. McBeth, in essence, marginalized the Landmarkers as rigid, exclusive, imbalanced, intolerant, and insecure "ultraconservatives" who tried to inject their "high church ecclesiology" into the SBC.[30] On the other hand, he followed Barnes in comparing Landmarkers and Roman Catholics: "Perhaps the Landmark movement is best understood as a Baptist equivalent of nineteenth-century Roman Catholicism. The two groups show remarkable similarity in doctrine and spirit. For Landmark Baptists, the principle of church succession plays the same role as apostolic succession for Catholics, validating their claims to be the only true church. Both claimed to have the only true ordinances or sacraments, and both embraced a doctrine of 'high churchism.'"[31] Although this statement omitted any reference to the Episcopal Church, it was otherwise vintage Barnes. McBeth likewise followed Barnes—and Baker—in the judgment that Landmarkism jeopardized the integrity and survival of the SBC as a denomination.[32]

Hence, the Southwestern "school of historiography"—especially Barnes and McBeth—served to mold the high-church perspective on Landmarkism.[33] These historians taught at a Cooperative Program seminary and released their major works through the SBC's official publishing house. It is, therefore, not surprising that one practical effect of their scholarship was to uphold the "party line" of the denominational establishment that had turned away Landmarkist threats to the SBC's institutional agenda from 1859 until the early twentieth century. In the final analysis, the Landmarkers were ecclesiastical losers and were treated as such by SBC historians. It remains an open question, however, whether this high-church portrait of Landmarkism illuminates or muddles the subject.

Landmarkism as an Innovative Ecclesiology

A second interpretive schema for explaining the Landmark movement derived largely from James E. Tull's massive, seven hundred–page dissertation, "A Study of Southern Baptist Landmarkism in the Light of Historical Baptist Theology."[34] The length of the late author's work can be partially ascribed to the beefy documentation that he invoked to sustain one of his major theses: the nineteenth-century Landmarkers put forward an innovative ecclesiology that departed significantly from historic Baptist principles. In other words, Tull gave heavy emphasis to historical discontinuity in his analysis of Landmarkism.

Tull, who taught theology for twenty-five years at Southeastern Baptist Theological Seminary, apparently found one of his first clues about Landmark innovations in an article written in 1855 by W. W. Everts. This Baptist pastor in Louisville faulted the Landmarkers for their controversial spirit, high churchism, and legalism. Moreover, he dismissed their uncompromising position on non-Baptist "societies" as decidedly not an "old landmark": "We regard it rather as a new stake, which can be set down and maintained only in sectarian arrogance. A few may be found in earlier periods of our denominational history maintaining this high-church ground: but far more who never acknowledged it."[35] Thus, Everts merged attacks on both Landmarkism's high-church ecclesiology and innovative character in his appraisal of the movement; for his part, Tull focused more on the latter criticism and expanded it well beyond the Landmarkist refusal to accept non-Baptist bodies as legitimate churches.

The Baptist theologian's assessment of Landmarkism, which contained a wealth of useful historical information, nonetheless suffered because of its grudging and muted recognition of any continuities between Landmark ecclesiology and its Baptist precursors. Whether the topic was successionism, the nature and authority of the church, the ordinances, or the relationship of Baptists to other Christians, Tull opted to depict Landmarkism as alien to the most definitive Baptist traditions of the seventeenth and eighteenth centuries. For example, he correctly ascertained that church succession was the core Landmarkist doctrine, but proceeded to attribute its prominence to J. R. Graves's ignorance and "eclectic theological opportunism." At the end of his evaluation of successionism, Tull summarized what he saw as the Landmark founder's main weaknesses: "The more one studies the thought of Graves the more convinced he becomes that he really did not know Baptist traditions. In point after point, Graves seized uncritically upon ideas which were floating on the current of discussion in his own time, making these ideas central to his system."[36] Although Graves certainly clung to some dubious ideas—including successionist history—it is not clear that he did so because he was patently ignorant of his Baptist forebears or could not think critically.

In a subsequent examination of the Landmarkist rebuff of alien immersion, Tull again pointed to an innovative creativity that was chiefly a response to the movement's constricted frontier context:

The extremist position which the Landmarkers occupied was a substantial departure from contemporary Baptist thought, and from Baptist tradition, and, if it had precedent at all, this precedent was found first in the immediate, bitterly sectarian foreground of the environment from which Landmarkism sprang, and secondly, in radical individuals and groups who sprang up in the course of Baptist history, without deep rootage in the genuine Baptist tradition. Even in these, the particular constellation of elements, such as the necessity of baptismal succession, and the lodgement of an exclusive authority for baptism in a local Baptist church, were hardly to be found. The Old Landmark embodied elements of conspicuous novelty.[37]

Like the historians who viewed Landmarkism through the lens of high churchism, Tull marginalized the Landmarkers as being hopelessly out of the Baptist mainstream. Furthermore, as historian Harper noted, Tull overlooked discussions of irregular immersions that had taken place in the Philadelphia Association between 1707 and 1807, well before the emergence of the Landmark movement.[38]

A more serious difficulty, however, is Tull's reference to "the genuine Baptist tradition." In his commentary on Southern Baptist *stories*, Bill Leonard has fittingly warned that some approaches to the past can oversimplify the rich complexity of the Baptist heritage: "Baptists should not succumb to the fallacy of origins, that noble but naïve belief that there exists a pristine, systematic, and unified source of Baptist identity in the beginning that need only be discovered and installed. In fact, there are multiple Baptist traditions—theological, regional, and institutional—from which churches may choose."[39] Ironically, Tull appears to be guilty of the same historical selectivity that the Landmarkers practiced.

In his 1966 doctoral dissertation at Southwestern Seminary, LeRoy Hogue challenged Tull's take on Landmarkism as innovative and novel by demonstrating some American antecedents of Landmarkism in a number of geographical contexts from the colonial period to the early nineteenth century. In particular, he found notable continuities between the ecclesiology of the earlier New England Separate Baptists and that of Graves and other Landmarkers. Hogue, who later served as a Southern Baptist missionary in Taiwan, indeed concluded that well before the 1850s, "there was a substantial part of the Baptist denomination in the United States that held to a strictly local ecclesiology, that maintained the independency and authority of every local church as a scriptural concept, and that insisted upon a strict observance of the ordinances in their relationship to the authority of the local church."[40] Although Hogue conceded that Landmarkers might have pushed some ideas beyond what their Baptist predecessors intended, his revisionism still offered an important corrective to Tull's innovation thesis and an overall more compelling historical account of the Landmark phenomenon. For some strange reason, Tull totally ignored Hogue's study in his later writings on Landmarkism, including the short redaction of his Columbia dissertation.[41]

The interpretation of Landmarkism as an innovative novelty may ultimately tell us more about Tull than about the Landmarkers. As he narrated the polemically charged war of words that occupied religious periodicals in the 1850s, Tull clearly took sides; in fact, his advocacy approach to history prompted Keith Harper to remark that "Tull's work was a vindication of that element among Southern Baptists who did not embrace Landmarkism."[42] Tull grew up in Arkansas, a state that many Baptist historians would see as part of the "Landmark Belt." As he moved on to graduate work at Baylor University, Southern Baptist Theological Seminary, and Columbia University between 1936 and 1960, he may well have decided that Landmarkism represented an awkward or embarrassing piece of the Southern Baptist heritage. Later at Southeastern Seminary, he was identified with the more liberal ethos that prevailed there even for a period after the launch of the SBC conservative resurgence in 1979.[43] Thus, it is probably not a stretch to suggest that his interpretation of Landmarkism contained a perceptible dose of historical reframing. His susceptibility to ideologically driven history became even more noticeable when he transitioned into the third hermeneutical model for explaining the Landmark movement.

Landmarkism as Proto-Fundamentalism

In the epilogue of his dissertation, James Tull reviewed post-1905 developments in the history of the Landmark movement, including a brief sketch of the fundamentalist controversy that beset American Protestantism during the 1920s and 1930s. Even though this conflict appreciably engaged the Northern Baptist Convention, Tull noted that its effects on the SBC were relatively minor. To be sure, issues such as evolution and personalities such as J. Frank Norris created a few ripples of debate, but they did not seriously endanger the peace and unity of the convention. Furthermore, Tull maintained that (1) the limited fundamentalist agitation in the SBC was unrelated to Landmarkism; and (2) extreme fundamentalists in the convention could not remain consistent Landmarkers. On the latter point, he made a perceptive observation: "The non-denominational nature of fundamentalism has led the fundamentalists into a kind of ecumenical movement of their own—a movement which in the Southern Baptist Convention has tended to ignore and to disrupt denominational lines."[44] Any true Landmarker would normally resist movements such as fundamentalism that held the potential for concealing denominational distinctives.

By the late 1980s, however, Tull significantly altered his assessment of the relationship between Landmarkism and fundamentalism. At the end of his seminary teaching career, he and many of his colleagues found themselves on the losing side of a major SBC controversy that ostensibly began in 1979 with the election of Memphis pastor Adrian Rogers as convention president.[45] For several years before that, SBC conservatives had become alarmed at what they perceived as a doctrinal drift in the convention. In particular, they focused on the issue of biblical authority and inerrancy, which they felt had been compromised in some of the colleges and seminaries. They passed resolutions at some of the SBC annual meetings—particularly in response to controversial Old Testament commentaries that had been published by Broadman Press—but did not sense that these actions had produced any measurable change.

As part of a strategy—often attributed to Paige Patterson and Paul Pressler—to generate a course correction in the SBC, the conservative victory at Houston was followed by a series of triumphs in which men such as Bailey Smith, Charles Stanley, Jerry Vines, and Morris Chapman ascended to the SBC presidency. Conservative presidents appointed conservative trustees to the boards of SBC agencies, including the six Cooperative Program seminaries. In less than fifteen years, the conservative resurgence, which their moderate opponents labeled a "fundamentalist takeover," had succeeded in transforming the ethos, theological orientation, and organizational life of the Southern Baptist Convention. This more recent SBC controversy clearly eclipsed the earlier Landmark disputes in both scope and denominational impact.

Tull, who experienced the SBC conflict as an embattled seminary professor, plainly did not welcome the outcome. Because he died in 1989, what he wrote about possible parallels between fundamentalism and Landmarkism in *High-Church Heresies in the South* (2000) had to reflect, in part, his reaction to the first decade of conservative-moderate discord. In that context, he moved beyond the analysis in his original dissertation and now sought to uncover "Landmark characteristics" in the SBC "fundamental-ist" resurgence. After acknowledging that SBC "fundamentalists" focused on biblical inerrancy, which was not an issue in the Landmark debates, Tull then staked out the most likely common ground between the older and more recent movements:

> The present movement has also exhibited the same belligerent at-titude of older fundamentalism, and is exclusive in that it has no kind words for other Protestant denominations, that is, the anti-affiliationism of the Landmarkists. The leaders of this current fun-damentalist movement come from the heart of the Landmark Belt. The present fundamentalist control of the Southern Baptist Con-vention is not a Landmark movement, yet it claims to go back to a universally held Baptist position, similar to the 'Old Landmarks' of Landmarkism, and calls up earlier Baptist leaders to buttress these claims, and reinterprets history to support the claims, as did the Landmarkers.[46]

The spirit and strategies of the Landmarkers, according to Tull, thus re-surfaced in the arrogance, exclusivism, and intimidation tactics of the SBC "fundamentalists." Evidently, the movement that once had been de-feated in the SBC had returned with a vengeance; or, as Tull wistfully ex-pressed it, the mean disposition of the Landmarkers toward non-Baptists "has been assimilated in general Southern Baptist life until it is not spe-cifically a 'Landmark' characteristic any longer."[47]

Except in a most general way, however, does Landmarkism really shed much light on the most recent disruptions in SBC life? The issues in the second half of the nineteenth century were very different from those that erupted into open conflict in 1979. The central foci of the Landmark-ers were ecclesiology and a successionist view of Baptist history, which were conspicuous by their almost complete absence in the conservative-moderate dispute. In fact, when ecclesiology came up, it was usually in the setting of moderate alarms about the SBC endangering the autonomy of local churches who might challenge the prevailing SBC consensus on matters such as women's ordination or homosexuality.[48] Hence, Tull's con-clusion to High-Church Baptists in the South is unconvincing and laced with non sequiturs; moreover, it takes on the character of special plead-ing, or worse, an emotional venting at what had transpired in the SBC since 1979.

At the very least, Tull was culpable of carelessly interchanging two very different historical contexts. Where his innovative approach, moreover, stressed *discontinuity* between Landmarkist ecclesiology and "historic" Baptist principles, his updated slant posited substantial *continuity* between Landmarkers and "fundamentalists." For consistency, he might have suggested that both movements epitomized innovative departures from normative Baptist life, but he did not pursue that line of thought.

Since Tull, other Baptist historians have attempted to link Landmarkism and fundamentalism. First, Belmont University professor Marty Bell found parallels between J. R. Graves and late twentieth-century SBC "fundamentalists." Because Graves's agenda differed considerably from his alleged ecclesiastical descendants, one can only assume that some connection might be uncovered in Bell's description of the Landmark patriarch as "excessively disputatious, outrageously arrogant, extremely bigoted, and at times desperately paranoid."[49] In other words, Bell concentrated more on common attitudes than on specific ideas or beliefs. Second, Leon McBeth twice labeled Landmarkers as "ultraconservative" in the beginning paragraph of his short 1994 dictionary article on the subject. Even though this echoed a description in his earlier textbook treatment, it appeared to be rather passionate—if not anachronistic—language for a reference tool and may have confirmed a subtle agenda based on his view of the SBC's conservative-moderate controversy.[50] Finally, William Brackney, in a Festschrift for McBeth, made a tantalizing statement that Landmarkism "laid the groundwork for later fundamentalism" without any explanation of what he meant.[51]

A glaring weakness in the historiography since the late 1980s is the paucity of documentation in support of the thesis that Landmarkism somehow anticipated or paved the way for contemporary "fundamentalism" in the SBC. The limited evidence, in fact, accounts for why the protofundamentalist interpretive angle remains imprecise and undeveloped. It shows scant scholarly promise because one of its explanations of the Landmark movement is filtered through the still festering residue of a late twentieth-century denominational ruckus. In short, the historical assessment of Landmarkism suffers when it becomes captive to presentist agendas.

Conclusion

In an insightful essay on the writing of history, Duke University professor Grant Wacker contrasts two approaches: (1) "the straight story" (i.e., "understanding the past for its own sake"); and (2) "an ethically accountable narrative, history with homiletic overlay" (i.e., "using the past for present needs"). While judiciously weighing the strengths and pitfalls of each mode, he observes that those choosing the latter should be mindful that "whenever historians make a self-conscious decision to make the story appeal to or repel the reader, they impose value judgments above and beyond what is presented in the materials."[52] Moral advocacy can have merit; it just needs to be done sensitively and responsibly.

The historians who have interpreted Landmarkism as high churchism, an ecclesiological novelty, or protofundamentalism all went beyond the evidence that they found in their sources and probably sought to "repel" their readers concerning the Landmark movement. They displayed institutional and ideological agendas that ultimately colored their evaluations of Landmarkism. Unfortunately, their "homiletic overlays" served to reframe the Landmarkers in such a way as to create historical caricatures of them. The protofundamentalist thesis has been arguably the worst in this regard.

The Landmarkers themselves never really learned that history can be messy, as their successionist dogmas illustrate. On the other hand, some modern Baptist historians have refused to appreciate the complex nature of the Landmark movement and the individuals who composed it. In a day when issues relating to Baptist identity are being heatedly debated, it will simply not do to assign to the Landmarkers the lion's share of the blame for what is troubling in Southern Baptist life and thought. When that happens, historical understanding suffers at the hands of those who prefer to use the past for other purposes.

Notes

1. Joseph Bottum, "The Judgment of Memory," *First Things*, no. 181 (March 2008): 30.

2. Lynn S. Neal, "Christianizing the Klan: Alma White, Branford Clarke, and the Art of Religious Intolerance," *Church History: Studies in Christianity and Culture* 78 (June 2009): 370–76.

3. For a critical discussion of a representative Landmark understanding of Baptist history, see James A. Patterson, "James Robinson Graves: History in the Service of Ecclesiology," *Baptist History and Heritage* 44 (Winter 2009): 72–83. Successionism was popularized in J. M. Carroll, *The Trail of Blood* (Lexington, KY: American Baptist Publishing Company, 1931).

4. Joe Early Jr., "The Cotton Grove Resolutions," *Tennessee Baptist History* 7 (Fall 2005): 41. The most thorough historical and theological analysis of Landmarkism is James E. Tull, "A Study of Southern Baptist Landmarkism in

Light of Historical Baptist Ecclesiology" (Ph.D. dissertation, Columbia University, 1960). This was reprinted in typescript as *A History of Southern Baptist Landmarkism in the Light of Baptist Ecclesiology* (New York: Arno Press, 1980).

5. The text of the resolutions initially appeared in *Tennessee Baptist*, July 19, 1851, [2]. Graves originally posed them as questions to be answered in the affirmative or negative by the audience at Cotton Grove.

6. J. R. Graves, " An Old Landmark Reset," *Tennessee Baptist*, 1854, [3]; and J. M. Pendleton, *An Old Landmark Re-Set* (Nashville: Graves & Marks, 1854). It was also reprinted in J. R. Graves, ed., *The Southern Baptist Almanac and Register, for the Year 1855* (Nashville: Graves & Marks, 1855), 3–22. For a useful recent study of Pendleton, see Thomas White, "James Madison Pendleton and His Contributions to Baptist Ecclesiology" (Ph.D. dissertation, Southeastern Baptist Theological Seminary, 2005). For a summary of the key differences between Pendleton and his Landmark colleagues, see Keith E. Eitel, "James Madison Pendleton," in *Baptist Theologians*, ed. Timothy George and David S. Dockery (Nashville: Broadman Press, 1990), 198.

7. See [A. C. Dayton], "Theodosia Ernest," *Tennessee Baptist*, September 1, 1855, [3] for the first installment; and Dayton, *Theodosia Ernest; Or, The Heroine of Faith* (Nashville: Graves & Marks, 1856). Dayton eventually completed a trilogy, which also included *Theodosia Ernest: Ten Days Travel in Search of the Church* (Nashville: Graves & Marks, 1857), and *Emma Livingston, the Infidel's Daughter* (Nashville: Graves & Marks, 1859). For scholarly analysis of Dayton, see James E. Taulman, "Amos Cooper Dayton: A Critical Biography" (Th.M. thesis, Southern Baptist Theological Seminary, 1965); and Taulman, "The Life and Writings of Amos Cooper Dayton (1813–1865)," *Baptist History and Heritage* 10 (January 1975): 36–43.

8. Graves, *Old Landmarkism: What Is It?*, 2nd ed. (Texarkana, TX: Baptist Sunday School Committee, [1880] 1928), 38–39.

9. Ibid., 121–30. For documentation of Baptist perpetuity, Graves relied heavily on G. H. Orchard, *A Concise History of Baptists from the Time of Christ Their Founder to the Eighteenth Century* (Nashville: Graves & Marks, 1855), the edition for which Graves wrote an introductory essay. Orchard's book was originally published as *A Concise History of Foreign Baptists* (London: George Wightman, 1838).

10. Graves, *Old Landmarkism*, 183–238 and 262–65.

11. Ibid., ix–xi, 51, 80–85, 105–20. See also Graves, *Intercommunion Inconsistent, Unscriptural, and Productive of Evil* (Memphis: Baptist Book House, Graves, Mahaffy, 1881).

12. On the schisms caused by Landmarkers in the late nineteenth and early twentieth centuries, see Tull, *A Study of Southern Baptist Landmarkism*, 569–

77 and 618–28. For more specific material on the American Baptist Association, see Christopher Bart Barber, "The Bogard Schism: An Arkansas Baptist Agrarian Revolt (Benjamin Marquis Bogard)" (Ph.D. dissertation, Southwestern Baptist Theological Seminary, 2006); and J. Kristian Pratt, "A Landmark Baptist Ecclesiology: Ben Bogard and Local Church Protectionism" (Ph.D. dissertation, Baylor University, 2005). On a similar split in the Lone Star State, see Joseph E. Early Jr., *A Texas Power Struggle: The Hayden Controversy* (Denton: University of North Texas Press, 2005).

13. For a case study of an editorial war, see William Terry Martin, "Samuel Henderson and His Response to J. R. Graves and Landmarkism through South Western Baptist, 1857–1859" (M.A. thesis, Samford University, 1977). On the conflict between Graves and Howell, see Kenneth Vaughn Weatherford, "The Graves-Howell Controversy" (Ph.D. dissertation, Baylor University, 1991). These two types of disputes actually overlapped as some Baptist editors who opposed Graves on other grounds rose to defend Howell against Graves's attacks.

14. Bill J. Leonard, "Whose Story, Which Story? Memory and Identity among Baptists in the South," in *History and the Christian Historian*, ed. Ronald A. Wells (Grand Rapids, MI: Eerdmans, 1998), 136.

15. For a helpful survey of the historiography pertaining to Landmarkism, see Louis Keith Harper, "Old Landmarkism: A Historiographical Appraisal," *Baptist History and Heritage* 25 (April 1990): 31–40.

16. William Wright Barnes, *The Southern Baptist Convention: A Study in the Development of Ecclesiology* (Fort Worth, TX: William Wright Barnes, 1934), 61.

17. Ibid., 78.

18. Barnes, *The Southern Baptist Convention, 1845–1953* (Nashville: Broadman Press, 1954), 100. Prior to the release of this volume, a Southwestern student who may have worked with Barnes averred that Landmarkism brought high churchism into the SBC through an exaggerated concept of local church autonomy. See Eugene Tillman Moore, "The Background of the Landmark Movement" (Th.M. thesis, Southwestern Baptist Theological Seminary, 1947), 66. It is possible that Barnes used Moore's thesis, but he did not cite it in his footnotes or bibliography.

19. Barnes, *The Southern Baptist Convention*, 100–8.

20. Ibid., 108.

21. Ibid., 117.

22. Michael Williams, "Enduring Legacy: William Wright Barnes and Church History at Southwestern Baptist Theological Seminary," *Baptist History and Heritage* 37 (Winter 2002): 23.

23. Graves, "High Churchism," *Tennessee Baptist,* November 12, 1853, [2]. Barnes found evidence in the *Western Recorder,* April 25, 1855, 2, that "Graves himself refers to the position opposed to his as 'low church practices,' thus indirectly calling his own position 'high church.'" See Barnes, *The Southern Baptist Convention,* 100n5. But Barnes failed to reference Graves's "High Churchism" editorial.

24. Mark A. Noll, *America's God: From Jonathan Edwards to Abraham Lincoln* (New York: Oxford University Press, 2002), 56.

25. Graves, introductory essay to G. H. Orchard, *A Concise History of Baptists* (Lexington, KY: Ashland Avenue Baptist Church, [1855] 1956), xviii–xix.

26. For Graves's animus toward Methodism's episcopalian polity as both anti-American and despotic, see Graves, *The Great Iron Wheel; or, Republicanism Backward and Christianity Reversed,* 9th ed. (Nashville: Graves & Marks, 1855), 159–60 and 167–68. For my discussion of his republicanism and related issues, see Patterson, "The J. R. Graves Synthesis: American Individualism and Landmarkist Ecclesiology," *Tennessee Baptist History* 7 (Fall 2005): 9–18.

27. Leonard, *Baptist Ways: A History* (Valley Forge, PA: Judson Press, 2003), 184. For an insightful study of Landmarkism's relationship to frontier populism and democracy, see Marty G. Bell, "James Robinson Graves and the Rhetoric of Demagogy: Primitivism and Democracy in Old Landmarkism" (Ph.D. dissertation, Vanderbilt University, 1990). A weaker side of Bell's work is discussed in the last major section of this chapter.

28. Leonard, "Communidades Ecclesiales de Base and Autonomous Local Churches: Catholic Liberationists Meet Baptist Landmarkers," in *Poverty and Ecclesiology: Nineteenth-Century Evangelicals in the Light of Liberation Theology,* ed. Anthony L. Dunnavant (Collegeville, MN: Liturgical Press, 1992), 82.

29. Robert A. Baker, *The Southern Baptist Convention and Its People, 1607–1972* (Nashville: Broadman Press, 1974), 284. For his discussion of representation at conventions, which was more lucid than Barnes's, see ibid., 315–316. On Landmarkism and the search for authority, see Baker, "Factors Encouraging the Rise of Landmarkism," *Baptist History and Heritage* 10 (January 1975): 1–2, where he specifically cited Barnes.

30. H. Leon McBeth, *The Baptist Heritage: Four Centuries of Baptist Witness* (Nashville: Broadman Press, 1987), 459–61.

31. Ibid., 459.

32. Ibid., 460; and McBeth, "Cooperation and Crisis as Shapers of Southern Baptist Identity," *Baptist History and Heritage* 30 (July 1995): 39.

33. For other designations of Landmarkism as high church, see Chad Hall, "When Orphans Became Heirs: J. R. Graves and the Landmark Baptists,"

Baptist History and Heritage 37 (Winter 2002): 119–20; LeRoy Moore, "Crazy Quilt: Southern Baptist Patterns of the Church," *Foundations* 20 (January–March 1977): 18; John E. Steely, "The Landmark Movement in the Southern Baptist Convention," in *What Is the Church?: A Baptist Symposium,* ed. and comp. Duke K. McCall (Nashville: Broadman Press, 1958), 134–38, 143; and Hugh Wamble, "Landmarkism: Doctrinaire Ecclesiology among Baptists," *Church History* 33 (December 1964): 433.

34. Tull, "A Study of Southern Baptist Landmarkism." About a decade after his death, Tull's dissertation was condensed, revised, and published as *High-Church Baptists in the South: The Origin, Nature and Influence of Landmarkism,* ed. Morris Ashcraft (Macon, GA: Mercer University Press, 2000). Despite the revised title, Tull himself showed only two minor references to Landmark ecclesiology as high church (see 59 and 61). The new title seemingly was Tull's, although the editor cited high churchism three times in his just over three-page preface (see ix–xii).

35. W. W. Everts, "The Old Landmark Discovered," *Christian Repository and Literary Review* 37 (January 1855): 34, quoted in Tull, "A Study of Southern Baptist Landmarkism," 319. Everts may well have picked up on the high-church allegation made two years earlier by Presbyterian editor Hill, who was also based in Louisville. See discussion in the previous section and the reference in note 23. McBeth cites Tull's use of the Everts article, although his footnote gives the wrong page number in Tull's dissertation. See McBeth, *The Baptist Heritage,* 460.

36. Tull, "A Study of Southern Baptist Landmarkism," 320.

37. Ibid., 372–73.

38. Harper, "Old Landmarkism," 40n23.

39. Leonard, "Whose Story, Which Story?," 135.

40. LeRoy Benjamin Hogue, "A Study of the Antecedents of Landmarkism" (Th.D. dissertation, Southwestern Baptist Theological Seminary, 1966), 122–23. I have a forthcoming book on Graves, *James Robinson Graves: Staking the Boundaries of Baptist Identity* (Nashville: B & H Academic, 2012), in which I tie the Landmark patriarch closely to the Separate Baptist tradition of his native Vermont.

41. See Tull, "J. R. Graves—Champion of Baptist High Churchism," in *Shapers of Baptist Thought* (Valley Forge, PA: Judson Press, 1972; reprinted Macon, GA: Mercer University Press, 1984 and 2000), 129–51; Tull, "The Landmark Movement: An Historical and Theological Appraisal," *Baptist History and Heritage* 10 (January 1975): 3–18; and Tull, *High Church Baptists in the South.* For Hogue's qualifiers about continuity, see his "Antecedents," 142, 298. Contemporary Landmarkers evidently are using Hogue's disserta-

tion for their own apologetic purposes. See the digitized version at http://
landmarkism.tripod.com/index.html (accessed July 9, 2009).

42. Harper, "Old Landmarkism," 33. Harper currently teaches church history at Southeastern Seminary, where Tull once served.

43. For biographical information on Tull, see Morris Ashcraft's foreword and the about the author page in Tull, *High-Church Baptists in the South*, vii, xiii. Ashcraft was dean of the faculty at Southeastern until 1989.

44. Tull, "A Study of Southern Baptist Landmarkism," 678–79.

45. What follows on the SBC controversy is a summary based on my role as a participant-observer in SBC life since 1977. There is a wide body of literature on the post-1979 developments in the SBC. For a nonconservative perspective, see David T. Morgan, *The New Crusades, the New Holy Land: Conflict in the Southern Baptist Convention, 1969–1991* (Tuscaloosa: The University of Alabama Press, 1996). For an account by a recognized SBC conservative, see Jerry Sutton, *The Baptist Reformation: The Conservative Resurgence in the Southern Baptist Convention* (Nashville: Broadman & Holman, 2000).

46. Tull, *High-Church Baptists in the South*, 172. Editor Ashcraft sounded a similar note in his preface, ix, by commenting that "some students of Baptist history see the present situation [the 'fundamentalist takeover'] as a resurgence of the fundamentalist 'high churchism' of the nineteenth-century Landmark Movement."

47. Ibid., 173.

48. For example, see Carolyn D. Blevins, *Women's Place in Baptist Life* (Brentwood, TN: Baptist History and Heritage Society, 2003), 16–19.

49. Bell, "James Robinson Graves and the Rhetoric of Demagogy," 240, 274ff. This dissertation was completed shortly after Tull's death.

50. *Dictionary of Baptists in America*, s.v. "Landmark Baptists." The article in the parent volume was written four years earlier by Marty Bell without the derogatory language. Cf. *Dictionary of Christianity in America*, s.v. "Landmark Movement."

51. William H. Brackney, "A Turn toward a Doctrinal Christianity: Baptist Theology, a Work in Progress," in *Turning Points in Baptist History: A Festschrift in Honor of Harry Leon McBeth*, ed. Michael E. Williams and Walter B. Shurden (Macon, GA: Mercer University Press, 2008), 81.

52. Grant Wacker, "Understanding the Past, Using the Past: Reflections on Two Approaches to History," in *Religious Advocacy in American History*, ed. Bruce Kuklick and D. G. Hart (Grand Rapids, MI: Eerdmans, 1997), 160, 162.

10

Is There a River?

Black Baptists, the Uses of History, and the Long History of the Freedom Movement

Paul Harvey

Writing to Ralph McGill in 1962, a black Georgian queried the white southern moderate editor of the *Atlanta Constitution* on the unconscious assumptions that distorted the views of even the best-intentioned white southerners. In a previous editorial, McGill had excoriated religious institutions for doing "nothing at all" to address the region's social ills. With clergymen delivering sermons that were "routinely irrelevant," the South's churches had "placed themselves on the sidelines." The correspondent quickly pointed out that McGill, of course, referred to white churches. Had so many black ecclesiastical buildings "been burned and bombed because they were on the sidelines?" he inquired. "Have they not provided the meeting-places, theme-song, and leaders for the center of the non-violent protest." In McGill's language, "Christianity" and "the churches" unconsciously signified "white" in both cases. "When one views the churches and Christianity without regard for color," the letter concluded, "it becomes strikingly clear that Christianity and the churches have never been more relevant (taken as a whole)—or less on the sidelines."[1]

This correspondent speaks to the common understanding that black churches and activist ministers sparked a moral crusade to redeem America. Such a view captures part, but only part, of the complicated and ambiguous relationship between religion and the civil rights movement. Other stories from the era suggest more ambiguity in the relationship of black Baptist churches to the history of the civil rights struggle. Activists contended with the reality that "the black church" was not, as a rule, behind the movement. "We have learned, and our students 'learned' with us, that deacons and preachers, especially in the wealthier churches, are generally conservatives," a Mississippi civil rights volunteer wrote of his trying experiences seeking places to hold freedom schools.[2]

Leaders of the freedom struggle knew firsthand of the numerous congregations that closed their doors to movement meetings. "The preachers, number one, they didn't have nothing to do with it," two local activists recalled of the movement in Mississippi. "Teachers number two, they didn't have nothing to do with it. Until things got when they could tell they wasn't gon' kill 'em, and then they went to comin' in." In Holmes County, a Mississippi civil rights worker reported, "we got turned down a lot of times from the black minister. . . . He mostly was afraid because they [whites] whooped a few of 'em and bombed a few churches. The preacher didn't want his church burned down, and them old members was right along in his corner." There was good reason for this fear. In the early summer of 1964, forty-one black churches in Mississippi, of various denominations and geographic locations, went up in flames.[3]

Thus, the relationships among religion, race, and rights during the 1960s are more complicated than often portrayed, particularly in the recent deification (and oversimplification) of Martin Luther King's life and work. Whether because of fear, indifference, coercion, and the implicit threat of terrorism, black Baptist churches as a whole were less involved in the struggle than was, and is, commonly perceived. A white student stationed in southwest Georgia in 1965 tellingly concluded that the movement was "saturated with religion," but for him the "most shocking discovery . . . (because it is at such variance with the impression one gets from the national news media) was to find how conservative and separate from the movement are most Negro churches." He generally found religious leaders "far more conservative than the people in many cases." Black churches were a "very active" stumbling block, another activist observed, often still beholden to a theology "based on a heaven-centered world view coupled with a demeaning view of the power of man. These two tenets fulfill the function of keeping the Negro in his place." The long-time South Carolina NAACP organizer Septima Clark understood that the tenure of local black ministers often depended on the approval of whites. Even with their congregations' support, they could be "run out of town if the white power structure decided they ought to go." Ministers who shied away from involvement were not necessarily opposed to the movement but might have been "just afraid to join it openly. It's simply a contradiction: so many preachers support the Movement that we can say it was based in churches, yet many preachers couldn't take sides with it because they thought they had too much to lose."[4]

Since the King years, as historian Taylor Branch refers to the period from the Montgomery Bus Boycott to the Selma march, black churches and ministers have stood in as iconic emblems of the civil rights struggle. And black church leaders have cultivated that view of their own history, for it is a narrative that places black churches at the center of one of the most important moments of American history. Black Baptists historically have composed the largest segment of the black churchgoing population. In some understandings, they always have been in the vanguard of civil rights, always freedom fighters. In this view, a movement based on secular ends, namely the extension of citizenship rights in the American nation-state, drew its sustenance from spiritual understandings, language, and motivations. It was a fundamentally Protestant imagery of Exodus, redemption, salvation that inspired the revivalist fervor of the movement. And it was church activists—most visibly Martin Luther King Jr., but also black Baptist leaders such as Fred Shuttlesworth, John Lewis, and Fannie Lou Hamer—who infused the struggle with their religious passion and steely commitment. This view is captured best by Vincent Harding's *There Is a River*, a work that places the beginnings of the civil rights movement with rebellions aboard slave ships and moves forward from there. In this telling, activism in freedom struggles moved like a river current through black history. The recent historiographical move to stress the "long history of the civil rights movement" follows that river current through the *longue durée* of black history, part of a larger project to reperiodize our concept of the civil rights movement away from the "Montgomery to Memphis" paradigm.[5]

Activists in the 1960s held a more chastened view, and others looking for church leadership against segregationism also ran into historic obstacles. Most black Baptist congregations—often rural, with few resources, and with part-time ministers—remained outside the social fray altogether, at least as much as they could. Even black Baptist churches without such institutional constraints had to learn to put their theology into social action; it did not arise naturally from Baptist theology, or from a history that naturally compelled them in that direction. Black evangelical theology focused on the state of the soul, and black Baptist polity focused on the local and congregational. Given the emphasis on the individual, both presented obstacles toward larger efforts at social organization. In this rendering, there was no fast-flowing current in the long river of activism. The Baptist tradition of local and congregational democracy, moreover, placed ministers in precarious positions, another factor that discouraged troublemakers.

This chapter will examine the ideas by which "the black church" has evolved and how ideas of civil rights grew slowly and haltingly from black Baptist congregations often resistant to participating in the struggle. This chapter also will discuss how black churches came to understand their own history, creating a master freedom narrative out of a set of institutions aptly referred to by James Melvin Washington as a "frustrated fellowship."[6] How such a frustrated fellowship evolved (in the minds of many) into a civil rights phalanx—how black ministers (led by black Baptists) leading an interreligious march across the bridge at Selma came to be the dominant image of the civil rights era—involves understanding the evolution of the historiography of black churches and civil rights. Black Baptists had to weave a version of their own history out of a complicated tangle of threads, not all of which were particularly amenable to the civil rights narrative. Once they did so—once they created a usable past—they helped to bring about the greatest social revolution of twentieth-century American history. And to do so, they had to engage in narrative acts that allowed people to see themselves as part of a river of protest. They did not have to invent a tradition, but they needed at least to embellish it and make it a coherent narrative. They had to place themselves within a usable past, and to do that they had to revivify part of, and break from the shackles of other parts of, the history of black Baptist churches.

The Burden of Black Baptist History

The dichotomy of what the black church represented—and the very notion of "the black church" itself—arose from a discourse that also singularized "the Negro," as Curtis Evans has shown in his landmark study *The Burden of Black Religion*. Evans's work historicizes the concepts by which African American religious expressions in any form have come to be understood. The categories imposed on the black church have given it a burden that no institution could bear. It had to be all things to all black people, something no institution could do. In the nineteenth century, cultural understandings, which George Frederickson called "romantic racialism," understood African American people as embodying a simplistic but sincere evangelical emotion. This "natural" spirituality of the Negro appealed to those troubled by the crasser forms of market materialism that dominated American life. Later, the social science–defined abstraction of the "Negro Church" used by black scholars (starting with DuBois and continuing on through E. Franklin Frazier and Benjamin Mays) effectively pathologized the black church, diagnosing its ills as a symptom of larger woes of African American life in the Jim Crow world. Rural black Baptist churches harbored an affecting but ineffectual "compensatory religion." These social science views dominated the nascent scholarly literature of black religion during the interwar years and explained the church's seeming quietism, its otherworldliness. In the 1960s and forward, the neo-romantic racialist concept of "soul" turned into virtue what the social scientists had condemned as illness. African American religious emotion now embodied authenticity, rather than acting as a symptom of pathology. In their own ways, all of these views have been distorting mirrors by which Americans have used black religion to reflect back on themselves. Later scholars, especially DuBois, created the idea of the Negro Church as a "normative discourse" designed to "mine these new tools of social science to radically transform the nature of black religious life," in Evans's words, even while "Northern white artists and dramatists sought to mine the folk wisdom and alleged primitive religiosity of this rural black Southern culture."[7]

From possessing an almost frightening power, to languishing as frustrated fellowship, the black Baptist church came under scrutiny both for its potential and its problems. The poetic and the sociological modes of exploration both struggled to understand how spiritual power implicit in the black churches could be unlocked and then unleashed into a social world whose entire premise rested on the degradation of African Americans. Philosophers, preachers, and scholars contemplated the black church as a spiritual force, a potential base for power, and a sociological drag on progress.

Evans's work also helps us understand and further contextualize James Melvin Washington's concept of black Baptists as a "frustrated fellowship." Through all periods of American history, Evans argues, the "burden" of black religion has been that it has been forced to carry too much weight; it has produced "overly robust notions of agency" that ignore the "difficult and constricting social spaces in which African Americans have practiced their religions." It is those constricting social spaces that frustrate fellowships and have led to once-prevalent ideas (best articulated in Gayraud Wilmore's *Black Religion and Black Radicalism*) of the "deradicalization of the black church."[8]

Evans would have scholarship "move beyond the black church and free up scholars to construct more interesting and empirically grounded narratives," stories that would not be forced into dichotomous straitjackets of "protest versus accommodation."[9] But in fact, these concepts are so deeply grounded that this is unlikely. The role of black Baptist churches in the civil rights movement solidified the liberationist view, even as it tightened the straitjacket that has burdened interpretations of black religious history. By the early twentieth century, this discourse was so deeply inscribed that the black scholars who pioneered modern-day histories of African American religious institutions had to use the very language that, inevitably, distorted their subjects. Moreover, from W. E. B. DuBois forward, those who studied black religious institutions (dominated by black Baptist churches) oscillated between visions of liberatory potential and sociological explorations of why these poetically powerful institutions so often apparently failed to act as engines of social progress. DuBois pioneered this in his essays in *Souls of Black Folk* as well as his landmark sociological study *The Negro Church*.[10] In his poetic essay and in his sociological studies, DuBois effectively brought into the twentieth century the two modes of discourse that continued to dominate black history and historiography. The first depicted the black church as a force of emotional power that helped Negro people transcend the dismal conditions of Jim Crow America; the second depicted the black church as an institutional hindrance to the recognition by black Americans of their own social power. The very language in which these studies were conducted forced academic debate into sterile categories and still does so to a considerable degree— hence words such as *liberationist* or *accommodationist* to encompass wildly diverse institutions ranging from sharecroppers' churches in the middle of Mississippi's cotton fields to Gothic structures on Chicago's Southside housing thousands on a Sunday listening to western classical music. How was a normative narrative empowering a freedom struggle to be built from such divergent histories, institutional contexts, and ideological structures?

If Vincent Harding's *There Is a River* traced an unbroken stream of black religious activism and radicalism from the earliest days of slavery through to the civil rights movement, Gayraud Wilmore's *Black Religion and Black Radicalism* showed the disjunctures in this history. For Wilmore, black religion through the Civil War and Reconstruction era provided consolation for suffering slaves, as well as power for those seeking to break the shackles of bondage. The central role of black churches during Reconstruction, moreover, showed how the subterranean power of African American religious practices in the invisible institution could become visible and very public when African Americans were given the opportunity for a public life. Nowhere was this more the case than in the low country of Georgia in January 1865, when Baptist minister Garrison Frazier led a delegation of black Georgians in a colloquy with General William Tecumseh Sherman and Oliver O. Howard, soon to be head of the Freedmen's Bureau.

In January 1865, African American ministers from Savannah and the Georgia low country advised Union war officers on assisting the refugees set free by Sherman's march. Long-time Baptist pastor Garrison Frazier counseled William Tecumseh Sherman and Secretary of War Edwin Stanton that "the way we can best take care of ourselves is to have land and turn it and till it by our own labor . . . and we can soon maintain ourselves and have something to spare." Frazier suggested as well that a decided preference to "live by ourselves" rather than "scattered among the whites," over the objections of the Methodist James B. Lynch, who took the view that ex-slaves and southern whites "should not be separated." Sherman set aside for black war refugees lands in the Georgia and South Carolina low country and Sea Islands, a decision soon transformed in the prevailing folklore ("forty acres and a mule") as a governmental promise to provide land for the freedpeople. Ulysses L. Houston, one of those who had met with Sherman, was another influential Baptist clergyman in the area. Brought to Savannah as a house servant, he worked at the city's hospital and earned extra income by hiring out his time. White sailors helped him learn to read and write. From 1861 to 1880, he pastored the Third African Baptist Church and served twice as president of the black Baptist convention in Georgia. Houston also helped to plan a village for the freedpeople on Skidaway Island.[11]

Throughout the South, black religious leaders followed Houston's lead, actively shaping African American life under freedom and realizing the implicit social power of the newly visible black church. James Simms, too, pursued an active career as a minister-missionary and politician. Born a slave in Savannah, he purchased his freedom in 1857 with money raised from working as a master builder. During Reconstruction, he worked with the Freedmen's Bureau and the American Baptist Home Mission Society, served as a Union League organizer, and later won election to the Georgia House of Representatives. During that time, he became the only black district judge in the state. His political success left him vulnerable to Klan attacks that eventually chased him from the low-country region into Atlanta. As Simms later explained, socially conscious black clergymen of that time "had to leave their flock and legitimate field of labor to enter the arena of politics to secure right and justice for their people . . . notwithstanding the white citizens among whom they lived and served, and the late owners, [who] constantly spoke disparagingly of the ministers who served in these positions." At one meeting concerning black suffrage, Simms subverted the attempts by white ministers to "manage every thing their own way." He said that "it was the first time he ever had such an opportunity of speaking to white men, and should improve it to tell them *some plain truths*. . . . For once, at least, they heard the unvarnished truth." Simms also testified before Congress on behalf of the freedpeople and edited the Savannah-based *Freedmen's Standard*. His ministerial colleague Thomas Allen, a politician in Jasper County, reminded his congregants that the Yankees had freed them and that "they ought to vote with them; to go with the party always. They voted just as I voted."[12]

Scholarship on Reconstruction emphasizes the power of the black church; scholarship focusing on the Jim Crow era has tended to emphasize its impotence, highlighting instead the "constricted social spaces" described by Curtis Evans. Scholars searching for an activist tradition in black church politics hardly could hide their dismay at the role of the church during the long and dismal interregnum between the demise of Reconstruction and the advent of the civil rights movement. What was the role of the church in the rural South during Jim Crow? For many students of the subject, it appeared to be little, at least measured by the standards of public activism during Reconstruction. Black religious practices appeared to be "compensatory," allowing for emotional enthusiasms that "compensated" for the lack of any real social agency in this world. Black religion had been depoliticized, or deradicalized in Wilmore's terms. *The Negro's God*, to quote the title of Benjamin Mays's study of the subject, seemed a psychic projection of a fantasy from another world, an alternative universe in which black southerners could exercise some control over their own lives. Allowed to worship such a God on Sundays, the Negro then returned to his labors the next morning, with spiritual consolation to withstand another week of humiliation.

Though scholars such as Harding could find precious little water flowing in the "river" metaphor of black religious activism through the Jim Crow era, students such as Wilmore found it difficult to explain the uprisings of the 1950s and 1960s. In those revolutionary years, black Baptists in frustrated fellowships, now apparently reradicalized, led the transformation of a nation. It was even more difficult to understand within the world of the National Baptist Convention, the single largest black religious Protestant denomination. Led from 1953 to 1982 by Joseph H. Jackson, black ministers high up in the world of the NBC practiced patronage politics, accepting favors from local politicians (especially in Chicago) in exchange for token plums of power. Jackson bitterly resisted Martin Luther King, refusing even to meet with him when the son of the South engineered a freedom movement in Chicago. Jackson's tenacious hold on the presidency of the NBC, and his refusal to employ this fellowship of black Baptists in active support of King and the nonviolent civil rights struggle in the South, led King and his followers out of the convention. They formed the Progressive National Baptist Convention, in the second major split that the NBC had experienced in the twentieth century (the first being in 1915, in a dispute over who would control the National Baptist Publishing Board, then the largest black-owned publishing house in the nation).[13]

In short, black Baptists had a history to which they could appeal, especially the history of black religio-political activism in the era of Reconstruction. But black Baptists, and black Christians in America, also had a complex history, one in which, as Evans states, constricted social spaces restricted social activism. In other words, the river sometimes flowed in a torrent, and sometimes—very often, in fact—was dammed up by the powerful forces of white supremacy and by the divisive internal politicking that substituted for power struggles that would matter in the larger world. History was no uncomplicated ally for those looking for a usable past to empower civil rights protests in the 1950s and 1960s.

History was not always an ally in another sense as well—black history had yet to be recognized more generally as part of American history. In many ways, to paraphrase Hegel, African Americans remained (not so much in their own communities, as seen by the larger society) a people without history. The civil rights revolution of the 1950s and 1960s certainly transformed the practice of studying African American history and rapidly brought it into the forefront of the rewriting of American history more generally. But history was the cart and the movement the horse. That is, the transformation in the understanding of African American history followed the civil rights revolution; it did not precede it.

Since the nineteenth century, black Americans had written their own histories, creating a sacred narrative in which black people figured centrally in God's plan. In *God Requires That Which Is Past*, religious studies scholar Laurie Maffly-Kipp has combed through a surprisingly extensive literature of "black history" written by African American authors from the late Revolutionary era to the early twentieth century. She traces the story of African American "sacred narratives." The history of the narration of black history, she concludes, "resulted in the affirmation of a group identity that came to be seen as 'natural' and inevitable rather than humanly constructed, denying its own genesis in a particular historical circumstance." The writing of black history from the late eighteenth century to the era of W. E. B. DuBois helped to create black peoples' sense of themselves *as* a people. The narration of race, in other words, helped to create race; it fostered a unified sense of blackness in America that overrode the multiple ways in which actual African American people were divided—by class, skin tone, personal histories of slavery and freedom, literacy, gender, and denomination.[14]

Black Baptist authors were part of this process of narration, most especially in the works of twentieth-century pioneers of Negro history such as Carter Woodson and Benjamin Mays. Perhaps more importantly, black Baptist leaders in the post–Civil War era adopted the language of the grand narrative, placing black people in classical as well as sacred traditions, from the ancient world through to their era. Blacks had a history, they knew, and African American history, as they perceived it, should be empowering in the contemporary social world. The early black historians, including Woodson and moving on through the generation of E. Franklin Frazier and Benjamin Mays, adopted the language of the Negro Church in part because it imparted a sense of history and peoplehood to African American institutions. The limitations of these kinds of singularized concepts would become more apparent later, when scholars had to deconstruct some of the monolithic views that earlier had been constructed by those seeking to place blacks within history at all. Black Baptist ministers of the civil rights era, then, drew from a tradition of history both of their own denomination as well as from a larger sacred narrative of the meaning of Africans becoming Americans. Increasingly, they could use a professionalized historiography as well, which drew from modern norms of historical research that brought African Americans into the larger world of American history. C. Vann Woodward's classic *Strange Career of Jim Crow*, for example, came to be called the "bible of the civil rights movement," precisely because it historicized segregation. By showing segregation's relatively recent origin, it placed the South's history in a context that showed how easily history could be changed. Institutions falsely portrayed as immutable custom or tradition were instead imminently changeable.[15]

Black Baptists, Black History, and Civil Rights

Black Christians who formed the rank-and-file of the civil rights movement demolished the political structures of segregation. Key to their work was a transformation of Protestant thought in ways that deftly combined the social gospel and black church traditions, infused with Gandhian notions of active resistance and "soul force," as well as secular ideas of hard-headed political organizing and the kinds of legal maneuverings that led to *Brown v. Board* and *Loving v. Virginia,* the latter declaring unconstitutional laws prohibiting interracial marriages.

The religion of the southern folk appeared to be apolitical. Critics called it "otherworldy" or "compensatory," and to some extent, doubtless it was. But W. E. B. DuBois pointed out that whereas religion might be seen as "mere symbolism," to the freedpeople "God was real. They knew Him. They had met Him personally in many a wild orgy of religious frenzy, or in the black stillness of the night." As a scholar and social scientist, DuBois was often critical of the black church as an institution for its increasing insularity, its focus in the twentieth century on internal growth and power politicking, and its inability before the civil rights movement to use its enormous resources effectively on behalf of African American people. At the same time, however, DuBois as a poet and sensitive essayist understood the kind of powerful work going on in the rituals and the ostensibly "otherworldly" preaching emanating from black pulpits.[16]

As DuBois's work suggests, the implicit potential of southern folk religion—what contemporary scholars might call the "hidden transcript" contained in religious behavior—bears close scrutiny. The historian Robin D. G. Kelley has argued that "we need to recognize that the sacred and the spirit world were also often understood and invoked by African Americans as weapons to protect themselves or to attack others. . . . Can a sign from above, a conversation with a ghost, a spell cast by an enemy, or talking in tongues unveil the hidden transcript?" To which one might add, can one's private and communal prayer when facing down racist sheriffs, voting registrars, or snakes thrown on one's front porch embolden resistance, and serve as the antidote to the opiate of the people fed by Jim Crow's spokesmen? In Mississippi and Alabama, and other places in the 1950s and 1960s, the "hidden transcript" came to the surface. The assassins who bombed the 16th Street Baptist Church in Birmingham and numerous other ecclesiastical buildings through these years recognized this as clearly as anyone. White racists somehow understood that the moral arc of black Baptist history would tend toward justice, and they aimed, at least, to interrupt it.[17]

The civil rights movement had legislative aims; it was, to that extent, a political movement. But it was more than that as well. It was a religious movement, sustained by the deeply Protestant religious imagery and fervor of southern black churches. Black Baptists were part of a movement to undermine the historic Christian mythic grounding for destructively hierarchical ideas of whiteness and blackness; or perhaps to sacralize blackness in a way that whiteness historically had been deified. The historically racist grounding of whiteness as dominant and blackness as inferior was radically overturned in part through a reimagination of the same Christian thought that was part of creating it in the first place. As one female sharecropper and civil rights activist in Mississippi explained in regard to her conversion to the movement, "Something hit me like a new religion."[18]

In the 1950s and 1960s, the "silent South" spoke, black Baptists loudest of all. Black Baptists had been active earlier, as may be seen in a figure formerly unknown but now resurrected by Taylor Branch's popular history *Parting the Waters:* the Reverend Vernon Johns, surely the least-known important black religious figure of the twentieth century. One of the last of his pulpits was in Montgomery, Alabama, where "the man who started freedom" and the feisty orator prepared the way for the young and studious Martin Luther King, who in 1954 was still a doctoral student at Boston University. King's quiet demeanor contrasted sharply with Johns's penchant for picking fights and pointing out the faults of the congregants, and of the black church generally, too often and too publicly.

As he took over his Baptist pulpit in Montgomery, Martin Luther King had no idea of the history that was about to overtake him, but long-time community activists quickly recognized the usefulness of the young doctoral candidate. The story in elaborate detail has been told most fully, and for a popular audience, in Taylor Branch's trilogy. David Garrow's *Bearing the Cross* provides a landmark scholarly biography that places King firmly in the context both of his southern religious roots as well as his northern theological training and his connections with political organizers outside the church world such as the pacifist radical Bayard Rustin. Garrow places much emphasis on King's visionary spiritual experience in the mid-1950s, a second version that steeled him for the numerous attempts on his life and the constant internecine struggles within movement organizations.[19]

Much early civil rights scholarship followed a great-man-theory-of-history approach, not surprisingly given the attention paid in the media to designated spokesmen such as King, Malcolm X, and a few others. But scholars, in the midst of the social history revolution soon uncovered and analyzed the "local people" who did much of the actual work of the movement, most especially women, a great number of whom could be found in Baptist pews every Sunday. One model emulated in future studies was Aldon D. Morris's *The Origins of the Civil Rights Movement: Black Communities Organizing for Change* (1984). He begins his story not with Montgomery but with an earlier boycott led by black Baptist pastor T. D. Jemison in Baton Rouge, Louisiana, in 1953, an action that set the stage for mass mobilizations to come. Morris refers to the Southern Christian Leadership Conference (SCLC) as the "decentralized arm of the black church." Morris argues strongly for the central role of churches in organizing and carrying out the black freedom struggle, noting that only an indigenous organization such as the church could have served so effectively as an agent of mass mobilization.[20]

The argument advanced by Morris is furthered by Andrew Manis's memorable biography of Fred Shuttlesworth, *A Fire You Can't Put Out* (1999), which shows the long-time Baptist pastor in Birmingham at the forefront of civil rights crusades in this most brutally racist of southern cities long before the more well-known names from SCLC showed up in 1963. No one represented the movement's fire—a "fire you can't put out," as his biographer has expressed it—more than the Reverend Fred Shuttlesworth, who served in Birmingham during fateful crusades in the infamously tough industrial town. Shuttlesworth gradually made his name locally first in Selma, and later in Birmingham, as a willful preacher with a "'combative spirituality.'"[21]

Electrified by the *Brown* decision and his sense of God's hand moving in history, Shuttlesworth's civil rights career blossomed in the 1950s. He felt divinely inspired to defy a response to the banning of the NAACP in Alabama imposed by the state authorities. Resisting more senior ministers who urged moderation, Shuttlesworth and his followers organized the Alabama Christian Movement for Human Rights. He saw the new group as part of a "worldwide revolution which is a divine struggle for the exaltation of the human race." Repeated attempts on his life only enhanced his personal authority and charisma. In 1957, white terrorists exploded dynamite at his home, nearly killing his wife and children. Shuttlesworth emerged from the severely damaged building uninjured.[22]

After the sit-ins at lunch counters in Greensboro and the birth of the Student Nonviolent Coordinating Committee (SNCC), Shuttlesworth met with former SCLC executive director Ella Baker and told her to inform King that Birmingham was the thing that could "really shake up the world." Even while sitting in an Alabama jail, Shuttlesworth smuggled out pieces of writing, including a petition signed by inmates to desegregate courthouse facilities in the county. Following his release, Shuttlesworth led an interracial conference assembled at the Gaston Motel in Birmingham on "Ways and Means to Integrate the South." The success of the gathering convinced Shuttlesworth to pressure King and the SCLC leadership to choose Birmingham for their next crusade. "There are certain places that have symbolic meanings," as one participant put it, including the town infamously known as "Bombingham." After the meeting, true to form, bombers struck Bethel Baptist Church (where Shuttlesworth had preached) for the third time since 1956. Shards of shrapnel sprayed everywhere. Shuttlesworth later said, "I have always been a symbol of the Negro freedom movement here, and that is why the church where I used to be pastor has been bombed again. This is Birmingham's shame and America's tragedy."[23]

Shuttlesworth threw his energies into the civil rights movement, and as one of his congregants said, "everything he did and said spoke to that." Shuttlesworth told black Birminghamians that he possessed no "magic wand to wave nor any quick solution by which the God of segregation can be made to disappear," but had only "myself—my life—to lead as God directs." After suffering a severe beating while trying to enroll his daughter in a school, he lay near death on the ground but heard the voice of God telling him, "you can't die here. Get up. I got a job for you to do." Though considered headstrong and even neurotic for his apparent desire for martyrdom, Shuttlesworth reminded supporters of how many of the "Biggest Preachers (I'll call no names) pleaded with me to call off the Mass Meeting; how many tried to take a stand against the Movement, and would have publicly except for public sentiment. . . . You cannot imagine how tedious and painstaking it has been to forge together this organization in Birmingham; nor how difficult to keep in line moving forward." Of his courageous actions, he later reflected, "I really tried to get killed in Birmingham. I exposed myself deliberately, and I felt [that] if I did give my life that the country would have to do something about it." Shuttlesworth placed himself squarely in the "contest for justice and righteousness" from the Old Testament to the present, seeing the biblical parable of good and evil being waged "between God and Eugene [Bull] Connor." During the Birmingham demonstrations in 1963, Shuttlesworth reminded his colleagues frequently that "this is my town, and I know this town; I know them rednecks." When James Farmer of the Congress of Racial Equality came to Montgomery, Shuttlesworth escorted him through a mob surrounding a church. Miraculously, the crowd of hostile whites opened up and allowed them to pass. Farmer attributed this to Shuttlesworth's well-deserved reputation for near insanity in pursuit of justice. For Shuttlesworth, it was more akin to God opening up the Red Sea.[24]

Civil rights activists such as Shuttlesworth mixed the language of evangelicalism with the tenets of American civil religion. The two were inseparable, and in both cases, historical narrative could be invoked as an ally for those in the freedom struggle. Both the Bible and American history were full of freedom struggles. They were also inseparable in the mind of Fannie Lou Hamer, who personified the fortitude and vibrant religious imagery of the movement. Daughter of a sharecropper in Ruleville, Mississippi, she experienced sexual abuse and later sadistic torture at the hands of local policemen. Hamer rose to prominence in the 1960s as a liaison between "local people" and national civil rights leaders. With her wicked sense of humor, spirited singing voice, and uncompromising stance on justice, Hamer articulated a liberation theology that sustained her through years of struggle and turmoil. "She compares herself frequently to Job . . . without a trace of self pity or some warped sense of pride," wrote one northern admirer serving in Mississippi. "Her faith in God is pervasive and in a sense dominates her life. . . . There is a prophetic, messianic sense about her—an awareness, an electricity, a sense of mission which is very rarely absent." As a girl, Hamer had joined the Strangers Home Baptist Church in her hometown. She quoted the Bible expertly and led congregational song, qualities that served her admirably in the 1960s. In 1962, at a SNCC meeting in a rural church, Hamer and a few others volunteered to register for voting. This serious act of political defiance against the state regime earned them a beating in the county jail. After their release, they experienced economic and verbal harassment. For example, the mayor of Ruleville canceled the tax-exempt status of Williams Chapel Missionary Baptist Church, Hamer's congregation, reasoning that by welcoming in SNCC field secretaries the congregation had been using the building for "purposes other than worship services." Hamer eventually won a seat in the Mississippi Freedom Democratic Party's delegation, originally sent as a protest against the all-white official state delegation, to the Democratic National Convention of 1964. Hamer incited Lyndon Baines Johnson's special ire as she delivered an impromptu national address explaining why the Freedom Democratic Party would not settle for the compromise of taking two seats on the official state delegation. Queried by reporters, Hamer responded with an extemporized narration of black Mississippians who had risked their lives simply for trying to exercise citizenship rights. Hamer led the participants in her favorite freedom song "This Little Light of Mine," a tune known by Sunday schoolers everywhere.[25]

Hamer's political stance required spiritual sustenance. "Before 1962," as she later wrote, "I would have been afraid to have spoken before more than six people. Since that time I have had to speak before thousands in the fight for freedom, and I believe that God gave me the strength to be able to speak in this cause." She used her knowledge of the Bible in public rebukes of the timid. As she told one group of black Mississippians, "we are tired of being mistreated. God wants us to take a stand. We can stand by registering to vote—go to the court to register to vote." Christ would side with the sharecroppers in Mississippi during their struggle. Answering the inevitable charges that civil rights workers were agitators and communists, she retorted, "if Christ were here today, he would be branded a radical, a militant, and would probably be branded as 'red.'" Christ was a "revolutionary person, out there where it was happening. That's what God is all about, and that's where I get my strength." Summing up her life's work, she explained, "we can't separate Christ from freedom, and freedom from Christ." She criticized southern churches for doing "too much pretending and not enough actual working, the white ministers and the black ministers standing behind a podium and preaching a lie on Sunday." It was "long *past* time for the churches to wake up" and address fundamental issues of justice. Ephesians 6:11–12 provided sufficient evidence for the spiritual basis of the freedom struggle: "Put on the whole armor of God, that ye may be able to stand against the wiles of the devil. For we wrestle not against flesh and blood, but against principalities, against powers, against the rulers of the darkness of this world, against spiritual wickedness in high places." Women such as Fannie Lou Hamer "placed Jesus where his experiences, as passed through the traditions of the Black church, could be used in the freedom struggle."[26]

Both Shuttlesworth and Fannie Lou Hamer came out of very specific church traditions. And both recognized that their traditions were there not only to be used, but also when necessary to be rebuked, or simply to be overcome, gotten over. Hamer was not shy about issuing ultimatums to her pastors and congregants when they shied away from involvement in the movement, and Shuttlesworth was not hesitant to do the same to his own congregants. Both saw the church as an instrument of liberation, but they had to overcome much of their own training in the church to do so. History was their ally, but only if a version of that history that separated church from everyday struggles was bypassed in favor of a vision of churches like their role in Reconstruction. They were successful to the degree that the churches, and black ministers, became iconic symbols of the civil rights struggle. They were also successful to such a degree that the church's liberationist potential could become another heavy burden, as increasingly seemed to be the case in an allegedly postracial America.

Black Baptists and History in the Post–Civil Rights Era

Studying the history of the black church in American public life presents a paradox. On the one hand, thinking of the role of black churches during the Civil War and Reconstruction, during the Progressive era, or in the civil rights movement suggests that the African American church historically has taken an activist and progressive role in the public realm. Yet in all the cases cited herein, only a minority of churches and clergymen were ever involved, with the majority of churches remaining relatively quiescent or content to minister to internal spiritual or local communal needs and stay at some remove from the realm of public policy. Thus, despite the great collective power of African American churches, they have remained a "frustrated fellowship." As R. Drew Smith writes in his collection *African American Churches and Public Policy in Post–Civil Rights America*, "a consistent refrain is that there is a potential for—or at least an expectation of—black church public policy influence that has been, to this point, largely unfilled." Admittedly, this is a significant burden to put on churches that are often placed within beleaguered communities, but "it is one that they inherited as a result of their civil rights movement involvements." The authors in this collection draw from data collected from a survey of 1,956 African American churches (details of which are included in the book's appendix) conducted as part of the Public Influences of African American Churches Project, centered at Morehouse College. The thrust of this book, and of the project, is to study the public involvement of black churches in the post–civil rights era. Moving through a series of essays that describe the black church's response to issues such as affirmative action controversies in Florida, welfare reform under Clinton, antiapartheid activism, health issues and the AIDS crisis in the black community, and the "Boston Miracle" of crime reduction and improved police relations in the 1990s, the authors collectively demonstrate that, even though "a relatively small percentage of African American congregations have been actively engaged in public policy activism in recent years," nevertheless that activism "has been characterized by greater diversity with respect to issue orientation and the organizational channels through which it has moved," including especially a "greater emphasis on Africa-related policies and women's rights." But this very diversification of issues also means that the relatively small core of activist churches will have their influence spread thinly, especially in comparison to the civil rights years of earlier decades, with its focus and moral force. In short, even after acknowledging the impressive array of black church activism in difficult contemporary issues, Washington's image of a "frustrated fellowship" remains apt.[27]

The image carries over in part because of the successful invocation of history during the days of the civil rights freedom struggle. Once black churches became identified with "the movement," once history became an ally in supporting movement politics, then the burden of black religion (seen here through the lens of black Baptist churches), voluntarily accepted rather than imposed from without, became heavier. It remains so today in the era of faith-based politics, when churches are expected to carry the weight of public policy initiatives in addressing issues of poverty, crime, rural depopulation, and urban decay. The usable past of a "river" flowing into the freedom struggles of the twentieth century can leave churches in the middle of a torrent that few have the resources to control or withstand. C. Vann Woodward's famous phrase "the burden of southern history" is something black Baptist churches historically have understood perhaps better than the subjects on which Woodward based his thesis.

Notes

1. C. Edwards (Macon, GA) to Ralph McGill, September 22, 1962, in Ralph McGill Papers, box 24, folder 4, Special Collections Library, Emory University.

2. Vicki and Martin Nicklaus, open letter dated December 25, 1964, in Vicki and Martin Nicklaus Papers, WHS.

3. Jay MacLeod, ed., *Minds Stayed on Freedom: The Civil Rights Struggle in the Rural South, An Oral History* (Boulder, CO: Westview Press, 1991), 54.

4. Randy Sparks, *Religion in Mississippi* (Jackson: University Press of Mississippi, 2001), 227; "1965 Report Student Interracial Ministry," and "Statement by Edward A. Feaver on Student Interracial Ministry," in Charles Sherrod Papers, box 3, Amistad Research Center, Tulane University, New Orleans, Louisiana; Frederick Harris, *Something Within: Religion in African American Political Activism* (New York: Oxford University Press, 1999), 88.

5. Vincent Harding, *There Is a River: The Black Struggle for Freedom in America* (Boston: Houghton Mifflin Harcourt, 1993); Jacquelyn Dowd Hall, "The Long History of the Civil Rights Movement and the Political Uses of the Past," *Journal of American History* 91 (March 2005): 1233–63.

6. James Melvin Washington, *Frustrated Fellowship: The Black Baptist Quest for Social Power* (Macon, GA: Mercer University Press, 1986).

7. Curtis Evans, *The Burden of Black Religion* (New York: Oxford University Press, 2008), 176; E. Franklin Frazier, *The Negro Church in America* (New York: Shocken Books, 1954); Benjamin Mays and Joseph Nicholson, *The Negro's Church* (1933; repr., New York: Negro Universities Press, 1969); Mays, *The Negro's God, as Reflected in His Literature* (1938; repr., New York: Negro Universities Press, 1969).

8. Evans, *The Burden of Black Religion,* 280; Gayraud Wilmore, *Black Religion and Black Radicalism* (Garden City, NY: Doubleday, 1972).

9. Evans, 280.

10. W. E. B. DuBois, *Souls of Black Folk* (1903); DuBois, *The Negro Church. Report of a Social Study Made under the Direction of Atlanta University; Together with the Proceedings of the Eighth Conference for the Study of the Negro Problems, Held at Atlanta University, May 26th, 1903* (Atlanta: Atlanta University Press, 1903), http://docsouth.unc.edu/church/negrochurch/menu.htmlpublishing info. For an interpretation of DuBois's complex religious thought, see Edward J. Blum, *W. E. B. Du Bois, American Prophet* (Philadelphia: University of Pennsylvania Press, 2007).

11. Andrew Billingsley, *Mighty Like a River: The Black Church and Social Reform* (New York: Oxford University Press, 1998), 30–34; Steven Hahn, *A Nation under Our Feet: Black Political Struggles in the Rural South from Slavery to the Great Migration* (Cambridge, MA: Harvard University Press, 2003), 145.

12. William Montgomery, *Under Their Own Vine and Fig Tree: The African American Church in the South, 1865–1900* (Baton Rouge: Louisiana State University Press, 1993), 157, 179. For another example, Holland Thompson of

Montgomery, Alabama, see Howard Rabinowitz, "Holland Thompson and Black Political Participation During Reconstruction," in *Southern Black Leaders of the Reconstruction Era*, ed. August Meier (Urbana: University of Illinois Press, 1982), 249–79.

13. For an interpretation of Jackson's career, see Wallace D. Best, "'The Right Achieved and the Wrong Way Conquered': J. H. Jackson, Martin Luther King Jr., and the Conflict over Civil Rights," *Religion and American Culture: A Journal of Interpretation* 16, no. 2 (Summer 2006): 195–226.

14. Laurie Maffly-Kipp, *Setting Down the Sacred Past: African American Race Histories* (Cambridge, MA: Harvard University Press, 2010).

15. Carter Woodson, *The History of the Negro Church* (Washington, D.C.: Associated Universities Press, 1921); Albert Raboteau and David Wills, "Retelling Carter Woodson's Story: Archival Sources in Afro-American History," *Journal of American History* 77 (June 1990): 183–99; C. Vann Woodward, *The Strange Career of Jim Crow* (1955; Commemoration ed., New York: Oxford University Press, 2001).

16. W. E. B. DuBois, *Black Reconstruction: An Essay Toward A History of the Part Which Black Folk Played in the Attempt to Reconstruct Democracy in America, 1860–1880* (1935; repr., New York: Russell and Russell, 1999), 124.

17. Robin D. G. Kelley, "'We Are Not What We Seem': Rethinking Black Working-Class Opposition in the Jim Crow South," *Journal of American History* 80 (June 1993): 88. For more on freedom songs, see Kerran Sanger, *"When the Spirit Says Sing": The Role of Freedom Songs in the Civil Rights Movement* (New York: Garland Press, 1995).

18. See Paul Harvey, *Freedom's Coming: Religious Cultures and the Shaping of the South from the Civil War through the Civil Rights Era* (Chapel Hill: University of North Carolina Press, 2005), and David Chappell, *Stone of Hope: Prophetic Religion and the Death of Jim Crow* (Chapel Hill: University of North Carolina Press, 2004), for analyses of civil rights "conversions" and the civil rights movement as a religious revival.

19. David Garrow, *Bearing the Cross: Martin Luther King Jr., and the Southern Christian Leadership Conference* (orig. 1987; repr., New York: Harper Perennial, 1999); Taylor Branch, *Parting the Waters: America in the King Years, 1954–1963* (New York: Simon & Schuster, 1989).

20. Aldon Morris, *The Origins of the Civil Rights Movement: Black Communities Organizing for Change* (New York: Free Press, 1986).

21. Andrew Manis, *A Fire You Can't Put Out: The Civil Rights Life of Birmingham's Reverend Fred Shuttlesworth* (Tuscaloosa: The University of Alabama Press, 1999), 24, 26–27, 42.

22. Manis, *A Fire*, 79, 97, 112.

23. Manis, *A Fire*, 230–31, 296, 314.

24. Manis, *A Fire*, 141, 152, 196–99, 221, 231, 265, 347, 328.

25. Robert Jackall, diary entry for May 25 and 26, 1967, in Robert Jackall Papers, Wisconsin Historical Society, Madison, Wisconsin; John Dittmer, *Local People: The Struggle for Civil Rights in Mississippi* (Urbana: University of Illinois Press, 1995), 137; Chana Kai Lee, *For Freedom's Sake: The Life of Fannie Lou Hamer* (Urbana: University of Illinois Press, 2000).

26. Fannie Lou Hamer, "Sick and Tired of Being Sick and Tired," *Katallagete* (Fall 1968), 26; Fred Hobson, *But Now I See: The White Southern Racial Conversion Narrative* (Baton Rouge: Louisiana State University Press, 1999), 17.

27. R. Drew Smith, ed., *Long March Ahead: African American Churches and Public Policy in Post-Civil Rights America*, vol. 2 of *The Public Influences of African American Churches*, ed. R. Drew Smith (Durham, NC: Duke University Press, 2004), 3, 25.

11
Symbolic History in the Cold War Era
Alan Scot Willis

In February 1945, the Southern Baptist Training Union, an organization dedicated to training Baptists to live their faith in their daily lives, provided a carefully planned "tea party" social for Juniors, who were typically between the ages of nine and eleven. The evening's festivities unfolded around the story of George Washington and the cherry tree, followed by the story of the Boston Tea Party, and closed with a "George Washington Tea Party."[1] In this program, Southern Baptists manipulated two great symbols of American freedom—the Boston Tea Party and George Washington—in an effort to encourage youngsters to have an abiding affection for their nation. George Washington was not, of course, at the Boston Tea Party, but the program fit perfectly with the symbolic history of the United States that Southern Baptist leaders wished to teach, one that focused on the great truth of American history: America was a Christian and a chosen nation, shaped by great men acting according to God's will.

As World War II ended and the Cold War took shape, Southern Baptists saw an aggressively expanding, and avowedly atheistic, communism become an archenemy of Goliath proportions, threatening to stamp out Christianity and religious freedom everywhere. Only a truly Christian nation could counter such a menace. Within that context, Baptist leaders intensified their patriotic efforts and constructed an American history that demonstrated the Christian and the chosen nature of the United States. Baptist leaders, however, intended to do much more than teach history. By manipulating patriotic and religious symbols, Baptist leaders sought to meld the national and religious destinies of the United States and build an abiding affection for the nation's Christian past. They also sought to fill Southern Baptist youth with a desire to fulfill the nation's destiny to spread Christianity throughout the world. As the Cold War subsided and the Culture Wars emerged, the New Christian Right tapped into that same desire, in an effort to reclaim the wayward nation from the clutches of secularism.

Historians—including historians of the Southern Baptists—have offered surprisingly few insights into how history was taught within religious institutions. As Jeremy Black argues in *Using History,* religion is "one of the most significant non-governmental spheres for the creation and presentation of historical views." Nevertheless, Black contends that historians have overlooked the significance of religion in shaping people's views of *history.* He claims that the history taught by religious institutions engages in two types of analysis that professional historians typically eschew: It sees divine intervention as not only legitimate causality but as the ultimate cause of the course of history, and it engages an "eschatological dimension" that compresses the timeline of history and links the past with the present, and the future.[2]

The Southern Baptists' construction of American history clearly fits within Black's paradigm for history taught by religious institutions, and it offered a very different narrative of American history than the ones that came to dominate professional historical scholarship during and, especially since, the Cold War era. The history Southern Baptists taught made God the central causal agent in history and clearly linked the nation's past with its present and the future, showing America to be on a specific, divinely ordained path. America was a Christian nation because of its past, and a chosen nation because of its future. As each generation fulfilled its Christian destiny, it provided a Christian heritage for future generations to build on.

The Baptist teaching of history in Training Union and mission education organizations sponsored by the Woman's Missionary Union—the Sunbeam Band (for preschool children), the Girl's Auxiliary (approximately 8 through 12 years of age), the Young Woman's Auxiliary (teenagers, but always unmarried), and the Royal Ambassadors for boys (Juniors roughly age 8 through 12 and teenagers in the Intermediates)—clearly employed both religious symbols and symbols of national freedom to create among their youth a fervent patriotism and an affection for the nation's Christian heritage.

America's stature as a Christian nation was of critical importance in both the Cold War and the later Culture Wars. As Courts Redford of the Home Mission Board put it, America was "God's chosen vessel" for bringing Christianity to the troubled world of the Cold War. Years later, after the Cold War had been all but won, Pat Buchanan, a conservative Catholic culture warrior, argued during his presidential campaign, "There is a religious war going on in our country for the soul of America. It is a cultural war, as critical to the kind of nation we will one day be as was the Cold War itself."[3] In both the Cold War and the Culture Wars, the contest over America's Christian heritage pitted secular and religious histories against each other.

Baptist leaders believed that their teaching the history of the United States as a Christian nation provided a necessary corrective to the secular history being taught in public schools and universities. Penrose St. Amant, professor of Christian history and theology at New Orleans Seminary, argued that secular historians underestimated the role of religion in American society, focusing instead on economics and politics. Baptists held that professional and public school history fell short of demonstrating the one fundamental truth of American history: "the fact of the matter is that Christianity was the crucial factor which led to the founding of the colonies, the freedom we have won, and the development of this commonwealth." The Southern Baptist Training Union and mission education organizations, such as later conservative Christian academies and the Christian home schooling movement, provided a forum where the fundamental truth of America as a Christian and a chosen nation could safely be taught.[4]

As editor of the *Baptist Training Union Magazine* for over thirty years, Jerry Elmer Lambdin carefully planned the lessons for the organizations, and coordinated the assigning of particular lessons to trusted authors. His notes indicate the level of intentionality in the design of the historically based programs, which linked faith with patriotism and civic action. For example, in planning the lessons for November 1949, Lambdin noted that they should have "interesting incidents in the history of our country which will inspire new appreciation of the pioneers who gave us this land and which will stimulate Intermediates to hold high their ideals." This was typical. Lambdin's goals for the July programs in 1954 were "to help the Intermediate to rethink his debt to his country and to feel new pride in it," as well as to inspire the Intermediate "to make a contribution to the future of his country through personal integrity and loyal citizenship."[5]

If America had been blessed by God and had been given a divinely ordained mission, communism was equally guided by the supernatural. In

Los Angeles, in 1948, Billy Graham announced, "Communism is a religion that is inspired, directed, and motivated by the Devil himself." Similarly, in his book, *Christianity and Communism*, noted theologian John C. Bennett warned that communism operated as both an economic system and a religion; in September 1949, Southern Baptist leaders included *Christianity and Communism* on a list of recommended readings for youth involved in the Royal Ambassador and Girl's Auxiliary programs.[6]

Baptist youth got their leaders' message—and caught their hubris—casting the Cold War as an apocalyptic battle between good and evil. In his project for the Royal Ambassadors' program, Don Harbuck wrote, "Yes, this is the secret weapon of America—the Christian Youth of America. And they are more than a match for any weapon Satan can hurl at them."[7] In the Cold War, Satan's chosen weapon was communism, and America's Christian youth stood ready to defend the nation's Christian heritage and spread the blessings of religious liberty to the ends of the earth.

Southern Baptists believed that religious freedom undergirded all other freedoms, and, thus, the *true* story of American history began at Plymouth, not Jamestown, under the guiding hand of God. Norman Cox, former head of the Historical Commission, and C. Aubrey Hearn of the Sunday School Board, wrote in the *Baptist Training Union Magazine* that "few people understood that God held back the colonization of our Atlantic Seaboard until the first hour when he had a people who could come here with an open Bible in their hands."[8] Southern Baptist leaders emphasized the centrality of Plymouth to the meaning of the United States by conflating the colony with the nation and making little distinction between the founding of Plymouth and the founding of the nation. For Southern Baptists, the Pilgrims' landing at Plymouth Rock became the national creation myth, with an active God as the primary agent.

When Crea Ridenour, a missionary to Colombia, wrote for the Girls' Auxiliary in 1945 that "our nation is not old," she directly engaged that national creation myth. She explained that North America had been a stretch of wilderness inhabited only by tribes of Native Americans; then the Pilgrims came ashore at Plymouth Rock; and, Ridenour told the girls, "Our nation was born." In 1949, Helen Conger, the Sunday School Board librarian, explicitly conflated the Pilgrim Fathers with the Founding Fathers and other American leaders. Although her program focused on the Pilgrims and religious freedom, Conger suggested listing names of later leaders like George Washington, Patrick Henry, and Abraham Lincoln above pictures of the Pilgrims.[9]

Undoubtedly, Ridenour and Conger both knew that more than 150 years had passed between the *Mayflower*'s landing and the founding of the United States, but the eschatological timeline of divinely guided history, as noted by Jeremy Black, tied the Pilgrim past not only with the Founding Fathers but also the Cold War present. Perhaps no one made that point better than the prominent pastor W. A. Criswell, who told his congregation at First Baptist in Dallas, "As long as there is a strong America, the communists will not triumph. Even the Puritans went to church leading a child by one hand and carrying a musket in the other."[10]

By encouraging children and youth to participate in historical lessons filled with patriotic and religious symbols, Baptist leaders compressed the historical timeline to impress on their charges a sense of "oneness" with earlier generations, and they wedded the sacred and temporal histories of America. In doing so, they made the lives of earlier generations accessible to their youth. At various Thanksgiving socials, often decorated with symbols of America's past—*Mayflower* cutouts and a large boulder symbolizing Plymouth Rock—Baptist youth were reminded that the "stern" Pilgrim had engaged in a variety of games with Native Americans. One social, "The Pilgrims' Progress," began with the welcoming lines, "The *Mayflower* has landed in the New World and we greet our Indian Friends." Baptist youth then played "build the fort" and "catch the turkey." At the "Plymouth Rock Party," Baptists played games such as "Squanto's Maize Planting," using candy corn, and the "horn of plenty." Such events typically ended with more somber thoughts. The "Plymouth Rock Party" closed by remembering that the Pilgrims "thanked God for bringing them safely through the first year and for his love and guidance" and asking those present to name something for which they were thankful.[11]

The Pilgrims, and the Puritans who followed, may have come to North America to worship God as they so chose, but they proved reluctant to extend the same privilege to dissenters within their colonies. Indeed, as historian John Murrin noted, "One of the most enduring American myths—I intend nothing pejorative by this term, which I use in the anthropological sense of a body of folklore or a series of stories that organizes the way a particular culture tries to understand the world—remains the belief that this country was peopled largely by settlers fleeing religious persecution and yearning for the opportunity to worship openly and without fear. It was never that simple." Baptist leaders also knew it was never quite so simple. In publications for older readerships, especially *The Baptist Student*—which circulated among college students—Baptist writers engaged in more of the complexities of history than they did in programs for younger readers. Hence, although Penrose St. Amant saw the search for religious liberty as central to the colonization of America, he acknowledged that the Puritans did not grant that liberty to dissenters despite claiming it for themselves. For St. Amant, however, religious intolerance in the Puritan colonies was part of God's plan for America because it gave rise to the most salient event in the Baptist symbolic American history: the expulsion of Roger Williams, which led to his founding of Rhode Island on the principles of religious liberty.[12]

Saxon Rowe Carver, a prolific writer of Baptist books for young readers, told members of the Young Woman's Auxiliary that Roger Williams headed the list of "American founders of religious freedom," but her story did not end there. Carver explained Williams's ideal of religious liberty had been embodied in the Constitution. To bring Williams to life, Helen Falls, Young People's secretary for Kentucky, recommended that girls— dressed in costume for the Freedom Party picnic—enact a scene with Williams being put on trial for religious freedom, a symbolic representation of Williams's actual tribulations in Massachusetts.[13]

Reenactments of the past, manipulated as they were, led Baptist youth to understand that religious freedom could come under attack in the Cold War present just as it had in the Puritan era. In his project for the rank of ambassador extraordinary in the Royal Ambassadors program, Carvel Baker noted that early American history was replete with battles for religious freedom. That mattered in the Cold War because, Carvel noted, religious freedom was being "menaced" by communism.[14] The battles for religious freedom fought by the Pilgrims and Roger Williams were of the same cloth, if not scale, as the herculean struggle against the devil's own religion, communism, and Cold War Americans could look to the colonial past for inspiration and guidance. Without a concern for "covering" the whole of American history, Baptist leaders were free to focus on only those events that reinforced their vision of the United States as a Christian and a chosen nation: From Roger Williams, they leaped ahead to George Washington.

Southern Baptists presented George Washington as kneeling in prayer at Valley Forge, which became symbolic of national submission to God's will. Like the landing of the *Mayflower*, Valley Forge also provided evidence of God's guiding hand in history. In her winning oration for the Speakers' Tournament at the Ridgecrest Assembly, a Baptist retreat house, Bettye Flo Attebery announced: "As we think of the history of our nation, time and time again we are reminded of God's constant protective care. In hours of oppressive trial we have felt the delivering power of his boundless grace, as at Valley Forge, Jamestown, [and] Plymouth. We somehow forget to realize that God is actually in history, that with his mighty arm he is keeping watch over his own."[15] Attebery had imbibed the Baptists' version of American history. In her telling, God's guiding had intervened as a causal agent in history. More importantly, if God kept watch over "his own"—clearly the Americans—in their fight against the British, surely God would keep watch over "his own" in the Cold War against the atheistic communists.

Because the Baptists' national creation myth focused on the Pilgrims, Baptists often associated George Washington—the Father of the Country—with New England. Certainly, the "George Washington Tea Party," that placed Washington at the Boston Tea Party, did this. Similarly, program writer for the Woman's Missionary Union, Jane Carroll (Mrs. J. T.) McRae, outlined a program for Sunbeam Band leaders that placed Washington squarely in the New England tradition. She suggested that the preschool-aged children be shown pictures of Pilgrims while the Sunbeam leaders explained that "people first came here to find a peaceful land where they could worship God" and follow that idea by showing a picture of George Washington kneeling in prayer at Valley Forge.[16]

Still, without the establishment of religious liberty throughout the newly forged nation, victory in the Revolutionary War might well have been pyrrhic. The work of securing religious liberty in the United States fell, ironically, to Virginians as Massachusetts clung to its established church. In the July 1945 program for eight-year-olds, the Training Union recommended placing a picture of Thomas Jefferson and Monticello alongside a biblical map showing Egypt, the Sinai Wilderness, and the Promised Land of Canaan in an effort to increase interest in the biblical story of Moses. This conflation of patriotic and religious imagery offered an extraordinary example of the melding of biblical and national symbols in the Baptists' construction of the American historical narrative. America was the modern Promised Land, free of the spiritual and intellectual slavery of communism—that "materialistic religion"—and dedicated to the greatest of all freedoms, religious liberty. And Thomas Jefferson was America's Moses.[17]

Jefferson achieved his Moses status with the Declaration of Independence, which announced the political arrival of a new nation and, with it, the ideals of equality and liberty. For the Intermediate assembly program

in July 1958, Mildred Williams, a frequent writer of Training Union programs, recommended having one of the members explain that the Declaration made the United States a free nation. He or she was to add, "As an
American citizen I am free to worship God and to stand for what I believe
is right," demonstrating again the Baptist view that religious liberty lay at
the core of all American freedoms, because the Declaration, the document
under consideration, only addressed liberty in general, not religious liberty
specifically.[18]

Baptists argued that the Declaration of Independence, along with the
Constitution, had to be Christian documents because they brought forth
a nation dedicated to religious liberty. Even though Oklahoma pastor
Max Stanfield realized that the signers of the Declaration were not religiously orthodox, he argued that the document set "forth ideals of equality
and human brotherhood that only the teachings of Jesus could have produced." John Wesley Raley, president of Oklahoma Baptist University,
agreed, calling the Declaration "poetic in prose and Christian philosophy
in fact." As a result, "the stamp of Christian philosophy undeniably and
indelibly marks the beginnings of American institutions."[19]

Baptists tended to overlook Jefferson's less-than-orthodox religious
views as they constructed the history of a Christian America for their
children. As Agnes W. Thomas, a schoolteacher, noted, "Thomas Jefferson and other early Americans realized that God has a place in our government as well as in our churches. God is mentioned in the Declaration
repeatedly," but, she lamented, "Teachers sometimes fail to stress the religious significance of this document."[20] Baptist youth needed instruction
in the nation's Christian history and mission because schools and secular
historians often failed to teach that history. For Baptists, neither Jefferson's own religious heterodoxy nor secular Enlightenment influences could
explain the Declaration of Independence's enshrining of liberty. Only
Christianity could.

Baptists also saw the Constitution as a Christian document. Mrs. T. G.
Murphree clearly demonstrated the way Southern Baptists approached
these documents in her Training Union programs for Young People (typically in their late teens or early twenties). For the July 1960 program, she
suggested that leaders explain, "Democracy is the outgrowth of the religious conviction of the sacredness of every human life. On the religious
side, its highest embodiment is the Bible; on the political, the Constitution. As has been said so well 'the Constitution is the civil bible of Americans.'" Perhaps most telling, she recommended that leaders ask the mem-

bers of the Training Union if they agreed that the United States was founded on Christian principles, and then to ask them to "verify" their answers.[21] Clearly, given the thrust of the lesson, and all other lessons in Training Union materials, only affirmative answers could be verified. She thus encouraged young people to search for the evidence proving that the Constitution was, in fact, founded on Christian principles, but the conclusion was already drawn and beyond debate.

The Constitution was Christian because it enshrined religious liberty, and Baptists claimed that as their greatest contribution to the country. Baptists claimed Roger Williams as one of their own and saw a direct line between Williams's efforts in Rhode Island and the inclusion of religious liberty in the Constitution. When explaining how religious liberty came to be part of the Constitution, Southern Baptists focused their history on two eighteenth-century Baptist ministers—Isaac Backus and John Leland—who led Baptists to support James Madison only after he took a public stand for religious liberty. William McElrath explained to Royal Ambassadors that "Leland, in 1788, could practically decide whether James Madison would be elected [to Congress] or not." Hence, in McElrath's telling, Leland's insistence on religious liberty forced Madison to publicly support amending the Constitution. Southern Baptists, thus, proudly claimed the Bill of Rights as "a Baptist Trophy." For Norman Cox, with the passing of the Bill of Rights, "victory crowned their [Baptists'] efforts."[22]

Helen Conger, who had helped plan the "George Washington Tea Party," brought the Pilgrims, the Constitution, the Bible, and the Cold War together in a history lesson perfectly suited for a Christian and a chosen nation. She suggested that local leaders show a picture of the Pilgrims and explain, "Our country is beautiful because it was established by people who came to worship God." Leaders should then continue with: "We have a wonderful heritage. The Constitution is based on the Bible. The Liberty Bell has part of a verse of Scripture on it," and read the appropriate passage from Leviticus. Conger's preparatory remarks for counselors showed the lesson's explicitly Cold War context. She instructed counselors to show the girls "how we can strengthen our nation from within by being Christian" so that "communism will have no chance with our people." Conger's lesson thus blended the patriotic and religious symbols of the Pilgrims, the Constitution, the Liberty Bell, and the Bible into a single history lesson that would inspire Christian girls to defend the nation against communist infiltration.[23]

Christianity and religious liberty formed the bulwark against atheistic and tyrannical communism, and Baptists employed patriotic symbols to remind youth to preserve the heritage of religious liberty that they had inherited from the Founding Fathers. The July 1953 Bible Drill section for Intermediates included a silhouette of Washington under which appeared the caption: "The 'Father of Our Country' loved the truth; Our Heavenly Father is the truth, Read his Word daily." The *Baptist Training Union Magazine* for July 1946 included a silhouette of Jefferson embossed on the Liberty Bell, with the instructions, "Keep religious liberty alive by practicing it: read God's word daily."[24] Baptists here clearly melded the sacred and secular, conflating the "Father of Our Country" with "Our Heavenly Father." They also used Jefferson—who had rewritten the Bible to remove the supernatural and irrational—to inspire Bible reading; clearly, though, they intended their youth to read an orthodox version of the Bible, not Jefferson's.

Just as they had with the Pilgrims, Baptists sought to make the Founding Fathers real by engaging youth directly in their lessons. They manipulated various patriotic symbols, especially the Liberty Bell and George Washington. The "Patriotic Birthday Banquet," the Junior social for February 1950, included pantomimes of Washington's crossing of the Delaware River, as well as pantomimes of his signing of the Declaration, which he had not actually done, and the fictional, but ever-popular, story of his chopping down of the cherry tree. At another Training Union social, Juniors played "mend the Liberty Bell" and had a "ringing the Liberty Bell" relay, after which they pledged allegiance to the American flag, the Christian flag, and the Bible.[25]

Baptists also included the much-later-acquired Statue of Liberty in their symbolic celebrations of American freedom. Hilda Hall Drake, a program writer for the Woman's Missionary Union, suggested that counselors of the Young Woman's Auxiliary prepare the first February meeting of 1949 to emphasize the responsibilities of freedom by displaying symbols of American freedom—the American flag, the Liberty Bell, and the Christian flag—and recommended that counselors outline the Statue of Liberty on the cover of the program folders. Drake then conflated Christianity and American freedom by explaining, in the same program, that the Statue of Liberty "has become a symbol of freedom" and advising program leaders to "discuss that freedom comes by following Jesus." To conclude, Drake proposed that counselors "pray that America will appreciate her responsibility as a Christian nation, that we should not feel free from service to all in our own country and to people in the entire world." Using the Statue of Liberty in a more dramatic presentation, the Intermediate Training Union program for July 1957 revolved around a girl draped as the Statue of Liberty while another girl, hidden from view, reminded the Intermediates that "Christ has given his all to make America the land of the free."[26]

Celebrating the spirit of the "land of the free," O. K. Armstrong, a Republican U.S. Senator from Missouri and occasional author for Baptist publications, offered readers of the July 1954 *Training Union Magazine* an article exuberantly titled "It's Great to Live in a Christian Nation." Taking the well-known inalienable rights outlined in the Declaration, Armstrong exulted, "Liberty—equality—happiness! Those are great and important words in our American heritage. Where did we get them? They took root in Christian faith and grew as men put Christian teachings into practice." Armstrong realized, however, that the nation had been slower to achieve equality and liberty for all its people.[27]

"And what of equality—that second great blessing of life in a Christian country?" With that, Armstrong introduced Abraham Lincoln, "who preserved the Union and would have been the South's best friend had his life been spared." Lincoln thus joined the Pilgrims, Roger Williams, George Washington, and Thomas Jefferson as one of the giants of American history. Armstrong also elevated the Gettysburg Address to sacred status, not unlike the Declaration of Independence. He quoted Lincoln, saying America was "conceived in liberty, and dedicated to the proposition that all men are created equal."[28]

The Baptist telling of history rarely referenced the Reconstruction amendments. Baptists credited Lincoln and the Emancipation Proclamation, not the Thirteenth Amendment, with the end of slavery. A Congress filled with politicians and led by a gang of Radical Republicans could hardly fit the symbolic history they told. The martyred Lincoln fit perfectly. For J. I. Bishop, director of the Royal Ambassadors program, Lincoln's "vision of the wrongness of any soul or body, regardless of color, being owned by anyone other than God and the individual for whom it was created certainly must have come from the Great Emancipator of all races."[29] In Bishop's narrative, Lincoln merely acted as God's agent, implementing God's will in America.

Activities for children nurtured this idyllic image. In Story Time meetings for toddlers, Training Union leaders explained, quite simply, that Lincoln had come to hate slavery after witnessing a slave market in Mississippi, and then he set the slaves free. Just as Baptist youth were encouraged to engage directly in the history of the Pilgrims and the Founding Fathers, so too did they engage in lionizing Lincoln. Richie Harris, author of *The Baptist Junior Union Manual,* planned the "Penny Party," to be decorated with silhouettes of Lincoln, oversized paper Lincoln pennies, and streamers of red, white, and blue.[30]

From Lincoln, Southern Baptists skipped ahead to Booker T. Washington and George Washington Carver. Baptists offered a presentation of African American history that highlighted specific individuals, always Christians, who had accomplished greatness despite racism and discrimination, which emphasized the guiding hand of God. That version of African American history fit easily with their telling of the American narrative. Southern Baptists held up Booker T. Washington because he was a Christian and because he believed in African American self-help through education. H. Cornell Goerner, a professor of missions at the Southern Seminary in Louisville, Kentucky, and typically one of the convention's more progressive leaders on the race question, wrote in 1948 that Tuskegee was a "worthy project" and that industrial education was still needed because "the Negro needs to learn how to do things with skilled hands, in order to make a better living." Writing in the 1960s, Robert Hastings, editor of the *Illinois Baptist,* cited Booker T. Washington as an exemplar of "reaching up" by African Americans. Hastings stressed the "progress" made since Emancipation, particularly in education, reporting that, prior to the end of the Civil War it had been widely illegal to teach slaves to read or write, but since the war ended, literacy rates had increased to nearly 95 percent by 1954.[31] Still, George Washington Carver fit even better than Booker T. Washington did with the Baptist version of American history.

Writing about George Washington Carver for *Ambassador Life,* John Carter, a professor at Howard College, a Baptist institution in Birmingham, Alabama, claimed that "by depending on God's leadership each day, he [Carver] was able to make one new product after another from peanuts, until he had discovered 300 different ones."[32] Carver's work with the peanut demonstrated that God's hand guided work of a Christian professor just as it had guided the Pilgrims to America and the founders of the nation. Carver, like the Pilgrims and the founders, was merely God's tool; God was the driving force in history.

Nevertheless, Southern Baptist leaders knew that race restricted millions of people's access to quality educational opportunities. A. T. Greene, a denominational leader from South Carolina who served as a state sec-

retary for the Royal Ambassadors, analyzed the impact of unequal education on African American students for Junior Royal Ambassadors in 1948.
Greene used the eponymous George Turner to represent African American boys of the same age in his fictitious story "The Negro Responds."
He noted that equipment in the school Turner attended was "not nearly
so nice as that in the white school in his town." He compared the one-
room schoolhouse with its broken windows and squeaking seats to the big
brick school for white children, with its gym, lunch room, maps, and a play
ground. Greene tied this straightforward comparison of unequal schools
to history by saying, "George would like to learn. He is a boy of ambition. He has heard of George Washington Carver, and what he did for his
country. He, too, would like to amount to something but what chance does
George have?"[33]

In his story, Greene placed Carver in the mainstream of United States
history, not merely of African American history, by noting that his eponymous George Turner knows what Carver did for his *country*, not for his
race. Greene also tied Turner's ambition to history, to his desire to emulate
the past great leaders. Finally, and maybe most significantly, Greene defied
the myth that the Southern racial system allowed African Americans of
ambition and drive to rise as far as their ability would take them. Greene's
African American exemplar, George Turner, was ambitious, but had little
chance of making a contribution to the country. Unequal schooling made
that impossible.[34] The nation had not yet fulfilled that part of its destiny
pointed to by the martyred Lincoln.

Although Greene and other leaders recognized the nation's shortcomings in race relations, the plantation myth of the Old South occasionally
surfaced in Training Union activities, and, like other symbolic aspects of
American history, was sometimes enacted by Baptist youth. The setting
for the Sweetheart Banquet held at the First Baptist Church of Indianola,
Mississippi, clearly romanticized the Old South and plantation life. Organizers decorated each table with a "Negro cabin" bearing labels such as
"Aunt Jemima's Wedding Hut." Décor included round-headed clothes-
pins painted to be black faces with white eyes and red mouths, and the
evening's entertainment included a choir whose blackfaced members sang
Negro spirituals. The plantation myth also occasionally appeared in centrally planned programs. In 1963, long after most publications for youth
took a consistently progressive view on race, the Training Union outlined
an Intermediate banquet titled "Land That We Love." Predictably, the
program offered images of the landing of the Pilgrim Fathers to represent

the Northeast. For the South, however, the program drew directly on the plantation myth, offering a scene of African Americans singing in the cotton fields.[35]

America's racial symbolism also included persistent misrepresentations of Native Americans, which Southern Baptists occasionally tapped into for their youth programs. In the first quarter of 1956, leaders of the Sunbeam Bands wrote programs promoting mission work among Native Americans, but the activities recommended were peculiar choices. In one, Sunbeam Band leaders recommended that counselors "make a 'river' by drawing a line on the ground with a stick. Let the children stand on the bank a reasonable distance from the 'river' and throw 'Indians' over the 'river.' The 'Indians' can be little stones or stick."[36] Thus, Indian Removal, the process of pushing Native Americans from the heart of the expanding young nation across the Mississippi River into what became Oklahoma, was enacted as church-sponsored children's game.

Such representations of racism infiltrated the Southern Baptist version of history, which sanctified the past as the nation's Christian heritage. Such a view of history could lead adherents to the belief that America was wholly Christian. For many Southern Baptists in the Cold War era, that belief meant that racial segregation, because it existed in a Christian society, must be itself *Christian*. Even though progressives like H. Cornell Goerner and A. T. Greene promoted that same version of history, they rejected the idea that America was, now, wholly Christian and instead offered a version of the present that rejected racism and segregation as *unchristian* because they interfered with fulfilling the nation's chosen destiny.[37]

Racism in the United States presented a problem for a Christian and a chosen nation because it inhibited Christian America's ability to spread religious liberty to other lands and played into the hands of the communists. Communism promised to eliminate all racial distinctions and give freedom to those who still, even after two world wars, labored under the yoke of colonialism. However, Goerner explained, communism offered only the path of "bloody revolution, bitterness, and hatred." Christianity, on the other hand, offered the path of peace in solving those same problems. Still, progressive Southern Baptists argued that communists were able to exploit racial tensions in the United States to undermine Christianity in much of the world. In his tract, *America Must Be Christian,* Goerner argued that "Race prejudices hamstring American missionaries everywhere. We cannot go much farther in persuading others to become Christian until we are willing to go deeper in applying Christian principles in our land." Racial tensions in America were easy for communists to exploit because technology allowed increasingly rapid communications. Goerner believed that news of racial problems in the United States spread especially quickly, and that such news could undermine the "good will and understanding which the missionary has laboriously built up over the years and may create embarrassments and problems which greatly hinder his work."[38]

The answer to both racism and communism—indeed, to "all the isms that infest and infect civilization today"—was a more Christian America. Training Union and mission education programs reiterated that theme throughout the 1950s. For example, the November 1955 Intermediate lessons were designed to encourage a discussion "of the religious aspects of communism, as compared with the freedom of our country." For her program for Intermediate Girls' Auxiliaries in November 1956, Helen Fling, later president of the Woman's Missionary Union, constructed a fictional interview about religious freedom in communist countries. After realizing that both Russia and China denied Baptists freedom of worship, the eponymous young interviewer concluded that she wished to do more "than just write." Denominational leaders assured her that she could do more: She could support the missionary program through the Lottie Moon Christmas Offering, an annual Christmas-time collection that provided substantial financial support for the convention's foreign mission work.[39]

Giving to the Lottie Moon Christmas Offering, however, was not enough. Howard G. McLain of the South Carolina Christian Action Council told Royal Ambassadors that Christian citizenship meant: "We must keep on working to spread the spirit of Christianity into all aspects and areas of the American way of life." Indeed, even though Baptist leaders were certainly patriotic, they also issued dire warnings that the nation was not Christian *enough* to fulfill its God-ordained mission. Hence, though history demonstrated the nation's Christian heritage and God's guiding hand, America had to be *continually made* Christian; the current generation had to provide the Christian heritage of future generations, just as prior generations had done for it. Reflecting on the demands of Christian citizenship, Mrs. Warren F. Jones, whose husband was president of Union University in Jackson, Tennessee, wrote, "Our forefathers left us a rich spiritual legacy. This legacy must be replenished with each generation, even with each individual."[40]

Many people were not doing enough to replenish the nation's spiritual legacy, perhaps because they were comfortable with America's position of power, or they were satisfied that America was truly Christian. Even though Southern Baptist leaders agreed that America was the world stronghold of Christianity, they argued that too many people believed that America was too strong to be destroyed. Such belief was folly. As program writer for the Woman's Missionary Union, Mary Dobbins reminded readers that the ancient Israelites had believed themselves to be invulnerable and had, thus, ignored the warnings of the prophet Amos. A mere thirty years later, their nation was in shambles. Reminding readers of God's hand in American history and destiny, Dobbins asked, "What has God done for our land in the past? How grateful are we now? Is the nation as a whole a Christian nation or indifferent toward the church?"[41]

Other Southern Baptist writers went so far as to suggest that God was already sorely disappointed in America. Ruth Boone Fusselle, a writer of programs for the Girl's Auxiliary, provided an example, noting that America had more Bibles and more churches than any other nation, but half the population was not Christian, and many of the self-identified Christians were poor Christians indeed. Citing the false gods of communism and materialism—which were vying for the soul of America— Fusselle noted, "God's heart must be sad as he looks to America as his nation to lead the world to the Kingdom of God." She was not alone in suggesting that America had failed God. J. B. Lawrence, executive secretary of the Home Mission Board, worried that some twenty-seven million Americans under the age of twenty-one were growing up "without any religious training of any kind—growing up to join the already large army of adult pagans." Having dedicated his life to mission work, Lawrence no doubt would have agreed with Fusselle's conclusion that God "must long for a more Christian nation."[42]

Baptist leaders consistently impressed on youths the need for action. John L. Hill of Nashville, whose Sunday School lessons were broadcast on WSM radio for over twenty-five years, reminded youths to be constantly vigilant, because "no other young people in the world are blessed with such a glorious heritage. This fact alone carries with it the solemn responsibility to know, to cherish, to defend and to preserve our liberties." Similarly Woman's Missionary Union leader Hermione Dannelly Jackson wrote that "every YWA [Young Woman's Auxiliary] member wants to live in a Christian nation which will lead toward a Christian world," and she explained that young women could help the United States become Christian by being loyal and courageous Christians. Denominational leaders assured Baptist youths that, beyond providing financial support for missions, living a Christian life and working for the Christianization of the country were well within their power. Nancy Lou Story of Houston, Texas, got the point. In her letter to *Tell,* she explained: "Although I am only an Intermediate girl, in a city of over one million people, if my life is wholly dedicated unto God, I can surely have a part in making my community Christian."[43]

America's hope, and the world's, lay in Christian youths, like Story, who could win the world to Christ. Maxie Collins, the politically active South Carolina pastor, assured readers of *The Baptist Students* that winning the nation and the world to Christ was possible. Realizing that some young people would be awed by the magnitude of the task, he reminded his readers that Jesus had started with a mere dozen followers. Collins wrote, "We too can begin small, each working in his own community, standing steadfast for the things we know to be right. And as more and more take such a stand America will conform more fully to the will of God."[44]

The times were urgent. As Collins explained, "Today America holds the destiny of mankind in the palm of her hand." Such times required Christian citizens, and Baptists often melded being a good American with being a good Christian. John L. Hill was blunt. Writing for *The Baptist Student,* he declared, "Strictly speaking, one cannot be a good American and not believe in God." But Baptists worried that fewer and fewer Americans were following the Christian path. Laura Young Monroe, wife of prominent pastor James Monroe, lamented, "It seems that every day our nation gets farther and farther from the Christian standard and the ideals of Jesus Christ. The Pilgrims came over to this country on the *Mayflower* for freedom of religion. But, as many have said, it seems that we have freedom *from* religion instead."[45]

In the later 1960s, it seemed the nation moved even further from the Southern Baptist vision of a Christian nation. Liberal movements propelled themselves forward with increasing radicalism. The civil rights movement spawned the black power movement. The free speech movement and antiwar movement suggested that youth had learned something other than respect for authority and patriotism. Eastern religions became fads. Press coverage made hippies, though few in number, seem to pop up everywhere; their call for dope use, relaxed sexual morals, and a rejection of traditional religion prompted the Christian Heritage Center to announce, "The hippies are the anti-Christ." For many evangelicals, women's liberation and the sexual revolution, combining to bring forth *Roe v. Wade* in 1973, undermined the core of American society. America was not becoming a more Christian nation; it was not fulfilling its God-ordained mission or living up to its Christian heritage.[46]

Conservative evangelicals fought back in the 1970s. Organizations like the Moral Majority and the Christian Coalition, along with Christian academies and the Christian Homeschooling Movement, formed the cornerstones of the New Christian Right. The Southern Baptist Convention, by then the largest Protestant denomination in the United States, provided both leaders and numerous adherents for this emerging ideological camp. The relationship between the Christian Right and the Southern Baptists only increased throughout the 1980s as the convention itself underwent a significant shift to the right.[47]

By the late 1970s, those Southern Baptists who had attended youth programs during the height of the Cold War were adults. When they heard leaders of the New Christian Right expounding on America's Christian heritage, it likely struck a chord reminiscent of their youth. The arguments had changed very little. Advocates of recovering America's Christian heritage believed that public school textbooks and mainstream historians had secularized America's history, smeared the Founding Fathers with accusations of deism, and failed to recognize God's guiding hand in America's past—all echoes of Penrose St. Amant's lamentations about the historical profession years earlier.[48]

While evolution and sex education snared more headlines, history was clearly contested ideological terrain. The textbook *The American Republic for Christian Schools* proffered a question that Norman Cox and Aubrey Hearn would have easily answered: "Who, knowing the facts of our history, can doubt that the United States of America has been a thought in the mind of God from all eternity?" Cox and Hearn had known that God had held back the founding of America until the Pilgrims were ready to cross the Atlantic with open Bibles. Voicing another perspective, however, Michelle Goldberg, a critic of the Christian Right, characterized the history texts for Christian academies and homeschooling as describing "a past in which America was founded as a Christian nation, only to be subverted and debased by God-hating liberals bent on perverting the Country's heritage." Both sides are clearly dedicated to their own positions, and their incompatibility has contributed to a striking rift in American education. As historian Allan Lichtman points out, between 1989 and 1999, evangelical Christians increasingly turned to homeschooling and Christian academies, accounting for three-quarters of all new private school enrollment during those ten years. Even so, some leaders feared that too many Christian children were still being left to public education; they promoted "Exodus 2000," a call for Christian parents to remove their children from public schools.[49]

The use of history by the New Christian Right extended far beyond the homeschooling and Christian academy movements. Politicians of the New Christian Right, like Mike Huckabee, the Baptist minister turned Arkansas governor, announced that Christian Heritage Week would be observed in Arkansas. In Missouri, conservative legislators proposed a resolution "declaring that the founding father 'recognized a Christian God' and established the nation on God's principles." Under the influence of party insider and Christian heritage crusader David Barton, the Texas Republican state platform for 2004 confirmed that "the United States is a Christian nation" and was founded on biblical principles, a position mirroring that in John Hill's article "Reflecting the Faith in Citizenship" from fifty years earlier, when Hill announced, "the government was inaugurated according to the principles of the Bible; its teaching found expression in the political principles and framework of our government of free people."[50]

Worried about the divisions created by the Culture Wars, Ray Suarez, senior correspondent for National Public Radio, looked back on his Cold War upbringing from the vantage point of the twenty-first century. He wrote: "what I was *not* taught, even in those intensely patriotic Cold-War decades, was that God had chosen America as the instrument for His Will in the world . . . that Christianity was not an American religion, and the American state was *not* necessarily Christian." But if Suarez had been raised attending Southern Baptist youth programs and meetings, he indeed would have been taught those very lessons; the seeds of the Culture Wars were sown early, and the ideological divisions—at least in the presentation of American history—have only increased since the Cold War.[51]

As a profession, history has become even more balkanized than it was when St. Amant lamented the influence of the political and economic. Those years have seen the rise of social history and cultural history, as well as the increasing importance of such subdivisions as African American history, women's history, labor history, gay and lesbian history, and so forth. Even older fields of history—political and religious history, for example—changed significantly under the influence of social and cultural history. Historians, particularly cultural historians, have reevaluated the very ideas of objectivity and truth in ways anathema to those preparing texts for Christian academies and Christian homeschooling, and possibly unimaginable to those Southern Baptists who prepared the history lessons for the Training Union and mission education organizations. Thus, students taught their American history in Christian academies or via Christian homeschooling guides may well share a country with students learning their American history in public schools and from professional historians in secular universities, but it can hardly be said they share a *history*.[52]

Notes

1. Mrs. Henry H. Dorris and Helen Conger, "George Washington Party for Juniors," *Baptist Training Union Magazine,* February 1945, 46–47.

2. Jeremy Black, *Using History* (London: Hodder Arnold, 2005), 40–41.

3. Courts Redford quoted in Alan Scot Willis, *All According to God's Plan: Southern Baptist Missions and Race, 1945–1970* (Lexington: University Press of Kentucky, 2005), 93; Pat Buchanan quoted in Allan J. Lichtman, *White Protestant Nation: The Rise of the American Conservative Movement* (New York: Grove Press, 2008), 406.

4. Penrose St. Amant, "Christianity and History," *The Baptist Student,* May 1953, 5–6; Lichtman, *White Protestant Nation,* 387–88; Michelle Goldberg, *Kingdom Coming: The Rise of Christian Nationalism* (New York: Norton, 2006), 5; Jeff Sharlet, "Through a Glass Darkly: How the Christian Right Is Reimagining U. S. History," *Harpers,* December 2006, 35–37.

5. "Intermediate Union Lessons—1949," Jerry Elmer Lambdin papers, box 2, folder 15, Southern Baptist Historical Library and Archives, Nashville, Tenn.; "15 and 16 Intermediate Training Union Lessons—1954," Lambdin papers, box 2, folder 15. See also "15 and 16 Intermediate Union Lessons—1955," Lambdin papers, box 2, folder 15.

6. Billy Graham quoted in Willis, *All According to God's Plan,* 58; John C. Bennett, *Christianity and Communism* (New York: A Haddam House Book, Association Press, 1948); "Read about Russia," *World Comrades,* September 1949, 3.

7. Don Harbuck, "America's Secret Weapon," *Ambassador Life,* June 1946, 9.

8. Norman Cox and C. Aubrey Hearn, "How to Observe Baptist Heritage Week," *Baptist Training Union Magazine,* April, 1958, 14.

9. Crea Ridenour, "Junior Girls Auxiliary: Fourth Meeting," *World Comrades,* March 1945, 35; Helen Conger, "Christ the Answer to Godless Ideas," *World Comrades,* September 1949, 29.

10. Criswell quoted in Oran P. Smith, *The Rise of Baptist Republicanism* (New York: New York University Press, 1997), 41. See also, Charles Wells, "What the Pilgrim Fathers Had," *Ambassador Life*, November 1952, 19.

11. Joe Holbert, "*Mayflower* Masquerade," *Baptist Training Union Magazine*, November 1963, 59; Florance L. Enloe, "Young People's Fellowship: Pilgrims' Progress," *Baptist Training Union Magazine*, November 1958, 33; Louise Berge, "Plymouth Rock Party," *Baptist Training Union Magazine*, November 1958, 49; Black, *Using History*, 37.

12. John M. Murrin, "Religion and Politics in America from the First Settlements to the Civil War" in Mark A. Noll, ed., *Religion and American Politics: From the Colonial Period to the 1980s* (New York: Oxford University Press, 1990), 19; St. Amant, "Christianity and History," 6.

13. Saxon Rowe Carver, "Programs, 2nd Week: Sounds of Jubilee," *The Window of the YWA*, March 1959, 32–33; Helen Falls, "This Month's Programs, First Week: His to Command," *The Window of the YWA*, February 1961, 25.

14. Carvel Baker, "We Must Give Our Best to Him," *Ambassador Life*, November 1952, 1.

15. Bettye Flo Attebery, "Christ above All in Our Citizenship," *Baptist Training Union Magazine*, January 1947, 26.

16. Mrs. J. T. McRae, "My Country's Story," *World Comrades*, July 1945, 29.

17. Mrs. Emmett Golden, "Consider Your Eight-Year-Olds," *Baptist Training Union Magazine*, July 1945, 40; Robert Shapiro, "Christianity, Democracy, and Communism," *The Baptist Student*, February 1954, 8.

18. Mildred Williams, "These Rights We Hold," *Baptist Training Union Magazine*, July 1958, 37.

19. Max Stanfield, "I Pledge Allegiance," *Baptist Training Union Magazine*, July 1946, 3; John Wesley Raley, "The Dynamics of Democracy," *Home Life* (June 1952), 24–25.

20. Agnes W. Thomas, "Religion in American Schools," *Home Life* (September 1958), 46.

21. Mrs. T. G. Murphree, "Assembly Programs for Young People" *Baptist Training Union Magazine*, July 1960, 36.

22. William N. McElrath, "Twelve Trailblazers," *Ambassador Life*, July 1963, 18; Davis C. Woolley, "The Bill of Rights—A Baptist Trophy," *Baptist Training Union Magazine*, July 1960, 6–7; Norman Cox, "Baptist Development in America," *The Baptist Student*, April 1963, 26.

23. Conger, "Christ the Answer to Godless Ideas," *World Comrades*, September 1949, 20.

24. Mrs. Ernest Hale, "Bible Drill Suggestions," *Baptist Training Union*

Magazine, July 1953, 35; Unsigned, untitled editorial cartoon, *Baptist Training Union Magazine,* July 1946, 33.

25. L. H. Johnson Jr., "Junior Social a Bang-up Patriotic Picnic," *Baptist Training Union Magazine,* July 1954, 52–53; Mrs. C. A. Dabney, "Junior Social: A Patriotic Birthday Banquet," *Baptist Training Union Magazine,* February 1950, 45.

26. Hilda Hall Drake, "Your YWA programs, First Meetings: 'Lend Me Thy Masses,'" *The Window of the YWA,* February 1949, 28–29; Sara Hine, "Assembly Program for Intermediates," *Baptist Training Union Magazine,* July 1957, 34.

27. O. K. Armstrong, "It's Great to Live in a Christian Nation," *Baptist Training Union Magazine,* July 1954, 10.

28. Ibid., 10.

29. J. I. Bishop, "Life Lines . . . Freedom," *Ambassador Life,* February 1951, 3.

30. Bethann F. Van Ness, "Abraham Lincoln," *Baptist Training Union Magazine,* February 1947, 37; Richie Harris, "Penny Party," *Baptist Training Union Magazine,* February 1948, 45.

31. H. Cornell Goerner, "A Worthy Project," *Ambassador Life,* September 1948, 17–19; Robert J. Hastings, "A Race Reaches Up: Education," *Ambassador Life,* May 1962, 17.

32. John Carter, "The Scientist Who was Traded for a Horse," *Ambassador Life,* May 1962, 4.

33. A. T. Greene Jr., "The Negro Responds," *Ambassador Life,* September 1948, 22.

34. Ibid.

35. Grace Lovelace, "Sweetheart Plantation Banquet," *Baptist Training Union Magazine,* February 1951, 24; Irene Jones, "Land That We Love," *Baptist Training Union Magazine,* August 1963, 64.

36. "Indian Games to Play Outdoors," *Sunbeam Band Activities,* January—February—March 1956, 49.

37. H. Richard Niebuhr, *Christ and Culture* (New York: Harper Torchbook Edition, 1975); Willis, *All According to God's Plan.*

38. H. Cornell Goerner, "Meetings for Intermediate Royal Ambassadors, Fourth Intermediate Meeting: Communism and World Missions," *Ambassador Life,* September 1949, 18; H. Cornell Goerner, *America Must Be Christian* (Atlanta: Home Missions Board, 1947), 21, 105. Willis, *All According to God's Plan,* 45–46, 57–59.

39. J. B. Lawrence, "Missions and the March of Events: The Answer to Communism," *Home Missions,* December 1948, 2; "15 and 16 Intermediate

Union Lessons—1955" Lambdin papers, box 2, folder 15; Helen Fling, "First Intermediate Meeting: Our Freedom, Their Bondage," *Tell*, November 1956, 31–32.

40. Howard G. McLain, "1st Intermediate Meeting: the Meaning of Christian Citizenship," *Ambassador Life*, Oct 1952, 14; Mrs. Warren F. Jones, "Building Better Programs," *Baptist Training Union Magazine*, July 1955, 33.

41. Mary Dobbins, "Program, 3rd Meeting: Right in Our Own Backyard," *The Window of the YWA*, July 1952, 36–37.

42. Ruth Boon Fusselle, "1st Meeting for Intermediates: A New Type of Living for Youth," *Tell*, September 1954, 26; Lawrence quoted in Willis, *All According to God's Plan*, 94.

43. John L. Hill, "Lord Make Us Thankful," *The Baptist Student*, November 1950, 3; Hermione Dannelly Jackson, "Programs, First Week: America the Beautiful," *The Window of the YWA*, March 1953, 27; Nancy Lou Story, "My Part in Leading My Community," *Tell*, May 1956, 7.

44. Maxie Collins, "Don't Sell America Short," *The Baptist Student*, May, 1948, 7.

45. Ibid.; Hill, "Lord Make Us Thankful," 3, emphasis in original; Laura Young Monroe, "How Christian Is America," *World Comrades*, February 1950, 14.

46. Lichtman, *White Protest Nation*, Christian Heritage Center quoted on p. 268.

47. Lichtman, *White Protestant Nation*, 402; Smith, *The Rise of Baptist Republicanism*; Dan Gilgoff, *The Jesus Machine: How James Dobson, Focus on the Family, and Evangelical America Are Winning the Culture War* (New York: St. Martin's Press, 2007), 80–82; David T. Morgan, *The New Crusades, The New Holy Land: Conflict in the Southern Baptist Convention, 1969–1991* (Tuscaloosa: The University of Alabama Press, 1996).

48. Kurt W. Peterson, "American Idol: David Barton's Dream of a Christian Nation," *The Christian Century*, October 31, 2006, accessed July 12, 2009, http://www.questia.com/PM.qst?a=o&d=5018509208; Gilgoff, *The Jesus Machine*, 191.

49. Goldberg, *Kingdom Coming*, 5; Lichtman, *White Protestant Nation*, 387–88; *The American Republic for Christian Schools*, quoted in Sharlet, "Through a Glass Darkly," 36; Rob Boston, "The Public School Bashers," *Church and State*, October 1998, accessed July 29, 2009, http://www.questia.com/PM.qst?a=o&d=5001377805.

50. Smith, *The Rise of Baptist Republicanism*, 56; John L. Hill, "Reflecting Faith in Citizenship," *Baptist Training Union Magazine*, July 1954, 4; Peterson, "American Idol."

51. Ray Suarez, *The Holy Vote: The Politics of Faith in America* (New York: Harper Collins, 2006), 70, emphasis added.

52. David Cannadine, ed., *What Is History Now?* (London and New York: Palgrave Macmillan, 2002, 2004); Richard J. Evans, *In Defense of History* (New York: W. W. Norton, 1999); Joyce Appleby, et al., *Telling the Truth about History* (London, 1994).

12

Southern Baptists and the F-Word

A Historiography of the Southern Baptist
Convention Controversy and What It Might Mean

Barry Hankins

In 1992, an article appeared in *Church History* titled "The Strange Career of J. Frank Norris: Or, Can a Baptist Democrat be a Fundamentalist Republican?."[1] Norris identified himself as both a fundamentalist and a Baptist, and he claimed to be a Democrat while almost always supporting Republican candidates for president. The author of this article argued that it was just as difficult to be a fundamentalist and a Baptist as it was to be both a Democrat and a Republican. I wrote the article, and I no longer believe its central argument.

When the Southern Baptist controversy (1979–1991) was at its fever pitch, the moderate position was essentially what I had argued in *Church History:* Fundamentalism and Baptist history are irreconcilable.[2] In this view, fundamentalism is historically creedal and accommodationist on church-state matters, whereas real Baptists are anticreedal and strict separationists. Norris himself often made a distinction between "convention Baptists" and "fundamental Baptists," drawing clear lines between the two groups, but he argued that only fundamentalists were real Baptists, an inverse version of the irreconcilable thesis that moderates used in the 1980s and 1990s.

Eventually, the thesis of the *Church History* article on Norris began to look doubtful. The first step in this metamorphosis came when I submitted a book manuscript on Norris to a major university press. The irreconcilable thesis was central to the book, as it had been in the *Church History* article. The editors were kind enough to give the manuscript a thorough review and return a scathing critique. While I viewed the book as thesis-driven, the press editors believed it was agenda-driven, something of a propaganda piece for the moderate side of the Southern Baptist controversy. Clearly, for scholars outside of the fray, the stark contrast between Baptists and fundamentalists made little sense. Following revisions, the eventual result was *God's Rascal: J. Frank Norris and the Beginnings of Southern Fundamentalism*—sans irreconcilable thesis.

Following the Norris book, the second step toward a more nuanced understanding of Baptists came in an article on Southern Baptist Conservatives' views of religious liberty and church-state separation. When I arrived at Baylor's J. M. Dawson Institute of Church-State Studies in 1996, I attempted to answer the question moderates often asked of the conservatives in the denomination. "Why have conservatives, or fundamentalists, jettisoned the traditional Baptist understanding of religious liberty and church-state separation?" It seemed the best way to find out would be to ask them, so I conducted a series of interviews with key conservatives that resulted in an article titled, "Principle, Perception, and Position: Why Southern Baptist Conservatives Differ from Moderates on Church-State Issues."[3] In the article, I argued that Southern Baptist Convention conservatives rejected the notion that they have jettisoned historic Baptist principles. They were as fervent in their articulation of Baptist principles as moderates were, but conservatives had a different perception of the cultural situation, which led them to take different positions on key church-state issues. In short, if one believes as conservatives do that Christians are living in a hostile culture with a secular establishment, then pushing for government accommodation of religion would seem in keeping with the historic Baptist plea for religious liberty against similarly hostile governments of the past. This was not the moderate perception of the situation, and it was not mine, but the conservative position seemed at least plausible.

The final step in my change of mind about the wideness of Baptist history came in conjunction with the book *Uneasy in Babylon: Southern Baptist Conservatives and America Culture,* which grew out of the article "Principle, Perception, and Position." As part of the research for the book, I conducted many more interviews with Southern Baptist conservatives and read everything they had written on public issues. One of these items was the 1984 book coauthored by former SBC president James Draper and former public school superintendent Forrest Watson titled, *If the Foundations Be Destroyed.* The book was a fairly standard Christian Right jeremiad concerning America's lost Christian heritage, essentially a Southern Baptist version of Francis Schaeffer's *A Christian Manifesto,* which had been published two years before Draper and Watson's book. Evangelical his-

torians Mark Noll, Nathan Hatch, and George Marsden had answered
Schaeffer in their book *The Search for Christian America,* arguing against
the Christian America idea. In a veiled reference to Noll, Hatch, and
Marsden, Draper and Watson criticized "supposedly Christian historians"
who write "anti-Christian history."[4]

Draper and Watson included the standard litany of spurious facts about
Christian founding fathers and their intent to form a Christian nation, but
they also addressed Baptist history and made claims about Isaac Backus
that I had never heard. Draper and Watson wrote that unlike the more separationist John Leland, Isaac Backus argued for an end to the established
church of Massachusetts but still favored laws that promoted Christianity.
Specifically, they charged, Backus supported a theistic test oath for state
officeholders, government licensure of Bible translations, and state aid to
missionaries taking the gospel to Native Americans. Draper and Watson believed that Backus had gone too far in his government accommodation of religion, but they did not get his alleged Baptist anomalies from
Francis Schaeffer, Christian America lecturer David Barton, or any other
pop culture warrior. Rather, they took this information from the works of
William McLoughlin, the eminent historian of New England Baptists.
On state aid to missionaries, Draper and Watson were technically in error, as Backus was dead by the time that issue was debated, but many of
Backus's New England Baptist associates favored the aid. As McLoughlin
wrote in the late 1960s, "Though Backus' views of church and state are
often equated with those of [John] Leland, it is clear that the two had distinctly different positions on many aspects of the question."[5] McLoughlin
may have been responding to popular twentieth-century Southern Baptist authors such as J. M. Dawson, T. B. Matson, and others who obliter-
ated the differences between Backus and Leland, as did Baptist historian
William Estep. Estep argued that Leland's views were the logical extension of Backus's views. This position seemed a tacit admission of the differences between the two but written in a progressive vein that attempted
to show how Baptists of the past were always on the road to strict separation, which was the only proper Baptist position. Historical theologian
Stanley Grenz also took issue with McLoughlin's interpretation, suggesting that McLoughlin had ignored how Backus himself developed pro-
gressively toward a thoroughgoing separationist position. Still, the question of contrast between Backus (even a younger Backus) and Leland
seemed at the least a contested question.[6]

Confronted with the possibility that Baptists had approached religious
liberty in a variety of ways, I began to question also whether one could say

with assurance that Baptists at all times in history had been anticreedal. Moreover, being a historian of fundamentalism and evangelicalism, I had to consider just how many professed Baptist fundamentalists I was willing to read out of Baptist history. By the time *Uneasy in Babylon* came together, which was a decade after the *Church History* article on Norris, I had concluded that whatever constituted the historical Baptist tradition, it was wide enough to include liberals, moderates, modernists, fundamentalists, creedalists, anticreedalists, church-state accommodationists, church-state separationists, and a lot of other folks as well. It seemed historically problematic to read out of Baptist history any gathered body of believers who were baptized in the name of Jesus Christ; claimed that they were Baptists; revered the Bible, however they interpreted it; and advocated religious liberty, no matter how they understood the proper relationship between church and state.

Rejecting the irreconcilable thesis puts one in good company. Southern Baptist historian Bill Leonard wrote an article in 1990 entitled "Southern Baptist Relationships with Independent Baptists." Leonard focused on how the fundamentalist Independent Baptists differed from Southern Baptists, but he did not go so far as to say that the former were not really Baptists. Rather, he argued that Southern Baptist confessions were broad enough to include both fundamentalist and nonfundamentalist Baptists and that the SBC had members of what historian Sam Hill called the "truth party" and the "conversion party." In a 1981 essay, Hill identified four types of southern evangelicals: (1) the truth-oriented truth party, properly called fundamentalists; (2) the conversion-oriented party that emphasizes evangelism; (3) the spiritually oriented party that emphasizes inward experience and nearness to God; and (4) the service-oriented party that works for justice and racial reconciliation. Hill counted Southern Baptists as the clearest example of the conversion party, whereas Independent Baptists represented best the truth orientation. He stressed, however, that denominations often exhibit features of more than one party, leaving Leonard to write a decade later that Southern Baptist history has been wide enough for both the truth and conversion parties. Like Leonard, Hill pointed out the difference and tension between different kinds of Baptists, but he made no attempt to write fundamentalists out of Baptist history.[7]

Moderate Scholars and the Irreconcilable Thesis

Southern Baptist historian E. Glenn Hinson went the other direction, arguing not only that Baptists and fundamentalists were of a different species, but that Southern Baptists were not evangelicals. In a book coauthored with James Leo Garrett and James Tull titled *Are Southern Baptists Evangelicals?*, Hinson answered with a resounding "no," whereas Garrett gave a qualified "yes." Hinson was an influential historian among Southern Baptist moderates, but in the historiography bearing directly on the SBC controversy, Walter Shurden did more than anyone to shape the moderate party's irreconcilable thesis. Among his efforts was the edited volume *Going for the Jugular: A Documentary History of the SBC Holy War*, which is a collection of primary documents on the controversy spanning the period 1979 to 1996. Shurden took his title from a comment made by conservative movement architect Paul Pressler at a meeting of conservatives in Lynchburg, Virginia, in 1980. Pressler told his audience that in their attempts to reshape the denomination, conservatives should go for the jugular, by which he meant the boards of the various SBC agencies and seminaries. Pressler acknowledged in his 1999 memoir that the statement was "unwise."[8]

In his introduction, Shurden considered the various names that were used for the two sides of the controversy. Among these were the cumbersome monikers used briefly by Baptist Press, "Fundamentalist-Conservatives" and "Moderate-Conservatives." Given that both groups claimed to be conservative, Shurden believed the terms had little meaning. "The most accurate terminology," he wrote, "is 'fundamentalists' and 'moderates.'"[9] While insisting on the problematic term *fundamentalist*, Shurden also characterized the controversy as a "clash of Baptist cultures" and a battle between two different kinds of Baptists. By the end of the book, however, Shurden had moved to a full-throated irreconcilable view.

In his conclusion, Shurden appropriated Sam Hill's four types of southern evangelicals: (1) the truth-oriented party, (2) the conversion-oriented party, (3) the spiritually oriented party, and (4) the service-oriented party. Shurden argued that types two, three, and four are "inclusive, relational, and nonabsolutist." By contrast, the truth party of fundamentalists "tends to be "exclusive, rationalistic, and dogmatic." "It is a descriptive not a derogatory statement to say that this is the very nature of the type of fundamentalism that captured the Southern Baptist Convention," Shurden wrote. "The uncompromising, nonnegotiating aspect of fundamentalism can only be understood in light of their passionate conviction that fundamentalists and fundamentalists alone are the truth-people."[10] Shurden acknowledged that some fundamentalists were "more convicted by a particular understanding of truth than they are mean in spirit." Nevertheless, "their passionate and unbending and inflexible understanding of truth makes them appear mean in spirit."[11] While claiming that the term *fundamentalist* was not necessarily "derogatory," he argued that as the denomination had been *"fundamentalized,"* it had also been *"centralized," "chauvinized,"* and *"sectarianized."* Then came the trump card: "[T]he SBC has been *debaptistified."*[12] Shurden elaborated by classing SBC conservative leaders such as Pressler, Paige Patterson, Adrian Rogers, and Charles Stanley as being closer to independent fundamentalists such as Jerry Falwell and "the descendents of J. Frank Norris" than to "traditional Southern Baptists" such as George Truett, E. Y. Mullins, and Herschel Hobbs. Debaptistification was evident in fundamentalist creedalism, the emphasis on pastoral authority, the denigration of the "priesthood of all believers," the denial of congregationalism, and the rejection of separation of church and state. This was the essence of the irreconcilable thesis. SBC conservatives were not real Baptists; they were fundamentalists.

Shurden argued that truth was never at risk during the SBC controversy, "unless by the fundamentalists themselves."[13] Here he was alluding to the multivolume conservative history of the controversy entitled *The Truth in Crisis.* Written by journalist James Hefley, this five-volume popular interpretation is the most comprehensive narrative of the controversy. Hefley wrote under the pretense of journalistic objectivity, and his friend Louis Moore of the Houston *Chronicle* wrote in the foreword to the first volume that while many will view the book as an apology for the conservative side, it really is an evenhanded work.[14] Early on, however, Hefley tipped his hand as to where his sympathies lay. Hefley's autobiographical introductory chapter is entitled "The Education of an Innocent," where he portrays himself in the 1960s and 1970s as naively flummoxed by conservative "heresy hunters." He simply could not understand what the fuss was about on the right wing of the denomination. By the time Hefley wrote *The Truth in Crisis,* however, he had been educated, convinced that the heresy hunters were correct.

Hefley's own conservative point of view comes through clearly in the rest of his work. For example, while describing a debate between conservative leader Paige Patterson and moderate Kenneth Chafin, Hefley wrote, "Many observers felt Patterson won by sticking to the issues, while Chafin digressed with attacks on the motives of the conservatives."[15] There is no footnote showing who the "many people" were who thought Patterson had won. In another passage, Hefley discussed the claim that conservative churches baptize more converts than moderate churches did. Apparently, in an effort to be evenhanded, he covered both sides—the conservative claim, and the "excuses" moderates use for why their churches baptize fewer people.[16] Examples such as these could be multiplied many times throughout Hefley's five volumes. Still, *The Truth in Crisis* and its sequels are very useful year-by-year accounts of the most important period of the Southern Baptist controversy, 1979–1990.

The conservative Hefley wrote more on the controversy than any other author, and until Jerry Sutton's *The Baptist Reformation* appeared in 2000, Hefley's work was the stand-alone conservative history of the controversy. Conservatives, however, authored three books exploring the theological issues related to the controversy, and these could be interpreted as attempts to show the need for a conservative course correction in the denomination.[17] Taken together, therefore, before Pressler's memoir in 1999, there were eight books on the conservative side of the SBC controversy, five of them by Hefley. According to my calculations, moderates, moderate sympathizers, and other nonconservatives wrote sixteen books on the controversy during that same period, almost all of them historical or sociological. This tally includes an edited volume by Nancy Ammerman that contains one essay by the conservative Timothy George. It appears that with the exception of Hefley, conservative scholars tended to write theology, whereas moderates wrote history.[18] This phenomenon was consistent with the nature of the controversy itself, where moderates on the popular level emphasized the irreconcilable thesis based on what they perceived to be historical Baptist distinctives, and conservatives stressed theological renewal and confessional uniformity.

There was one book that cannot be reckoned in the literary contest because it was written by moderates and conservatives together. Edited by conservative David Dockery and moderate Robison James, *Beyond the Impasse? Scripture, Interpretation, and Theology in Baptist Life* contains chapters by eight scholars, four from each side. Although this book defies the scorecard, it also serves as a qualifier for the generalization that moderates wrote the early history whereas conservatives stuck to theology. All the chapters in this book are theological, the moderate as well as the conservative. As far as the effort to move "beyond the impasse," one reviewer wrote that the volume was too little by too few and too late.[19] That assessment was certainly accurate as far as any attempt to find accommodation between moderates and conservatives within the denomination, but today one would have to reassess the reviewer's claim in light of Dockery's presidency at Union University in Jackson, Tennessee, and George's long tenure as dean of Beeson Divinity School. These and other institutions have moved beyond the Southern Baptist impasse toward creative intellectual engagement done from an evangelical and Baptist perspective.

Some of the authors who were not Southern Baptists nevertheless wrote from a point of view that is closely attuned to the irreconcilable thesis. These books range from the decidedly nonconservative to the blatently antifundamentalist. Joe Barnhart's *The Southern Baptist Holy War* appeared the same year as Hefley's first volume, making it one of the earliest books on the controversy.[20] Barnhart grew up Southern Baptist and even held a degree from Southern Baptist Seminary. By the time he wrote his book, however, he was no longer affiliated with any wing of the denomination and, therefore, played no role whatsoever in the controversy. While not a participant observer, he was a scholar, holding a long-time position in the department of philosophy and religion at the University of North Texas. Although not a moderate per se, he sympathized with the moderates and was even identified wrongly as a moderate in the *New York Times* review of his book. He was motivated to write *Holy War* by what he perceived as the fundamentalist threat to society, specifically to the separation of church and state and the Baptist tradition of religious liberty, positions with which he identified strongly. While disagreeing intellectually with moderates on many matters of theology, he did not view them as a threat because their views on church-state separation were in line with what Barnhart took to be a proper reading of the First Amendment.[21]

Writing in the mid-1980s, Barnhart recognized implicitly the legitimacy of the claim that conservatives represented a large segment of the denomination, perhaps the majority, and, therefore, deserved to control at least some of its institutions. He suggested a divorce scenario where the convention's property would be divvied up, each side taking a few of the seminaries and other denominational bodies. Barnhart argued that the denomination did not need the Peace Committee it formed in 1986 but rather a "Divorce Arbitration Committee" instead. Because there was still hope of resolving the conflict at the time he wrote, divorce sounded a bit extreme, and Barnhart duly noted that such a move might be impossible.[22] Given that the conservatives eventually won control of the entire denomination, Barnhart's divorce scenario looks better from a moderate perspective than what actually happened. As one moderate leader said after an important convention meeting, "I feel like I've been locked out of my own house."[23]

Arguing that fundamentalists pose a threat to society and that they have strayed from the Baptist view of religious liberty, Barnhart articulated clearly the irreconcilable thesis. In his own view, he wanted to turn the light of research and argumentation on the SBC fundamentalist movement in hopes that it would not bear up under scrutiny. He sought to issue a warning that something of value was being lost in America's largest Protestant denomination. This sense of impending loss motivated him to write. When asked a decade after his book appeared why he believed the conservatives were not writing much about the controversy, Barnhart responded that he believed it likely that they were reluctant to put their ideas or their interpretation of events before the scholarly public because this would necessitate deep reflection over issues such as orthodoxy and liberalism. Such reflection might dilute their absolutist position, causing conservative leaders to run afoul of their own constituents.[24] Put another way, perhaps the conservative winners of the controversy had little to gain and much to lose by writing their own history, whereas the moderates who had lost everything were motivated to record the sad tale for posterity.

In the historiography of the controversy before 2000, the two most influential scholarly books were sociologist Nancy Ammerman's *Baptist Battles* and Bill Leonard's *God's Last and Only Hope: The Fragmentation of the Southern Baptist Convention.* Ammerman's book was based on painstaking sociological research conducted throughout the 1980s. The book combined the curiosity of a sociologist with the passion of a life-long participant in the denomination. "All I can promise," Ammerman wrote in the preface, "is that my own involvement may give passion and life to the story and that my sociological discipline may yield insight that my involvement alone would not have revealed."[25] Ammerman imposed rules on herself as she conducted field work at SBC meetings and other venues. Because she knew many moderates, she deliberately spent most of her time at conventions with conservatives. In the process, she wrote, "I learned to appreciate their grievances." Given her position at the Candler School of Theology at Emory University at the time she wrote the book, Ammerman could claim believably, "I really did not have a stake in which side won." Moreover, by the time she wrote, Ammerman identified with the breakaway Southern Baptist Alliance and not with moderates still in the convention.[26]

As for terminology, Ammerman acknowledged that the conservatives detested the name fundamentalist. "It seems to them to connote narrow, moralistic, backwoods rednecks, or perhaps even terrorist fanatics," she wrote. Nevertheless, claiming no pejorative intent, Ammerman used the term because she believed it was historically accurate.[27] Fundamentalism developed in the early twentieth century as a Protestant defense of traditional ways of interpreting the Bible against liberal theology, Ammerman pointed out. Southern Baptist conservatives were doing likewise at the end of the century. Ammerman then addressed the moderates, acknowledging their diversity but also maintaining, "Almost all of those on the left are committed evangelicals, believing that a life-changing encounter with Jesus Christ is necessary for salvation." Still, most on the left resisted "required traditional orthodoxy" and held a general attitude that sought to "accommodate change." Such accommodation, in Ammerman's view, was the reason the fundamentalists opposed the moderates.[28]

Ammerman largely achieved the evenhandedness she set as her goal, so much so that even conservative leader Paige Patterson praised the book lavishly. In his *Christianity Today* review, the architect of the conservative movement wrote that the most unfortunate aspect of Ammerman's book is that "it will not make its author a millionaire."[29] Patterson believed that Ammerman's research showed that virtually every concern voiced by conservatives over the previous thirty years was justified. While praising her research, however, he did take one swipe at the sociologist when he wrote that his enthusiasm for the book will seem curious, especially "in light of the inaccuracies and misrepresentations of conservatives and their views that crop up occasionally in the book."[30] By contrast to Patterson's enthusiasm, Ammerman said the book angered some moderates because it documented that there were real theological differences between them and the conservatives. Many moderates claimed that the controversy was merely political and that the theological differences were insignificant. *Baptist Battles* showed otherwise.[31] Moderate activists might also have been dissatisfied with Ammerman because she used the term *fundamentalist* but did not indulge the irreconcilable thesis; SBC fundamentalists were still Baptists, in her view.

Ammerman placed her sociological data against the backdrop of Southern Baptist history, proving to be as fine a historian as she is sociologist. (She was, in fact, a high school history teacher before doing her doctoral work in sociology at Yale.) Ammerman followed up *Baptist Battles* with an edited volume titled *Southern Baptists Observed,* which contains chapters by other scholars, both Southern Baptist and non, some of whom were participant-observers as well.[32] Ammerman also helped train at least one other scholar who published a book on the controversy. Arthur Farnsley served as a research assistant for *Baptist Battles,* then wrote his own book analyzing the democratic processes of the SBC and how majoritarian politics worked in the midst of theological conflict.[33]

Ellen Rosenberg's *The Southern Baptists: A Subculture in Transition* stood in stark contrast to Ammerman's sensitivity toward history and theology and Ammerman's empathy toward southerners and Southern Baptists. Rosenberg grew up in a New England Unitarian environment and was an anthropologist at Western Connecticut State University when she did her work on Southern Baptists. She made clear early on in her book that she believed the roots of ideology and theology could be found in race, class, and gender. For Rosenberg, theology usually served as a cover for these more basic phenomena. Rosenberg believed that to be southern was to be "hyper-American: hyper-rural . . . , hyper-patriotic . . . , hyper-also in indifference to history and anti-intellectualism, . . . and hyper-racist, and sexist."[34] Such a view raised questions about her fair-mindedness toward the South, Southern Baptists, and even religion itself. Rosenberg had even less at stake in the controversy than Ammerman did and was little interested in what constituted a "real Baptist" and whether they were different from fundamentalists. For her, all such theologies were epiphenomenal. As she put it: "I knew that theology was largely ideological, that religious groups select for emphasis those aspects of their tradition which are congruent with their class interests, express their prejudices, reinforce their identity, or at the very least support their claims to authority."[35] Although her writing contains that crusty skepticism that often renders books readable, one might say she was hyper-skeptical about religion in the South.

Even though Ammerman had moved on to the Southern Baptist Alliance by the time she completed her book, Leonard was still laboring as a scholar within the denomination when he wrote on the controversy. His title, *God's Last and Only Hope,* was a paraphrase of a statement made by a denominational leader in the 1940s.[36] The author of the quote claimed that the SBC was God's last and only hope for evangelizing the world. Using the phrase somewhat whimsically in his title, Leonard chronicled the denomination's fragmentation and became the first Southern Baptist church historian to write a book on the controversy.[37]

Acknowledging that as a moderate insider he could not claim objectivity, Leonard argued that "both warring factions—fundamentalists and moderates—must bear common, though different, responsibility for the current denominational state of affairs." Leonard defined fundamentalists as those in the convention "who accept a doctrine of biblical inerrancy as the only method for defining biblical authority and who seek to participate in a concerted movement to make that doctrine normative, particularly for those employed by the convention-supported agencies and institutions."[38] Moderates consisted of the diverse group of Southern Baptists who were unified by their resistance to the fundamentalist efforts. Although many moderates involved in the political battles argued that conservatives were motivated exclusively by political concerns emanating from a desire to seize power within the denomination, Leonard took seriously the theological disagreements between the two factions. Moreover, he traced the roots of the controversy not to the development of twentieth-century fundamentalism, but back to the founding of the SBC in 1845.

When the SBC began, the basic tenets of orthodox theology could be taken for granted within almost all mainline Protestant denominations. Evangelical theology had not yet been challenged by modernity. With little need to maintain orthodoxy, Southern Baptists were free to develop organizationally rather than confessionally. This led to the "the Grand Compromise." "The convention was a means to accomplish an evangelical end," Leonard wrote.[39] That end was evangelism and missions. In short, theological disagreement was held at bay so that Southern Baptists could win the world for Christ. Still, at the popular level, many Southern Baptists assumed that they were united doctrinally and that the denomination was theologically homogenous. The Grand Compromise worked until the response to modernity on the part of some moderate Southern Baptists brought theology to center stage, challenging the assumption of doctrinal uniformity. As that happened the Grand Compromise became inherently unstable, and the controversy erupted. The surprise was not that the SBC was fragmenting, but that it stayed intact as long as it did. As Leonard put it, "Our 'intactness' endured longer than anyone had a right to expect."[40] Although Leonard used the term *fundamentalist* for the conservative side of the controversy, he did so judiciously and descriptively, just as he did in his 1990 article on Southern Baptists and Independent Baptists. Like Ammerman, he eschewed the irreconcilable thesis.

The phrase "God's Last and Only Hope" was not unique in the annals of Southern Baptist triumphalism. In 1953, an SBC denominational relations committee registered an official statement that claimed, "When our Baptist doctrines are properly understood and applied in all realms of life, Communism will be demolished, dictators dethroned, ecumenicalism destroyed and liberalism defeated." E. Luther Copeland argued that such triumphalism was a natural but sinful outgrowth of a denomination founded on the basis of proslavery racism. His book, *The Southern Baptist Convention and the Judgment of History*, was an attempt to locate the root problems of the denomination in an original sin that went much deeper than anything moderates and conservatives actually understood or acknowledged. Both groups, in Copeland's view, were guilty of racism, sexism, and denominational chauvinism that can be traced back to the SBC's founding. Copeland's book was provocative, to say the least, as he argued that the controversy and the distress it caused may have been God's judgment for the aforementioned sins.[41]

Written in the late 1980s, Leonard and Ammerman's books were superseded by David Morgan's *The New Crusades, The New Holy Land: Conflict in the Southern Baptist Convention, 1969–1991*, a book that appeared in 1996. Morgan was a historian at the University of Montevallo in Alabama. Taken together, the books by Barnhart and Morgan serve as bookends, bracketing a decade of historiography that was sympathetic to the moderate cause. Morgan stressed in this work that the fundamentalist takeover that began with Patterson and Pressler in 1979 was the second such attempt. Laying the foundation for that successful movement were the failed efforts of M. O. Owens and William Powell who attempted in the 1970s to capture the denomination for the conservatives. Given that the controversy essentially ended in 1991, when it was clear that the conservatives had won and the moderates were no longer fighting, Morgan's book had the advantage of five years of hindsight that Ammerman and Leonard did not enjoy.[42] When asked why he wrote a book on the controversy, Morgan responded: "I wrote about the controversy because I have always been a Southern Baptist, and I have always been interested in controversies. . . . I am sympathetic to the moderate position, but all fundamentalists and perhaps many moderates would call me a liberal. Even though I do not like the fundamentalist mindset, I respect their right to hold their views and to play the political game—even if I am sorry it turned out the way it did."[43]

With these sympathies, Morgan's work was more balanced than Barnhart's and apparently even earned begrudging praise from Owens, one of the old-time Southern Baptist conservatives from the 1960s and 1970s. Owens allegedly told his daughter that Morgan was fairly objective—"for a liberal historian."[44] As with Barnhart, however, one can detect the wistful sense of loss in Morgan's statement, "I am sorry it turned out the way it did."

The most forthright statement of this sense of loss can be found in theologian Fisher Humphreys's title, *The Way We Were*. The controversy forced Humphreys to move from New Orleans Baptist Theological Seminary to Beeson Divinity School at Samford University. Tragically, in his view, the SBC lost some of its most important defining characteristics: democratic polity in congregations, vigilant defense of the separation of church and state, the priesthood of believers, and opposition to creedalism. In short, this was a soft version of the irreconcilable thesis. Humphreys identified tension between fundamentalism and the Baptist way and duly noted how the conservative movement changed the denomination. As a result of the fundamentalist takeover, Southern Baptists had lost the distinctives of Baptist history that Humphreys listed. In place of these, the denomination took on militant opposition to liberalism, an overwrought insistence on inerrancy, and literalistic premillennialism. At the time he wrote, Humphreys had decided to stay within the SBC because he believed that the denomination still held many basic doctrines in common with historic Christianity. Posing a question often used by presidential candidates, Humphreys asked Southern Baptists rhetorically, "Are you better off since 1979 than you were before?" He answered "no" and concluded his book as a sad loser but not a sore loser, writing, "So, for me, this story is one of sadness. Others are persuaded that things are going to be much better for Southern Baptists in the future than they were in the years leading up to 1979. I pray that they are right and I am wrong."[45]

Humphreys's colleague at Beeson Divinity School, Timothy George, was supportive of the conservative redirection of the SBC, arguing that for only the second time a major denomination heading toward theological liberalism turned back to its conservative and evangelical roots (the other was the Missouri Synod Lutherans). Though not writing a book on the controversy, George's thoughtful and plausible arguments appeared in articles in *Christianity Today* and in Ammerman's edited volume.[46]

These highlights illustrate some basic features of the historiography of the Southern Baptist controversy before 2000. When it comes to scholarly work, the losers and their sympathizers wrote most of the first draft of history, and they were usually motivated by a sense of loss concerning what happened in the denomination. Some used the irreconcilable thesis, arguing that SBC conservatives were fundamentalists and, therefore, not real Baptists, a ubiquitous view at the popular level among moderates engaged in the battles. Other scholars did not go so far, viewing the controversy as an honest fight between two different types of Baptists. In this category, Ammerman and Leonard stand out.

Conservative Historiography

From 1985 until 2000, moderates dominated the historiography of the Southern Baptist controversy. Even today there is no book-length history of the controversy written by a scholar from the conservative camp who is a professional historian—that is, a historian who makes his or her living in an academic setting. The closest we have is Jerry Sutton's *The Baptist Reformation: The Conservative Resurgence in the Southern Baptist Convention.* With a Ph.D. from Southwestern Baptist Theological Seminary, Sutton served many years as pastor of Two Rivers Baptist Church in Nashville, Tennessee, and in various capacities in the SBC. After retiring in 2008, he went on the pastoral theology faculty at Liberty Baptist Theological Seminary in Lynchburg, Virginia.

James Draper wrote the foreword for *The Baptist Reformation* and remarked accurately that most of the authors who had written on the controversy before Sutton were opposed to the conservative movement. Sutton, Draper says, "writes from a strongly conservative perspective, yet he has done so in a very fair way."[47] Sutton acknowledged up front, "I am not dispassionate about the outcome. Neither am I neutral, although I maintain that I have been objective. I have endeavored to substantiate all conclusions."[48] He says that he learned while writing his dissertation that there is no such thing as "absolute objectivity," and that whatever one's point of view, "the ultimate assessment of our work awaits us at the final judgment."[49] In the meantime, it might be said, book reviews and a historiographical essay will have to suffice.

Although claiming fairness and at least partial objectivity in the top half of the first page of his book, by the bottom half, Sutton acknowledged that his book was actually a "polemic in the sense that I am convinced that conservatives were right and the moderates were wrong." He bristled at the term *fundamentalist,* which he believes was used "pejoratively and incorrectly," and also at any suggestion that conservatives need apologize for the dissension they caused. In his view, "If any apologies need to be made, they should come from the moderate side of the aisle for ever letting the Convention get into the shape it was in—both theologically and bureaucratically." The final solution for Sutton is for "those who have questioned the authority, accuracy, and inerrancy of God's Word" to change their minds.[50]

Writing in the late 1990s and having his book published in 2000, Sutton was able to interact with the moderate scholars from the controversy's early historiography. He engages virtually all of the moderates their fellow travelers discussed in the preceding text—Ellen Rosenberg, Nancy Ammerman, Arthur Farnsley, David Morgan, and, especially, Bill Leonard and Walter Shurden. Similar to Paige Patterson's review of Ammerman, Sutton believes that the problem with Leonard's interpretation of Southern Baptist history is that it is correct. In the Grand Compromise, the convention organized around missions and evangelism, which "gave opportunity for theological diversity that moved beyond the bounds of normative Southern Baptist theology."[51]

In discussing Shurden, Sutton turns to the 1988 SBC resolution "On the Priesthood of the Believer."[52] Sutton wrote the resolution as part of his role as chair of the Resolutions Committee that year. Conservatives pushed the resolution through largely because they believed the priesthood of the believer doctrine had been blown out of proportion, misappropriated to "justify wrongly the attitude that a Christian may believe whatever he so chooses and still be considered a loyal Southern Baptist," and misused to undermine pastoral authority.[53] Shurden claimed in *Going for the Jugular* that the resolution passed by 54.75 percent. Oddly, Sutton calls this exact percentage a "guestimation by those who represent the moderate vote based on their conjecture of the show of hands." Sutton offers as a more accurate figure "a two to one majority" reported by the "*Baptist Recorder*."[54] Further complicating this matter, there is no *Baptist Recorder*, leaving one to wonder if Sutton meant Mississippi's *Baptist Record*, North Carolina's *Biblical Recorder*, or Kentucky's *Western Recorder*.

Whoever reported the vote tally and whatever that tally was, all are agreed there was a majority in favor of the resolution. The resolution goes to the crux of Sutton's argument that the conservative resurgence was necessary because theologically the denomination was moving away from Christian Orthodoxy. From the conservative perspective, the priesthood of the believer concept had become a cover for doctrinal drift. Just how important is the priesthood of the believer for Baptists? So important, apparently, that there is even debate over how to phrase the term. Is it "the priesthood of believers," "the priesthood of the believer," or "the priesthood of all believers"? Much is at stake over whether one believes the doctrine to mean that each individual Baptist stands alone before God, or whether in order to be priests to each other, Baptists must exist in community. As one can see from Sutton's characterization of the doctrine, conservatives believed moderates used the priesthood idea as license to interpret all theology for oneself.

Shurden spoke for those who believe that the priesthood of the believer is central to Baptist identity. For him, the resolution was an example of "revising the Baptist heritage . . . , presented by and voted for by people who simply did not know the Baptist heritage."[55] Sutton denies this charge. The first two "Whereases" of the resolution say, respectively: "None of the five major writing systematic theologians in Southern Baptist history have given more than passing reference to the doctrine"; and "The Baptist Faith and Message preamble refers to the priesthood of the believer, but provides no definition or content to the terms."[56] In other words, moderates have blown out of proportion the importance of the doctrine and have also misinterpreted it. As Sutton put it, "[M]oderate historians revised history and acted offended when their bluff was called." He added that while the "priesthood of all believers" was "sound doctrine," its recent teaching "clearly exceeded what was warranted in the biblical materials."[57] Turning the tables on Shurden and others who argue the irreconcilable thesis, Sutton concludes his book by arguing that "the Conservative Resurgence was a struggle to define or reclaim Southern Baptist identity."[58] In other words, conservatives are the real Baptists.

Although in many ways historical, Sutton's book has the trappings of a well-researched memoir and an apologetic, the latter aspect of the book acknowledged in its preface. *The Baptist Reformation* stands with Paul Pressler's *A Hill on Which to Die* that came out the year before. Both books were written by conservative insiders who were active in the controversy. The counterpart to these is *What Happened to the Southern Baptist Convention?: A Memoir of the Controversy* by long-time moderate leader Grady Cothen.[59]

Among Southern Baptist conservatives, perhaps the leading historian is Greg Wills of Southern Baptist Seminary in Louisville. Wills was converted while attending that bastion of fundamentalism, Duke University. He then did his masters degree at Gordon-Conwell before moving on to Emory University's Candler School of Theology where he was mentored by the prominent religious historian Brooks Holifield. While standing on opposite sides of the denominational controversy, Wills and Leonard share an identity as Baptist historians working in the mainstream of academic scholarship. Wills's two books have been published by Oxford University Press, just as Leonard's recent history of Baptists was published by Columbia University Press and his *God's Last and Only Hope* by Eerdmans.[60]

Even though he has not written a history of the SBC controversy, Wills devotes essentially four chapters of his history of Southern Baptist Seminary to the prelude, the controversy itself, then its aftermath. His interpretation is judicious, sympathetic, and at times critical of both moderates and conservatives. Undergirding Wills's narrative is the well-documented argument that the scholars at Southern Seminary were more progressive theologically than typical Southern Baptists were. The faculty at Southern, Wills writes, accepted "the historical-critical scholarship, the liberal view of inspiration, and progressive social views." Because the denominational leaders also supported such views, the seminary's scholars came to the erroneous conclusion that rank-and-file Southern Baptists favored progressive Christianity or were at least open to its presence in the denomination. Such was not the case, Wills argues. When the gap between the beliefs of grassroots Baptists and those in the denominational leadership and on the seminary faculties grew too wide, the conservative revolution ensued. As Wills writes, "The spread of progressive views throughout denominational leadership ultimately provoked the Southern Baptist people to support revolution against the progressive denominational leadership, especially against Southern Seminary, the headquarters of the denomination's progressive wing."[61]

In telling his story, Wills includes moderate uses of the irreconcilable thesis, citing moderate Baptist newspaper editors, moderate activists, and denominational scholars, many of whom appropriated Shurden's view that the conservatives were fundamentalists and, therefore, not Baptists. In particular, Wills cites former Southern Seminary president Roy Honeycutt who delivered a convocation address in 1984 that became known as the "Holy War" sermon, a sermon that appears in Shurden's edited collection of primary documents. Honeycutt portrayed SBC conservatives as "independent fundamentalists," "unholy forces," "Judaizers," "political bosses, and demagogic tyrants," who sought "autocratic and dictatorial control" of the denomination.[62]

Wills made little effort to refute the irreconcilable thesis, taking for granted that the controversy was an honest fight between different kinds of Baptists. He had already argued in his first book that there is a substantial history of Baptists in the South who were creedal, theologically exclusivist, and proponents of ecclesiastical authority exercised by democratically organized congregations. His first book was titled, *Democratic Religion: Freedom, Authority, and Church Discipline in the Baptist South, 1785–1900*. Wills took as his primary case study the Baptist churches in Georgia during the nineteenth century. In comparing those churches to mid-twentieth-century Southern Baptists, he put the case this way: "In 1850, Southern Baptists understood democracy largely in terms of ecclesiastical authority. In 1950, they understood it primarily in terms of individual freedom."[63] Nineteenth-century Baptists believed that congregations should be organized democratically with each member having an equal voice. At the same time, however, those democratically organized congregations enforced doctrinal conformity and believed, as Wills puts it, "that orthodoxy was a source of church life more important than tolerance."[64] "Their democratic communities rejected much of the individualism that rose in tandem with the populist republicanism that swept the young nation," Wills wrote in the preface to *Democratic Religion.* "They honored their clergy, they were unashamedly authoritarian, they were stubbornly creedal, and they defended orthodox Calvinism."[65] Nineteenth-century congregations routinely disciplined their members for lax morals or deviant theology, and Baptist associations disfellowshipped congregations. At the same time, associations "disclaimed power to enforce their advice" on individual congregations, and associations "did not deny that the churches were independent and free to do as they pleased." Still, as Wills argued, "[C]hurches could not retain membership in the association while they deviated from orthodoxy."[66]

Taken together, Wills's *Democratic Religion* and Leonard's *God's Last and Only Hope* point to a tension that existed in Southern Baptist history during the nineteenth and early twentieth centuries. On the one hand, churches and associations sought doctrinal conformity and often disciplined and even disfellowshipped members for theological deviance. On the other hand, the SBC took orthodoxy for granted and in its Grand Compromise unified around evangelism and missions, leaving theological controversy to the congregations and associations. Put this way, one might argue that SBC conservatives did on the national level what formerly had been done on the congregational and associational levels—that is, enforce confessional orthodoxy. Moderates can argue plausibly that this was a new phenomenon in Southern Baptist history, especially the specificity of the conservative emphasis on the inerrancy of scripture and the vigor with which conservatives enforced it. On the other side, conservatives can cite as precedent for denomination-wide confessional identity the Baptist Faith and Message statement adopted by the SBC in 1925 and revised in 1963. We are left with an interesting set of questions: Is it fundamentalist and therefore un-Baptist to do on a denomination-wide basis what Baptists have been doing on the congregational and associational levels for four centuries? Does doing so make one a fundamentalist? Can a fundamentalist be a Baptist?

What Is Fundamentalism?

For nearly a third of a century, historians have adhered to a consensus definition of fundamentalism articulated by George Marsden in his important 1980 book *Fundamentalism and American Culture*. "Briefly," wrote Marsden, "[fundamentalism] was militantly anti-modernist Protestant evangelicalism." Moreover, he continued, "Fundamentalists were evangelical Christians, close to the traditions of the dominant American revivalist establishment of the nineteenth century, who in the twentieth century militantly opposed both modernism in theology and the cultural changes that modernism endorsed."[67] Many early twentieth-century Baptists fit this definition and are properly called Baptist fundamentalists or fundamentalist Baptists. J. Frank Norris, John Roach Straton, William Bell Riley, Mordecai Ham, and others were viewed as Baptists and fundamentalists in their own time and are viewed as such by historians today.

In the twenty-five-year anniversary edition of his book, Marsden added a new concluding chapter in which he discussed among other developments the rise of the South and its importance in twentieth-century fundamentalism. He also considered how to categorize politically active fundamentalists in the Christian Right. They pose a bit of a problem for Marsden's interpretation because in addition to militant defense of Protestant orthodoxy, fundamentalism was also marked by theological and cultural separatism. Throughout much of the twentieth century, most real fundamentalists, those who claimed the term for themselves, separated from all forms of liberalism and secularism and eschewed political engagement in the process. Jerry Falwell's 1965 sermon "Ministers and Marchers" was a typical fundamentalist denunciation of religious political activism in the civil rights movement. After 1980, Falwell and many other self-defined fundamentalists entered the political fray, raising the question, is a fundamentalist still a fundamentalist if he or she is culturally engaged? In a fundamentalist version of the irreconcilable thesis, Bob Jones Jr. said "no" and called Falwell a "pseudo-fundamentalist" for engaging in political action alongside Catholics, Jews, and secular conservatives. In other words, Jones believed, Falwell forfeited his fundamentalist status when he became non-separatist. Marsden suggested that perhaps we need a new term, "fundamentalistic evangelical," to describe such folks. They are neo-evangelical in their desire to engage culture, but they retain the militant fighting spirit of fundamentalism. Although the term rolls off the tongue with some difficulty, it provides nuance.

There cannot be an airtight definition of evangelicals because there are so many different types. This is true of denominations as well. There are fundamentalist, moderate, and liberal Presbyterians; conservative and liberal Methodists; traditional, liberal, nominal, and lapsed Catholics; and women-ordaining, gay-friendly Episcopalians and others in that communion who oppose these. Baptists do not need a highly restrictive historical definition of themselves any more than these other groups do. Given their robust diversity, one might argue that Baptists should have the least restrictive self-identity. Ironic in the extreme is a definition of Baptists that includes Southern, Northern, Calvinist, Arminian, General, Particular, Charleston, Sandy Creek, Primitive, Two-Seed in the Spirit, and a Heinz-57 variety of other types of Baptists, but at the same time excludes fundamentalists. In short, Baptists need adjectives too. "Fundamentalist Baptist" would work just fine had not the word been ruined by its rhetorical use as an "othering" agent, to use terminology employed by anthropologist Susan Harding. Harding wrote in 1993 that modern scholars sometimes othered SBC conservatives in the same way they did fundamentalists in the Scopes trial of 1925. "It is difficult to find anyone willing to explicitly declare themselves modern," she wrote, "but the modern point of view is still hard at work implicitly." Modern scholars must explain SBC conservatives, no less than the fundamentalists of the Scopes trial, because in the modern, progressive view of history, fundamentalists refuse to accept that history has passed them by.[68]

Modern Words

In light of the conservative victory in the SBC, one might say that rhetorically the F-word has lost its othering ability. Shurden explained this by saying, "By the 1980s America, indeed the world, appeared to be moving away from toleration."[69] There is a slightly different explanation, however. In the wake of the postmodern critique of modernity, liberal tolerance looks less tolerant than it used to. Liberal tolerance as it developed from the eighteenth through the late-twentieth centuries—say, from John Locke to John Rawls—came to mean leaving everyone free to decide for themselves what is true and good. Such a view is posited on a belief in the autonomy of the individual. Each person, unencumbered by authority, has the right to decide for himself or herself what good to pursue. As political liberals such as Rawls argued, in a pluralistic culture no one's comprehensive doctrine (i.e.,worldview) should be imposed on anyone else because such an imposition is a denial of individual freedom (i.e., autonomy).[70]

Picking a fight on the inerrancy of scripture may have been good rhetorical strategy in a populist setting such as the SBC. In framing the fight this way, however, Southern Baptist conservatives played the role of militant defenders, leaving themselves open to the moderate charge that they were fundamentalists from a bygone era. Another way of framing the critique of moderates was to claim they had confused Baptist freedom and tolerance with liberal freedom and tolerance, that moderates could not tell the difference between American democracy and Baptist democracy, between democratic politics and democratic religion. Wills argued in his first book that nineteenth-century Baptists believed in democratic congregations that exercised authority over the individual believer. Individual Baptists did not have the right to decide for themselves what was theologically true. In other words, they were not autonomous individuals, as modern liberal theory argues. This is close to what conservatives argued in the Resolution on the Priesthood of the Believer, and the move was risky because they were taking on George Truett, E. Y. Mullins, and other twentieth-century moderate Southern Baptist patriarchs. On this issue, conservatives risked looking even less Baptist than moderates portrayed them to be.

In a 1911 sermon titled "God's Call to America," which would be a chapter in Truett's 1923 book by the same title, the venerated Dallas pastor wrote, "The triumph of democracy, thank God, means the triumph of Baptists everywhere."[71] Far from an anomalous utterance during some isolated July 4th celebration, this equation of American democracy and Baptist democracy was Truett's and Mullins's studied view. Both made similar claims throughout their careers, Mullins writing in his revered book *The Axioms of Religion*, "We may regard American civilization as a Baptist empire for at the basis of this government lies a great group of Baptist ideals."[72] James McClendon, Barry Harvey, Curtis Freeman, Beth Newman, other signers of the Baptist manifesto, and non-Baptists such as Stanley Hauerwas and John Howard Yoder argue that such a view obliterates the difference between political democracy and Christian freedom and turns Baptist congregations into mini-Americas—all done in the name of the separation of church and state.

When conservatives responded to the F-word with the L-word, they meant that moderates were theological liberals, which left unexplained why so many moderates were Jesus-loving supernaturalists who believed in the virgin birth, resurrection, and eventual Second Coming of Christ. When they used the L-word, conservatives should have argued that moderates imbibed political liberalism—not in the popular sense of the Democratic Party but in the classic or academic sense of John Rawls and the notion of the free-standing, unencumbered, autonomous individual. The Baptist manifesto group has argued that premodern Baptists said the king should not tell a congregation of Baptists what to believe and should not exercise authority over the individual's conscience. The congregation, however, still exercised spiritual authority over the individual. Many twentieth-century moderates argued that no one has the right to tell an individual what to believe—not the state, not the denomination, not the association, not the congregation, not Christian history, and not the historic confessions written and adopted by Baptists through the ages. Indeed, "nobody but Jesus gonna tell me what to believe," as the saying goes. Such a thoroughly modern idea put moderates at the popular level in position to label premodern notions of corporate authority *fundamentalist* in an attempt to other the conservatives out of Baptist history. The postmodern question is: Why is modern better than premodern?

Such an argument is the thing of academic conferences, difficult to make in a populist movement such as the conservative resurgence. Much more useful for both sides were words that delegitimize, and none work better on a popular level than *fundamentalist* and *liberal*, however one defines those terms. But such words only reinforce one's own side of the fight; few outside the fray find such terms persuasive. Perhaps now that the SBC controversy is a matter of history, the debate over Baptist identity can move on to more edifying conversations, free of F-bombs. One can always hope.

Notes

1. *Church History* 61, no. 3 (September 1992): 373–92. Some of the essay you are currently reading is an updated and otherwise expanded version of "History Is Written by the Losers: A Case Study in Historiography and Religious Conflict," *Fides et Historia* 29 (Fall 1997): 50–65. Used by permission.

2. A key example here was E. Glenn Hinson's section of James Leo Garrett Jr., E. Glenn Hinson, and James E. Tull, *Are Southern Baptists "Evangelicals"?* (Macon, GA: Mercer University Press, 1983).

3. *Journal of Church and State* 40 (Spring 1998): 343–70.

4. Barry Hankins, *Uneasy in Babylon: Southern Baptist Conservatives and*

American Culture (Tuscaloosa: The University of Alabama Press, 2002), 62–63; James T. Draper and Forrest Watson, *If the Foundations Be Destroyed* (Nashville: Oliver Nelson, 1984); Mark Noll, Nathan Hatch, and George Marsden, *The Search for Christian America* (Westchester, IL: Crossway Books, 1983). Noll, Hatch, and Marsden's book was a response to Schaeffer's *A Christian Manifesto*. For a discussion of Schaeffer's relationship with Noll and Marsden, see Barry Hankins, *Francis Schaeffer and the Shaping of Evangelical America* (Grand Rapids, MI: Eerdmans, 2008), 209–25.

5. William McLoughlin, *Isaac Backus on Church, State, and Calvinism: Pamphlets, 1754–1789* (Cambridge, MA: Harvard University Press, Belknap Press, 1968), 50–51.

6. See Joseph M. Dawson, *Baptists and the American Republic* (Nashville: Broadman, 1956); T. B. Matson, *Isaac Backus: Pioneer of Religious Liberty* (Rochester, NY: American Baptist Historical Society, 1962); Stanley Grenz, *Isaac Backus: Puritan and Baptist* (Macon, GA: Mercer University Press, 1983), 4–5n9; and W. R. Estep, *Revolution within the Revolution* (Grand Rapids, MI: Eerdmans, 1990).

7. Bill Leonard, "Southern Baptist Relationships with Independent Baptists," *Baptist History and Heritage* 25, no. 3 (July 1990): 49–50; and Samuel S. Hill Jr., "The Shape and Shapes of Popular Southern Piety," in *Varieties of Southern Evangelicalism,* ed. David E. Harrell Jr. (Macon, GA: Mercer University Press, 1981), 99–103.

8. Paul Pressler, *A Hill on Which to Die: One Southern Baptist's Journey* (Nashville: Broadman & Holman, 1999), 112.

9. Walter B. Shurden and Randy Shepley, eds., *Going for the Jugular: A Documentary History of the SBC Holy War* (Macon, GA: Mercer University Press, 1996), xx.

10. Ibid., 273.

11. Ibid.

12. Ibid., 277. Italics Shurden's.

13. Ibid., 273.

14. James Hefley, *The Truth in Crisis,* 5 vols. (Dallas: Clarion Publications, and Hannibal, Missouri: Hannibal Books, 1986–1990), vi.

15. Ibid., 83.

16. Ibid., 19.

17. The three are: L. Russ Bush and Tom J. Nettles, *Baptists and the Bible: The Baptist Doctrines of Biblical Inspiration and Religious Authority in Historical Perspective* (Chicago: Moody Press, 1980); James Draper Jr., *Authority: The*

Critical Issue for Southern Baptists (Old Tappan, NJ: Fleming H. Revell, 1984); and W. Wiley Richards, *Winds of Doctrine: The Origin and Development of Southern Baptist Theology* (Lanham, MD: University Press of America, 1991).

18. Bill Leonard also believes that the conservatives do better with theology than with history. Leonard, e-mail to author, August 5, 1996.

19. Robison James and David Dockery, eds., *Beyond the Impasse? Scripture, Interpretation and Theology in Baptist Life* (Nashville: Broadman Press, 1992). The review cited here is: S. Mark Heim, "Talking the Truce Line: Southern Baptists in Dialogue," *Christian Century,* April 14, 1993, 402–4.

20. Barnhart, *The Southern Baptist Holy War* (Austin: Texas Monthly Press, 1986).

21. Joe B. Barnhart, phone interview by author, August 21, 1996.

22. Barnhart, *The Southern Baptist Holy War,* 236–37, 246. At one time, Paige Patterson himself considered the idea of dividing the six Southern Baptist seminaries between moderates and fundamentalists.

23. Moderate leader Cecil Sherman confirmed in a 1997 telephone conversation with Brett Lattimer that he did make this statement. I have read the quote but have been unsuccessful in tracking it down. Lattimer was a doctoral fellow in the J. M. Dawson Institute of Church-State Studies, Baylor University.

24. Joe B. Barnhart, phone interview by author, August 21, 1996.

25. Nancy Ammerman, *Baptist Battles: Social Change and Religious Conflict in the Southern Baptist Convention* (New Brunswick, NJ: Rutgers University Press, 1990), xi.

26. Ibid., xii.

27. Ibid., 16.

28. Ibid., 16–17.

29. Paige Patterson, "Help for Confused Baptists," *Christianity Today,* January 14, 1991, 33. Patterson lists the following as results of Ammerman's research that justify the conservatives: (1) the SBC national bureaucracy had become totally pervasive; (2) the vast majority of Southern Baptists are conservatives; (3) "Moderates in the SBC tend to be more liberal than their conservative counterparts on ethical issues, with many moderates imbibing alcohol and even swearing;" (4) moderates view evangelism as less important than conservatives do; (5) moderates are almost exclusively from the elite classes; (6) influential moderates tend to be from large, historic churches whereas conservatives hail from smaller churches and the so-called megachurches; and (7) during the 1950s and 1960s, conservatives were isolated and excluded from denominational leadership positions.

30. Ibid.

31. Nancy Ammerman, e-mail to author, August 8, 1996. The criticism Ammerman received from moderates was in person as opposed to print. Ammerman, e-mail to author, August 8, 1996, second letter.

32. Ammerman, ed., *Southern Baptists Observed.*

33. Arthur Farnsley, *Southern Baptist Politics: Authority and Power in the Restructuring of an American Denomination* (University Park: Pennsylvania State University Press, 1994).

34. Ellen Rosenberg, *The Southern Baptists: A Subculture in Transition* (Knoxville: The University of Tennessee Press, 1989), 5.

35. Ibid., xi.

36. Bill Leonard, *God's Last and Only Hope: The Fragmentation of the Southern Baptist Convention* (Grand Rapids, MI: Eerdmans, 1990), vi.

37. Leonard, *God's Last and Only Hope*, x. I have heard Leonard tell Southern Baptist college students that just as Martin Luther happened to live in an era of religious upheaval, so must this generation of Southern Baptists endure their own controversy.

38. Ibid., 7.

39. Ibid., 29.

40. Ibid., xii.

41. E. Luther Copeland, *The Southern Baptist Convention and the Judgment of History* (Lanham, MD: University Press of America, 1995). The quote from the denominational relations committee is on p. 77. The official name of the committee was the Committee on Relations with Other Religious Bodies.

42. David T. Morgan, *The New Crusades, The New Holy Land: Conflict in the Southern Baptist Convention, 1969–1991* (Tuscaloosa: The University of Alabama Press, 1996).

43. David Morgan, e-mail to author, August 15, 1996.

44. Morgan, e-mail to author, August 27, 1996.

45. Fisher Humphreys, *The Way We Were: How Southern Baptist Theology Has Changed and What It Means to Us All* (New York: McCracken Press, 1994), 153–66, 173–74; quotes on 173 and 174. Humphreys expected that Patterson, Pressler, or Adrian Rogers would one day write a memoir telling us much more than we now know about the organization of their work. Humphreys, to author, August 29, 1996.

46. Timothy George, "The Southern Baptist Wars: What Can We Learn From the Conservative Victory?," *Christianity Today*, March 9, 1992, 24–27; "Passing the Southern Baptist Torch: Preserving a Rich Theological Heritage, *Christianity Today*, May 15, 1995, 32–33; and "Toward an Evangelical Fu-

ture," in *Southern Baptists Observed*, ed. Ammerman, 276–300. George cites the Lutheran Missouri Synod as the other denomination that was turned back to conservatism.

47. James T. Draper, foreword to *The Baptist Reformation: The Conservative Resurgence in the Southern Baptist Convention*, by Jerry Sutton (Nashville: Broadman & Holman Publishers, 2000), xiii.

48. Sutton, *The Baptist Reformation*, xv.

49. Ibid., xv.

50. Ibid.

51. Ibid., 34.

52. One has to be careful how he or she words this concept as much can be made over whether one calls it "the priesthood of believers," "the priesthood of the believer," or "the priesthood of all believers."

53. Shurden and Shepley, *Going for the Jugular*, 237. Shurden included among the documents he collected and edited: "Document 44: SBC Resolution on Priesthood of All Believers," 237.

54. See Shurden and Shepley, *Going for the Jugular*, 231; and Sutton, *The Baptist Reformation*, 430.

55. Shurden and Shepley, *Going for the Jugular*, 230.

56. Ibid., 237.

57. Sutton, *The Baptist Reformation*, 437.

58. Ibid., 458.

59. Grady C. Cothen, *What Happened to the Southern Baptist Convention?: A Memoir of the Controversy* (Macon, GA: Smyth and Helwys, 1993).

60. Gregory A. Wills, *Democratic Religion: Freedom, Authority, and Church Discipline in the Baptist South, 1785–1900* (New York: Oxford University Press); Gregory A. Wills, *Southern Baptist Theological Seminary, 1859–2009* (New York: Oxford University Press, 2009); Bill J. Leonard, *Baptists in America* (New York: Columbia University Press, 2005).

61. Wills, *Southern Baptist Theological Seminary*, 436.

62. Ibid., 446. For the entire address see Shurden and Shepley, *Going for the Jugular*, 124–34.

63. Wills, *Democratic Religion*, 139.

64. Ibid., 137.

65. Ibid., vii.

66. Ibid., 101–2.

67. George Marsden, *Fundamentalism and American Culture* (New York: Oxford University Press, 1980), 4. A twenty-five-year anniversary edition of the book appeared in 2005.

68. See Susan Harding, "Epilogue: Observing the Observers," in *Southern Baptists Observed*, ed. Nancy Tatom Ammerman (Knoxville: University of Tennessee Press, 1993), 331.

69. Shurden and Shepley, *Going for the Jugular*, 274.

70. See John Rawls, *A Theory of Justice* (Cambridge, MA: Belknap Press of Harvard University Press, 1971); and John Rawls, *Political Liberalism* (New York: Columbia University Press, 1993).

71. Quoted in Lee Canipe, *A Baptist Democracy: Separating God and Caesar in the Land of the Free* (Macon, GA: Mercer University Press, 2011), 139. See George Truett, "God's Call to America," in *God's Call to America* (New York: George H. Doran Company, 1923), 19.

72. Quoted in Canipe, 119; See E. Y. Mullins, *The Axioms of Religion* (Philadelphia: Judson Press, 1908), 255.

Contributors

James P. Byrd is associate dean for graduate education and research at Vanderbilt University Divinity School, Nashville, Tennessee.

John G. Crowley is professor of history at Valdosta State University, Valdosta, Georgia.

Edward R. Crowther is professor of history and chair of the Department of History, Government, and Philosophy at Adams State College, Alamosa, Colorado.

Christopher H. Evans is professor of the history of Christianity and Methodist studies at Boston University School of Theology, Boston, Massachusetts.

Elizabeth H. Flowers is assistant professor of religion, Texas Christian University, Fort Worth, Texas.

Curtis W. Freeman is research professor of theology and director of the Baptist House of Studies, Duke University Divinity School, Durham, North Carolina.

Barry Hankins is professor of history, Baylor University, Waco, Texas.

Keith Harper is the author of *The Quality of Mercy: Southern Baptists and Social Christianity, 1890–1920*, and editor of *American Denominational History: Perspectives on the Past, Prospects for the Future*.

Paul Harvey is professor of history and Presidential Teaching Scholar, University of Colorado, Colorado Springs, Colorado.

Bill J. Leonard is professor of church history and professor of religion at Wake Forest University Divinity School, Winston-Salem, North Carolina.

James A. Patterson is university professor and associate dean of the School of Theology and Missions, Union University, Jackson, Tennessee.

Jewel L. Spangler is associate professor of history at the University of Calgary, Calgary, Alberta, Canada.

Alan Scott Willis is associate professor of history, Northern Michigan University, Marquette, Michigan.

Index